Islamic Economics: Theory and Practice

(Revised Edition)

Islamic Economics:
Theory and Practice

(Foundations of Islamic Economics)

Muhammad Abdul Mannan

M.A. (Bangladesh), M.A. (Econ.) Mich., Ph.D. (Michigan)
Certificate-in Dev. (U.S.A.)
Professor, Islamic Research and Training Institute
Islamic Development Bank, Jeddah

WESTVIEW PRESS
Boulder, Colorado

HODDER AND STOUGHTON

THE ISLAMIC ACADEMY, CAMBRIDGE

Dedication To: Nargis

Distributed by
Westview Press, Inc.
5500 Central Avenue
Boulder, Colorado 80301

Mannan, Muhammad Abdul, 1938–
  Islamic economics.

  Includes bibliographies and index.
  1. Economics—Religious aspects—Islam.   2. Islam—
Economic aspects.   I. Title.
BP173.75.A17918   1987   330.1   87-2106
ISBN 0-8133-0479-2

Mannan, Muhammad Abdul
  Islamic economics: theory and practice.
  1. Economics—Religious aspects—Islam
  I. Title
  330.1   BP173.75

  ISBN 0 340 36046 1

New and revised edition 1986

Printed and bound in Great Britain for
Hodder and Stoughton Educational,
a division of Hodder and Stoughton Ltd,
Mill Road, Dunton Green, Sevenoaks, Kent,
by Richard Clay Ltd, Bungay, Suffolk

Phototypeset by Macmillan India Ltd., Bangalore-25.

Contents

PART II. ISLAMIC APPROACHES TO ECONOMIC FUNCTIONS COMMON TO ALL SYSTEMS

Foreword to the revised edition

I am indeed pleased to write the foreword of the revised edition of Dr M. A. Mannan's academic-award-winning book, *Islamic Economics: Theory and Practice*, the first edition of which was published in 1970 when few scholars in the Muslim world showed serious interest in the study of Islamic economics as a distinct branch of knowledge.

However, during the 1970s, the introduction of Islamic economics as a course of study in various universities around the Muslim world, the establishment of the Islamic Development Bank and a number of other Islamic Banks and Investment Companies indicate the rejuvenation of the Islamic economic system. Therefore, the publication of this book in its revised form would be helpful in broadening the understanding of Islamic economics as a social science.

I hope the new edition of the book will be as well received by those for whom it is intended as its first edition, which has been reprinted over twelve times in ten years and published in several languages including Arabic, Turkish and Bengali.

May I take this opportunity to thank all the brothers who undertook the task of publishing this book.

Lastly, I must say that Dr Muhammad Abdul Mannan deserves our deep appreciation for his efforts in promoting the cause of Islamic economics.

May Allah guide us to serve His *Deen*.

Amen.

Dr Abdullah O. Nasseif

Secretary General,
The Muslim World League,
Makkah Al-Makarramah,
Ex-President, King Abdulaziz University,
Jeddah, Saudi Arabia.

Introduction to the revised edition

Islamic economics is emerging as a distinct academic discipline. The revised edition of this book, *Islamic Economics: Theory and Practice*, will, I am sure, strengthen the process of development of Islamic economics as a social science. When this book was first published in English in 1970, its main objective was to give the reader a comprehensive account of Islamic economic values within the context of contemporary economic analysis in layman's language. The international recognition of the first edition of this book has indeed encouraged the author to revise this edition keeping its original objectives undisturbed.

It is indeed gratifying to note that, in the book's first edition, the author advocated the founding of a Muslim World Bank at least five years before the actual establishment of the Islamic Development Bank. This new edition provides a critique of the actual operations of the Islamic Development Bank and other Islamic banks and offers a number of policy suggestions in Chapter 10.

Besides this new chapter, there is an additional introductory chapter dealing with some pertinent methodological issues, as well as necessary changes in almost all the chapters from Chapter 2 to Chapter 18 incorporating up-to-date facts and information wherever possible. Furthermore, at the end of each chapter a list of 'further reading' has been added to enhance the usefulness of this book to both the student and the teacher.

I am thankful to Dr Ghazi O. Madani, Vice President, King Abdulaziz University, Jeddah, and Dr Omar Z. Hafiz, Director of the International Centre for Research in Islamic Economics for the support I received from them during completion of this project.

I am thankful to Dr H. M. Hasanuzzman of the State Bank of Pakistan for his valuable comments on the first edition of the book.

My thanks are also due to Mr Liaquat Ali for his excellent typing and secretarial assistance.

I am obliged to my wife, Nargis Mannan, for her co-operation throughout the work.

Finally, I must say that the defects or deficiencies in this analysis, if any, are attributable to me.

May Allah help us to serve His *Deen*.

M. A. Mannan

Foreword to the first edition

It gives me immense pleasure to write a foreword to the book, *Islamic Economics: Theory and Practice*, by Dr M. A. Mannan. There is hardly any standard work on this subject covering such a wide range of topics. Although I am not competent to pronounce any judgement on Islamic Laws and Jurisprudence, yet, in my opinion, Dr Mannan's interpretation of the Islamic viewpoint in relation to modern economic theory and thought is worthy of consideration. His new synthesis is likely to provoke further analysis on the subject.

To me, there is an urgent need for synthesis between economic progress and preservation of moral and spiritual values. We must supplement the material reward which often results from economic development with non-material satisfactions and motivations through the creation of a more just society. This approach to development is especially significant in case of Pakistan—a nation committed to welfare concepts based on the ideology of Islam.

Moreover, I judge Dr Mannan, in explaining the Islamic tenets, has brought out the implication of various religious injunctions of Islam and their bearing on some of the very pressing issues confronting the Muslim world. In this connection also, he gives a number of practical suggestions. The most important point which the author has raised is the founding of a Muslim World Bank of Development to better utilise the vast resources of the Muslim countries. This is not a Utopian notion, but a practical and useful suggestion. If the Muslim countries join hands together and make serious efforts in this direction, this scheme could be fully transformed into a great reality.

Dr Mannan deserves our appreciation for his contribution in this field.

(Dr) CHARLES S. BENSON

University of California
Berkeley, U.S.A.

Preface to the first edition

The book *Islamic Economics: Theory and Practice* seeks to give my learned readers an insight into the economic values of Islam in the context of modern economic thought. It is, therefore, primarily analytical. In this book an attempt has been made to examine whether Islam could give a workable code of conduct and a blueprint of the socio-economic framework; thus, in addition to theoretical analysis of various economic problems of the Muslim world, a number of practical suggestions based on Islamic values of life have been put forward for policy decisions. As, for instance, I have advocated founding a Muslim World Bank on the model of I.B.R.D., the Asian Bank and the African Bank; I have suggested setting up of a network of consumers' co-operatives to solve the problem of consumption loans and price inflation; I have underlined the need to establish a "People's Zakāt Trust," and emphasised the urgency of associating the '*Ulamā*' with development planning by setting up of "Mosque Community and Farm Guide Centres", and so on. Since Pakistan is committed to Welfare State concepts based on the ideology of Islam, I have also discussed many economic problems of Pakistan in the light of Islamic values.

In writing this book, works of many eminent authorities have been freely consulted and quoted not only to emphasize certain ideas but also to give them an authoritative impression. I am grateful to all of them. Many verses of the Holy *Qur'ān* and *Hadīths* have also been repeated here and there for the purpose of analysis. A part of the book was also published in the form of articles in various national and international journals with a view to ascertaining the reaction of the learned readers. I have taken note of their reactions at the time of final preparation of the manuscript.

With a feeling of humility I must appreciate the unfailing encouragement I used to receive from my father-in-law, Mr K. A. Hossain, ex-Member of the Bengal Civil Service, from time to time which has greatly stimulated my interest in writing this book.

I express a deep sense of gratitude to Dr Mahbubul Haq, Mr Raihan Sharif, Dr Moinuddin Baqai, Dr M. A. Sattar, Mr M. A. H. Khandkar, of Planning Commission, Government of Pakistan, for their help in several ways.

I am also grateful to Dr Charles S. Benson, Professor, University of California, Berkeley, U.S.A., for the trouble he has kindly taken in writing a Foreword to my book. He is an educationist of international repute and author of a number of books on Economics of Education.

I must record my thanks to Mr M. M. R. Chowdhury of the Ministry of Education, Dr Abdun Noor of the Planning Commission, Mr Mosharraf Hussain of Military Accounts Service, Mr Mahmood-i-Elahi and Mr Aurangzeb Khan of the Ministry of Foreign Affairs, Mr Bazlur Rahman and Mr Abdul Ghani Alvi of the Ministry of Finance and Mr W. Rasool, ex-Editor, *Sandhan*, of Islamic Research Institute, for their encouragement.

I am grateful to the Planning Division for permission to publish this book in my personal capacity.

I am greatly indebted to my renowned publisher, Sh. Muhammad Ashraf, for his kind co-operation and help. But for the help of Mr Ashraf Darr it could not have been possible to publish this book so soon and in such a presentable way.

I am also obliged to my wife, Mrs Nargis Mannan, B.A. (Hons), M.A., for her invaluable co-operation. This is not merely a routine acknowledgement of her help.

My thanks are also due to my Steno, Mr Nurul Islam Bhuiyan, for his help.

Finally, I would like to confess that I am not a scholar in Islamic literature. The present work which is the outcome of private study is based on my conviction that the Socio-Economic System of Islam could serve as a guide for the ailing Muslim world, nay, the world at large. My labour will, however, be amply rewarded if some of my thoughts and recommendations, as reflected in the book, find an echo in the hearts of those for whom this book is intended.

In this connection it may be mentioned that the Punjab and Karachi Universities have recently introduced a paper in their M.A. classes on "Economic Values of Islam". Although I started this work long before the introduction of the paper in question, this book is expected to cover more than 90 % of the syllabus of the course. I hope, this book will be of great help to all serious students of Economics.

However, the views expressed in the book are purely personal and do not in any way reflect the views of the Planning Commission. The defects or deficiencies in the analysis, if any, are entirely attributable to me.

M. A. MANNAN

Islamabad
1 September, 1970

PART I

The Concept of Islamic Economics

CHAPTER 1

Introduction

CHAPTER 2

Islamic Economics: A Comparative Review

CHAPTER 3

Islamic Economic Laws

CHAPTER 1

Introduction

1.1 Aims and Assumptions of the book

1.2 Steps in the development of Islamic Economic Science

1.3 The Methodology of Islamic Economics

1.4 Conclusion

1.5 Selected Further Reading

"O you who believe! Do not forbid yourselves the good things which Allah has made lawful for you, and do not exceed the limits."

Al-Qur'ān.

"The best of you are those who have the most excellent morals."

The Prophet (peace be upon him) (Bukhari)

1.1 Aims and Assumptions

This chapter seeks to state the main aims and objectives of this book and to demonstrate how Islamic Economics as a science begins, thereby explaining some of the methodological issues which are needed to understand the process of formulation of Islamic theory and policy.

This book is one of the poineering works in Islamic Economics, covering a wide range of topics as it is intended to expore the potentialities of the social and economic ethics of Islam in the development of Islamic economics as a distinct discipline of knowledge. As such, the book tries to explain the theoretical and practical policy implications of various Islamic socio-economic values.

The main aims and objectives of this book are:

(i) to give beginner students of Islamic economics as well as non-economists a systematic exposition of Islamic socio-economic values and their meaning in economics as far as practicable in layman's language;

(ii) to increase understanding of the internal dynamism of the Islamic economic system and Islamic way of life in economic matters;

(iii) to provide the down-to-earth operational policy implications of diverse Islamic socio-economic values wherever possible;

The book, which assumes no prior knowledge either of economics or of matters of the Sharī'ah on the part of the reader, is based on the author's conviction that there is a unique Islamic economic system and science capable of explaining the economic problems confronting the Muslim communities of today. The book recognizes the need for the reconstruction of Islamic thought processes as well as for the reappraisal of old values in the light of new social and economic realities in order that a creative synthesis may emerge.

Thus, the analysis is based on the assumption that the underlying assumptions on which the neoclassical orthodox paradigm or the Marxist-radical paradigm are based are considered either inappropriate or inadequate or incapable of explaining the Muslim worldviews on economic matters, although these systems may, in the opinion of their protagonists, work well within their respective socio-economic contexts and value framework. This is not to suggest that every institution and practice operating in these systems is un-Islamic in character. The fact is that in every system of thought, there will be some assumptions and ideas in common with other systems of thought. It is only through emphasis or de-emphasis, modification or rejection that an identity is established. Seen in this light, Islamic economics has its own identity. Let us now discuss briefly the steps needed for the development of Islamic economics as a science.

1.2 Steps in the Development of Islamic Economic Science

In my view, there are at least seven steps in the formulation and development of Islamic economic science. They are interlinked with each other. The first step is to identify an economic problem or an issue. It is to be followed by a search for the explicit or implicit guiding principles of the *Sharī'ah* through which we should seek solution of the problem in question. These principles, which can be derived or deduced from the *Qur'ān* and the *Sunnah*, can be seen as timeless. But at an operational level the knowledge on which these principles are based need to be formulated and conceptualized first. This is where a process of theoretical formulation of the problem begins: the starting point of Islamic economic science. They are relative to space and time. Because "why", "how", "what", "for whom" and "which" questions are to be linked to the principles so identified. These questions need to be examined in terms of available options and alternatives having space and time dimensions.

From this follows the prescription of policy. It is to be clearly recognized at this stage that an "ought" statement of what should be is to be linked not only with the level of theoretical formulation but also with the level of prescription of the policy package. Here both the ethical judgements, being among the more permanent components of the system of values based on the *Sharī'ah*, and the value judgements on the basis of one's intuitive feelings or individual opinions concerning specific events may influence both the description of concepts and the prescription of the policy.

Although Islam recognizes the role of the individual value judgement it should always be subordinated to the ethical judgement. Now, the policy which emerges from theoretical analysis is to be implemented. So is the need for an appropriate institution without which an idea cannot take shape. But any gap between the achievement or the actual and the perceived goal or target represents the inadequacy of the theoretical formulation and consequent policy prescription. It calls for the review of the principles. It is also indicative of the need for reconstruction of Islamic economic theory and policy. This is a continuous process. As such, there are unlimited possibilities for the growth of Islamic economic science.

The following table summarizes the steps involved in the development of Islamic economic theories, policies and institutions. This table coupled with the explanatory notes should be helpful in understanding the evolution of Islamic economics as a social science.
It is important to offer some explanatory notes on each of the steps as indicated in the table.
Step (1)   For the sake of simplicity we have identified three basic economic functions – consumption, production and distribution – common to all economic systems irrespective of their differences in ideologies.

*Table 1 Showing the Steps in the Development of Islamic Economic Theory and Practice.**

Step(1)	Step(2)	Step(3)	Step(4)	Step(5)	Step(6)	Step(7)	Remarks
Basic functions common to all systems	Timeless Islamic imperatives rooted in the Sharī'ah	Alternatives having space and time dimension. Questions: Why; how what, for whom, which? to be linked with step (2)	Alternative Policy choices subject to Individual / Social / Moral } constraints	Transfers & Exchange	Integrated view: dual notion of individual and aggregative welfare: (maximise welfare)	Feedback	Steps 2, 3,4 are so interlinked that attempts to distinguish between normative &
	(Principles)	(Process)	(Policy)	(Operation)	(Goal)	(Gap)	
Consumption	Moderation	*Describe: what?* concepts, functions, variables, behaviour etc. Choice of variables based on (2): Formulation of theory starts	*Prescribe:* identity of basket of goods and services? —its composition; —its content; —to achieve (2)	*Implementation.* 3+4 influence —Institution building for transfer payments & exchange	*Achievement* of goal/target/or perceived	*Review with reference* to (2) *Reconstruct* (3) (4) (5)	

		Describe	Prescribe			
Production	"... seek the bounty of Allah" (Qur'ān) work, produce	*Describe: how?* function, variables, behaviour, etc. output why, which method —co-operation —competition —control —trade-off :Formulation of theory	*Prescribe: which?* —price —non-price —market —non-market —demand + supply :choice of policy	do	do	positive economics becomes unnecessary.
Distribution	"equitable, *not* equality; (*al-Adl*)	*Describe: For whom?* concepts, function, trend etc. —poverty line —guarantee of a minimum level of income/living: —individual and family level —community level —international level	*Prescribe: how?* —minimum income cash or kind; —minimum wage; —subsidy; —transfer payments;	do	do	do

* Explanatory notes for steps (1) to (7) are given on the following pages.

Step (2)   Some of the fundamental principles governing these basic functions which are timeless Islamic perspectives rooted in the *Sharī'ah*. Take the example of "moderation" in consumption. This principle of "moderation" is to be reflected in the consumption behaviour of Muslims both at microeconomic and macroeconomic level. This principle has *no* time dimension: it is essentially based on the Islamic worldview in economic matters (i.e, normative values).

Step (3)   Now there is a need to identify the method of its operation (i.e. process); this "knowledge" needs to be formulated or conceptualized. This is where the development of the theory starts and where Islamic economic science begins. Thus the choice of variables or the use of ethically-based economic reasoning are to be directed to infer behaviour patterns appropriate for the achievement of pre-selected objectives (i.e., moderation). Thus, in explaining the consumption function in an Islamic economy it should be possible to identify variables rooted in the *Sharī'ah*. This theoretical formulation has a time dimension. It can be *replaced* or modified by superior theoretical formulations, which are value-loaded indeed.

Step (4)   It follows that once this concept of "moderation" is formulated, we need to prescribe a definite basket of goods and services to achieve the goal of "moderation" either at individual or at aggregate level. Its contents and composition are changeable; it depends on the level of social and economic conditions of the society concerned.

Step (5)   This step refers to implementation of the policy chosen in step (4). This implementation can be done either by exchange through price mechanism or by transfer payments. This is where we need the development of institutions for the implementation of the policy.

Step (6)   This step indicates the need for evaluation in terms of predetermined or perceived goals or targets of how we intend to maximize welfare within the overall framework of principles as set out in step (2) as well as within the dual notion of return—economic and non-economic, making the positive and normative considerations relatively indistinguishable and unimportant.

Step (7)   This step gives the result of the evaluation. This feedback is needed to determine the gap between actual implementation of policy (step (5)) and perceived achievement. This is where the interpretation of the principles (as indicated in step (2)) on which the Islamic economic theory on which development of the policy and institution is based starts (as stated in step (3), (4) and (5)).

Following the logic and reasoning advanced in steps (2) to (7), consumption, production and distribution processes as indicated in the table can be further explained.

1.3 The Methodology of Islamic Economics

Steps discussed so far in the development of Islamic economic science are indeed connected with methodological issues. (In some places, the treatment may call for some prior knowledge of elementary economics.)

Despite the fact that methodological issues are controversial, this discussion is not just an academic exercise motivated by sheer intellectual curiosity; it is fraught with meaning for those who are determined to make a contribution towards the development of value-loaded Islamic theory, thereby influencing the policy direction of an Islamic economy. Therefore, this study can be of great practical consequence. Despite the fact that there are many methodological questions and issues in Islamic economics, here I would like to confine my discussion to the following three questions only:

(a) Is Islamic economics a positive or a normative science or both?
(b) Do we need an Islamic economic theory in view of the absence of an actual Islamic economy?
(c) Is Islamic economics a "system" or a "science"?

Let us now discuss the first question.

(a) Is Islamic Economics a Positive or Normative Science or Both?

There is a clear methodological controversy as to whether Islamic economics is a positive or a normative science.

Generally speaking, positive economics studies economic problems as they are. Normative economics concerns what ought to be. It is argued that scientific enquiry in modern Western economics is usually confined to positive questions, rather than to normative questions, which depend on value judgements about what is good and what is bad at least at the level of theoretical formulation. Some Muslim economists have, however, also tried to maintain the distinction between positive and normative science, thereby moulding the Islamic economics analysis in the intellectual framework of the west. Other positivists simply say that Islamic economics is a normative science. To me, it is neither a positive nor a normative science. In Islamic economics, the normative and positive aspects of the science are so interlinked that any attempt to separate them could be misleading and counter-productive. This is not to suggest that Islamic economics will not have any distinguishable normative and positive components. In fact, the *Qur'ān* and the *Sunnah* which are treated primarily as a source of normative statements, have many positive statements. This does not, however, qualify us to declare Islamic economics either as a positive or a normative science.

The reasons why we would like to treat it as an integrated social science are as follows:—

(i) It has already been demonstrated that steps (2) to (7) as indicated in the table are linked so intimately that the distinction between positive and normative economics is unimportant both at the level of theory and policy, because values can be reflected both in theory and policy. Since theory provides the framework for policy choice, values cannot simply be reflected in policy to the exclusion of theory. Viewed from this angle, the separation of the positive from the normative is not relevant to Islamic economics; they are both inextricably bound up with Islamic life, philosophy, and cultural and religious positions. (1) In fact, this is true in the case of most economies, for, "value judgments of one sort or another lie at the basis of *all* the premises of economic reasoning".[2] Most economic arguments or disagreements over positive economics are about value differences, not about analytic techniques. This is evident, because in secular economics the welfare function, which influences investment decisions, originates from sources inside the society in the sense that generally it represents the will of those who control the political power. In Islam, such a function essentially originates from a source outside the society itself, meaning the will of Allah. This constant exogenous variable provides a valid frame of reference to an Islamic model of economic structure. The flexibility of endogenous variables is, of course, subject to the principle of the *Sharī'ah*.

(ii) It follows that when values enter into both theory and policy, the distinction between positive and normative becomes blurred or else breaks down completely, if pushed to its limits. When examined carefully, apparently normative propositions reveal positive questions and *vice versa*. Again, most positive assertions or theories which are based on so-called factual evidence or actual observations are not value-free. The question "What government policies will reduce unemployment or prevent inflation?" is a positive one, because it could be tested by an appeal to empirical observation. Similarly the question "Ought we to be more concerned about unemployment than inflation?" cannot be settled merely by an appeal to facts.[3] Thus we see that positive and normative questions can be the obverse and reverse of the same coin. The point we are making is that economic problems and issues should be viewed in their *totality*. This is particularly true in the case of Islamic economics where the usefulness of the model or hypothesis and the validity of their theorems are to be determined by examining the correspondence between assumptions of the model and the principles of the *Sharī'ah*. Thus, in Islamic economics the volume of private investment is *neither* negatively *nor* positively related to the real rate of interest as advocated by the Keynesian model. For the *Sharī'ah* has prohibited interest for ethical and various economic reasons. Again, from the Hicksian indifference-preference hypothesis, we can deduce the conditional theorem: "if a person buys more of a good when his real income rises then he will also buy more of that good if, *ceteris paribus*, its price falls".[4] Even in such an apparently value-free theorem an "ought" statement can be built into the theory. The question of "how much" or "which good" can be related to the Islamically acceptable level of "moderation". Thus it is possible to conceive that in a properly run Islamic community a consumer may *refuse* to buy "more of a good", when prices are falling or incomes rising, when he thinks that he is exceeding the limits of "moderation" as prescribed by the *Sharī'ah*. At this point of refusal, his moral preference is indeed "revealed". Since this is an objective assessment of his subjective notion, this may consequently influence the shape of his demand curve.[5]

We may give a few more examples to demonstrate how Islamic values can enter into the very heart of the theoretical formulation of apparently value-free concepts. In explaining the nature of a "consumption function", we are required to identify variables having roots in the *Qur'ān* and the *Sunnah* right at the level of theoretical formulation. Generally we say that consumption is a function of income (i.e. $C = fYa$ where C = consumption and Ya = disposable income). Beyond personal income, there are other variables such as intrafamily income, intracommunity level of consumption and income etc., which need to be incorporated or estimated to understand the true nature of a consumption function in an Islamic economy. Again, when factor prices and a production function are to be explained within the Islamic framework, it should be understood very clearly that a firm which may be guided by the multiplicity of objectives may not *always* require to satisfy the first or second order conditions of maximization as taught in Western secular economics, because the first and second order conditions are to be fulfilled only when the firm or enterprise is aiming at maximization of profit. But in an Islamic framework it should be possible to conceive of a firm which may require to satisfy only the first order condition (i.e., considering the relationship between the quantity "Q" of a commodity marketed by some firm and the total profit 'R' which accrues to it, the derivative condition $dR/dQ = O$ can be satisfied not only where profit is at its maximum but also where profit is at its minimum). This is because a firm may aim at a minimum target level of profit only for some broader Islamically justified non-pecuniary social considerations. Thus we need not *always* go for fulfilling the second order conditions (which require that the slope of the dR/dQ must be negative.)[6] The fact is that the choice of variables and their classification into endogenous and exogenous variables as well as the mode of operation of the firm—competitive, cooperative or guided—must be made with reference to the timeless framework given by the Islamic value system.

(iii) Any attempt to distinguish between positive and normative may perhaps backfire in the sense that it may eventually give rise to the birth and growth of "secularism" in Islamic economics. The tendency to test everything with limited human knowledge and bias may destroy the basic foundations of Islamic economics. By secularization is meant "the process whereby religious thinking, practice and institutions lose social significance".[7] We must not forget the history of the growth of "secularism" and the struggle between the Church and the State in the West. The Christian Church lost its battle to secularists even on the question of charging interest (i.e. usury). It is common knowledge that both Aristotle and Plato condemned the charging of interest. Roman law was against it in its early stages. In the Middle Ages, the Christian Church prohibited the practice of usury and the charging of interest was against the principles of Common Law. Despite these hard facts of history, secularists won the battle; interest payment revived with all its social, economic and moral consequences in the Western Christian world, not to speak of the Muslim world and Third World countries. Though the evidence differs, the loss of religious influence in Western societies is basically similar. There are several historical reasons for this decline. But the positivists' pre-occupation with empirical tests and immediate results, the dominance of economic costing over spiritual aspiration, and the testable criteria of efficiency are, among others, responsible for the loss of influence of religious institutions, organizations and institutionalized belief systems in the Western societies.[8] Herein lie the lessons of experience for Islamic economists determined to make a serious beginning. It is now evident that any attempt to classify Islamic economics either as a normative or a positive science may defeat the very purpose for which it is designed, just as any attempt to separate the eighty per cent of the human body which is made up of water from the rest may very well destroy the body itself. Thus, issues in Islamic economics are to be understood and evaluated within the framework of integrated social science without splitting them into normative and positive components.

(iv) Lastly, it follows that we should try to get out of the intellectual stranglehold of the positivists as far as practicable. It is not always necessary or even desirable to mould our thought processes in an intellectual framework which suits the positivists' neoclassical orthodox paradigm. Once we allow this distinction to go to its logical extreme, it is likely to affect adversely the fundamental institutionalized belief system of Islam, because a number of issues in Islamic economics canot be settled solely by an appeal to observations, or they are not subject to empirical observations.
Let us now discuss the following related question in some detail:

(b) Do We Need an Islamic Economic Theory in View of the Absence of an Actual Islamic Economy?

My categorical answer is: Yes. It is the plea of the positivists that there is no need to develop Islamic economic theory because of the absence of an actual Islamic economy where ideas could be tested against actual problems. It is argued that the theory must explain the facts as they are. As such it is said that there is no case for an Islamic economic theory, as it has nothing to explain and predict from the existing socio-economic reality of contemporary Muslim societies. To them, the test of a theory lies in its ability to explain and illuminate reality, although every theory distorts reality by simplifying it.

The above-mentioned arguments of the positivists clearly show a lack of appreciation of the role of diverse theories emerging from respective ideologies in the development of economic society and institutions.

It is well documented that it is *not* always necessary to have theories to explain realities and predict their behaviour. I shall list a few examples from the economic and political history of the world to support the above contention.

The rapid period of innovations which followed the rise of Islam is a spectacular example of how innovations in religion and its economic values liberate society from its previous equilibrium and expose it to all the consequences of the dynamics of economic life. "Indeed the most important innovation in any society is the *idea* of innovation itself."[9] Thus, Islamic prohibition of interest coupled with imposition of *Zakāt* has a profound impact on the development of Islamic theories of money and public finance. The ethical concept of "moderation" coupled with intrafamily and intracommunity obligations is significant in understanding Islamic theory of consumption function and consumer behaviour. The concept of "*al-Adl*" (justice) is, among others, linked to the theory of distribution of income which, in its turn, is the centre of theories of growth and economic development. The fear of Allah and the consequent dual notion of return can be directly related to cost-benefit analysis. These innovations in social and economic theory were not originally designed to explain the reality existing when they were introduced. In fact, in an important sense they pave the way for innovations in Islamic economic theory and economic life in subsequent generations.

Let me give a few more specific examples to demonstrate that theoretical development can take place to explain the *perceived reality*. When in 1776 Adam Smith wrote *The Wealth of Nations*, freedom of trade was *not* the order of the day. But he could foresee the need for it in view of the social and economic transformations which were taking place in Britain. What the *Wealth of Nations* claimed was freedom of trade, freedom from the tariffs and bounties, prohibitions and monoplies and all the other restrictions which governments imposed upon manufacturers and merchants. The book with its profound argument became a classic, for it contains much else beside a defence of free trade. However, it established the modern science of economics. "For centuries *before* 1776, it had been taken for granted, in Britain as elsewhere, that the task of government was to regulate trade in what it is thought to be the best interest of the community. The most obvious feature is mercantilism, as the system of regulations".[10]

Again, in 1867 the first volume of *Das Kapital* by Karl Marx was published. It began the modern science of socialism and communism. Marxism become the gospel of the Bolsheviks of Russia who carried out the October Revolution of 1917—exactly 50 years after the publication of *Das Kapital*.

Besides, the doctrine on popular sovereignty of Rousseau[11] and its impact on French revolutionary thought and the influence of Lock's work[12] on the development of philosophical and political theory, have been incalculable. These political theories were designed to explain the *expected* reality. It should be possible to produce more evidence from world economic and social history to support my hypothesis.

It is now abundantly clear that the presence of an actual economy (i.e. reality) where ideas could be tested against actual problems is not really needed for the formulation of a social and economic theory, the development of which may be needed to explain both the reality of the present and the perceived reality of the future. A theory can contribute to contradiction by walking away from the facts.

In the case of Islam however, it would be a mistake to assume that an Islamic economic system and science had never been implemented. Even in our contemporary societies many economic theories such as the Islamic concept of banking, *Zakāt* etc. are being implemented. There are at least three reasons to develop Islamic economic theory: (i) to draw from the lessons of past experience by identifying the reasons for the adequacy or inadequacy of explaining past economic behaviour and practices by Islamic economic theory; (ii) to explain the actual economy however fragmented it might be; (iii) to identify the *gap* between ideal Islamic economic theory and the practices of contemporary Muslim societies so that an attempt can be made to reach an ideal situation. To me, these tasks of Islamic economic theory have historical significance during our time; it is much more important than the narrow view of economic theory as taken by the positivists. It is to be recognized very clearly that Islamic economic theory, being a science, draws its principles from the Islamic economic system. This brings us to the last question of whether Islamic economics is a science or a system.

(c) Is Islamic Economics a "System" or a "Science"?

There appears to be some confusion among some Muslim scholars on this question. Some regard Islamic economics as a "system" and some as a 'science'. To me, it is both. Although it is essentially *a part of* a "system", a fine case can, however, be made for Islamic economics as a "science". The word "system" is defined as a "complex whole: a set of connected things or parts" and "science" as "systematic and formulated knowledge".[13] Similarly, the word "science" is defined as "the organized body of knowledge concerning the physical world, both animate and inanimate", but a proper definition would also have to include "the attitudes and methods through which this body of knowledge is formed".[14] Following the definition of a "system", we can easily say that Islamic economics is certainly a part of a complete code of life based on four distinct parts of knowledge: "revealed knowledge" (i.e. the *Qur'ān*), the then existing practices of the society as adopted by the Prophet (peace be upon him) and his actual sayings (i.e. the *Sunnah* and the *Ḥadith*) subsequent analogical deductions, interpretations and the consequent consensus of the community or doctors of religion (i.e. *'Ijmā'*). The "system" provides a built-in mechanism for fresh thinking (i.e. *'Ijtihād*) on new issues and problems so that a solution(s) can be found out. It is permissible as long as it does not come into conflict with the system's basic components, (i.e. the *Qur'ān* and the *Sunnah*). Thus we see that a "system" provides a set of principles governing the entire code of life. These principles should be seen in a timeless framework. (See table, step (2)). Out of these principles, a conceptual framework is to be developed which can be related either to explain past economic behaviour or the present reality (actual economy) or expected and perceived future reality. For the failure to perceive socio-economic change is an obstacle to change itself, as it will bring stagnation in the process of development and evolution of Islamic economics as a science. This evolutionary process clearly has space and time dimensions (Step (3) in the table); it is entirely possible, though, that a new and competing conceptual framework can redefine a number of puzzles and may also generate new puzzles. It is evident that an Islamic economic theory can be replaced or modified subject to the timeless framework of the *Sharī'ah*.

1.4 Conclusion

Taken all in all, it can be said that the Islamic economists determined to make a serious beginning should now be able to have a broad understanding of the deductive or inductive method of enquiry in formulating Islamic theory and policy. For, there is a valid case for an ideal value-loaded Islamic theory which may have time and space dimensions. It is needed to explain the past, present and perceived future of economic behaviour, institutions and organizations. But it must be understood within the broader timeless framework of the *Qur'ānic* principles and the *Sunnah*. While Islamic economics is a part of a "system", it is a science too. The distinction between normative and positive economics is neither necessary nor desirable; in some senses, it could be misleading. It is to be noted however, that the method of enquiry can be deductive or inductive or a combination of both. The deductive method as developed by the Muslim jurists can be applied to Islamic economics in deducing the principles of the Islamic system, from the sources of Islamic laws. The inductive method can also be utilized to find solutions for the economic problems by reference to valid historical precedents. It is to be recognized, though, that much more work still needs to be done to bring the treatment of the subject to a comprehensiveness and further refinement which is beyond the scope of this chapter.

Notes

[1] Mannan, M. A. "Scarcity, choice and opportunity cost: their dimensions in Islamic economics", *Journal of Social Science*, a special issue on the Fifteenth Hijra Century, Kuwait University, 1981, pp. 170–171.

[2] Heilbroner, R. L. and Thurow, L. C. *The Economic Problem*, 4th edn, Prentice Hall Inc., p. 77.

[3] Lipsey, R. G. *Positive Economics*, Weidenfeld and Nicholson, London, 1975, p. 22.

[4] Mishan, E. G. *Introduction to Normative Economics*, Oxford University Press, Oxford, 1981, p. 22.

[5] This situation cannot be explained in terms of "Giffen goods" (when prices rise, consumption also rises and when prices fall, their consumption also falls) or "inferior goods" (a rise in a consumer's income causes a fall in demand, a fall in income causes a rise in demand).

[6] Baumol, W. J. *Economic Theory and Operation Analysis*, 4th edn, Prentice Hall, 1977, p. 55.
[7] Wilson, B. *Religion in a Secular Society*, C. A. Watts and Co. Ltd., London, 1966, p. xiv.
[8] Wilson, B. p. xvi.
[9] Boulding, K. E. *Beyond Economics*, The University of Michigan Press, Ann Arbor, U.S.A., 1970, p. 202.
[10] Hill, C. P. *British Economic and Social History, 1700–1975*, 4th edn, Edward Arnold Ltd., London, 1978, p. 85.
[11] Rousseau, J. (1712–1778). Swiss–French philosopher, author, political theorist and composer. Famous for his *Social Contract*.
[12] Lock, J. (1632–1704). English philosopher, founder of British empiricism. Famous for his *Two Treatises on Civil Governments* and other works.
[13] *The Oxford Pocket English Dictionary*, Oxford University Press, U.K.
[14] *The Oxford Pocket English Dictionary*.

1.5 Suggested Further Reading

Boulding, K. E. *Beyond Economics*, The University of Michigan Press, Ann Arbor, U.S.A., 1970.

Masumi, S. H. *The Role of Reason in Islam*, vol. 1, ed. by M. A. Khan, International Islamic Conference, Islamic Research Institute, Karachi, 1970.

Rahman F. *Islamic Methodology in History*, Islamic Research Institute, Islamabad, Pakistan, 1966.

Zarqa, A. "Islamic Economics: An Approach to Human Welfare" in *Studies in Islamic Economics*, ed. by K. Ahmed, International Centre for Research in Islamic Economics, I.C.R.I.E., King Abdul Aziz University, Jeddah, Saudi Arabia.

CHAPTER 2

Islamic Economics – A Comparative Review

2.1 Meaning, Nature and Scope of Islamic Economics

2.2 The Origin of Islamic Economics

2.3 Selected Further Reading

"And when the Prayer
Is finished, then may ye Disperse
through the land,
And seek of the Bounty
of Allah."
    Al-Qur'ān, Sūrah LXII. 10

"No one eats better food than which he eats out of the work of his hand."

The Prophet Muhammad
(peace be upon him) (Bukhari)

2.1 Meaning, Nature and Scope of Islamic Economics

The main objective of this section is to explain the nature and scope of Islamic economics and to offer a comparative analysis with modern secular economics.

To me, Islamic economics is a social science which studies the economic problems of a people imbued with the values of Islam. This is not to suggest that Muslims are prevented from studying the economic problems of non-Muslims. On the contrary, those who are imbued with the values of Islam are required by the *Sharī'ah* to study the economic problems of a non-Muslim minority in an Islamic state in particular, and of humanity in general. So this apparently narrow definition has a wider implication.

Besides, this definition of Islamic economics is in striking contrast to the modern definition of economics which is a "study of mankind in the ordinary business of life". To put it more clearly in the words of Professor Robbins: "Economics is a science which studies human behaviour as a relationship between ends and scarce means and which have alternative uses." The aptness of this definition is not incontrovertible, but it provides at any rate a very good description of the subject matter of modern economics which is primarily a study of man living in a society. If sociology is a genus, economics is a species of the same genus. No doubt, Islamic economics is a part of sociology. But this is a social science in a restricted sense. Because here we are not studying every individual living in society. Islamic economics is the study of man—not of an isolated individual but of a social individual having faith in the Islamic values of life. Like modern economics, Islamic economics does not study the world consisting of men like Robinson Crusoe, because the phenomenon of exchange, either as a fact or as a possibility, is to be included in both schools of economics although Islamic economics deals with the provision of "non-exchangeables (i.e. transfer payments) which frequently exist under the conditions of relative social concern and moral responsibility as opposed to indifference and selfishness."

Islamic economics deals mainly with problems involving money. There is, indeed, an increasing number of economists who endorse the view that economics is concerned with that aspect of human behaviour which is concerned with money-getting and money-spending. But classical writers and their present-day followers are inclined to go behind the money veil and to depict the economic problem in non-monetary terms. The fundamental economic problem of mankind owes its origin to the fact that we have wants and that these wants cannot generally be satisfied without the expenditure of our limited resources of human energy and material equipment. If we had unlimited means for the satisfaction of all kinds of wants, the economic problem would not have arisen. So far as this basic problem of scarcity is concerned, there is hardly any difference between Islamic and modern economics. If there is any difference, it lies in its nature and volume. That is why the main difference between these two systems of economics can be found with regard to the handling of the problem of choice. The question of choice arises from the fact that our resources are limited so that the satisfaction of some kind of want is at the expense of some other want which must go unsatisfied. The eternal conflict between multiplicity of wants and scarcity of means forces us to make a choice between our wants, to fix up a list of priorities and then distribute our resources in such a manner as to be able to secure maximum satisfaction of wants. In modern economics, this problem of choice is greatly dependent on the whims of individuals. They may or may not take into account the requirements of society. But in Islamic economics, we are not in a position to distribute the resources in any way we like. There is a serious moral limitation imposed by the Holy *Qur'ān* and the *Sunnah* on the powers of the individuals in this respect. The entire circle of economic activity may be explained with the help of the following two charts:

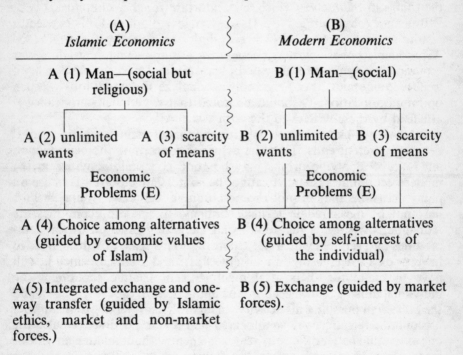

(A)	(B)
Islamic Economics	*Modern Economics*

A (1) Man—(social but religious)   B (1) Man—(social)

A (2) unlimited wants   A (3) scarcity of means   B (2) unlimited wants   B (3) scarcity of means

Economic Problems (E)   Economic Problems (E)

A (4) Choice among alternatives (guided by economic values of Islam)   B (4) Choice among alternatives (guided by self-interest of the individual)

A (5) Integrated exchange and one-way transfer (guided by Islamic ethics, market and non-market forces.)   B (5) Exchange (guided by market forces).

Thus to sum up, in Islamic economics we study not only the social individual but also man with the religious bent of man [A(1)], whereas in modern economics we are primarily interested in a people living in a society [B(1)]. It is because of a multiplicity of ends [A(2)/B(2)] and scarcity of means (A3/B3), that the economic problems have arisen (E). This problem is basically the same in both modern and Islamic economics. But the difference arises with regard to choice. Islamic economics is guided by the basic values of Islam [A(4)] and modern economics, based on a capitalist socio-economic framework, is greatly controlled by the self-interest of the individual B(4). What makes Islamic economics really distinctive is that the integrative system of exchange and one-way transfer influence the allocation of scarce resources, thereby making the process of exchange immediately relevant to the total welfare of man (A/5) as distinguished from mere economic well-being (B/5).

This difference gives rise to the controversy whether Islamic economics is concerned with ends or whether it should be neutral between different ends. Because modern economics is indifferent between ends, it discusses the economic problems as they are, not as they ought to be. In other words, modern economics is not concerned with value-judgments. Thus Professor Robbins observed: The subject-matter of economics is essentially a relationship between ends conceived as tendencies to conduct, on the one hand, and the technical and social environment on the other. Ends as such do not form part of the subject-matter. Nor does the technical and social environment. It is the relationships between these things and not the things in themselves which are important for the economist.

But some recent writers like Hicks, Lange, Kaldor and others tried to restore at least a part of welfare economics on a strictly scientific basis. According to these writers, economic welfare is maximized if our economic resources are allocated in an optimal manner. The task of welfare economics, then, is simply to analyze the conditions of such optimum allocation. It should be noted that no ethical significance is attached by these writers to the term "welfare".

Whether we like it or not, Islamic economics cannot remain neutral between different ends. Thus the activities concerning the manufacture and sale of alcoholic drinks may be good economic activities in the modern economic system. It cannot be so in Islamic States. Because on many occasions they do not promote human welfare—a welfare which may not be measured in terms of money. In modern economics the individual's welfare is regarded as an increasing function of the commodities and services which he, according to his scale of values, likes to have, and as a decreasing function of efforts and sacrifices which he will have to make for their attainment. But in Islamic economics the individual must take into account the injunctions of the Holy *Qur'ān* and the *Sunnah* in pursuing his activity. In Islam, social welfare is maximized if economic resources are so allocated that it is impossible to make any one individual better off by any rearrangement without making anyone or some others worse off within the framework of the *Qur'ān* and the *Sunnah*. Anything which is not expressly prohibited in the *Qur'ān* or the *Sunnah* but is consistent with the spirit of the same may be styled as Islamic. We find no harm in having such activities carried out in the Islamic economic system.

Though Islamic economics, like modern economics, is not merely concerned with that aspect of human behaviour which is related to money-getting and money-spending, yet they form a great part of our economic activities. It is really surprising that even fourteen hundred years ago Islam tried to bring about a lasting balance between earning and spending in order to achieve the target of the maximum social advantage. Islam has always emphasized lawful earning of livelihood. All unlawful means of acquiring property are prohibited as these, in the end, destroy a people (Qur'ān *Sūrah* IV. 30). It has, therefore, laid down certain rules which govern and determine the form and intensity of the wealth-earning activities of man. They are so restrained as to be in complete harmony with the peace and well-being of society as a whole. At no stage are these economic activities to be free from the yoke of moral consideration. To this effect the Holy *Qur'ān* says:

"O ye people!
Eat of what is on earth,
Lawful and good;
And do not follow
The footsteps of the Evil One,
For he is to you
An avowed enemy."

Sūrah II. 168

Thus an Islamic State can encourage only those legitimate activities which are in complete harmony with social good. It follows that Islam views with extreme disfavour a monopoly of resources by a few capitalists (*Sūrah* LIX.7) and the stress is always on socially beneficial spending only. The Holy *Qur'ān* says

"And spend (in Charity)
Out of what We have provided
For them, secretly and openly,
Hope for a Commerce
That will never fail."

Sūrah XXXV. 29

In fact, niggardliness is condemned as a negative and destructive quality. Wealth of the misers, instead of bringing them any advantage, becomes a handicap and arrests their moral and spiritual development (*Sūrah* III. 180). The other extreme, extravagance, is equally condemned. He commands:

"But waste not
By excess, for God
Loveth not the wasters."

Sūrah VI. 141

"Verily spendthrifts are brothers
Of the Evil Ones;
And the Evil One
Is to his Lord (Himself)
Ungrateful."

(*Sūrah* XVII. 27)

The fact is that Allah is Alone and All-Sufficient. It is men who are needy, and prosperity is achieved not through miserliness or holding back but through beneficent spending in the cause of Allah, that is, in the service of His creatures (*Sūrah* XLVII. 38)

In this way, Islam harmonizes the money-earning and money-spending activities in such a way that they may promote the welfare of the people.

Thus in one sense, Islamic economics is more restricted and, in the other sense, it is more comprehensive than modern economics. It is restricted, because it is concerned only with those people who have faith in the Oneness of Allah and His moral teachings as reflected in the Holy *Qur'ān* and the *Sunnah*. It is also restricted, because an Islamic State cannot encourage any and every economic activity. The activities which cannot promote human welfare cannot be encouraged in an Islamic State. But the concept of human welfare cannot be static, and is always relative to changing circumstances. The point is that the concept of welfare must be in harmony with the universal principles of Islam—principles which will remain valid for all times to come just as the sum total of one plus one will remain true to all ages.

Again, it is comprehensive because Islamic economics takes cognizance of non-economic factors like political, social, ethical and moral factors. In a sense it is like applied economics which also takes cognizance of non-economic factors—the roughness and frictions of the actual world which tilt the balance of a practical decision. Thus the scope of Islamic economics seems to become the administration of scarce resources in human society in the light of the ethical conception of welfare in Islam. It is, therefore concerned not only with the material causes of welfare, but also with immaterial matters subject to the Islamic prohibition on consumption and production.

Neither the consumer nor the producer are sovereign in Islam. The behaviour of both is to be guided by the general, individual and social welfare as understood in the *Sharī'ah*.

2.2 The Origin of Islamic Economics

The main purpose of this brief section is to establish the hypothesis that although the fundamental principles of Islamic economics owe their origin to the *Qur'ān* and the *Sunnah*, the interpretation and re-interpretation of those principles (governing a variety of subjects such as value, division of labour, the price system and concept of "fair price", the forces of demand and supply, consumption and production, population growth, government expenditure and taxation, the role of the state, trade cycles, monopoly, price control, household income and expenditure etc.) by a number of Islamic scholars and economists from the very beginning of Islam provided the operational basis of Islamic economics and a continuity of economic ideas. Muslim scholars such as Abū Yūsuf (731–

798), Yahyab Ibn Adam (d. 818), El Harīri (1054–1122), Ṭūsī (1201–1274), Ibn-Taimiya (1262–1328)[1], Ibn Khaldūn (1332–1406), Shāh Walīullah (1702–1763), not to mention Abu Darr Ghifari (d. 654), Ibn Hazm (d. 1064), al-Ghazālī (1059–1111), Farabi (d. 950) and many others contributed to the development of the science of economics.

It is perhaps not out of place to mention briefly the contribution of a few of them. Abū Yūsuf's contribution to public finance, his emphasis on the role of the state, public work and the development of agriculture has its validity even to-day.

Ibn Taimiya's notion of the "price of the equivalent", his understanding of market imperfections and price control, his emphasis on the role of the state to ensure the fulfilment of the basic needs of the people, and his notion of ownership provide us with a number of interesting clues in understanding the theory of Islamic economic policy in our own times. Tūsī's definition of economics clearly underlined the importance of the value of exchange, division of labour and welfare of the people. Thus Tūsi, in his famous Persian work *Akhlaq-i-Nāṣirī*, wrote: "If every person had to remain occupied in producing his own food, clothing, shelter and tools respectively . . . he could not have survived because of becoming foodless during the (long) period required (for supplying the above things) . . . However, since people co-operate with each other and everyone adopts a particular profession, producing more than what is sufficient for his own consumption, and since the laws of justice take care of the matters pertaining to the exchange of one's surplus output with the products of other people, economic means and goods become available to all . . . . Thus God in His wisdom diversified people's activities and tastes so that they might adopt different occupations (to help each other) . . . . It is this division of work which brings into existence international structure and mankind's economic system. Since human existence does not acquire a shape without mutual co-operation, it cannot take place without social contact, hence man by nature is dependent upon society."

Again Ibn Khaldūn, the celebrated Arab scholar of Tunis who is universally recognized as the father of Social Sciences, has given a definition of economics which is broader in scope than that of Ṭūsī's. He saw more clearly than many later economists the intimate connection between economics and human welfare.

His reference to "the dictates of reason as well as ethics" shows that he considers economics both a positive and a normative science. Further, his use of the word "masses" (*al-jambūr*) is indicative of the fact that the purpose of the study of economics is to promote welfare of masses and not of individuals. It is so because economic and social laws operate on masses and cannot be significantly influenced by isolated individuals. It was Ibn Khaldūn who saw the interrelationship between economic, political, social, ethical and educational factors. Although his celebrated *al-Muqaddimah* deals with these factors separately, he considers them as inter-linked "aspects of civilization that affect human beings in their social organisation". He introduced a number of fundamental economic notions such as the importance of division of labour, recognition of the contribution of labour in the theory of value, theory of population growth, capital formation, public finance, trade cycles, the price-system etc.

Taken all in all, these Muslim scholars in general and Ibn Khaldūn in particular can be regarded as precursors of the mercantilists, physiocrats and the classical writers (e.g. Adam Smith, Ricardo, Malthus) and neoclassical writers (e.g. Keynes).

Notes

[1] Shaykh Al-Islam Ibn Taimiya, a Hanbali theologian, was one of the most outstanding scholars of Islamic history. His economic views are expressed mostly in his famous works: *al-Siyasah al-Shari'ah fi Islah al Rai wa'l Rai' ah* (Public and Private laws in Islam, English translation by Farrukh Omer; French translation by Henri Laoust) as well as *al Hisbah wa Masuliah al Hukumah al Islami'ah* (Public supervision of economic and social activities and role of the Islamic state)

2.3 Selected Further Reading

Ariff, M. "Islamic Ethics and Economics", Proceedings of the 7th Annual Conference of the Association of Muslim Social Scientists, Indiana, U.S.A., 1978.

Ben Shemesh, A. *Taxation in Islam* (Translation of *Kitab al-Kharaj* by Abū Yūsuf and Ben Adam) vol. 1 and vol. 2, Brill, Leiden, 1958 and 1965.

Mannan, M. A. "Scarcity, Choice and Opportunity Cost; their dimensions in Islamic economics" in *Journal of Social Sciences*, a special issue on the Fifteenth Hijra Century, Kuwait University, 1981.

Rozenthal, F. *The Muqaddimah: An Introduction to History* by Ibn Khaldūn, Routledge and Kegan Paul, London, 1967.

CHAPTER 3

Islamic and Economic Laws

3.1 Introduction

3.2 Nature of Economic Laws

3.3 Sources of Islamic Economic Laws

    (a) *The Qur'ān*

    (b) *Hadīth* and *Sunnah*

    (c) *Ijmā'*

    (d) *Ijtihād* or *Qiyās*

    (e) Other principles of law

3.4 The *Fiqh* Schools and Their Contemporary Implications

3.5 Conclusion

3.6 Selected Further Reading

"Hā-Mīm;
By the Book that
Makes things clear:
We sent it down
During a blessed night:
For we (ever) wish
To warn (against Evil);
In that (night) is made
Distinct every affair
of wisdom;
By command, from Our
Presence. For we (ever)
Send (revelations)."

Al-Qur'ān, (Sūrah XLIV. 1–5)

"Obedience is due only in that which is good".

The Prophet (peace be upon him)
(Bukhari)

3.1 Introduction

In this chapter my main objective is to establish that Islamic law (*Sharī'ah*) has the ability for evolution and development to face the contemporary issues of the world of Islam. The spirit and general principles of Islamic laws were valid yesterday, are valid today and will remain valid tomorrow. In most cases, the Islamic scheme of laws leaves the details to human reason. The reason, of course, has been tethered to revelation and a wide range has been provided to it for its function. It is this absence of details that gives Islam an amount of elasticity, unknown in any other system, and it is this elasticity and adaptability in details that make Islam a universal code, capable of being realized at all times. We can see the same principles running through all the teachings of Islam. As a wonderful combination of rigidity and flexibility is inherent in Islamic laws, there are some points of similarity and dissimilarity between Islamic laws and economic laws. Let us now confine ourselves to explaining the nature of economic laws.

3.2 Nature of Economic Laws

An economic law is a statement of tendencies—a statement of a causal relationship between two groups of phenomena. All scientific laws are laws in the same sense. If there is a combination of hydrogen and oxygen, other things being equal, we get water. So also in economics, other things being equal, if the price of a commodity rises, the demand for it will usually fall. If a law of chemistry be a natural law, an economic law is also a natural law in the same sense. But the laws of economics cannot be as exact as the laws of natural sciences. This is due to the following reasons.

First, economics is a social science and as such it has to deal with a multiplicity of men guided by a multiplicity of motives. This element in the situation is responsible for the fact that economic laws can give only average results. Secondly, not only are the economic data innumerable but they are themselves changeable over a period of time. Since men change in their attitudes, tastes and disposition over a period of time, the task of predicting how different men will react to a given change in circumstances on different occasions becomes extremely risky and precarious. Thirdly, there are many unknown factors in the situation. All the data cannot be known and prediction based on known data may be falsified or distorted by the influence of the unknown data. Economic laws may, however, be compared with the laws of tides rather than the simple and exact law of gravitation. The laws of tides explain how there is a rise and fall of tides twice a day under the influence of the sun and the moon, how there are strong tides at new and full moon, etc. In human activities, too, there are many unforeseen circumstances, as a result of which the expected course of action may not happen in the regular way.

"Economic laws," writes Seligman, in his *Principles of Economics*, "are essentially hypothetical". All economic laws contain the following qualifying clause "other things being equal," i.e. we assume that from a given set of facts, certain conclusions will follow, if no other change takes place in the meantime. But other things are not always equal and, consequently, in economics, definite conclusions cannot be predicted from a given set of facts. Economic laws are, therefore, described as hypothetical—hypothetical because their truth and operation depend upon so many factors which are variable and imperfectly ascertainable.

But it does not follow that because an economic law is hypothetical, it is unreal or useless. The laws of all other sciences are also hypothetical. Every science assumes certain causes and draws certain generalizations from those causes, assuming that nothing changes in the meantime. Moreover, all economic laws are not essentially hypothetical. There are some economic laws which may be regarded as true as physical laws and there are others which are true as axioms as we find in the case of the law of diminishing returns. Economics, unlike other branches of the social sciences, has got a common measuring rod of human motives in the shape of money. As Marshall has observed, "Just as the chemist's fine balance has made chemistry much more exact than any other physical science, so also the economist's balance,—the money measuring rod of human motives—rough and imperfect as it is—has made economics much more exact than any other branch of the social sciences." Thus economics, though much less exact than the physical sciences is much more exact than the other social sciences. Economics does not, generally speaking, give us a body of settled conclusions and doctrines. It imparts instead an apparatus of the mind, a technique of thinking, an outlook and an approach. Training in economic theory and economic analysis enables us to understand better concrete economic problems and thus equips us for finding a scientific solution to our problems. With this brief analysis of economic laws we may proceed to explain the basic concepts of Islamic laws and their ability for evolution to face the conflicting present-day problems.

3.3 Sources of Islamic Economic Laws

The uniqueness of Islamic laws lies in their comprehensiveness of principles, valid through ages in respect of the whole of mankind. The whole basis and sources of Islamic laws are a standing and perpetual miracle—miracle in the sense that Islamic laws may not only be compared with the laws of tides but also with the simple and exact law of gravitation. Because, while Islamic laws have always been found to yield new truths and fresh guidance in every age and at every level, guidance has also been furnished to mankind through a series of fundamental and eternal revelations vouchsafed by Allah to the Prophet (peace be upon him). It is at this stage necessary to go into the very basis and sources of Islamic Law to establish that it is a standing guidance for mankind for all times to come, We all know that the sources of Islamic Law are basically four: (*a*) the *Qur'ān*, (*b*) the *Sunnah* and *Hadīth*, (*c*) *Ijmā'* and (*d*) *Qiyās and Ijtihād,* but I shall try to explain each of these sources of law from the standpoint whether they could expound and explain all that is or may be needed by mankind for the complete fulfilment of life.

(a) The Holy Qur'ān.

The eternal and original source of Islamic Law is the Holy *Qur'ān* which is the very messages that Allah put in the mouth of the Prophet (peace be upon him) for the guidance of mankind. These messages are universal, eternal and fundamental. But there are certain misconceptions among some Muslim and non-Muslim scholars regarding the true meaning of the Holy *Qur'ān*. The first misconception arises from the controversy whether the *Qur'ān* is "created" or "uncreated". The Mu'tazilah school of thought along with some non-Muslim thinkers believed that the *Qur'ān* belongs to the created world and is not the eternal speech of God. They appear to have believed that the Holy Book was sent to the heart of the Prophet (peace be upon him) from where it emerged from time to time in the language and style of the Prophet (peace be upon him). Hence they held the view that the *Qur'ān* is "created". But on the authority of Shāh Walīullah and Iqbāl we can say that the Holy *Qur'ān* is "uncreated," an eternal message vouchsafed by Allah to the Prophet (peace be upon him). Undoubtedly, the Divine Revelation flowed through the Prophet's heart over a period of approximately twenty-two years, but the words, the idioms and the style are generated with the ideas *without the conscious control* of the Prophet (peace be upon him), the recipient of Revelation which is not an integral part of the "agent's mind". Herein lies the fundamental distinction between the mysticism of the Qur'ānic Revelation and the mystic inspiration of a philosopher, a poet and a scientist. Because, in the latter case, the organic relationship between feeling, ideas and words becomes complete with a life of its own; though this creative process of a philosopher or a scientist lies, in a sense, beyond the ordinary reach of the recipient, yet this creative new knowledge is an integral part of the "agent's mind". In this sense, the Divine Revelation does not form part of the creative mind of the Prophet (peace be upon him). Therefore, the *Qur'ān* is eternal. In his book *Islām*, Dr Fazlur Rahman, has also tried to establish the same. But his analysis gives us ample scope for intellectual confusion. At one place, he observes: ". . . That is why, his [Prophet's] overall behaviour is regarded by the Muslims as Sunna or the 'perfect model'. But, with all this, there were moments when he, as it were, 'transcends himself' and his moral cognitive perception becomes so acute and so keen that *his consciousness becomes identical with the moral law itself* "[1] (*my italics*). Again he says, "But if Muhammad, in his Qur'ānic moments, became one with the moral law, he may not be absolutely identified with God. These observations are inconsistent in the sense that if Muhammad (peace be upon him) "became (identified) with the moral law" even in the "Qur'ānic moments," that moral laws or religious values are then part of the agent's mind. But the Holy *Qur'ān* categorically forbids any attempt to associate a creature (*sharīk*) with Allah and the Prophet (peace be upon him) himself condemned any such move as the greatest sin. The fact is that the Holy *Qur'ān* is the universal record of the verbal revelation vouchsafed by Allah to Muhammad (peace be upon him) who was powerless to control the process of revelation consciously. Thus, the Holy *Qur'ān* is uncreated, it always yields, and will go on yielding, the needed guidance for mankind. This has been demonstrated through more than thirteen centuries, and that is a guarantee that it will continue to be demonstrated through the ages. In the words of Sir Muhammad Zafarullah Khan, we can say, "The Quran has proclaimed that falsehood will never overtake it. All research into the past and every discovery and invention in the future will affirm its truth (*Sūrah* XLI. 42). The Quran speaks at every level; it seeks to reach every type of understanding, through parables, similitudes, arguments, reasoning, the observation and study of the phenomena of nature, and the natural, moral and spiritual laws (*Sūrah* XVIII. 54–55; *Sūrah* XXXIX. 27; *Sūrah* LIX. 22);"[2]

Secondly, some modern scholars are under the wrong impression that a great part of the Qur'ānic revelation is "causal," because its appearance is based on the then Arab society. The norms and values are, therefore, to be derived from the various Qur'ānic injunctions. Thus in his book *Mohammedan Theories of Finance*[4] N. P. Aghnides observed: "The revelations of the second period [in Madinah], therefore, relate principally to questions of war and internal reorganisation such as spoils, Zakat, marriage, inheritance, usury, transgressions, etc. The general characteristic of these revelations is that they are *causal,* for they were revealed as the circumstances required, they were never meant to be, and they are, a well-rounded system of Law."
But the very term "causal" is objectionable, because this is against the spirit of the "uncreated" or eternal nature of the *Qur'ān*. If everybody starts thinking that the Qur'ānic revelations are generally "causal" in character, different people guided by a multiplicity of motives and values would derive different sets of norms and values suited to their own requirements. This will have a damaging and disastrous effect on the whole aspect of the universal revelations of the Holy *Qur'ān*. The fact is that the Qur'ānic Laws are to be enforced as they are. That does not mean that we are debarred from deriving norms and values by analogy in the problems for which we have no expressed or written solutions. The revelations which were obviously based on the condition of Arab society then prevailing are symbolic ones.

It is not also correct to assume that the Qur'ānic revelations were never meant to be a system of law. If by law we mean the present-day man-made system of law which is mostly one-sided and motivated mainly by consideration of exploitation in one way or another or apartheid policy or the like, then the *Qur'ān* does not clearly provide us with a code of Law. It is, of course, true that the *Qur'ān* is not a legal code in the modern sense of the term. It is not a compendium of ethics either. The Qur'ān, however, instead of mentioning the minutive, talks of the basic principles and draws attention to various Divine Attributes, their operation and the manner in which mankind may derive benefit from the knowledge thereof. In fact, all that is basic for the promotion of human welfare in all spheres, whether pertaining to principles or conduct, is set forth and compounded (*Sūrah* XVI. 90). We are reminded:

"O mankind! there hath come to you a direction from your Lord
And a healing for the (diseases)
In your hearts, – and for those who believe guidance
And Mercy.

(*Sūrah* X. 57)

Within this framework, man is free to accept the truth on the basis of understanding (*Sūrah* XII. 109). It is, therefore, not correct to assume that belief in Divine Revelation of fourteen centuries ago would tend to intellectual rigidity, rather it will stimulate the intellect and open all manner of avenues for the expansion of knowledge. The constant and repeated exhortation to reflect upon and ponder every type of natural phenomenon with which the *Qur'ān* abounds is an express urge in that direction.

The last, not the least, misconception about the *Qur'ān* arises from the incorrect presumption of N J. Coulson who made the following remark: "The primary purpose of the *Qur'ān* is to regulate not the relationship of man with his fellows but his relationship with his creator."[4] This observation is simply a half truth and betrays the author's sad ignorance of the spirit of the Qur'ānic Law which is intended to bring an equilibrium between the spiritual and material requirements of life. The verses revealed in Makkah, especially the oldest of them, all enjoin upon the people of Makkah belief in the resurrection, the last day of judgment and the final reward or punishment for human acts in the world to come. We have already noted that the revelations of the second period relate to the law of inheritance, rulings for marriage and divorce, the question of war and peace, punishments for theft, adultery and homicide, etc. Thus we see that the *Qur'ān* expounds not only the significance of establishing and maintaining communion with God but also explains all that may be needed for the complete fulfilment of social life. In fact, the *Qur'ān* emerges as a document that from the first to the last seeks to emphasize all those moral tensions that are necessary for creative human actions. Indeed, at bottom the centre of the Qur'ān's interest is man and his betterment. For this it is essential that men operate within the framework of certain tensions which, indeed, have been created by God in him. First and foremost, man may not jump to the suicidal conclusion that he can make and unmake moral law according to his 'heart's desire' from the obvious fact that this law is *for him*. Hence the absolute supremacy and the majesty of God are most strikingly emphasized by the *Qur'ān*. The Prophet (peace be upon him) was, to all intents and purposes, sent primarily to exemplify the teachings of the *Qur'ān* and present to the world a model of ideal practical life. The *Sunnah,* by its very nature, therefore, never goes against the *Qur'ān,* nor does the *Qur'ān* go against the *Sunnah,* the second important source of Islamic Law.

(b) Sunnah

In the context of Islamic laws, the Sunnah which literally means "way, custom, habit of life" refers to the exemplary conduct of the Prophet largely based on the normative practice of the early community. The concept of *Sunnah* came perforce to have the meaning of the living tradition in each succeeding generation.

Some jurists are of the opinion that both the *Sunnah* and the *Ḥadīth* were coeval and consubstantial in the earliest phase after the Prophet (peace be upon him) from whom they drew their normativity. But *a Sunnah* is to be distinguished from a *Ḥadīth*, which is a narrative, usually very short, purporting to give information about what the Prophet (peace be upon him) said, did, approved or disapproved, or of similar information about his Companions. Therefore, the *Ḥadīth* is something theoretical in nature, whereas the *Sunnah* is the very same report when it acquires a normative quality and becomes a practical principle for the Muslim. Whereas *Sunnah* was largely and primarily a practical phenomenon, geared as it was to behavioural norms, *Ḥadīth* become the vehicle not only of legal norms but of religious beliefs and principles as well.

The answer to the question as to why the *Sunnah* is a source of law lies in the Holy *Qur'ān*, which enjoins upon the Muslim to follow the conduct of the Prophet (peace be upon him). The *Qur'ān* asks the Prophet (peace be upon him) to decide the problems of the Muslims according to Revelations. (*Sūrah* V. 47–48) Again, the Prophet (peace be upon him) has been declared to be the interpreter of the Qur'ānic text (*Sūrah* IV. 16,44). The *Qur'ān,* for instance, mentions *Salāt* and *Zakāt*, but does not lay down their details. It is the Prophet who explained them to his followers in a practical form. Moreover, the *Qur'ān* directs the Muslims to follow the examplary conduct of the Prophet. Therefore, the *Sunnah* became a definite source of Islamic Law. In an effort to give *Sunnah* a very predominant position as a source of law there is a theory that the *Sunnah* which is a supplement to the *Qur'ān* can supersede the *Qur'ān* in case of its contradiction. We are not prepared to accept this contention simply because of shifting the centre of gravity from the *Qur'ān* to the *Sunnah*.

At this stage it seems necessary to explain why the *Sunnah* is dynamic and capable of handling the present-day problems arising from the complexity of life. In a living community, new moral tensions, various legal and administrative complications are bound to arise. In fact, many a serious controversy arose in the theological and moral sphere of the expanding Islamic society. But the concept of the ideal *Sunnah* was retained: new material was thought out and assimilated, because the process of interpretation began both tacitly and explicitly with the Companions themselves and various practical norms were deduced keeping in view the basic rulings of the Holy *Qur'ān*. F. Rahman has rightly mentioned that "after the period of the Companions (and in some cases of the following generation of the 'Successors') the Sunna could not be deduced from the actual practice but only from the expressely transmitted *Ḥadīth*. But it is most significant and remarkable that deductions by interpretation from a *Ḥadīth* in *any* period were called Sunnas. Thus Abū Dā'ūd (d. 275/888) after relating a *Ḥadīth* remarks, 'There are five *Sunnas* in this *Ḥadīth*,' i.e. five points with the character of practical norms can be deduced from this *Ḥadīth*,"[5]

Now is the time to interpret the *Ḥadīth* not merely in literal form but also in spirit. The interpretation of the *Ḥadīth* and the *Sunnah* must take into account their correct historical perspective and functional significance in a historical context. Because in a rapidly expanding society interpretation of the Holy *Qur'ān* and the *Sunnah* must serve as a guide for intelligent moral understanding and implementation, not for a mere rigid formalism.

In fact, through individual interpretation of the law and the dogma, the content of the *Sunnah* created a wealth of material which, although it was generally uniform in its essentials, except for certain extreme doctrines of the Khārijites and other sects, conflicted in its details on most points. This material was, in the next step, brought under the concepts of the "agreed practice" and the consensus, which is called "*Ijmā*'".

(c) Ijmā'

Ijmā'—the third source of Islamic law—is the consensus either of the community or of the doctors of religion. The conceptual difference between *Sunnah* and *Ijmā*' lies in the fact that while *Sunnah* is restricted mainly to the teachings of the Prophet and is extended to the Companions inasmuch as they are the source for its transmission, the *Ijmā*' which is a principle of new legal content that emerges as a result of exercising reason and logic in the face of a rapidly expanding society, such as the early Islamic one, begins with the Companions and extended to subsequent generations.

We find the justification of *Ijmā*' as a dynamic source of law both in the Holy *Qur'ān* and the *Sunnah*. The *Qur'ān* says: "It is this that We have made of you a nation of the right mean" (Sūrah II.143). The Prophet is also reported to have said: "My people shall never agree on an error." The fact is that *Ijmā*' is intended "not only for discerning the right at present and in the future, but also for establishing the past": it was *Ijmā*' that determined what the Sunnah of the Prophet had been and indeed what the right interpretation of the *Qur'ān* was. In the final analysis both the *Qur'ān* and the *Sunnah* were authenticated through the *Ijmā*'.

Therefore, it appears that *Ijmā*' is the most powerful factor in solving the complex belief and practice of the Muslims. At a given period of time it has supreme functional validity and power. If its verdict is final, it is final only in a relative sense, because *Ijmā'* has the potentialities of assimilation, modification and rejection according to the requirements of modern life. Herein lies its dynamism in Islamic Law. N. P. Aghnides has rightly mentioned that "the significance of ijma' in the Mohammeden law can hardly be overestimated. By its means, not only is controversy on many points forever done away with, but also, when new situations have been met by analogy or otherwise, the Muslims may be assured that they are not getting away from the old basis and drifting into heresy. Notwithstanding the unifying influence of *Ijmā'*, there remained indeed always a certain residuum of divergence of opinion on some minor question on which no consensus could be attained, but this was construed by the canonists to be an indication of God's grace to His people, for there is an *Ijmā'* on this very point too, namely, that such divergence is not to be depreciated, because it is a sign of God's grace. This *Ijmā'* is based on the *Ḥadīth* in which the Prophet said: The difference of opinion in my Community is an indication of grace from God's Part."[6]

It follows that there are points which have been universally accepted and agreed upon by the entire community. This sort of *Ijmā'*, which is obligatory in nature, is known as the *Ijmā'* of the community. On the other hand, there are certain rules which are agreed upon by the learned of a particular region, and not by the entire community. This is known as the *Ijmā'* of the learned, which may be used as a mechanism for creating a sort of integration among the divergent opinions which arose as a result of the individual legal activities of jurists.

Some doctors are of the opinion that it is impossible to ascertain the existence of *Ijmā'* simply because of the difficulty of ascertaining the consensus of opinion of the community. If it is possible to assess public opinion in huge democracies like the United Kingdom, the United States, India, etc., I find no reason why it would not be possible to ascertain the existence of *Ijmā'*. For having *Ijmā'*, we need not press for authoritative justification. If we did so, there would no longer be any use for the *Ijmā'* as an independent source of law. But the authority or evidence for the opinions which make up an *Ijmā'* may be a probable evidence such as *Qiyās*; or it may be an "individual" report or it may be a positive evidence, such as a verse of the *Qur'ān* or a *Sunnah*. It appears that *Ijmā'* which sets aside the stray opinion circulating in each locality as a dynamic force of a living community. A Muslim community which wants to keep pace with the modern world must give due importance to *Ijmā'* as a source of Islamic Law and jurisprudence. Because it helps us to derive a set of principles or a code of conduct exercising *Ijtihād*, the last but not the least basis of *Fiqh*.

(d) Ijtihād.

Technically, *Ijtihād* means "putting forth every effort in order to determine with a degree of probability a question of the *Sharī'ah*". The legal effect of it is that the opinion rendered is probably right, though there is the possibility of error. Obviously, the fundamentals of the religion of Islam like the Oneness of Allah, the sending of Prophets, etc. cannot properly constitute a subject of *Ijtihād*. According to al-Māwardī, the scope of *Ijtihād* after the Prophet's death includes eight separate heads. Seven of these consist in the interpretation of the revealed texts, by some method such as analogy, and the eighth is the derivation of a meaning from other than the revealed texts, e.g. by reasoning. It follows that *Ijtihād* believes partly in the process of interpretation and reinterpretation and partly in analogical deductions by reasoning. With the march of human civilization our life is, on the one hand, becoming more complex day by day, and new social and moral problems that emerge in the society from time to time require solutions. On the other hand, the mental and intellectual horizon is also widening with the advance of human knowledge. The result is that Islamic Law developed with the emergence of new problems since the days of the Prophet and was created and recreated, interpreted and reinterpreted in accordance with the changing circumstances Therefore, the Mu'tazilites' view that *Ijtihād* is always right can hardly be accepted. Since *Ijtihād* mainly deals with a question of the *Sharī'ah* that emerges in society from time to time, its ruling cannot be the same for all times to come. With the passage of time the concept of social requirements of life is, other things being equal, bound to change. Therefore, the process of rethinking and reinterpreting must be allowed to go undisturbed keeping in view the basic injunctions of the Holy *Qur'ān* and the *Sunnah*.

In the early centuries of Islam, *rā'y* (personal opinion) was the basic instrument of *Ijtihād*. But when the principles of law were systematically laid down it was replaced by *Qiyās*. The *Qur'ān* and the *Sunnah*, no doubt, provide us with the legal rules with regard to the individual and social life of the Muslims. But human life, living dynamics, requires laws that ought to change with the changing circumstances. Hence the necessity of *Ijtihād*. However, the famous controversy between the *Ḥadīth*-folk and the *rā'y*-folk is one of the most unfortunate phases of the struggle in the process of evolution of Islamic Law. In this connection let me quote N. P. Aghnides who has correctly observed:

"The jurists of Medina and Mecca, living in the cities in which Islam had its origins and early development and which were saturated with hadith associations laid emphasis on the preservation and the study of the hadiths and in deciding legal questions they referred to them or their standard. This they could easily do, because the cultural and legal conditions under which those hadiths had been uttered by the Prophet still remained practically the same and so the hadiths and local customs would be sufficient to decide the legal question that might arise, without resorting much to the use of analogy. But it cannot be said that this was true of the jurists of the conquered countries outside of Arabia, especially of Iraq. In Iraq the conditions were different and the jurists who lived there, being away from the home of the hadith lore and facing new situations, from the very first used and had to use personal opinion (rā'y) much more extensively. They are, therefore, called rā'y folk in distinction from the jurists of Hijaz who were known as hadith folk."

It is no surprise that this controversy was largely a matter of quibbling over words, both sides made free use of personal opinion although *Qiyās* has ultimately been admitted into most of the schools.

We have evidence to prove that the majority of the jurists and theologians considered *Qiyās* lawful not only intellectual matters but also in *Sharj'ah* matters. We also share the same view, although the Shī'ites and the Khārijites allowed the use of *Qiyās* only in *Sharī'ah* matters; and that the Hanbalites sanctioned its use only as regards applications of '*Fiqh*', in view of the need, for cases concerning which the *Qur'ān* is silent but denied its lawfulness as regards the determination of intellectual matter.

The role of *Qiyās* is to extend the law of the text to such cases as do not fall within the purview of its terms by reason of an "effective" cause which is common to both cases and cannot be understood from the expression (concerning the original case). According to the jurists, the extension of law by analogy does not establish a new rule of law, but merely helps us to discover the law. For instance, if a certain act has been prohibited in the *Qur'ān* and the *Sunnah*, other acts, common with that act in regard to the "effective" cause ('*illah*) for which the prohibition has been decreed, are likewise prohibited. It is necessary, however, that the acts to which the value is extended, should not be included in the meaning of the prohibitory expression, explicitly or implicitly, for in that case they would be prohibited by virtue of the prohibitory expression itself and not by virtue of *Qiyās* thereon.

The effective cause of a law may be the quality of a thing inseparable or accidental, manifest or hidden, a generic name or a rule of law. An effective cause may sometimes be determined by the consensus of scholars' opinion. The case in which the Prophet (peace be upon him) treated an obligation to perform pilgrimage as a debt is an example of an effective cause suggested by the fact of its being laid down in answer to a question.

The period of 'Umar's Caliphate abounds in instances which explain the dynamism of Islamic Law. His introduction of certain changes in the details of collection of *Zakāt*, his refusal to distribute the conquered land among the soldiers—a practice which was current during the lifetime of the Prophet (peace be upon him) and during the Caliphate of Abu Bakr and a host of other measures are indicative of the fact that while exercising *Ijtihād*, one should keep in mind the change of conditions and circumstances. This is the most important factor for legislation by means of *Ijtihād*.

During the medieval period it was said that the door of *Ijtihād* was closed and one should follow an established school of law, because the trend of "*taqlīd*", which means the servile acceptance of another opinion without evidence, dominated the people and they began to follow some jurists or some school of law. This is partly due to the fact that the founders of the schools were men of great ability and thoroughness who had practically exhausted the various logical alternatives within the limitations set by the revealed texts. It is true that the comman man who has no ability to derive the rule directly from the *Qur'ān* and the *Sunnah* has to follow some school of Law. This does not mean that the door of *Ijtihād* has been closed. The process of *Ijtihād* requires that priority should be given to each of the roots of Law according to their status. In solving a question of the *Sharī'ah*, the *Mujtahid* (i.e. a person exercising *Ijtihād*) must consult the *Qur'ān* and the *Sunnah* in the first instance. If the answer is not available there, then and then only one can have recourse to *Ijmā'* (consensus) of the community and, finally, he should exercise *Ijtihād*. It is also remarkable that right decisions are not necessary in *Ijtihād*. If one makes an effort to seek the truth, but does not reach the right conclusion, one will get the reward. According to the Tradition of the Prophet, while exercising *Ijtihād* a man who commits an error will get a single reward but a man who arrives at the truth will get double the reward. This Tradition keeps the door of *Ijtihād* open for all times to come. The only condition is that, while exercising *Ijtihād*, one should be well equipped with the knowledge of the injunctions of the *Qur'ān* and the *Sunnah*, their ethical discipline and prescribed duties.

(e) Other principles of law

So far the four bases of *Fiqh*, namely the sources of law which are accepted by all of the four most important schools as lawful, have been examined. There are, however, other principles of law accepted by only a few of them, which need to be briefly explained. They are (i) *Istiḥsān* (ii) *Istiṣlāḥ* and (iii) *Istiṣhāb*.

(i) Istiḥsān

Foremost among these three principles is *Istiḥsan*, advocated by the Hanafite School of Law alone. The word means literally, to hold something for good, right. According to the treatises on *"usul-al-Fiqh,"* *Istiḥsan* technically denotes the abandonment of the opinion to which reasoning by analogy (*Qiyās*) would lead, in favour of a different opinion supported by stronger evidence. Such a departure from *Qiyās*, may be based on evidence found in the *Sunnah*, or the *Ijma'*, on necessity (*darūrah*), or on what the upholders of *Qiyās* claim to be another kind of *Qiyās* which, though it does not so readily occur to the mind as the first *Qiyās*, in reality is stronger than it.[7] Thus we see that *Istiḥsan* appears to be "a more effective means than *Qiyās* for introducing new elements, since in its case the rules for determining the matter are even subtler than in the case of *Qiyās* and consequently afford greater possibilities. All that is needed is to discern in the new element whose introduction is desired some quality that is shared by a matter already approved or prohibited by the sources and the object is achieved."[8]

(ii) Istiṣlāh

Istiṣlāh consists in prohibiting or permitting a thing simply because it serves a "useful purpose" (*maṣlaḥah*), although there is no express evidence in the revealed sources to support such action. *Istiṣlāh* has been called by some "independent deduction" (*istidlāl mursal*), or simply "deduction" (*istidlāl*). Here the "useful purpose" is expressed in terms of an absolute necessity or in terms of mere expediency for the promotion of a good cause. Since this principle, which is used by the Malikite school of law, dispenses with the necessity of finding the supportive evidence in the sources, it is probably the most effective of all in dealing with a situation unheard of before.

(iii) Istiṣhāb

This principle was introduced by al-Shafi'i. According to *Istiṣhāb*, when the existence of a thing has been once established by evidence, even though later some doubt should arise as to its continuance in existence, it is still considered to exist. It is called *Istiṣhāb al-hāl*, if the present is judged according to the past, and *Istiṣhāb al-mādī*, if the converse is the case. This principle is admitted by Abu Hanifah, the founder of the Hanafite School of Law, also, but only to refute an assertion (*dawa*), that is, as an instrument of defence, (*daf 'dawa*) and not to establish a new claim (*dawa*). According to al-Shafi'i, however, it may be used for both purposes. This principle has, however, acquired considerable importance, especially in questions of *Fiqh*.

3.4 The *Fiqh* Schools and their Contemporary Implications in Economics.

So far, we have attempted to give a broad view of Islamic Law as a background for the understanding of economic laws and principles as well as for an intelligent determination of the extent to which non-revealed knowledge has gone into the making of *Fiqh* or Islamic laws. At this stage it should be clearly understood that the interpretation and application of both revealed and non-revealed knowledge have given rise to the emergence of different *Fiqh* schools. The differences between schools relate to all the various subjects of human interest on which the *Sharī'ah* has had something to say.

The most important of the *Fiqh* schools have been the ones founded by Abu Ḥanīfah 80/699–150/767 (known as the Ḥanafite school), Mālik Abu Anas, 95/713–179/795 (known as the Mālikite school), Muḥammad Ibn Idrīs al-Shāfi'i, 150/767–204/820 (known as the Shāfi'te school), Aḥmad Ibn Ḥanbal, 169/780–241/855 (known as the Ḥanbalites). Besides these prominent schools, other *Fiqh* schools have also been founded by scholars like Dawud Ibn 'Ali, al Awzā'i, Sufyān al-Thawri and Abu Thawr, during the same period.

Each of the schools is considered to be a full "*mujtahid*" and is supposed to have its own system of theory and application of laws. They have all been regarded as "orthodox" and they have considered one another as such. They are to be distinguished from the so-called "Shi'ites" and "Khārijites", etc., who are regarded as "heretical" by the former.[9]

However the diversity of views as presented by the different *Fiqh* schools provide us with a system of built-in flexibility in interpretation and application of *Fiqh*, which is the body of legal prescriptions concerning human affairs derived from the *Sharī'ah* – a generic name given to the complete collection of religious truths taught by the Prophet (peace be upon him).

This dynamism of the Islamic laws provides a system of diverse principles through which the various socio-economic problems confronting the modern Muslim states can be explained and Islamically justified solutions can be found.

The problem of economic development and planning, the operation of Islamic banking on the basis of profit-sharing, equity, participation and leasing, organization of Islamic financial markets, the problem of inflation, unemployment and social security, as well as a host of other modern economic problems can be examined in the light of Islamic values, once we understand the process of adjustment, compromise and rejection within the framework of the *Sharī'ah*.

Thus we shall see later on that the emergence of a new form of wealth in the form of stocks and shares and the imposition of *Zakāt* on them, the behaviour of the consumers and producers in an Islamic framework, regulation of a modern monopoly price, investment through Islamic banks without interest and the like can be directly attributed to the understanding of the process of rigidity and flexibility as permissible under Islamic laws.

3.5 Conclusion

Taken all in all, we can now conclude that in the dynamics of Islamic law, the *Qur'ān*, has its own identity, but the *Sunnah*, *Ijmā'* and *Ijtihād* stand in a very intimate relationship to one another. The *Sunnah* and *Ijmā'* especially, although disinct, pass into one another. The bridge, the inalienable link, is *Ijtihād* or *Qiyās*. This principle of systematic thinking, which not only interpreted the *Sunnah* of the Prophet (peace be upon him) into law but also integrated the new social and administrative institutions and practices with the *Sunnah* into "living tradition". Again, the *Ijtihād*, through the eternal process of compromise, adjustment and rejection, gradually crystallized into *Ijmā'* which exerts a tremendous influence in solving the conflicting requirements of material and spiritual life.

Needless to mention that Islam is living through a crucial moment in which the heritage of the past must become the herald of its future. The present, to be meaningful, must emerge out of the accumulations of the past. The emphasis is merely on accents. The slow dynamics of the past must give way to the swift acceleration of modern stresses, but the basic principles and the beaconlights would remain the same as truth is one and indivisible. Thus the Islamic principles of goodness and truth, justice and equity, fairness and righteousness are so dynamic and eternal in nature that they are quite capable of handling the various conflicting problems of modern life including socio-economic problems arising out of the complexity of present-day civilization.

Notes

[1] Rahman, F. *Islam*, Oxford University Press, Weidenfeld, 1966, p. 32.
[2] Khan, Sir Muhammad Zafarullah. Islam, *The Meaning for Modern Man*, p. 86.
[3] Aghnides, N. P. *Mohammedan Theories of Finance with an Introduction to Mohammedan Law*, The Premier Book House, Lahore, 1980
[4] Coulson, N. J. *A History of Islamic Law*, Edinburgh, 1964, p. 12.
[5] Rahman, F. *Islam*.
[6] Aghnides, N. P.
[7] Aghnides, N. P.
[8] Aghnides, N. P.
[9] Aghnides, N. P.

3.6 Selected Further Reading

Aghnides, N. P. *Mohammedan Theories of Finance with an Introduction to Mohammedan Law*. The Premier Book House, Lahore, reprinted 1980.

Rahman, Fazlur *Islamic Methodology in History, Central Institute of Islamic Research Karachi, Pakistan , 1965.*

Hamidullah, M. "*Sources of Islamic Laws* – A new approach" in *The Islamic Quarterly* vol. 1, London, 1954, pp. 205–211.

Horten, M. "The System of Islamic Philosophy" in *Islamic Studies*, vol. 12, Islamabad, Pakistan, 1973.

Iqbal, M. *The Reconstruction of Religious Thought in Islam*, Sh. Muhammad Ashraf, Lahore, Pakistan, 1960.

Schacht, J. *An Introduction to Islamic Law*, Clarendon Press, Oxford, 1979.

PART II

Islamic Approaches to Economic Functions Common to all Systems

CHAPTER 4

Consumption and Consumer Behaviour

4.1 Introduction: An overview

4.2 The Principle of Consumption in Islam

4.3 Islamic Injunctions on Food

4.4 Wants and the Islamic Order of Priorities

4.5 Nature of Consumer Behaviour

4.6 Conclusion

4.7 Selected Further Reading

"(Fasting) for a fixed
Number of days;
But if any of you is ill,
or on a journey,
The prescribed number
(should be made up)
From days later.
For those who can do it
(with hardship), is a ransom,
The feeding of one
That is indigent
But he that will give
More, of his own free will,
It is better for him.
And it is better for you
That ye fast,
If ye only knew."

Al- Qur'ān, Sūrah II. 184.

"Muslim Law brands as a form of squandering any consumption of wealth not required by real use. In its eyes, prodigality is a form of mental disease. It insists on moderation . . . ."

D. de Santillana, *The Legacy of Islam.*

4.1 Introduction: An Overview

Every society, irrespective of its ideological basis must have a mechanism to accomplish the complicated task of production. But the Islamic response to the solutions of these tasks is quite different from the responses of the market or the command economy. Although one may feel justified in saying that a society must undertake the tasks of producing first before it takes up the question of distribution, yet in an Islamic economy, it is the distribution which should activate production and consumption. In other words, the question "For whom shall goods and services be produced?" should be decided in the first instance. The other relevant questions—(a) "What goods and services will be produced?" (b) "How are they to be produced?"—should come next in order of priority. For, the Qur'ānic concern for the poor is so acute that the question of distribution comes into the very heart of economic activities.

As such, the consumption, production and distribution processes are indeed integrated in such a way that a simultaneous improvement in the quality of both material and spiritual life becomes possible. This brief introduction should be helpful in understanding the role of consumption, production and distribution in an Islamic society.

4.2 The Principle of Consumption in Islam

Consumption is to demand as production is to supply. The consumer's wants, present and anticipated, are the chief incentive for his own economic activities. They may not only absorb his income but also give him an incentive to increase it. This implies that the discussion of consumption is primary and that only as economists demonstrate an ability to understand, and explain the principles of both production and consumption, can they be considered competent to develop the laws of value and distribution or almost any other branch of the subject. The difference between modern and Islamic economics in respect of consumption lies in the approach towards satisfaction of one's wants. Islam does not recognize the purely materialistic bent of the modern pattern of consumption.

The higher we go up the ladder of civilization, the more overshadowed become our physiological wants by psychological factors. Artistic taste, snobbish limitation, exhibitionist impulses—all these factors play a more and more dominant role in determining the concrete outward form of our physiological wants. In a primitive society, consumption is very simple, because wants are also very simple. Modern civilization, however, has destroyed the sweet simplicity of our wants. The materialistic civilization of the West seems to take a peculiar delight in making our wants more and more varied and numerous, and a man's economic well-being is almost sought to be measured by the varied character of his wants which he tries to satisfy by means of special efforts. This outlook on life and progress is in striking contrast to the Islamic conception of values. The ethics of Islamic economics sought to reduce man's present excessive material needs in order to release human energy for spiritual pursuits. Inner development, rather than outward expansion, was held out to be man's highest ideal in life. The modern Western spirit, while not deprecating the need for inner perfection, however, seems to have shifted the emphasis to the amelioration of the material conditions of life. Progress now means higher and higher standards of living which imply a progressive enlargement of wants, increasing discontent and dissatisfaction with things as they are and a passionate yearning after higher and higher levels of consumption. From the modern point of view, then, the progress of a community is judged by the character of its material wants.

4.3 Islamic Injunctions on Food

With this general statement, we may now proceed to a further analysis of Islamic injunctions on consumption which are guided by five principles:
 (*i*) Principle of righteousness
 (*ii*) Principle of cleanliness
(*iii*) Principle of moderation
 (*iv*) Principle of beneficence
 (*v*) Principle of morality
   The first rule regarding consumption is contained in this verse of the Holy *Qur'ān*:

"O ye people
Eat of what is on earth,
Lawful and good

> (*Sūrah* II. 168).

   This condition carries the double significance of earning lawfully and not having been prohibited by law.
   In the matter of food and drink the prohibitions are: blood, the flesh of an animal that has died of itself, the flesh of swine, and the flesh of an animal on which the name of other than Allah has been invoked meaning thereby sacrifices made to idols or other gods, and offerings to saints or any being other than Allah. (*Sūrah* II.173; *Sūrah* V.4). The first three categories are prohibited because they are harmful to the body, and that which is harmful to the body is necessarily harmful to the spirit. The last prohibition relates to something which is directly harmful morally and spiritually, inasmuch as it amounts to association of others with God. A relaxation is made in the case of a person who is driven by necessity and to whom no other means of sustenance and nourishment is for the time available. He may partake of a prohibited article of food, using only that much which he considers necessary for his immediate need.
   The second condition laid down both in the Holy *Qur'ān* and the

Sunnah regarding food is that it should be good or fit for eating, not unclean or such as offends the taste. Therefore, not all that is permissible may be used as food and drink in all circumstances. Of all that is permissible only that may be used as food and drink which is clean and wholesome. The tradition of the Prophet (peace be upon him) also runs that cleanliness in all respects is half of our "*Imān*". Salman reported, the Messenger of Allah (peace be upon on him) said: "The blessing of food is washing of hands before it and washing of hands after it" (Tirmidhī; *Mishkāt*). Moreover, the Prophet has instructed that drink and food must not be blown into and must be covered. It is related on the authority of Abū tādah who said: The Messenger of Allah (peace be upon him) said, "When one of you drinks, he should not blow into the vessel" (Bukhārī).

Again, Jābir reported Abū Humaid brought a cup of milk from Naqī. The Messenger of Allah (peace be upon him) said to him, Why didst thou not cover it? Thou shouldst have placed a piece of wood on it" (Bukhārī). Again, it is related on the authority of Jābir who reported: The Messenger of Allah (peace be upon him) said: "When you go to sleep, put out the lamp and shut the doors and cover the food and drink" (Bukhārī). In the light of these *Ḥadīths* the importance of cleanliness can hardly be overestimated.

The third principle governing the conduct of man in respect of food and drink is moderation which also implies that no food should be used to excess. The *Qur'ān* says:

"Eat and drink:
But waste not by excess,
For God loveth not the wasters."

(*Sūrah* VII. 31).

Again:

"O ye who believe!
Make not unlawful
The good things which God
Hath made lawful for you,
But commit no excess."

(*Sūrah* V. 90).

The significance of these verses lies in the fact that as underfeeding affects the build-up of mind and body, so does also the overloading of the stomach. Self-denying practices by which a man deprives himself of certain kinds of food are expressly denounced in Islam.

The fourth principle is the principle of beneficence. Thus, subject to Islamic injunctions there is neither harm nor sin in eating and drinking of the good things provided by God out of His beneficence, so long as the objective is that life may be sustained and health promoted for the purpose of carrying out God's will through firm faith in the guidance that

He has provided, and righteous action in accordance therewith, which ensures conformity to all His commandments (*Sūrah* V. 96). Here, then, is a gradation which is elastic and takes account of the immediate as well as the ultimate purpose of food and drink. That which is on the whole harmful is prohibited altogether.

An intoxicant cannot, therefore, be used even in small quantities unless, of course, it is used as a medicine to save life, for which purpose the Holy *Qur'ān* expressly allows the use of prohibited foods:

"But if one is forced by necessity,
Without wilful disobedience,
Nor transgressing due limits.
Then he is guiltless."

(*Sūrah* II. 173; VI. 119).

The last, not the least, principle regarding consumption is the condition of morality. Not only the immediate purpose of food and drink but also the ultimate purpose, namely, the promotion of moral and spiritual values, must be kept in view. A Muslim is taught to start taking food with the mention of the name of Allah and to give thanks to Him after having finished it. He thus feels the Divine presence when satisfying his physical desires. This is significant because Islam stands for the happy blending of the material and spiritual values of life.

All intoxicants are also prohibited. It is recognised that some people may derive some pleasure or advantage from the use of liquor or other prohibited articles, but such use is prohibited because the harm that it might do is greater than any pleasure or advantage that might be derived from it (*Sūrah* II.219). The prohibition, however, is clear and total (*Sūrah* V.91). The *Qur'ān* points out that indulgence in liquor tends to create dissension and enmity and that people who indulge in it are liable to neglect prayer and the remembrance of Allah (*Sūrah* V.94).

Again, in the month of Ramādan, during the period of fasting there is abstention even from that which is lawful and permissible food and drink, which sustains life, and marital intercourse, which promotes the continuance of the species. It is a symbolical pledge or covenant that a worshipper enters into, signifying that if in the course of his duty of submission to the will of God he should be called upon to put his life in jeopardy or to sacrifice the interests of his progeny, he would not hesitate to do so.

4.4 Wants and the Islamic Order of Priorities

It is customary to classify human wants under three headings: necessities, comforts and luxuries.

"Necessities" usually include all things required to meet wants which must be satisfied.

"Comforts" may be defined as commodities the consumption of which adds to the efficiency of the worker but not proportionately to the costs of such commodities.

Lastly, "luxuries" refer to commodities and services the consumption of which does not add to one's efficiency and might conceivably diminish it. Costly dress and ornaments, expensive motor cars, costly furniture, palatial buildings, a large array of domestic assistants and retainers—all these constitute luxuries for most people.

Now the question arises as to the order of priorities of wants in an Islamic state and whether an Islamic state should encourage the production of luxury goods under the present circumstances.

As regards the order of priorities, the Islamic injunction on food and drink should be the guiding principle which has already been discussed in some detail. As to the second question, whether an Islamic state should encourage the production of luxury goods under the present capitalistic social framework of Muslim countries, our answer will have a relative validity. One school of thought opines that Muslim states, ever under the present circumstances, cannot encourage the production of luxury goods simply because consumption of luxuries is economically wasteful and their consumption does not add to one's efficiency and may rather diminish it in certain circumstances.

Viewed positively, it is, they say, socially injurious in that it absorbs many factors of production in wasteful occupations which, if they could be released from their present employment, might help to add considerably to the stream of useful goods and services.

The above line of reasoning, however, is not as sound as it seems to be. It neglects the vital fact that all employment depends upon the state of "effective demand" and that it is impossible to add to the existing stream of necessaries and comforts unless steps are first taken to divert the surplus purchasing power now in the hands of the few rich into the pockets of the many poor. The mere prohibition of the production and consumption of luxury goods, unaccompanied by a scheme of planned redistribution of wealth and income, is not at all likely to ease the economic problem for the masses. It is more likely to add further and distressing complications. At present, under the capitalistic system of almost all the Muslim countries a disproportionately large part of the total volume of purchasing power remains concentrated in the hands of the rich. The demand for luxury goods on the part of the rich is thus a big constituent of the total "effecctive demand" for society as a whole. If, therefore, the consumption of luxury goods is prohibited, —and nothing is done to make the rich less rich and the poor less poor—unemployment is bound to ensue on a large scale and the poor would become poorer still. If the consumption and, therefore, the production of luxury goods ceased altogether, the released factors of production would just swell the existing volume of chronic involuntary unemployment; they would not find their way to new and more useful channels of employment. The traditional view that the "released" factors of production would be automatically absorbed in more useful lines of employment rests on the assumption of perpetual or at least long-run full employment, an assumption for which there is apparently no empirical justification.

It follows that the consumption of luxury goods is not altogether economically wasteful. Its validity is relative only to the existing capitalistic structure of Muslim countries characterized as it is by glaring inequalities of wealth. In almost all the underdeveloped Muslim countries the monopoly element is in existence in a varying degree in almost all sectors of the economy. Therefore, if the economic order is changed and a more egalitarian system of economic society based on Islamic values is established, the factors of production, at present employed in luxury goods industries, would be automatically diverted to the production of useful commodities for which the effective demand will then be very high.

To my mind, prohibition of consumption of luxury goods in the Islamic economic system need not be necessary simply because nobody will find it worthwhile to produce such items for which no market exists. But it is the duty of the Muslim countries to create an environment where a deep sense of moral responsibility develops among the people. In the transitional period Muslim countries may, if need be, take some coercive measures in the larger interests of the society as a whole.

4.5 Nature of Consumer Behaviour

The preceding discussion of Islamic injunctions on food and the order of priority in consumption provides us with some interesting insights into understanding the nature of consumer behaviour in Islam. In the course of analyzing consumer behaviour one may take a narrow and static view by saying that consumer behaviour in an Islamic society is to be guided strictly by the list of prohibitions. (i.e. eating pork, drinking wine, wearing silk clothing and gold rings (for men) etc.), since the prohibitions have definite validity in the *Sharī'ah*, and Muslim consumers must not indulge in the consumption of such prohibited items for reasons of social discipline, Islamic unity and spiritual significance. The author is however inclined to take a wider view of consumer behaviour. To me, the key to its understanding lies not merely in prohibited items but in the concept of "moderation" in consumption guided by the altruistic behaviour of Muslim consumers. What is needed then is to determine whether the current consumption level in a community is below or above the moderation level. In the context of present Muslim societies, it would be naive to assume that the Islamic stress on moderation means lowering an already low level of consumption.

Consumption is essentially a positive concept in Islam. The pro-hibitions and injunctions concerning food and drink should be seen as a part of the effort to improve the quality of consumption behaviour. By discouraging wasteful and unnecessary consumption expenditure, Islam stresses altruistic behaviour on the part of the consumer. Moderation in consumption behaviour then comes as a logical outcome of the Islamic consumption style, which is relative and dynamic in nature.

4.6 Conclusions

(1) Islam does not recognize the pure materialistic bent of the modern pattern of consumption. The rationale of the consumption pattern in Islam is to reduce man's present excessive physiological wants arising from artificial psychological factors in order to release human energy for spiritual persuits.
(2) The Islamic injunctions on consumption are guided by the following principles:
  (i) Principle of righteousness
  (ii) Principle of cleanliness
  (iii) Principle of moderation
  (iv) Principle of beneficence
  (v) Principle of morality
(3) Generally, human wants are classified under three headings: (*a*) Necessities, (*b*) Comforts and (*c*) Luxuries. As for the order of priorities, the Islamic injunctions on consumption [mentioned above] should be the guiding principles. It is very difficult to give a categorical answer whether or not the Islamic State should encourage the production of luxury goods. To my mind, the mere prohibition of the production and consumption of luxury goods unaccompanied by a scheme of planned redistribution of wealth and income is not likely to ease the economic problems of the masses. What is needed is to establish a more egalitarian system of society based on the Islamic code of life.
(4) The key to understanding consumer behaviour in Islam lies not merely in knowing the prohibited items but in realizing the dynamic concept of moderation in consumption guided by the altruistic behaviour of a Muslim consumer. The Islamic prohibitions concerning food and drink should be seen as a part of the effort to improve the quality of consumption behaviour.

4.7 Selected Further Reading

Kahf, Monzer, "A contribution to the Theory of Consumer Behaviour in an Islamic Society" in *Studies in Islamic Economics*, ed. by Khurshid Ahmed, The Islamic Foundation, Leicester, 1980.
Khan, M. F. "Implications of Islamic Consumption Patterns for Saving, Growth and Distribution in Islamic Framework", a paper presented at the Second International Conference on Islamic Economics: Development, Finance and Distribution in an Islamic Perspective Islamic University, Islamabad, Pakistan, 19–23 March, 1983.

Mannan, M. A. "Consumption Function: its Nature and Scope in an Islamic Economy" in *The Making of Islamic Economic Society, Islamic Dimensions in Economic Analysis* by M. A. Mannan, Chapter 12, International Association of Islamic Banks, Cairo, 1984.

Mannan, M. A. "Institutional Setting of an Islamic Economic order", International Centre for Research in Islamic Economics, King Abdulaziz University, Jeddah, publication No. 8, 1981.

Maudoodi, S. A. *The Economic Problem of Man and its Islamic Solution*, Islamic Publications, Lahore, 1975.

Rahman, F (1969) "Economic Principles of Islam" in *Islamic Studies*, Islamabad, Pakistan, 1969.

CHAPTER 5

Factors of Production and the Concept of Ownership

5.1 Introduction: The Principle of Production.

5.2 Factors of Production: An Overview.

    (a) Land

    (b) Labour

    (c) Capital

    (d) Organization

5.3 The Concept of Private Ownership in Islam.

5.4 Conclusion.

5.5 Selected Further Reading.

10. "It is He Who sends down
    Rain from the sky:
    From it ye drink,
    And out of it (grows)
    The vegetation on which
    ye feed your cattle.

11. With it He produces
    For you corn, olives,
    Date-palms, grapes,
    And every kind of fruit:
    Verily in this is a Sign
    For those who give thought.

12. He has made subject to you
    The Night and the Day;
    The Sun and the Moon;
    And the Stars are in subjection
    By His command: Verily
    In this are Signs
    For men who are wise."

18. "If ye would count up
    The favours of God,
    Never would ye be able
    to number them: for God
    Is oft-Forgiving, Most Merciful."

    Al-Qur'ān, Sūrah XVI. 10–12, 18).

"Mohammadanism is not unequipped for survival in the modern world. . . . ."

Dennis Saraut, *History of Religion.*

5.1 Introduction: The Principle of Production

The basic principle of consumption already explained must be reflected in the productive system of an Islamic state. Because production means creation of utilities, just as consumption is the destruction of the same. Production does not imply the physical creation of something out of nothing, since nobody can create matter. All that man can do to make things useful and serviceable is said to be "produced" in the economist's sense. Now, we may address ourselves very briefly to the discussion of the principle of production.

The fundamental principle which is to be kept in view in the process of production is the principle of economic welfare. Even in the capitalist system there is a call for production of goods and services based on the principle of economic welfare. The uniqueness of the Islamic concept of economic welfare lies in the fact that it cannot ignore the broader considerations of general welfare which are involved in the questions of morality, education, religion and many other things. In modern economics, economic welfare is measured in terms of money. As Professor Pigou says: "Economic welfare may be defined roughly as that part of welfare that can be brought in relation with the measuring rod of money." Since modern economic welfare is materialistic in character, it is necessary to limit the scope of the subject-matter of the same.

In doing this we are naturally attracted towards that portion of the field in which the methods of science seem likely to work to the best advantage. This they can clearly do when there is present something measurable, on which analytical machinery can get a firm grip. The one obvious instrument of measurement available in social life is money. Hence, the range of our inquiry becomes restricted to that part of social welfare that can be brought directly or indirectly in relation with the measuring rod of money. This part of welfare may be called economic welfare (Pigou). Under the Islamic system of production the concept of economic welfare is used in a more comprehensive manner. To me, the Islamic concept of economic welfare consists in the increasing of income resulting from the increase of production of only beneficial goods through the maximum utilization of resources—both human and material—as well as through the participation of the maximum number of people in the productive process. Thus, improvement in the productive system in Islam implies increase not only in income, which can be measured in terms of money, but also improvement in maximizing our satisfaction at minimum effort keeping in view the injunctions of Islam on consumption. Thus, in an Islamic state mere increase in the volume of production will not ensure the maximum welfare of the people. The quality of the goods produced, subject to the injunctions of the *Qur'ān* and the *Sunnah*, must be taken into account in determining the nature of economic welfare. We should also take into account the unsatisfactory results which would ensue in connection with the economic development of forbidden foodstuffs and drinks. The prohibition of alcoholic drinks—sometimes mitigated, since the *Hanafites* tolerate alcohol and limit the prohibition of wine—has, however, had considerable repercussions on the cultivation of the grape-vine. In fact, in all the regions subject to the political control of Islam the high-quality vineyards disappeared. Grape-vine culture became essentially an occupation of hill or mountain people. It became more or less absorbed into the Mediterranean polyculture and the local way of life, but it could never produce enough for regular normal export. From the plains it retreated into the mountains, from the fields to the gardens. Therefore, attempts should be made to produce goods as cheaply as possible and to exploit resources—both material and human—so that full employment of the same can be achieved, because wastage of resources in any form is condemned in Islam. Lastly, an Islamic state will not merely be interested in increasing the volume of production but also in ensuring the participation of the maximum number of people in the productive process. In modern capitalistic countries we find gross inequalities of income simply because the method of production is controlled by a few capitalists. Even many Muslim countries of the world are not free of this criticism. It is the duty of every Muslim state to take all reasonable steps for the reduction of inequality of income resulting from the concentration of productive powers into a few hands. This has been sought to be done through (*a*) adoption of the system of progressive taxation of incomes, (*b*) levy of death-duties on inherited properties at progressive rates, and (*c*) distribution of the proceeds of the taxes, mainly collected from the richer classes, via the provision of social services among the poorer sections of the community.

To sum up, the productive system in an Islamic state must be guided by both objective and subjective criteria; the objective criteria will be reflected in the form of welfare which can be measured in terms of money, and the subjective criteria in the form of welfare which can be measured in terms of the economic ethics based on the injunctions of the Holy *Qur'ān* and the *Sunnah*.

5.2 Factors of Production: An overview

(a) Land

Islam has recognized land as a factor of production but not exactly in the same sense in which it is used in modern times. In classical writings land, which was regarded as an important factor of production, includes all the natural resources used in the process of production, e.g. the surface of the earth, the fertility of the soil, properties of air and water and mineral resources, etc. True, there is no evidence to prove that Islam does not approve of this definition of modern economics. While Islam recognizes land as a factor of production, it recognizes the creation of only those utilities which can maximize the economic welfare of the community—a welfare which takes into account the basic principles of economic ethics. The Qur'ānic Law and the Tradition of the Prophet are clear about this.

The method of utilization of land as a factor of production in Islam is unique in the real sense of the term.

Both the *Qur'ān* and the *Sunnah* lay much emphasis on the proper cultivation of land. Thus the Holy *Qur'ān* draws attention to the necessity of turning wasteland into gardens by making arrangements for watering it, and growing good crops. The *Qur'ān* says:

"And do they not see
That We do drive Rain
To parched soil (bare of herbage),
and produce therewith crops, providing food
For their cattle and themselves.

(*Sūrah* XXXII. 27).

We have evidence to indicate that impetus is given to the cultivation of wasteland. It is related on the authority of 'Ā'ishah who reported the Prophet (peace be upon him) to have said: "Whoever cultivates land which is not the property of anyone has a better title to it" (Bukhārī). Since Islam recognizes the noncultivator ownership of land, it is permissible to let it to another person for cultivation for a part of the produce or for money, but it is at the same time recommended that a person who can afford it should give land free of rent to some of his poor brethren.

Ibn 'Umar reported that the Messenger of Allah (peace and blessings of Allah be upon him) granted (the lands of) Khaibar to the Jews on condition that they worked thereon and cultivated them and they should have half of the produce (Bukhārī). Again, it is related on the authority of Rafī who reported: They used to have land cultivated in the time of the Prophet (peace and blessings of Allah be upon him), taking what grew on the water-courses or anything which the owner of the land reserved for himself. So the Prophet (peace and blessings of Allah be on him) forbade this. I (the reporter) said to Rafī', "How is it if it is done on payment of dinārs and dirhams?" Rafī' said, "There is no harm in taking dinārs and dirhams" (Bukhārī).

"'Amr said: I said to Ṭāwūs, Thou shouldst give up Mukhabrah for they say that the Prophet (peace and blessings of Allah be upon him) forbade it. He said, Ibn 'Abbās informed me that the Prophet (peace and blessings of Allah be upon him) did not forbid this but he only said: "If one of you gives it as a gift to his brother, it is better for him than that he takes for it a fixed payment"'" (Bukhārī, Muslim, and *Mishkāt*). Evidently this was the advice given to people who had vast tracts of land which they could not manage to cultivate themselves. It did not mean that land could not be let to a tenant.

Islam has attached great importance to irrigation for increasing agricultural production. Therefore, Islam has tried to impress upon its followers that a person having his land on a water channel is entitled to water his field but he must allow the water to pass on to other tracts when his need is satisfied. Even the digging of a well is considered to be a great act of merit. Abū Hurairah reported, the Messenger of Allah (peace and blessings of Allah be upon him) said: "Excess of water should not be withheld, arresting thereby the growth of herbage" (Bukhārī) The Prophet (peace and blessings of Allah be upon him) said: "Whoever digs the well of Ruma, for him is paradise" (Bukhārī) So 'Uthmān dug it.

It is surprising to note that even fourteen hundred years ago Islam realized the need for balanced growth—a balance between agricultural and industrial development. In Islam, land as a factor of production must be used in such a fashion that the objective of balanced growth is achieved in the long run. The *Sharī'ah* provides that if the people concentrate on a particular occupation to the neglect of other occupations and to the detriment of the community as a whole, the State can intervene to change habits. Thus where people concentrate on acquiring agricultural land and adopt cultivation only and neglect other types of occupation, industry or investment, the state can make rules to ensure that they spread their wealth evenly and engage in the trades or industries which would, in the long run, be to the benefit of the community.

It is reported about Abū Umāmah that he said that when the Prophet saw a plough and some other agricultural implements, "I heard the Prophet (peace and blessings of Allah be upon him) say: "This does not enter the house of a people but it brings ingloriousness with it" (Bukhārī). Bukhārī's heading of the chapter is "Warning against the consequences of engrossment with the implements of agriculture or going beyond the limit ordained." The *Ḥadīth*, therefore, implies that a nation which gives itself up entirely to agriculture neglecting other lines of its development cannot rise to a position of glory.

The utilization and maintenance of land as a factor of production can also be seen as a natural and exhaustible resource within the framework of an Islamic economic society.

Land as a Natural Resource

A Muslim can acquire ownership of natural resources after fulfilling his obligations towards society. The use and maintenance of the natural resources can give rise two components of earning. They are: (a) earning from natural resources on its own right (i.e., pure economic rent) and (b) earning from the improvement in the use of natural resources through human labour and capital. While the pure economic rent must be shared equally by all members of the community, one is entitled to proper compensation for human efforts (i.e. wage and profit). It is therefore important to separate pure economic return from compensation for other factors involving the use of natural resources.

Land as an Exhaustible Resource

It is the Islamic view that exhaustible resources belong to the present as well as to future generations. The present generation has no right to misuse exhaustible resources, which may cause harm to future generations.

From the above analysis the following hypotheses or policy guidelines can be derived:

(a) Agricultural development in Muslim countries can be accelerated through intensive and extensive methods of cultivation if it is supplemented by a programme of moral education, based on the teachings of Islam.

(b) The revenues generated from the use of exhaustible resources should be spent more on the development of social institutions (e.g. universities, hospitals) and on physical infrastructure rather than on current consumption.

(c) The pure economic rent may be spent more to meet the current level of consumption expenditure.

(b) Labour

Labour as a factor of production is recognized in all economic systems irrespective of their ideological bias. The peculiarities of labour such as perishability, inseparability from the labourer himself, short-run insensitivity to its demand, etc., which have a bearing on the determination of wages, are the same in all systems.

Nevertheless, the distinctive nature of this factor of production in Islam arises due to the fact that labour and, for that matter, all factors of production are not merely subject to a process of historical change, as we find in the case of modern secular economics, but also to a timeless moral and ethical framework under which all the factors of production need to operate. For many attributes of the labour capital relationship, the employee and employer's code of conduct and so on, are rooted in the *Sharī'ah*. As a result, labour as a factor of production in Islam is never divorced from moral and social life.

In Islam, labour is not simply an abstract quantity of effort or services offered for sale to bidders for manpower. Those who employ labour have moral and social responsibilities.

It is true that a modern worker has a property in his own labour which he is entitled to sell for as much as he can get. But in Islam he is not absolutely free to do what he wants to do with his own labour. He is not allowed to engage in professions not permitted in the *Sharī'ah*. Neither employee nor employer can exploit each other. All responsibility for labour does not end when an employee leaves the employer's factory; he has a moral responsibility to protect the legitimate interest, both of employers and less fortunate workers.

This moral and social dimension of labour as a factor of production is not clearly found in secular economics. In their book, *The Economic Problem*, Heilbroner and Thurow observed:

"It is that the factors of production, with which modern economic inquiry is concerned, are not eternal attributes of a natural order. They are the creations of a process of historical change, a change that divorced labour from social life and made it an abstract quantity of effort offered for sale to bidders for labour power: a change that has separated the value of land from its ancient prerogatives of status and power: a change that brought the idea of capital to a society which had always known wealth, but had never conceived of it as something whose form and shape were of no consequence, but whose yield was all important".[1]

Thus we see that in Islam labour is used in a wider and yet more restricted sense. It is wider, because it looks upon the use of labour services beyond the limits of purely monetary considerations. It is restricted in the sense that a worker is not absolutely free to do whatever he wants to do with his own labour.

(c) Capital

An Islamic economic system must be free of interest. In such a system interest will not be allowed to exert its adverse effects on employment, production and distribution. It is for this reason that capital has occupied a special place in Islamic economics. Here we are inclined to consider capital—"produced means of production"—not as a fundamental factor of production, but as an embodiment of past land and labour. In fact, capital is produced by the expenditure of labour and the use of natural resources. It is, in the works of Wicksell, "a single coherent mass of saved-up labour and saved-up land which is accumulated in the course of years."[2] In an interest-free society capital cannot, therefore, be treated in the sense it is used in capitalistic production.

Now, we shall confine ourselves to an analysis of the problem of accumulation of capital in the Islamic economic system. Such an analysis may, however, be preceded by a brief reference to the broad classification of capital, which may be regarded from the standpoint of society and from the standpoint of individuals. From the social angle, all things, other than land, which yield income are to be regarded as capital, including things in public ownership. Private capital is anything from which the individual expects to derive an income.

In the modern sense, a Government war loan is capital from the standpoint of the persons giving such a loan but it is not capital from the social standpoint.

Since an Islamic economic system stands for a balanced society, the distinction between private and social capital is immaterial. But this is not the case in the present-day capitalist society. The Islamic state has the right to intervene when private capital is used to the detriment of society. There is grievous punishment in store for those who abuse their riches to the detriment of society. God commands:

(The stern command will say):
"Seize ye him,
And bind ye him,
And burn ye him,

In the Blazing Fire.
Further, make him march
In a chain, whereof
The length is seventy cubits!"

(*Sūrah* LXIX. 30–32).

Islam promotes the basic moral conscience by inculcating a fear of God which in practice means scrupulous avoidance of anti-social behaviour in all shapes and forms.

Capital grows out of savings from which the creation of capital goods is possible. But the creation of capital goods is contingent upon the presence of two opposites: reduced current consumption and expectation of increased future production. Thus, as Keynes has observed, we are reminded of the "Fable of the Bees"—the gay of tomorrow are absolutely indispensable to provide a *raison d'etre* for the grave of today.

Now the question arises why in an interest-free Islamic economic system people will abstain from consuming the whole of the available consumer goods to save for the future, because writers like Marshall were of the opinion that the rate of interest was one of the factors which govern the volume of savings. The higher the rate of interest, i.e. the larger the reward for saving, the higher will be the propensity to save and *vice versa*. But many writers like Keynes have cast serious doubts on the connection between the rate of interest and the volume of savings. In their opinion, a high rate of interest will depress economic activities and lead to a smaller volume of investment. As a result, the aggregate money income will shrink, and given the same propensity to save, the volume of savings will be reduced. The fact is that if individuals are rational, they are likely to save more out of their incomes when the rate of interest is high. A high rate of interest means higher rewards on saving, and, therefore, on purely rational grounds, people will save more. But saving is one of the least rational of all things; it is surrounded by all sorts of social customs and inhibitions. There are several motives which induce an individual to save. Impelled by the motive of prudence and foresight he may save with a view to building up a reserve against unforeseen contingencies or rainy days or to make adequate provisions for the future education of his children, or the marriage of his daughters, or for his old age. Moneyed men enjoy great honour and prestige in our society, and so he may dream to be counted rich one day and to enjoy power and prestige (the motive of pride). Lastly, he may be guided by the spirit of pure miserliness with an unreasonable dread of spending money on anything whatsoever (the motive of avarice). These motives may be summed up as motives of prudence, foresight, improvement, family affection, pride and avarice.

In modern communities, a considerable portion of savings comes from such institutions as joint-stock companies. The people in charge of these institutions save because of the motive of prudence and enterprise.

Here the point we are making is that capital can grow even in an interest-free society. One must not forget that Islam allows profit which also acts as an incentive to save. Moreover, only an Islamic economic system can make a true and proper use of capital, because under modern capitalist systems, we find that the benefits of technical progress achieved by science can be enjoyed only by relatively wealthy communities whose incomes allow a good margin above the level of subsistence. Those who live from hand to mouth must necessarily remain condemned to eternal poverty, since we can provide for an increasing stream of output tomorrow only by consenting to reduce consumption today, and we cannot do so unless our current income leaves some margin above subsistence. A comparatively wealthy community is thus in an advantageous position for becoming wealthier still, while a poor community finds itself in a vicious circle from which it is difficult to get out. But even wealthy communities have their own problems, no less baffling than poor communities. Where the systems of private property and private enterprise prevail there is a tendency towards the accumulation of too much wealth in the hands of a small minority, and since consumption does not increase as fast as income increases, the second condition for capital creation, namely, the expectation of increased consumption in future, is generally not fulfilled. This factor goes a long way to explaining why the benefits of technical progress are not fully reaped even by rich communities and why unemployment develops even though there is no lack of resources for giving employment to all the unemployed factors of production.

But Islam safeguards the interests of the poor by imposing moral responsibility upon the rich to look after the poor. Secondly, while Islam recognizes the systems of private property in a restricted way, any tendency towards undue accumulation of wealth in the hands of a few is condemned. Thus the Holy *Qur'ān* tries to impress upon the rich that they should spend for the benefit of society, because wealth is for proper circulation. The *Qur'ān* says:

"And spend (in Charity)
Out of what We have provided
For them, secretly and openly.
Hope for a Commerce
That will never fail."

(*Sūrah* **XXXV**. 29)

Again:

"In order that it (wealth) may not
(Merely) make a circuit
Between the wealthy among you."

(*Sūrah* **LIX**. 7)

At the same time extravagance is condemned in the Holy Book which says:

"But waste not
By excess; for God
Loveth not the wasters."

(*Sūrah* VI. 141)

In this way Islam brings a happy compromise between two opposites of capital creation, reduced current consumption and increased future consumption, and allows capital to play its true role in the productive process.

The preceding discussion should not lead one to believe that capital as a factor of production is less important in Islam than its counterpart in a secular economic set-up. Its added importance arises because of Islamic concern not only for the present generation but also for future generations. Although interest is prohibited, it does not mean that there is no cost of capital which can be expressed in terms of its alternative uses. Therefore the rate of return on a particular economic enterprise can, among others, be used as one of the allocative devices for capital.

(d) Organization

In a conventional secular economic analysis, profit is associated with the earnings of an entrepreneur. It is considered to be the reward of the manager, responsible for management of both human and non-human resources. This is how organization as a factor of production emerges. Here the crucial question arises: what is "Islamic" about organization as a factor of production? What are the distinctive features of Islamic organization?

At first glance, there appear to be no special characteristics which can be attributed to organization in an Islamic framework. The following distinctive features may however, be noted to understand the role of organization in an Islamic economy.

Firstly, in an Islamic economy, being essentially equity-based rather than loan-based, managers tend to manage the enterprise concerned with a view either to sharing dividends among the share-holders or to sharing profit among the partners of an economic enterprise. The motivational properties of such organization are quite distinctive in the sense that they tend to generate co-operative forces through diverse forms of investments based on partnership in varying forms (i.e. *mudāraba, mushārika,* etc.).

Secondly, it follows that the notion of normal profit has a wider meaning within the Islamic economic framework, since interest on capital can no longer be charged. The human capital offered by the conventional manager needs to be integrated with the money capital. Thus the entrepreneur, investor and businessman become an integral part of the organization, in which normal profit becomes the joint concern of all. This added dimension of business experience in the management of an enterprise is again unique because of the importance of altruistic behaviour which Islam introduces to influence the producer's behaviour in an Islamic society. The altruistic behaviour on which Islam places so much importance may be at variance with the facts and with management strategy, except in those cases in which the actual behaviour of the organization happens, by chance, to coincide with the action necessary for profit maximization. This is not to say that the management will not strive for profit in an Islamic framework. What is in fact implied is that Islamic organization as a factor of production differs from its counterpart in secular economics, both at a conceptual and an operational level, with its attempt to harmonize a multiplicity of goals subject to profit constraints.

Thirdly, it is owing to this integrative nature of organization that the demand for moral integrity, punctuality and honesty in accounting are perhaps more severely needed than in any secular organization where the owners of the capital may not be part of the management. Islam stresses honesty, punctuality and sincerity in commercial dealings, for they reduce the cost of supervision and control.

Lastly, it follows that the importance of the human factor in production and business strategy is perhaps more clearly recognized than in other management strategies based on the maximization of profit or sales.

5.3 The Concept of Private Ownership in Islam

The uniqueness of the Islamic concept of private ownership lies in the fact that in Islam the legitimacy of ownership depends on the moral sign attached to it, just as that of a mathematical quantity depends on the algebraical sign attached to it. Here, again, Islam differs from capitalism and communism, as neither of them has succeeded in harmoniously setting the individual in a social mosaic. Private property is the life-blood of capitalism; its abolition is the blazing kernel of the socialist creed. Unrestricted ownership of property under capitalism can hardly escape censure for being responsible for the gross maldistribution of wealth and income because the actual course of economic development under capitalism almost everywhere, has increased the power and influence of gigantic trusts, cartels and monopolies. This unrestricted ownership has made the rich richer and the poor poorer. Here we find the sovereignty of the consumers, the tyranny of the price system and the quest for profits. Thus Professor Harold Laski, a noted British political scientist, has rightly observed:

"The present system of capitalistic production stands condemned from almost any angle of analysis. It is psychologically inadequate because for most, by appealing mainly to the motive of fear, it inhibits the exercise of those qualities which make for rich life. It is morally inadequate also, for it confers rights upon those who have done nothing to earn them and where these rights are related to efforts; this, in turn, has no proportionate relevancy to social value. It makes a part of the community parasite upon the rest; and it deprives most of the opportunity to live on a human plane of existence. It is also economically inadequate because it fails so to distribute the wealth it creates as to offer the necessary conditions of right living to those dependent on its processes."

Again, communism which has been organized on the basis of collectivism or State-ownership of everything believes in the liquidation of private property. While totalitarian planning guided by the concept of ownership of collectivism can help remove unemployment, maldistribution and many other shortcomings of capitalism, it is not free from certain limitations of a serious character, which revolve round the issue of incentives and the issue of personal liberty. Under communism the actual course of economic development has reduced man to a machine. Similarly, fascism ensures a bare livelihood to the individual, but it first destroys his independent entity by merging him with a demoniacally mechanized national whole. The individual has to pay a heavy price for "the mess of pottage". The communists live for the "proletariat" and the fascists for the "nation". They are symptoms of the same disease.

Islam maintains a balance between exaggerated opposites not merely by recognizing private ownership but also by securing the widest and most beneficent distribution of wealth through institutions set up by it and through moral exhortation. This will be clearer if we explain the fundamental rule as well as the eight specific rules of the *Sharī'ah* concerning the right of private ownership of property and the method of use of the same.

Basic Rule

The *Qur'ān*, the basic of all Islamic laws, categorically states that absolute ownership of everything belongs to Allah alone (*Sūrah* III. 189). Man is simply the vicegerent of Allah on earth. This absolute ownership does not mean that Allah has created everything for Himself. The Qur'ānic verse: "It is He Who hath created for you all things that are on earth" (*Sūrah* II. 29) is pregnant with great significance. It emphasizes that what Allah has created belongs collectively to the whole of human society. Legal ownership by the individual, that is to say, the right of possession, enjoyment and transfer of property is recognized and safe-guarded in Islam, but all ownership is subject to the moral obligation that in all wealth all sections of society, and even animals, have the right to share (*Sūrah* LI. 19). Part of this obligation is given legal form and is made effective through legal sanctions, but the greater part is secured by voluntary effort put forth through a desire to achieve the highest moral and spiritual benefits for all concerned. In fact, this supplementing of legal obligations which secure the irreducible minimum with moral obligations to be discharged through voluntary effort runs through every part of the Islamic society."

The Eight Rules of the *Sharī'ah*

Let us now discuss in some detail the eight rules of the *Sharī'ah* governing the private ownership of property.

Utilization of property. The first rule laid down by the *Sharī'ah* is that the non-use of property is not allowed in Islam. The Prophet (peace be upon him) is reported to have said that "the person who seizes land belonging to nobody would cease to have any right to such land if he did not reasonably exploit it after three years of possession." This doctrine of ownership gathered momentum during the reign of the great Caliph 'Umar who is said to have taken back some of the lands which the Prophet (peace be upon him) had given to Bilāl ibn al-Hārith simply on the ground that he (Bilāl) did not utilize all the lands given by the Holy Prophet. Thus, impetus is given to the cultivation of wasteland. 'Ā'ishah reported; the Prophet (peace be upon him) said, "Whoever cultivates land which is not the property of anyone has a better title to it" (Bukhārī).

The wisdom of this policy is quite obvious even today, because in many Muslim countries vast tracts of agricultural land have remained uncultivated or unutilized for years mainly because of bad land tenure system which has encouraged the growth of landlordism or the like. Since the non-use of property is wasteful and impoverishes the owner as well as the community as a whole, the Islamic state can intervene and deprive the owner of ownership to the extent of the land remaining unutilized. The state would pay compensation for this dispossession only where property was acquired by lawful means, not wrongfully. If this policy is adopted, there may be an increase in agricultural production as a result of extensive cultivation. The food problem which is a standing puzzle for all the Muslim countries of the world may be solved to a great extent.

The rule about continuous utilization of property also applies to the method of utilization. The teachings of Islam require that whoever undertakes a task must perform it in the best possible manner. If the owner utilizes the property in a wasteful and unproductive manner or if the people concentrate on acquiring a particular type of property to the neglect of other types of property, industry or investment, or if there has been an unduly heavy concentration of wealth in the hands of a small section of the people to the detriment of the community as a whole, the Islamic state has the right to intervene to secure a balance of economic interests and activities. It is reported by Abū Umāmah that, when the prophet (peace be upon him) saw a plough and some other agricultural implements, he said: "This does not enter the house of a people but it brings ingloriousness with it" (Bukhārī). Here Maulānā Muhammad Ali observed, "This hadīth, therefore, implies that a nation which gives itself up entirely to agriculture neglecting other lines of development cannot rise to a position of glory." Islam stands not only for balanced growth but also for balanced distribution of wealth. In fact, the object of the Islamic economic system is to secure the widest and most beneficent distribution of property through institutions set up by it and through moral exhortation. Wealth must, according to the Holy Qur'ān (*Sūrah* LIX. 7), remain in constant circulation among all sections of the community and should not become the monopoly of the rich. The general rule is that property should be used at all times and used in a rightful way for one's own benefit as well as for the benefit of the community.

Payment of Zakāt. The second rule of the *Sharī'ah* in regard to the conduct of the owner of private property is that he must pay *Zakāt* in proportion to the property owned. "Gold, silver, currency of any kind, agricultural produce, cattle, trading enterprises and everything owned by a man during his life is 'property' for the purposes of Zakāt. And everyone who does not have enough to satisfy basic needs, who cannot work, is 'poor and needy' for the purposes of Zakāt. And, finally, all that is directed to the benefit of the Muslims as a whole and not solely towards the satisfaction of personal needs is 'in the cause of God' for the purposes of Zakāt." (Maḥmūd Shaltūt, *al-Quḍḍh wa-al Sharī'ah*).

As a matter of fact, the categories of property defined in the early days of Islam should not be accepted as final. The reason is that the forms of property known in modern times are in many ways different and much more complicated and subtle than those known fourteen hundred years ago. The problem has been carefully studied by a group of eminent Islamic jurists in a comprehensive report on social solidarity in the Arab world which was presented in a meeting organized by the Arab League held in Damascus in December 1952. The view is held that *Zakāt* would now be due on all kinds of property not known in the early days of Islam. Such things as industrial machinery, bank notes, profits of professions and trades and rents would now be subject to *Zakāt*. Without going into details it can be said that the Arabia of fourteen hundred years ago and the world of today reveal a fundamental change in the socio-political and socio-economic pattern of society. So there is no reason to believe that items taxed and rates charged were meant to be unchangeable with the changing circumstances since the door of *Ijtihād* is never closed in Islam. One school of thought held the view that the rate of *Zakāt* cannot be changed as it has been fixed by the Apostle of Allah himself. But if we look to the spirit of *Zakāt*, there is not the least difficulty in concluding that in fixing the rate of *Zakāt* the Islamic state may introduce an element of elasticity to face the inflationary tendencies of the economy. If the exchange value of the existing rate of *Zakāt* is reduced to zero, *Zakāt* will lose its significance in bringing an element of socialism in society.

Beneficent Use. The third rule in regard to the conduct of the owner of private property gives emphasis to the beneficent use of property which means utilization of wealth "in the way of God," which, in its turn, means all causes beneficial to the community as a whole and conducive to its prosperity and welfare. The object of the beneficent use of property has so many aspects that they can be better appreciated in the juxtaposition in which the *Qur'ān* puts them. The following excerpts contain the whole philosophy of spending, giving and using property on which no detailed commentary is necessary:

(*a*) The similitude of those who spend their wealth for the cause of Allah is like the similitude of a grain of corn which grows seven ears, in each ear a hundred grains. Allah multiplies even more for whomsoever He pleases. Allah is Bountiful, All-Knowing

(*Sūrah* II. 261).

(*b*) Whatever of wealth you spend it is to the benefit of your own selves, while just spend not but to seek the favour of Allah. Whatever of wealth you spend, it shall be paid back to you in full and you shall not be wronged.

(*Sūrah* II. 272).

(*c*) Those who spend their wealth by night and day secretly and openly, have their reward with their Lord: on them shall come no fear, nor shall they grieve.

(*Sūrah* II. 274).

A similar sentiment is expressed in several other verses of the *Qur'ān*, and the Sayings of the Prophet (peace be upon him) emphasize this theme. Now, what is beneficial to the community is relative to the needs of the community and this changes with changing circumstances. Therefore, it is difficult to lay down any hard and fast rules in this regard. Time was when *Zakāt* used to meet all the requirements of the society, specially during the time of the Holy Prophet (peace be upon him), but nowadays we require more than the *Zakāt* revenue. Owing to the complexity of modern life the concept of welfare is changing with the changing values of life. What is more important for us is not to discourage this changing attitude towards life, but to welcome this change which is consistent with the basic spirit of Islam. Therefore, the beneficent use of property cannot initially be interpreted as implying an obligation to spend a specific portion of property on the welfare of the community. The obligation can never be absolute; it is always relative to the needs of the society and values of life. To my mind, the best way of utilizing property "in the way of Allah" is to formulate a fiscal policy which ensures levying from rich people that which is their just contribution and using the proceeds for the promotion of the public good. It is true that the Muslim world is poor and backward. Therefore, utilization of property "in the way of Allah" is highly significant because this is, I am sure, one of the basic conditions by which the Muslim community can prosper. If the Muslim States of the world want to achieve the goal of "Welfare State" in the true sense of the term, the leaders who are at the helm of affairs in the Muslim world must ensure that their countries' wealth and resources are all used for beneficent purposes.

Harmless Use. Fourthly, when Islam gives emphasis to the beneficent use of property it imposes upon the owner of property the duty not to use it in such a way as to cause harm to others or to the community. Absolute ownership of everything belongs to Allah; every individual, rich or poor, has the inherent right to use it. Therefore, when harm is done to others, this would be aggression which is forbidden. The Holy *Qur'ān* says:

"Fight in the cause of God.
Those who fight you,
But do not transgress limits;
For God loveth not transgressors.

(*Sūrah* II. 190).

There are several other verses in the Holy *Qur'ān* in a similar vein, and the traditions and sayings of the Prophet (peace be upon him) also emphasize this theme. Thus Abū Hurairah reported, the Messenger of Allah (peace be upon him) said: "Excess of water should not be withheld, arresting thereby the growth of herbage." (Bukhārī). The significance of this *Ḥadīth* lies in the fact that without water there would be no herbage, hence owners of land situated on water courses are required to allow the flow of excess water to other people's land or even to barren tracts which would thus become grass fields for cattle. This is a reminder as well as a warning to those who do not allow water to pass on to others when their needs are satisfied. In fact, the first Muslims were required to be very scrupulous in matters of other people's right to land. Ibn 'Umar reported, the Prophet (peace be upon him) said, "Whoever takes any part of land without having a right to it he shall be, as a punishment for it, sunk down into the earth on the Day of Resurrection to the depth of seven earths" (Bukhārī).

Nowadays in many Muslim countries we find that freedom of ownership appears to have resulted in some cases in an unduly heavy concentration of property in the hands of a few persons. It is certainly a state of affairs which the proper application of the teachings of Islam would not permit. Therefore, the government in a Muslim country should take active steps to prevent undue concentration of wealth in the hands of the few either by progressive taxation or by legislation. There is no hard and fast rule about this, but the guiding principle must be that property should not be made the special prerogative of a privileged few. The Islamic Law gives preference to the greater right of the community. The jurist Ibn al-Qayyim says on the subject: "If one contemplates the laws which the Almighty has ordained for His creation, one finds that they are all designed to ensure a balance of benefit and that where there is a conflict, preference is given to the more important as against the less important. The laws also seek to prevent the infliction of harm, but where harm is inevitable the lesser of the evils is preferred. These are the principles implied in the laws of God, which eloquently speak of His wisdom and compassion" (*Miftāḥ al-Sa'ādah*, p. 350). The basis of this rule is the maxim of "no harm is allowed whether the doer benefits from it or not," which is a saying of the Prophet (peace be upon him). Many subsidiary rules have been formulated upon this principle. The Muslim jurists have explained the distinction between the various types of harm, e.g. harm that befalls the entire community harm that is intentional, harm that is not intentional, harm of a serious nature, harm of a minor nature, harm that is inevitable, harm that is.very probable, etc. In all cases a balance is sought between the various interests, and the predominant intention is to promote benefits and prevent harm (see on this *al-Muwāfaqal* by al-Shātibī, Vol. II).

Islam promotes this basic moral conscience by inculcating the fear of God, which in practice means scrupulous avoidance of anti-social behaviour in all shapes and forms. The charter of human brotherhood outlined in the Holy Prophet's Farewell Address is far superior to the one envisaged in the *Communist Manifesto*. The great emphasis that Islam has laid on the social responsibilities of an owner of property has fascinated Western thinkers of whom Professor Massignon writes:

"Islam has the merit of standing for a very equalitarian conception of the contribution of each citizen by the title to the resources of the community. It is hostile to unrestricted exchange, to banking capitals, to state loans, to indirect taxes on articles of prime necessity, but it holds to the right of the father and the husband to private property and to commercial capital. Here again it occupies an intermediate position between the doctrine of capitalism and Bolshevist communism."

Lawful Possession. The fifth rule governing the conduct of the owner of property is contained in the Holy *Qur'ān* (*Sūrah* IV. 29) in which all such unlawful means of acquiring property are prohibited as these in the end, destroy a people. Acquisition of property or goods through falsehood falls into the same category. It is equally unlawful to seek to establish a title to property by obtaining judgment through corrupt means like bribery or false evidence (*Sūrah* II. 188). Since society is drifting towards materialism, many people resort to such devices as cheating, monopoly and usury for the purposes of increasing wealth. The *Sharī'ah* gives the state full powers to punish dishonest activities. As regards monopoly, Islam provides that property hoarded or monopolized would be punished because it puts wealth out of circulation and deprives the owner as well as the rest of the community of its beneficent use (*Sūrah* IX. 34). The jurist Abū Yūsuf (731–98 C.E.), a companion of Imām Abū Hanīfah, founder of the Hanafi school of thought, says: "If the withholding of anything from the public would harm it, then that act is wrongful, whether the commodity be gold or silver. He who hoards such commodities abuses his right of ownership. Whatever would harm the community, if withheld from it, should not be withheld. The hoarding of cloth is just as harmful as the hoarding of food. The reason for the prohibition of hoarding and monopoly is that harm should not befall the community. The community would suffer from the hoarding and monopoly of food as from the hoarding and monopoly of clothes. The community has various needs, and suppressing any of these needs would be wrongful."

Balanced Use. The sixth rule of the *Sharī'ah* in regard to the conduct of the owner of private property is that he should use the property in a balanced way. That is, the owner of the property should be neither prodigal or parsimonious in its use. The Qur'ān says:

"Make not thy hand tied like a niggard's to thy neck
Nor stretch it forth
To its utmost reach,
So that those become
Blameworthy and destitute.

(*Sūrah* XVII. 29).

Again, the Holy *Qur'ān* says

"For God loveth not,
The arrogant, the vainglorious;
(Nor) those who are niggardly
Or enjoin niggardliness on others,
Or hide the bounties
Which God hath bestowed
On them; for We have prepared,
For those who resist Faith,
A Punishment that steeps
Them in contempt."

(*Sūrah* IV. 36–37).

This is how Islam maintains a balance in the use of property. As regards prodigality, it can be said that goods and property lawfully acquired are a bounty of Allah which is provided by Him as a means of support. They should be properly looked after and should not be wasted through neglect. A person of defective judgment should not be allowed to squander his subsistence. It should be managed and administered for him, and provision should be made for his maintenance out of the income (*Sūrah* IV. 6). The duty of making such provision should normally appertain to the community or to the state. Prodigality does not necessarily mean wickedness or grave irresponsibility which does not harmonize with the prevailing needs of the community.

As regards parsimony, on the other hand, it must be admitted that some people, instead of putting their property into beneficent use in the service of their fellow-beings, have a tendency to hold back, not realizing that holding back renders a person progressively poorer in the true sense of the term inasmuch as he stultifies his faculties, and, by putting that which he possesses out of service and out of circulation, renders it completely barren and unfruitful. The Holy *Qur'ān* has repeatedly prohibited people from parsimonious holding back. For instance, the *Qur'ān* says, "Behold, you are those who are favoured by being called upon to spend in the way of Allah; but of you there are some who hold back, you who so holds back does so only to the prejudice of his own soul. It is Allah Who is All-Sufficient and it is you who are needy." (*Sūrah*

XLVII. 38). Though it is difficult to exercise effective control on it, one way of preventing undue parsimony is to impose heavy progressive taxes, which might persuade the parsimonious that it is not worthwhile to be too niggardly. Where parsimony becomes tantamount to the hoarding or monopoly of essential commodities, the state has every right to curb it either by legislation or by direct action.

Due Benefits. The seventh rule of the *Sharī'ah* gives emphasis to the use of property for the purpose of securing for the owner due benefits. It must be admitted that in practice many people utilize their property to secure for themselves undue special benefits in the political and economic spheres to the neglect of the larger interests of the community. This is obviously against the spirit of Islam. In many Muslim and Western countries, despite the removal of property qualifications for the franchise, it remains possible for the wealthy to secure for themselves special advantages in the political and governmental spheres. Money seems capable of persuading people to vote one way or the other, and of dissuading them from doing certain things. The control exercised by the wealthy minority over the main sources of the economy often leads to pressure being exerted to procure selfish advantages in politics and government. In Islam the state must ensure that property is never used for the attainment of such selfish objectives. The law would guarantee economic, social and political freedom and not subject it to financial control.

This last rule of the *Sharī'ah* gives emphasis to the interests of the living. Since the question of control and distribution of property after death of the owner does not arise, the due interests of the living will have to be secured by putting the Islamic laws of inheritance into practice.

Considering all these factors it may be repeated that the uniqueness of the Islamic concept of property lies in the ethical and moral injunctions attached to it—injunctions which provide opportunities for Muslim States to regulate the concept of private property. The religion of Islam contains principles which, if properly understood and applied, can be the best possible solution to the evils of both capitalism and communism and ensure happiness and property, order and justice.

5.4 Conclusion

The following major conclusions emerge from the preceding discussion:

(a) The productive system in an Islamic state must be guided by both objective and subjective criteria: objective criteria to be measured in material welfare, subjective criteria to be reflected in the welfare which should be judged in the light of the economic ethics of Islam.

(b) In Islam, the factors of production are not simply subject to a process of historic change, impelled by many background forces – the monetization of labour, land and capital, the rise of national states out of feudal principalities and so on, but also to a timeless moral and ethical framework as laid down in the *Sharī'ah*. As a result, the factors of production in general and labour in particular are never divorced from social and moral life. Land is not seen as an ancient prerogative of state and power; it is viewed as a means of increasing productivity to be used for individual and community welfare.

Both the *Qur'ān* and the *Sunnah* have laid much emphasis on the proper and efficient cultivation of land. Wastage of land in any form is condemned. But cultivation of land should not be the only occupation of the people in an Islamic state. The state can make rules to ensure that land as a factor of production is used in such a way that the objective of balanced growth is achieved for the benefit of the community. The Prophet tried to impress upon his followers the importance of cultivating land only themselves, making it a rule that a man should retain in his possession as much of the land as he cultivates himself.

Again, capital is not costless in Islam despite the fact that interest is prohibited. The cost of capital can be expressed in terms of opportunity cost in an Islamic framework. Islam does recognize the share of capital—a share which is variable. Thus, it is because of the presence of the element of profit that capital can grow even in the interest-free economy of Islam. Various injunctions of the *Qur'ān* go to prove that Islam can bring about a compromise between the two opposites of capital creation: reduced current consumption and increased future consumption, thereby allowing capital to play its true role in the productive process.

Lastly, the motivational properties of entrepreneurship in an Islamic framework are quite distinctive in the sense that they tend to generate co-operative forces through diverse forms of investment based on partnership in varying forms. This involves the integration of human capital with non-human resources.

(c) The Islamic concept of private ownership is unique in the sense that absolute ownership of everything on earth and heaven belongs to Allah alone (*Sūrah* III. 189). Man is simply the vicegerent of Allah on earth. Generally speaking, there are eight rules of the *Sharī'ah* governing private ownership of property. They are:

(*a*) continuous utilization of property;
(*b*) payment of *Zakāt* in proportion to the property owned;
(*c*) beneficent use of property;
(*d*) use of property without causing any harm to others;
(*e*) lawful possession of property;
(*f*) use of property not in a prodigal or parsimonious way;
(*g*) use of property for the purpose of securing for one-self due benefits;
(*h*) rightful application of the Islamic law of inheritance.

Notes

[1] Hellbroner and Thurow *The Economic Problem*, 4th edn, p. 20.
[2] Wicksell *Lectures on Political Economics*, vol. 1, p. 50.

5.6 Selected Further Reading

Ali, Mohammad Yousuf "Optimal Utilization of Resources and Maximization of Production in Islam," in *Thoughts on Islamic Economics*, Islamic Economics Research Bureau, 1980.

Faruqi, Islamil R. "Islam and Labour", in *Islam and a New International Economic order*, International Institute for Labour Studies, 1980.

Huda, M. N. "Economics Accepting Islam", in *World Muslim League*, Vol. 1, No. 3, Singapore, 1964.

Mannan, M. A. "Review of Risk Bearing and Profit-Sharing in an Islamic Framework", *Proceedings of International Seminar on Monetary and Fiscal Systems of Islam*, Islamabad, 1981.

Mustafa, Ahmad & Askari, H. "Economic Implications of Islamic Land Ownership and Land Cultivation", a paper presented at the Second International Conference on Islamic Economics: Development, Finance and Distribution in an Islamic Perspective, Islamic University, Islamabad. 19–23 March, 1983.

Siddiqi, N. "Muslim Economic Thinking – A Survey of Contemporary Literature", The Islamic Foundation, 1981.

Udovitch, Abraham L. "Labour Partnership in Early Islamic Law" in *Journal of the Economic and Social History of the Orient*, Vol. 1, Leiden, 1967.

Zarqa, M. A. "Capital Allocation, Efficiency and Growth in an Interest-free Economy" in *The Journal of Economics and Administration*, No. 16, King Abdulaziz University, Jeddah, 1967, pp. 43–58.

CHAPTER 6

Some Problems and Issues in Factors of Production

6.1 The Land Tenure System in Islam

6.2 Population Policy in an Islamic State

6.3 The Nature of Industrial Relations in Islam

6.4 Collective Bargaining and the Right to Strike in Islam

6.5 Conclusions

6.6 Selected further reading

APPENDIX:

(a) The Land Tenure System during 'Umar's Caliphate

(b) Some "Fatwas" on Family Planning

"The wages of a labourer must be paid to him before the sweat dries upon his body."

The Prophet (peace be upon him)

"The best earning is that of the labourers provided he does his job with care and regard for his employer."

The Prophet (peace be upon him)

6.1 The Land Tenure System in Islam

In a predominantly agricultural economy land tenure or the legal and customary relations based on land are of crucial importance from the point of view of production and distribution, because they influence incentives for production and techniques of farming and, through the pattern of ownership and tenancy, of ownership. Islam being a *"Dīn"* meaning thereby a code of life, instead of a *"Madhhab,"* i.e. a religion, cannot remain silent on the matter; rather, the laws of the *Qur'ān* and the *Sunnah* have laid down certain positive and fundamental principles from which it is quite possible to evolve a system of land-tenure suited to the requirements of the various Muslim countries of the world.

Qur'ānic Law and Peasant-proprietorship. The law of the *Qur'ān* regarding ownership of land is unequivocally in favour of peasant-proprietorship. According to the law of the *Qur'ān*, land is to be shared by all to the maximum good of human society; therefore, ownership and control over land which limits the benefits to a few, to the exclusion of the majority of the people, is contrary to the spirit of Qur'ānic Law. In Islam nobody can claim absolute ownership of land because land belongs to Allah. In fact, Qur'ānic Law does not favour the *zamīndārī* system, its essence being equitable distribution of land among all genuine cultivators. The *Qur'ān* says: "Said Moses to his people: Pray for help from God, and (wait)in patience and constancy; for the earth is God's to give as a heritage to such of His servants as He pleaseth; and the end is (best) for the righteous" (*Sūrah* VII. 128).

God has created the earth for the good of all people to enjoy its fruits and produce. "It is He Who has spread out the earth for (the benefit) of (His) creatures; therein is fruit and date-palms, producing spathes (enclosing dates)."

The obligation of providing sustenance to all rests on God Who is the Creator. All things that are on the earth are created by God Almighty for the benefit of the whole human race.

"There is no moving creature
On earth but its sustenance
Dependeth on God."

(*Sūrah* XI. 6)

"It is He Who/hath created for you
All things that are on earth."

(*Sūrah* II. 29)

The resources of the earth are to be shared equally by all.

"He set on the (earth).
Mountains standing firm,
High above it,

And bestowed blessings on
The earth, and measured therein,
All things to give them
Nourishment in due proportion,
In four Days, in accordance
With (the needs of)
Those who seek (sustenance)

(*Sūrah* XLI. 10).

Thus the sources of livelihood for human beings are so arranged by God Almighty that everyone is free to draw his share of sustenance by his own efforts and the law of God is that no one should get more than he works for.

Just as individuals vary in their physical and mental abilities, they also vary in their capacities to earn.

"God has distinguished you from one another, in (your capacities to earn) sustenance. Some can earn more than others, but it does not so happen that those who are more favoured give away (their extra earning) to those who depend on them, although they are all equal sharers in (the earnings). Then, are not such failing to acknowledge the favour of God?"

(*Sūrah* XVI. 71).

Commenting on the above verses, Maulānā Abul-Kalām Āzād says:
"It is clear that the Holy *Qur'ān* accepts the position that people are not alike in their ability to earn and consequently some possess more and some less; but the *Qur'ān* does not accept a situation in which some have too much and some nothing at all, of which the members are intimately concerned with the welfare of one another. They work in different spheres of life and earn more or less, according to their capacities, and though the better off among them do not give away all their earnings to those who are poor, yet they never become so unconcerned about the welfare of the poor but of them as to let them starve. Though the members have a right separately to their respective earnings, they have to pool them—regardless of the large or small share of each—in order to provide each of them with the necessities of life."[1]

The above exposition of Maulānā Abul-Kalām Azād shows clearly that if a man, by his possession over a large area of land, deprives others of their right to sustenance from God's earth, his possession would be considered illegal according to the Qur'ānic law.

Ḥadīth and Land Tenure System. Even from the Tradition of the Holy Prophet and the writings of many celebrated scholars of Muslim theology it can be proved beyond doubt that Islam disfavours the *zamīndārī* system or landlordism or feudalism as we call it, firstly, because this system of land tenure is the negation of the principle of equitable distribution of wealth and, secondly, because it may stand in the way of the proper utilization of land, as non-use of land is wasteful and impoverishes the owner as well as the community as a whole. No doubt, the Holy Prophet himself distributed land among his followers. Sources never implies that modern landlordism was present either in pre-Islamic days or afterwards. Not a single rich landlord could be found in that society because the nature of the country's soil precluded the existence of this form of land-ownership on account of the absence of rain and irrigation and the presence of sandy desert soil. As a result, Islam was never confronted with the problem of landlordism as it exists with all its evils in its modern form. So, land distributed by the Prophet around Madinah was not believed to have given rise to the evils of feudalism. The lands which previously belonged to the Jews were given to poor Muslims, especially to the *Muhājirīn*.

It was never the intention of the Prophet to encourage landlordism in any form to the detriment of society as a whole, because he tried to impress upon his followers the importance of cultivating land themselves. The Prophet is reported to have said: "A person who has a piece of land should cultivate it himself and should not leave it uncultivated. If he does not cultivate it, he should give it to another for cultivation; but if he does not cultivate, nor gives it to another for cultivation, he should keep it with himself—we do not want it". (Bukhārī).

The last sentence of the *Hadīth* is in a tone of displeasure at such a course of conduct. That is to say, if one does not give it to another for cultivation nor cultivates it oneself, let one keep it—"we do not want it". It was intended that one should retain in one's possession as much of the land as one cultivated himself.

This *Hadīth* has been quoted in *Sahīh Muslim* with a little addition: "if the other person refuses to take it, the person in possession may keep it with himself". In other words, if he offers it free to another who does not like to be favoured and wishes to have it on rent, he should rather keep it with himself than lease it on rent. The Holy Prophet has clearly prohibited the leasing of land on rent (cash or *batā'ī*). For this reason 'Abdullah ibn 'Umar, when he heard this *Hadīth* in the days of Amīr Mu'āwīyah, when capitalism had established its hold over Muslims, stopped accepting lease rent.

Another tradition of the Holy Prophet quoted by Imām Bukhārī runs as follows:

"Zafī' bin Khadīj says that his uncle Zubair bin Rafī'ah once stated that the Prophet had prohibited him from a lucrative business. Zafī' said that the Holy Prophet's orders must be just, upon which Zubair told him that he had been called and questioned by the Holy Prophet as to what he was doing with his land. He said he was leasing it on one fourth of the total produce, plus some quantity of dates and barley. The Holy Prophet replied: 'Do not do this; either cultivate it yourself or give it to another for cultivation (without any rent), otherwise keep it fallow with you.'"

This does not mean that one can keep one's land fallow for all times to come. The rule laid down by the *Sharī'ah* in regard to the conduct of the owner of landed property is that he should continue to use it all the time. The non-use of land is unproductive and wasteful. The Prophet is reported to have observed that the person who seizes land belonging to nobody, for the purpose of developing such land, would cease to have any right to the land if he does not reasonably exploit it after three years of possession.

This Islamic code is in contrast to French law, which prescribes the time limit as fifteen years and under which land is transferred to the cultivator, irrespective of whether he makes it productive or not. The superiority of the Islamic Law is inherent in this principle, for land is transferred only to those who are capable of making the fullest use of its productive capacity. There is a well-known saying of the Prophet which can be put forward in this context. The Holy Prophet said: "The person who brings dead land to life is its owner, provided it has no previous owner."

In case a person owns big tracts of land which are difficult for him to exploit property for their productive resources, the Islamic state is entitled to take any action against the owner, necessary for the proper use of land. Ibn 'Abidīn says: If taxable agricultural land is not utilized by the owner, or if it is not irrigated properly while improvement is possible, the government may levy taxes on the land and is, thereby, entitled to get its due share. In case the owner refrains from cultivating the land, the government may put another man in charge of the property so that it may get its due tax, or may let it on rent or operate it on its own account. Thus, freedom of ownership is not allowed to be misused. The action of Ḥaḍrat 'Umar in connection with the taking back of land given to Ḥaḍrat Bilāl is clear proof of this.

The aforesaid principle is a useful safeguard against the rise of feudalistic tendencies, for a person who owns more than he himself can manage stands in comparison with a capitalist seeking partnership of labour for the exploitation of his savings. So, the practice of letting out land on a fixed amount of produce—a counterpart of interest in the agricultural field—is unlawful. On the authority of Hasan Basrī, it is narrated that the practice during the period of Hadrat 'Umar was that the owner was bound to contribute some share in labour and investment so that his share might not constitute a return for the gift of Nature only. It may be noted here that Imām Abū Yūsuf, the Grand Qādī of Hārūnur-Rashīd, whose reign marked the climax of imperialism, is often quoted in support of the view that land can be leased on rent. But the consensus of opinion seems to dislike the idea, which may give rise to the zamīndāri system. Among the persons who condemned this system, the names of Imām A'ẓam, the great teacher of Imām Abū Yūsuf, Shāh Walīullah, Maulānā 'Ubaidullah Sindhī deserve special mention. Maulānā 'Ubaidullah Sindhī, a celebrated scholar of Muslim theology and a great exponent of the philosophy of Shāh Walīullah, writes in his commentary of *Ḥujjatullāh-ul-Bālighah*: "We are followers of Imām Abū Ḥanīfah who has prohibited the leasing of land on rent. According to him, a person should possess only so much area of land as he could cultivate himself. As a matter of fact, the system of leasing land in any form leads to great injustice to the tenants, and the landlords go on expanding their holdings over vast areas and making the poor tenants work like donkeys and oxen. They have no mercy for them and they starve them."

I also disfavour the idea of leasing land because it may help in creating a new capitalist class in society, the very existence of which is a threat to the basic economic ethics of Islam. Barring a few exceptions, the precepts of the *Qur'ān* in this regard have not been followed by Muslims throughout Islamic history. The capitalist class interpreted the Qur'ānic Law in a way that suited their interests and did not hamper the exploitation of poor people. Even today there are many Muslim countries where we find that some sort of feudalism is the order of the day. Only a handful of people are enjoying life with all the modern amenities we have, to the utter neglect of the vast majority of the masses. It is now time to think and act. Islam has faced the challenge of time.

6.2 Population Policy in an Islamic State.

A population control policy implies that the actual demographic situation is not satisfactory and that a more favourable one could be attained by pursuing the policy in question. Family planning through birth control is an integral part of a comprehensive population control policy, the full effect of which is not to prevent perpetual population growth but to bring about a happy marriage between population growth and economic growth for a nation as a whole. The objectives of family planning may be: (*a*) to protect the health and beauty of women by allowing a proper interval between two children, (*b*) to keep the family responsibility within the financial capacity of the parents, (*c*) to avoid the necessity of maintaining a large family through an illegal source of income. From the little study I have made it appears however, that the question of family planning has been a controversial issue in Islam. Clearly, there are two schools of thought; one looks with favour upon the idea of birth control and the other does not. Without entering into controversy, I would like to make a dispassionate analysis of the problem.

The opponents of family planning argue that, as problems of food and space are closely associated with the birth of a baby, people generally adopt a method of birth control because of economic considerations.

This motive for family planning is un-Islamic. Citing the verse from the Holy *Qur'ān* which says: "Slay not your children, fearing a fall to poverty; We shall provide for them and for you. Lo! the slaying of them is a great sin." (*Sūrah* XVIII. 13), they try to establish that Allah, being the creator of mankind, supplies food and other necessities of life according to our need. Any attempt to control birth artificially is, therefore, an act of disbelieving in His blessings. The present problem of food is, they argue, an artificial phenomenon and is bound to disappear if sincere efforts are made.

On the other side, the supporters of family planning do recognize the financial capacity of parents in adopting birth control, Besides, they argue that opponents of birth control have not fully appreciated the significance of the verse of the *Qur'ān* which declares: "Surely, Allah changes not the condition of a people, until they change their conditions." (*Sūrah* XII. 11). This verse, according to them, negates the idea of determinism and constitutes an assertion of man's free will. It is this "free will" which distinguishes man from animals, and in respect of sexual impulses nature is subordinated to man's will, whereas this is not the case with regard to animals. Therefore, they feel that men may utilize their sexual impulses for the production of the labour force according to their needs and financial ability.

Again, family planning is challenged on the ground that " '*Azl*" which was current during the Prophet's lifetime as a birth control device is not Islamic. ("'*Azl*" is an Arabic word, which originally means "putting a thing aside or away," and with reference to sexual relations it means "putting semen outside at the end of sexual intercourse.") It is argued against very forcefully on the authority of Zaoyama who reported: The Messenger of Allah (peace and blessings of Allah be upon him) said, "'Azl amounts to putting a living man into the grave". (Ṭahāwī). Besides this a number of *Hadīths* from Tirmidhī, Ibn Mājah, Abū Dawūd and *Ṣaḥīḥ Muslim* were cited against birth control. Again, in the course of expressing his opinion on different occasions in connection with '*Azl*, the Prophet (peace be upon him) is reported to have made the following statements: "When Allah wants to create any man, nobody can stop it."; "There is no soul that is to be till the Day of Resurrection but it will come to life." (Bukhārī); "It is the *Taqdīr* which determines everything." Quoting all these statements the opponents of birth control try to prove that any attempt to control population growth by artificial means is an act of disbelieving in Allah; whereas the protagonists of family planning have advanced a number of *Hadīths* in support of " '*Azl*" on the authority of Jābir, Abū Sa'īd, al-Ghazālī and others. In view of the conflicting *Hadīths* for and against " '*Azl*" or birth control, what is, to me, needed is to judge the correctness of these *Hadīths* by the exercise of our intellect with an unbiased frame of mind (i.e. *Ijtihād*), tempered by consideration of the opinion of most of the *Hadīth* commentators, because it is a verdict of history that a good number of false *Hadīths* manufactured by the so-called false Prophets and "*Munafiqs*" were mixed up with "*Ṣaḥīḥ Hadīths*" or true *Hadīths*.

Many '*Ulamā*' hold the opinion that new babies are not only the joint property of the family concerned but also an asset to society as a whole. Many others feel that new babies may turn out to be social parasites if they are not given proper education and training which is nowadays a costly affair.

The modern critics of birth control observe that the Malthusian theory which asserted that population tends to increase in geometrical progression (i.e. 1, 2, 4, 8, 16) while the supply of food tends to increase in arithmetical progression (i.e. 1, 2, 3, 4) was discredited by the actual course of events. All the mathematical propositions regarding the gloomy picture of population growth and food supply have been belied by events. These critics hold that Malthus did not foresee the great revolutionary developments which were destined to take place in the techniques of agricultural production and in the field of international transport. Every person comes to the world not only with a hungry stomach but also with a pair of hands. The increase in population which means the increase in the supply of labour makes possible better division of labour and better distribution. So, the problem becomes one of a ratio not between food and population but between wealth and population. They further observe that spending money on a family planning programme is a clear waste of resources. The amount of time and human energy spent on popularizing a family planning programme would be utilized more fruitfully in the mitigation of the economic ills of the people. Conversely, the protagonists of family planning argue that the objective of family planning is not to stop continual population growth, rather it aims at qualitative improvement of the labour force and helps in bringing harmony between population growth and economic growth.

It is agreed that the availability of artificial birth control has created the serious social problem of extra-marital relationships which have increased the incidence of adultery in society and consequently increased the numbers of illegitimate children, particularly in Western countries. But the supporters of family planning are of the opinion that if there is an increase in extramarital relationships in society, it is not merely because of the introduction of birth control but also because of the lowering of moral and spiritual standards and the changes of attitude towards life-philosophy.

The last, but not least, argument against family planning is that only the richer, educated sections of society, rather than the poorer, illiterate people, are interested in birth control, because they are more conscious of their standard of living; poverty and fecundity go together. As the standard of comforts increases, people find it difficult to earn a decent living till a very late period in life. Hence they are forced to marry late. They are also unwilling to have a large families, as this means a fall in their standard of living. "A baby or a car?"—this is a problem for the young couple and often the car is preferred. As a result of this there will be fewer children born to richer, educated parents, who are in a position to produce an effective labour force by imparting the best available training and educational facilities to their off-spring. Therefore, the progress of society is likely to be retarded. This is, indeed, a serious objection to family planning although its protagonists are of the view that family planning programmes, if properly implemented, would arrest the alarming rate of present population growth and help it to keep pace with economic growth, which, in its turn, implies the general well-being of the people.

Such, in brief, are the essential points for and against family planning or population control. I would now like say a few words about population control in poor Muslim countries from a purely economic standpoint.

At present, when the masses in many Muslim Countries are groaning under poverty due to the capitalistic system, birth control may be adopted as a temporary measure for alleviating their sufferings, even though partially. If the reported population increase of above 2.5 per cent per annum in rich and poor Muslim Countries such as Bangladesh and Pakistan be allowed to continue without any action being taken, the population will have doubled at the end of the present century.

There is a cry for economic growth in Muslim Countries. But we have seen that at the initial stage of economic development the death-rate is likely to fall. The limitation of deaths through health measures, although not pursued as a population policy, nevertheless, has demographic effects. In so far as health measures succeed in lowering the death rate while other demographic variables remain fixed, they tend to increase the population. Thus the seriousness of the situation lies in the fact that every improvement in medical aid will reduce the death-rate, and unless the birth-rate is reduced, the rate of population growth will be accelerated which will cancel the effect of the new development. The fall in the death-rate due to economic development will, of course, lead to the fall in the birth-rate after a lapse of time. Since this is a time-consuming process, control of population growth is of supreme importance.

Theoretically, there are two conceivable ways of reducing fertility quickly—one is birth control, the other is industrialization. The main disadvantages of industrialization as compared to a direct birth-control policy are twofold: (1) it is more difficult, (2) it is relatively slower. Although economic change seems more acceptable than birth-control measures, yet the truth is that any policy which rapidly industrialized Muslim Countries would be a far greater strain on the basic social institutions than would any policy that attacked fertility directly.

Moreover, we cannot pitch our hopes too high about industrial development which can absorb only part of our increased labour force. Besides, the mechanization of agriculture which is capital-intensive rather than labour-intensive cannot be applied to increasing extremely low agricultural productivity compared to other countries. Thus there will be more mouths to feed than there is food.

The excess labour force, according to Malthus, is historically corrected by Nature's positive checks such as war, epidemics, etc. The inevitable moral which Malthus draws from this gloomy picture is the need for the application of what he calls preventive checks, i.e. voluntary restrictions on birth, late marriage, etc.

A birth control policy is justified by the weakness of the other three alternative measures to combat the ills of over-population. Firstly, redistribution of population from thickly populated areas to areas of low density of population can be treated as one of the measures to overcome the problem of overpopulation, because there are wide variations in the density of population in the various regions of a country. This is not, however, an easy problem. Even Adam Smith was of the view that of all the forms of luggage, man is the most difficult to be transported. Besides the problems of language, customs, social institutions, many economic problems such as housing and settlement, water supply and health services arise with the redistribution of population. These require scientific planning and may only be a part of the country's overall plane.

Secondly, relief to the problem of relative overpopulation can be attempted through the redistribution of wealth by progressive taxation of the rich. But if taxation is too heavy, it may crush enterprise and reduce production, ultimately reducing national income. The purpose of redistribution will be defeated, if national income is reduced by the process of redistribution. Before cutting the cake for equal distribution, the size of the cake has to be increased. But the problem is *how* to increase its size.

Lastly, emigration as a population policy can be of some relief to the problem of overpopulation. But there are some practical difficulties in the way of its proper implementation, because even sparsely populated countries nowadays control immigration of foreigners with restrictive laws. Moreover, emigrants seldom leave in sufficient numbers to make a serious hole in the population. Not only that, emigrants often have higher skills than the average among the population that remains.

Apart from these factors, there are many social, physical and eugenic reasons which may be advanced in support of birth control or family planning in poor Muslim Countries.

(*a*) *Social.* Owing to the complexities of modern life, women have begun demanding more social and professional self-realization and as a result they have now begun taking an active interest in education. The more time and energy a woman puts into education, the more likely she is to continue with her own individual career. Though a few educated women forgo marriage and motherhood, many do not. There is a tendency, however, for those women who do marry to keep the family small enough to enable them to devote a part of their time to other activities outside the home.

(*b*) *Physical.* Many husbands feel it advisable not to have too many children in the interest of their wives' health. Physicians advise in the interests of the mother's health that the couple have at least a three years' gap between births, if they wish to produce healthy children and the mother to retain her vitality.

Although childbearing is a normal physiological function in the case of healthy women, it causes undue strain on those who suffer from certain diseases—such as heart disease and diabetes. Apart from any specific disease in the mother, continued childbearing with little or no interval between successive pregnancies may itself constitute an undue strain on her physical condition and the spacing of births so as to allow a return to normal health may prove to be a definite necessity.

(c) *Eugenic*. In the interests of the nation, it is very important that persons having transmissible or hereditary diseases should not have children. They should be checked from undertaking the venture of procreation by strict legislation, so that society is not full of imbeciles, idiots, infirms or social inadequates.

It is a matter of common knowledge that social customs in society are such that many of our eugenically fit cannot have families because of low incomes and a number of traditions to which the people are accustomed. Without doubt, thousands of these young men and women, physically and morally strong, would gladly marry if they knew that they could restrict their family so as to rear a few children well.

Thus, it is an undisputed fact today that the extended use of contraceptive measures is the most powerful weapon in population control and a direct means of controlling fertility without checking the enjoyment of sexual intercourse, besides eradicating and eliminating hereditary diseases from society.

Nevertheless, the conclusion that ideally emerges in order to maximize real income is that the population policy in poor Muslim countries should include at least three measures—a programme of strategic emigration, a sustained and vigorous birth-control campaign and a scheme for rapid industrialization, because none of these complex measures can be a substitute for the others or promise the maximum effect if pursued alone. Emigration should be encouraged with a view to losing as little as possible in terms of skills and capital. Birth control should be diffused with the help of films, radio, contraceptives, etc. Many of the prejudices against birth control are likely to disappear with wider education and vigorous propaganda. Lastly, industrialization should be pushed by central planning and control.

It should be noted here that we have so far talked of the quantitative aspect of our problem. A sound population policy will have to deal with the qualitative aspect which refers to the efficiency of the people; that is, the diseased and medically unfit should not be left free to perpetuate hereditary diseases of a dangerous character.

Thus the full effect of this comprehensive population policy would be, not to prevent perpetual population growth, but to bring about a happy marriage between population growth and economic growth.

Concluding Observation. The principle of benevolence and care for the poor, which is a universally recognized principle in Islam, should, I feel, be the guiding objective of population control and family planning. Therefore, if the population explosion, which we find in Bangladesh, Pakistan, Indonesia, and other countries, poses a threat to the economic growth which aims at raising the living standards of degraded humanity, a population control policy is perfectly justified just as the rationing of food, which aims at balanced distribution of food in a society, is justified: just as the prohibition on the slaughtering of cows and goats two days a week in Pakistan, *tempered* by consideration of the total welfare of the community, is justified in spite of the fact that these animals are quite "*Halāl*". But if the existence of a minority community in a state is at stake, both politically and economically, simply because of numerical strength, I shall definitely advocate the non-adoption of family planning, for this is also consistent with the principle of benevolence in so far as that community is concerned.

Broadly speaking, we are inclined to recommend population control policy, not only for the world of Islam, but also for the rest of the world with the exception of a few countries like Australia where there is a problem of underpopulation. But the success of a population control policy in countries like Pakistan or Bangladesh depends on the individual consciousness of social responsibility. If due to lack of this consciousness people do not react favourably to the policy of persuasion, the state has a right to intervene. If need be, the state can impose progressive taxes on a number of children beyond a certain limit. We have records to prove that, so far as the early history of the financial administration of Islam during the lifetime of the Prophet is concerned, there is a gradual evolution, beginning with persuasion and recommendation and culminating in obligations and duties enforced with all the power that the society could command. This has particularly happened with regard to *Zakāt*.

In fact, the Islamic state has a mission and vocation to fulfil—a mission to achieve social justice. If a population explosion creates a bottleneck in the way of attaining social justice, the Islamic state has a right to handle it accordingly.

6.3 The Nature of Industrial Relations in Islam.

The conflict between labour and capital is the bane of the capitalist world. The growth of workers' and employers' organizations during the last few decades has, therefore, been accompanied by a distinct increase in the number and extent of strikes and lockouts.

Since a strike is nothing but a withdrawal from work with the design of securing a return to the same employment under better conditions than are offered at the time by employers, it affects not only the consumers and producers but also the workers themselves. The consumers will be affected because of the artificial scarcity of goods resulting in a rise in prices. The producers will be affected because of disturbance caused in the continuity of production. Again, the stoppage of work owing to strikes means the loss of work and wages for the workers.

Similarly, a lockout which is the employer's answer to a strike is the act of closing a business enterprise by an employer for the purpose of forcing a decision on the employees. Obviously, a lockout causes a stoppage in production and creates the problem of unemployment. Thus the industrial conflict resulting in strikes and lockouts complicates the dual interests of consumers and producers, the socio-economic repercussions of which can hardly be overestimated. Many attempts have been made to bring a lasting compromise between labour and capital, but unfortunately, the capitalist system has failed to achieve any substantial results in this regard.

But Marx, the father of modern scientific socialism, represented a strong protest against the capitalist approach to the problem of the relationship between labour and capital. Following Smith and Ricardo, Marx developed his famous theory of value and surplus value. According to his theory of value, the value of any commodity is merely the amount of labour that is "socially necessary for its product". Thus, according to him, capital, being the embodiment of the past services of labour, is a "congealed labour". The capitalist sells the commodities in the market for a value equal to the full amount of labour used in their production. But the labourer gets his subsistence. The excess is the surplus which is pocketed by the capitalist; it measures the amount of exploitation of labour by capital. As time goes on this surplus value, according to Marx, gets concentrated in fewer and fewer hands and this results in the growing poverty and misery of the proletariat. In due course the workers will combine against their exploiters and will overthrow them. Thus will emerge a classless society which will end the class struggle.

But Marx's prophecy regarding this relationship between labour and capital is belied by the actual course of economic developments in various capitalist countries. Moreover, without going into details, it can be said that the labour theory of value itself is quite unsatisfactory, because it is not possible to reduce all labourers to one grade, as Marx and others have tried to do. The theory, which ignores the demand factor altogether and does not recognize the contribution of fixed capital in producing surplus value, cannot solve the problem of labour capital conflict.

Islam, on the other hand, does not recognize the exploitation of labour by capital, nor does it approve of the elimination of the capitalist class and the establishment of a classless society. Islam recognizes a diversity of capacities and talents resulting in a diversity in earnings and material rewards (*Qur'ān, Sūrah* IV. 33). It does not approve of dead-level equality in the distribution of wealth as this would defeat the very purpose of diversity. Naturally, Islam recognizes the existence of labour and capital in society. The two basic principles laid down in connection with this, both in the *Qur'ān* and the *Ḥadīth*, are that the servant shall do his work faithfully and to the best of his ability and that the master shall pay him fully for the service rendered. In fact, Islam brings about a happy marriage between labour and capital by giving the whole problem a moral bent; it will be clear if we analyze the main causes of industrial conflict and the Islamic injuctions. Industrial unrest arises mainly from economic and psychological factors.

The Economic Factor and the Islamic Viewpoint

The workers' share in production remains the cardinal cause of discontent. The workers, it is said, create the product of the industry, but they secure only a part of the production, the rest being held back by their employers. Similarly, the practice of overtime, especially when there is unemployment in the trade, has been responsible for much unrest. This practice is opposed, firstly, because it is retrogressive, secondly, because it might be used to cut down the standard day rates: thirdly, because it worsens the employment conditions; and, finally, because it adversely affects workers' health.

Here it is heartening to quote the Holy Prophet's (peace be upon him) observation: "Man has no right in his share in which God has no right. God's share is His command to give everyone his due and not to encroach on what belongs to another." The withholding of remuneration for service rendered is the gravest of sins. Abū Hurairah reported: The Prophet (peace and blessings of Allah be upon him) said, "Allah says there are three persons whose adversary in dispute I shall be on the Day of Resurrection: a person who makes a promise in My name, then acts unfaithfully: a person who sells a free person and devours his price; and a person who employs a servant and receives fully the labour due from him and then does not pay his remuneration" (Bukhārī). Again, it is related on the authority of Ibn Mājah that the Prophet (peace be upon him) said, "The wages of a labourer must be paid to him before the sweat dries upon his body."[2] But if it is not possible on the part of the master to pay the wages of the labourer for some valid reasons, it is permissible to invest the unpaid remuneration in some profitable business and the servant is entitled to all profits thus accruing. Ibn 'Umar said, "I heard the Messenger of Allah (peace be upon him) say: 'And the third man said, I employed labourers and I paid them their remuneration with the exception of one man; he left his dues and went away. So I invested his remuneration in a profitable business until it became abundant wealth'" (Bukhārī). It follows that employers are not entitled to utilize the unpaid wages of the labourers for their own purposes. Apart from the prompt payment of wages, Islam is quite alive to the welfare of labourers. Thus it is related on the authority of *Muhallah* of Ibn Hazm that the Prophet (peace be upon him) said, "It is the duty of the employers to take only such work from their employees which they can easily do. They should not be made to labour so that their health is told upon."[3] These *Hadiths* rule out all possibilities of capitalistic aggrandizement as well as forestall and supersede the Marxian methods of "expropriating the expropriators". Let us now pass on to the psychological causes of industrial unrest and the Islamic way of handling it.

Psychological Causes and the Islamic Viewpoint

In the present-day capitalist system, workers believe that the court, police and other administrative authorities are always prejudiced against them and are in favour of the employers. Whenever a dispute arises and a strike is called these authorities side with the capitalist employer; property rights seem to be more sacred than human rights. This remains a causal factor of industrial disputes.

In Islam, however, absolute ownership of everything belongs to God alone (*Qur'ān, Sūrah* III. 189). Man is Allah's vicegerent on earth. Thus legal ownership by the individual is recognized subject to the moral obligation that in all wealth all sections of society and even animals have a right to share (*Qur'ān Sūrah* LI. 19). In fact, "this supplementing of legal obligations with moral obligations to be discharged through voluntary effort runs through every part of the Islamic system." Moreover, the sovereignty of the state also belongs to Allah. The head of the state is His Caliph. As a matter of fact, the equality of the whole of mankind in the eye of Allah establishes a kind of rule of law which distinguishes the Islamic state from secular states. In such a scheme of society the court cannot interpret laws in the way it likes, the legislature may not pass any laws simply by majority. In fact, the whole code of conduct of the state must be consistent with the injunctions of the Holy *Qur'ān* and the *Sunnah*. In such a state of affairs there is no scope for exploitation and injustice. The interests of the labourers, nay, of the whole of mankind, are, therefore, safeguarded in the best possible way.

Employers' Interests and Islam

Again, Islam is quite alive to the interests of the employers, who can also make a positive contribution towards the welfare of society. Employers' interests, nay, the interests of the society as a whole, may be best safe-guarded: (*a*) if the employees, no matter whether they are industrial employees or Government employees, act faithfully and honestly, and (*b*) if the employees work with a high sense of the dignity of labour. Since modern society is drifting towards materialism to the utter neglect of the spiritual and moral values of life, it is difficult, or rather impossible, to imbue workers with a spirit of austerity of conduct and a high sense of the dignity of labour. Obviously, there is an eternal conflict of interests between classes in modern society. Islam is for the balanced growth of society for which the existence of a happy relationship between master and servant is considered an essential precondition. That is why Islam has tried to encourage the working class as a whole to work faithfully, honestly and with a deep sense of the dignity of labour. A number of authentic *hadīths* may be quoted in support of this contention.

Thus it is related on the authority of Ibn Mājah that the Holy Prophet (peace be upon him) said: "The best earning is that of the labourer provided he does his job with care and regard for his employer."[4] In fact, servants who carry out the orders of their masters faithfully are ranked with those who give charity. Ibn Mūsā reported that the Prophet (peace be upon him) said: "The faithful treasurer who pays what he is ordered with a willing heart is one of those who give charity." Moreover, it is really a duty of the servant to act according to the terms of the contract of service. The Prophet (peace be upon him) said that the Muslims shall be bound by the conditions which they make. Obviously, if conditions of service do not entitle the employees to take anything as a gift, they are entitled only to their wages or to remuneration. Abū Ḥumaid related that the Prophet (peace be upon him) appointed, from among the Azd, a man called Ibn al-'Utbīyyah, for the collection of *Zakāt*. When he came, he said, "This is for you and this was given to me as a gift." He (the Prophet) said: "He should have got down in the house of his father or the house of his mother, then he should see whether a gift is given to him or not" (Bukhārī).

Islam also condemns an employee's misappropriating or dishonestly taking any part of the master's property. Abū Hurairah said, "The Prophet (peace be upon him) stood up among us, and he spoke about dishonesty and he spoke of the enormity of its commitment. He said, 'I should not see any one of you on the Day of Resurrection there being on his neck a goat bleating, there being on his neck a horse neighing, so he should cry out "O Messenger of Allah! come to me," and I would say, "I do not control aught for thee. I delivered the message to thee."'" (Bukhārī).

The condition described here relates to Resurrection, hence it speaks of spiritual experience in physical terms, the significance being that every dishonesty, great or small, shall ultimately be brought to light and punished. From this it follows that in an Islamic state trade unions indulging in sabotage, which amounts to a number of activities ranging from "soldiering" to malicious destruction of plant and equipment, cannot be encouraged, rather, an Islamic state is quite competent to frame any laws prohibiting trade unions from indulging in anti-social activities. This is in accordance with the spirit of Islam.

Islam has also stressed the importance of the dignity of labour not only for the protection of the interests of the employees, but also for maximizing production. The Holy Prophet himself doing the work of tending of goats in his earlier days, even such a service is considered honourable and the Prophet's Companions did not disdain the work of a porter Abū Hurairah reported the Prophet (peace be upon him) having said, "Allah did not raise a Prophet but he pastured goats." His Companions said, "And thou?" He said, "Yes, I used to pasture them for the people of Makkah for some carts" (Bukhārī). Again, Abū Mas'ūd said: "When the Messenger of Allah (peace be upon him) commanded us to give charity, one of us went to the market and carried a load for which he got a *'mudd'* (a measure) and some of them are millionaires today." The importance of inculcating the spirit of the dignity of labour among different categories of the working class lies in the fact that the Muslim countries of today all over the world are underdeveloped. There is a crying need for development to improve the lot of common men, the vast majority of whom are still living at starvation level.

From the above analysis it can be said that Islam has tried to bring about a lasting compromise between labour and capital by giving the whole question of their relationship a moral bent and by making moral obligations on each side as part of the faith. Here, also Islam proves superior to secularism, which has not succeeded in harmoniously fitting labour and capital into a social mosaic.

6.4 Collective bargaining and the Right to Strike in Islam

Our discussion on the nature of industrial relations has established the fact that Islam has recognized the worker's right to a fair wage. If the employer tries to exploit the workers, they may opt for collective bargaining to secure Islamically-justified fair wages. For labour, being perishable, has a very weak bargaining power. Thus, a trade union can correct the bargaining weakness of labourers, eliminate capitalist exploitation and so enable labourers to raise their wages to the level of the full value of their marginal net product. It follows that in a properly-run Islamic society, there is no imperative necessity for the labour force to have collective bargaining power, because institutional arrangements will generate forces, whereby equitable and fair conditions of work tend to be established.

Around the question of the right to strike, a great controversy is still going on, as this problem is greatly influenced by one's attitude toward the existing industrial order. Those who regard private property and employers' management as indispensable will insist that strikes must be curbed, whilst those who advocate measures looking towards equalization of opportunities and possessions will favour a wide extension of the right to strike, since this is a means of curtailing the power of employers.

A strike is more than a merely collective refusal to enter into a contract of labour. It is a way of exerting pressure towards holding the old job on better terms. The betterment of the conditions may be in various directions: to obtain higher wages, to prevent a reduction of wages, to change working hours and any other conditions of work. The pressure may be defensive in that the wage-earners may be seeking to maintain the existing conditions that are being threatened, or it may be offensive in that an attempt is being made to improve upon existing working conditions. The essence of the striker's aim is to retain the same position. A strike, then, is a tactical procedure, a fighting move. It is mainly cherished and mainly used, because it constitutes an effective weapon of fighting. Sometimes, to aid the strikers, workers in other industries where conditions are acceptable may be called out in a *sympathetic strike*.

The economic significance of a strike lies in the fact that it affects every individual who has a dual interest in industry—an interest as a consumer and an interest as a producer.

Now, the question arises as to how far the right to strike shall be allowed to go. This is a question of the greatest intricacy and difficulty as there is no underlying set of principles to offer a satisfactory solution. As we have already pointed out, it all depends on one's point of view towards the existing scheme of things. A great deal depends on the warmth of one's social feelings, which vary greatly from individual to individual and from society to society. Obviously, there are two schools of thought—one group regards striking as old-fashioned and unnecessary and the other school favours the right to strike.

The main arguments of those who regard strike action as unnecessary may be summarized as follows:

Firstly, some people are of the opinion that labour's position under capitalism has been fundamentally changed. True, during the transition period of the industrial revolution a marvellous growth of material production was accompanied by an almost complete disregard for the well-being of the workers in the factories. The labourers worked from twelve to sixteen hours a day in dark crowded factories. Minor children of six to ten years of age laboured from dawn to dark. Under such conditions, some people argue, protest, in the form of strikes, was inevitable. But gone are those days. The effort to substitute peace for war in the conduct of industrial relations has given rise to several forms of machinery like conciliation, mediation, voluntary and compulsory arbitration, etc., for making amicable settlements. Moreover, the trend towards more labour legislation and increased government control of industry indicates a growing social conscience on the part of the general public. In the face of this, it is argued that strike action is old-fashioned and unnecessary.

Secondly, employers as a class regard it as unnecessary, because they think that they have the absolute right to manage their own businesses to suit themselves as opposed to their workers. Strike action is an unnecessary contravention of that right.

Thirdly, it is argued that strike action is the most effective fighting weapon of the trade union, which is itself unnecessary, because it cannot achieve the purposes for which it was created. Trade unions are, they argue, organized and controlled by a petty group of middle-class bourgeois intelligentsia. The poor labourers, who are living at starvation level, are being exploited by this group in the name of the welfare of the labourer. This is due to the fact that a trade union movement is incapable of developing an ideology for itself and, in consequence, the choice must be between allowing it to fall prey to the ideology of the middle class or indoctrinating it with socialist intellectualism. Under such conditions, workers become the yes-men of handful of middle class intellectuals.

Lastly, it is also pointed out that through strike action the trade union benefits only a small minority of industrial labourers, especially in the underdeveloped countries, by redistribution of income in their favour, because the majority of workers depend on agriculture for their living.

The main arguments of those who regard strike action as necessary may be summarised as follows:

They argue that strikes and the right to strike are not merely a matter of tactical procedure but of principle and fundamental right. If the right to discharge a worker is treated by employers as an inalienable right and if it is considered to be an indispensable part of the present industrial order of capitalism, then it stands to reason that the right to strike must be regarded as a fundamental right of workers.

It is thus pointed out that "discharge and strike" should be treated as cards of equal value in the game, the one to be set off against the other, and given up if the other is also given up. All conditions of employment may be subjected to some degree of control. If control is to be applied to the workman also, not only hiring but standard wages, piece rates, apportionment of taxes, the powers of foremen and shop rules may be settled by conference, agreement and contract, not by the employer at his untrammelled discretion. When methods of settlement such as participation in the contract of employment are established and in an effective position, strikes may be restricted to a greater limit than can be imposed in their absence.

Besides, the recognition of the right to strike may be necessary to further the cause of the democratic process, social justice and the implemention of development plans on the industrial front. It is further argued that no directives of the government or legislation by parliament can be a substitute for the social multiplier which the effective functioning of organized labour generates in the economy and in society.

But the most constructive approach to the problem calls for the development of an institutional process which can ensure such fair and acceptable conditions for work that disputes become rare. This implies that an effective channel must be opened through which the grievances of the workers are given a hearing and properly redressed. There may be organized, if possible, joint committees or work councils composed of representatives of workers and employers so that the former may have a voice in the determination of work conditions. If this institutional development takes place along with Islamic orientation and educational programmes on the rights and duties of employers and employees, then in the course of time the prohibition of strikes and lockouts becomes relatively unimportant and unnecessary.

In conclusion, it can be said that, given the existing order of industrial development, the right to strike and discharge may be recognized in principle, because any progress towards industrial development on Islamic lines calls for the fullest possible opportunities for both employers and employees. But how far should this right to strike and discharge be allowed to go? What degree of limitation would the Law exercise? It is an unanswerable question as no satisfactory answer can be given in absolute terms. The whole problem depends on a number of variables such as the existing level of concentration of industrial power, the level and stage of development of the labour movement, the level of social inequality and income, the level of Islamic awareness towards work ethics and so on.

It may however be repeated that if both workers and employers are imbued with the values of Islam, the whole question of strikes and lockouts would be relatively unimportant. But the fundamental problem is not how to prohibit or restrict strikes and lockouts, but how to inject Islamic values into the existing framework of industrial development in Muslim countries.

The crucial policy implication is that Islamic business ethics should form an integral part of either general or specific training designed for workers. There is also a need for an Islamic orientation training programme for management.

6.5 Conclusions

The main conclusions are as follows:

1. (*a*) The spirit of Qur'ānic law is undoubtedly in favour of peasant-proprietorship. Any land tenure system which limits the benefit to a few to the neglect of the majority of the people is un-Islamic. Islam condemns landlordism. But the actual form and type of peasant-proprietorship is relative to the needs of the community and is subject to change within the dynamic framework of growth. Peasant-proprietorship does not mean that everybody should have an equal portion of land for cultivation. Islam recognizes the differences in the abilities of men and the consequent differences in income. The *Qur'ān* does not accept any situation in which some have too much and some nothing at all.

(*b*) The practice of letting land on a fixed amount of produce—a counterpart of interest—from agricultural fields is unlawful in Islam.

(*c*) The land tenure system introduced by 'Umar the Great is a living testimony to the fact that the Qur'ānic law with regard to land is quite practicable. To save the Muslim society from the evils of feudalism, Ḥaḍrat 'Umar prohibited the purchase of land by Muslims in the conquered territories of Syria and Iraq. He also stopped not only the practice of distribution of land in the conquered territory among the Muslim soldiers, but also impressed upon the people the importance of cultivating the land. The Caliph 'Umar is reported to have taken back some of the lands which the Prophet had given to Bilāl on the grounds that he did not cultivate the entire lands given to him. He emphasized that one must lose one's right of ownership if one does not cultivate land within a term of three years. To my mind, if this condition of three years is linked to the right of ownership, agricultural production is likely to go up. However, Ḥaḍrat 'Umar introduced many reforms in the field of agriculture, Different kinds of land tenure systems were prevalent during the Caliphate of Ḥaḍrat 'Umar of which the following systems are the most important:

(1) *Iqṭāʻ* or individual ownership
(2) *Ḥimā*
(3) State-landlordism
(4) Peasant-proprietorship

2. The question of family planning in Islam is a very controversial issue because the silence of the *Qur'ān* on the matter and the absence of clear rulings from *Ḥadīths* have paved the way for various interpretations with the changes of time and circumstance. However, arguments for family planning appear to be more forceful than the arguments against. The author is inclined to recommend a comprehensive population control policy for the world of Islam.

3. Islam does not recognize the exploitation of labour by capital, nor does it approve of the elimination of the capitalist class from the social frame work as we find in the case of Marx's analysis of classless society. If the main causes of modern industrial conflict as well as the various

Islamic injunctions are analyzed side by side, one can easily say that Islam safeguards the interests of both labour and capital within its framework of a self-contained distinct organism. In fact, Islam brings about a union of labour and capital by giving the whole problem a moral bent. It is argued that once workers and employers are imbued with the values of Islam, the whole question of strikes and lockouts would be relatively unnecessary.

Notes

[1] Azād, Maulānā Abul-Kalān *Tarjumān-ul-Qur'ān*, Vol. II.
[2] Quoted in *Islām Ka Iqtiṣadi Niẓām*, p. 295
[3] Quoted in ibid.
[4] Ibid.

6.6 Selected Further Reading

Abu Sa'ud, M. "The Explanation of Land and the Islamic Law" in *The Islamic Review*, vol. 40, No. 9, London, 1952.

Abdul Kader, Ali, "Land Property and Land Tenure in Islam" in Islamic *Quarterly* vol. 5 (1–2), London 1959.

Abdul Kader Ali, "Land Property and Land Tenure in Islam", *The Islamic Quarterly*, vol. 5, London, 1960.

Al-Khatib, Syed Abdul Hamid, "Land Property and Ownership of Land in Islam" in *Some Economic Aspects of Islam*, Motamar, al Alam al Islami, Karachi, 1965.

Haque, Ziaul, "Landlord and Peasant in Early Islam", *Islamic Research Institute*, Islamabad, 1977.

Irving, T. B. "Ibn Khaldun on Agriculture", in *Islamic Literature*, vol. 31, Hyderabad, 1955.

Na qvi, Syed Habibul Haq, "Al Iqta – A Historical Survey of Land Revenue Administration in some Muslim Countries", in *Contemporary Aspects of Economic Thinking in Islam*, American Trust Publications, 1970.

Poliak, A. N. "Classification of Land in Islamic Law and its Technical Terms" in *American Journal of Semtic Languages and Literature*, 1957.

Rana, Ifran Mohammad, *Economic System under Omar the Great*, Sh. Muhammad Ashraf, Lahore, 1970.

Saleem, M. "Ethical Justification of Family Planning" in *Islamic Studies*, vol. VIII, No. 3. Islamabad, 1969.

Saud, Mohammad Abu. "The Exploitation of Land and Islamic Law", in *The Islamic Review*, vol. 40, 1952.

Schieffelin, Ilivia, (ed.) *Muslim Attitudes towards Family Planning*, The Population Council, New York, 1967.

Tabakoglu, A. "Labour and Capital Concepts in Islamic Economics", a paper presented at the second International Conference on Islamic Economics: Development, Finance and Distribution in an Islamic Perspective, Islamic University, Islamabad, 19–23, March, 1983.

APPENDIX (A)

(a) The Land Tenure System during 'Umar's Caliphate

At this stage it is really necessary to give a pen-picture of the land tenure system of 'Umar the Great, because the land system introduced by him bears ample testimony to the fact that a land tenure system based on the true spirit of Islam is not a mere figment of the imagination, but is quite practicable. In fact, this land system is quite suggestive to the modern Muslim states of the world where, in most cases, the *Qur'ānic* Laws with regard to land are honoured more in breach than in observance.

Though Arabia was not an agricultural country, yet the need for some permanent and lasting land system was felt during the caliphate of Ḥaḍrat 'Umar the Great, resulting from the conquest of Iraq, Syria, Iran and Egypt. 'Umar's revolutionary step of prohibiting the purchase of land by Muslims in the conquered territories of Syria and Iraq further proves the intention of avoiding the evils of landlordism within the Islamic social framework. Actually, it was the later Caliphs who were mainly responsible for giving big estates or fiefs free of rent to soldiers. Since regular salaries could not be paid to them, the awarding of estates in contrast to 'Umer's bold policy resulted in giving rise to the evils of feudalism in Muslim society.

Speaking of Ḥaḍrat 'Umar, Ameer Ali says, "With a farsightedness often wanting in rulers of later times, he perceived that the stability of the Empire and its material development depended upon the prosperity of the agricultural classes. To secure that object he forbade the sale of holdings and agricultural lands in the conquered countries. As a further protection against encroachment on the part of the Arabs, he ordained that no Saracen should acquire land from the natives of the soil. In the administration of the acquired countries, the improvement of the peasantry and the development of trade were persistently insisted upon." As a matter of fact the history of Islam records many incidents during the Caliphate of 'Umar which are indicative of his economic philosophy towards the land system. After the conquest of Iraq when soldiers requested the commander Sa'd to distribute the conquered land among them and Sa'd wrote to 'Umar, his reply was, "I have received your letter. People are demanding that you should distribute land and wealth among them. You should distribute the wealth among Muslims but let lands and canals remain for governors to pay Muslims. If we distribute the lands now, we will be left with nothing for coming generations."

The same controversy appeared at the time of the conquest of Egypt when people demanded of 'Amr bin al-'Āṣ, the victor, that he distribute land and he sought the Caliph's guidance. The details given by Qāḍi Abū Yūsuf show that a controversy had arisen because 'Abd al-Raḥmān b. 'Auf, Bilāl and some others were in favour of land distribution. At last Ḥaḍrat 'Umar called ten prominent people from the Anṣār and delivered a lecture to them. He said: "You heard the people who say I am depriving them of their right. I think that after the lands of Kisra (Chosroe) no lands will be left for conquest. God has granted us their wealth and lands. I have distributed wealth among Muslims, but I wish that lands be left with their tillers and I should impose *Kharāj* and *Jizyah*, which they would be paying us to meet the expenses of the army, children of Muslims and generations to come. You have seen the borders, we need the army to protect them; you have seen the big cities and to protect them a regularly paid army is necessary, and if I distribute the lands, how will they be paid?"

Having taken back some of the land which the Prophet had given to Bilāl ibn al-Ḥarith, 'Umar said to Bilāl: "The Messenger of God did not give you land so that you withhold it from the people. He gave you the land so that you can use it, so you must take only what you can utilize, and leave the rest." The wisdom of this policy is quite obvious. The intention is that land should be fully utilized, because the ownership of land is recognized in theory to be that of God and of the community, and the owner of property who does not utilize it for his own benefit, as well as for the benefit of the community as a whole, is not using land in the way God has ordained. Although the Holy Prophet had distributed land among Muslims, e.g. the Khaibar lands, the area of these lands was so small that there was not the slightest danger of landlordism; but the lands which came under Muslims after the conquest of Iraq and Syria were very vast and their distribution among Muslim soldiers would have led to landlordism with all its evils.

This bold departure illustrates the fact that the *Ḥadīth* of the Prophet should be interpreted not only in literal form but also in its spirit. The circumstances under which the Prophet distributed land were quite different in 'Umar's time. Therefore, 'Umar the Great did not follow the Prophet blindly: he exercised reason and logic on which the *Qur'ān* has laid much emphasis and took into account the total cost-benefit result. This provides food for thought even today, because modern man is trying to understand Islam in terms of modern language and terminology.

It is really interesting to note that 'Umar was convinced of the fact that a better land tenure system was needed for improvement in the production of agriculture. He introduced many reforms in the field of agriculture. "Irrigation canals were laid out in conquered lands, and a big department was organised for constructing dams, excavating tanks and for the building of canals and sluices for the distribution of water. According to Maqrīzī, in Egypt alone 120,000 labourers worked daily throughout the year on these works and were paid out of the public treasury. Juza'b. Mu'āwīyah built many canals in the districts of Khuzistān and Ahwāz with the permission of Ḥaḍrat 'Umar, which enabled many new lands to be brought under cultivation. Hundreds of other water courses were thus built, of which traces are found here and there in books of history." (Shiblī, *'Umar Fārūq*).

Forms of Land Tenure System during 'Umar's Caliphate.

Different kinds of land tenure system prevalent in the Muslim Empire during the Caliphate of Ḥaḍrat 'Umar b. al-Khaṭṭāb were as follows:

Iqṭā' or Individual Ownership System.

Iqṭā', also called fief, is an institution the origin of which can be traced back to the time of the Holy Prophet. This system had far-reaching effects upon the land system of Arabia which, owing to its bedouin life, was not much aware of the institution of landed property belonging to one individual. *Iqṭā'* means the act of bestowing or allotting a *qaṭī'ah* (a cut-off piece). Thus it includes giving state land as estates to individuals. The Holy Prophet gave *Iqṭā'*s to different individuals at different times to make arrangements for the livelihood of those who had left behind their relatives, families and in most cases their property also. Occasionally the grants were made according to the principle of *"Tālīf al-Qulūb"* (reconciliation of hearts), i.e. to pacify and to attack political opponents. The Prophet sometimes gave *Iqṭā'*s before a specific land was conquered. The grant of the fief of Tamīm ad-Dārī in Palestine is an instance of such grants. Grants of *Iqṭā'*s conferred proprietary rights on the beneficiaries. These *'Iqṭā'*s thus became *Iqṭā' Tamlīk*, i.e. a fief conferring the rights of property. The owners were therefore free to use the land in any way they liked and these rights in property were inherited by their descendants also.

There is a controversy as to whether 'Umar the Great followed the tradition of the Prophet in granting *Iqṭā'*s. True, there is evidence to indicate that 'Umar, following the tradition of the Prophet, granted fiefs even before the lands were conquered. But the consensus of opinion is that 'Umar disfavoured the idea of granting fiefs, because it may lead to the rise of new feudalism in society, which, in its ultimate analysis, may result in lowering the rate of agricultural production. He emphasized that if anyone did not cultivate his land within a term of three years, he must lose his rights of ownership. (We have seen how this was applied in the case of Bilāl.) I feel that the modern Muslim world may take a lesson from this bold step taken by 'Umar in an effort to improve the lot of poor people. To my mind, if the condition of three years' term is linked to the right of ownership, I hope—indeed, I believe—that, given sufficient encouragement, agricultural production is bound to go up. In addition to the application of modern knowledge in agriculture, this will, we are sure, help Pakistan in particular and the Muslim world in general in solving the age-old problem of food supply. Any future scheme of land reforms may derive benefit from it.

Ḥimā System.

Ḥimā land was owned by one or more than one tribe and cultivated or otherwise used for their collective needs, Individual possession of land was something unknown to the bedouin. This limited right of the bedouin to land had possibly been the origin of the development of collective reserves (*ḥimās*), where this right was made absolute, while other tribes were under obligation not to encroach upon it. The basis of *ḥimā* was mostly fodder and water. In the *ḥimā* usually one or more springs or watering places were found. Its nomadic character is clear from the fact that it was usually left untilled. At first the privileges of *ḥimā* were not of a permanent nature but afterwards, if they remained in the possession of a tribe for some longer period, they became their property. In every large *ḥimā* several tribes were often shareholders.

*Ḥimā*s paid '*Ushr* (tithe) on the produce. If the '*Ushr* was not paid, rights to the *ḥimā*s were forfeited, and other people occupied the property. The Government also had its own *ḥimā*s. Sometimes the *ḥimā*s which were necessary for military purposes or for the use of the common public were seized. From the above analysis of the *ḥimā* system it appears that the idea of co-operative farming existed in a crude form even during the caliphate of 'Umar the Great. The very concept of collective ownership is clearly suggestive for the Muslim world even today in so far as the question of agricultural development is concerned.

State Landlordism.

With the conquest of different countries, state landlordism also flourished. Under this system land belonged to the state and cultivators were its tenants. They did not enjoy proprietary rights and land could not be transferred to or sold by them. These (state) lands were classified into *Ṣawāfī*, i.e. proper state domains, and *Fai'*. *Ṣawāfī* were in fact public property and could not be disposed of in any way. Tenants tilled the land and paid a specific sum as revenue (*Kharāj*). They could not be ejected. There is no clear information but perhaps tenancy existed in the same family and was treated as inheritance. But these lands could not be sold by the tenants or by governors.

Fai', which also falls under crown lands, actually started with the Prophet. It included lands (and booty) which were left to the Prophet to be used by him at his own discretion. The first *Fai'* lands were the lands of Banū Naẓīr, Khaibar and Fadak. Later on during the caliphates of the Righteous Caliphs this included lands belonging to the state, which could be used by the Caliph in the way he wished. Fiefs were sometimes given out of these lands.

Another form of state land was *Diya*, which meant estates belonging to the state. The difference between *Ṣawāfī* and *Diya* is that the latter were private estates belonging to the state while *Ṣawāfī* were in the public domain.

State lands, whether *Ṣawāfī*, *Fai'* (excluding fiefs), *Diya* or *Waqf* paid *Kharāj*. *Kharāj* was treated more as the rent of the land than a tax because the tenant, irrespective of his religion, paid *Kharāj*. A non-Muslim tenant, even if he embraced Islam, had to pay *Kharāj*, although he was exempted from *Jizyah* in that case. In this system lands were owned by landlords who employed tenants to cultivate them. This system was prevalent in Arabia proper as well as in Syria and Egypt.

It is very surprising that even during Caliph 'Umar's caliphate the concept of state-ownership in land developed to a great extent. The modern idea of socialization of national wealth perhaps owes its origin to it. If people of a particular area of the country do not react favourably to agricultural development, the Muslim state has every right to intervene.

Peasant-Proprietorship.

In this system owners themselves tilled the land. This system was common in Arabia, especially in those parts which were arable and fertile. In Syria, there is evidence to prove that some small farmers cultivated as well as owned land. The land tenure system in different parts and provinces led to the emergence of the following classes of people.

Non-Cultivating Owner.

He represented an owner who possessed the land which was tilled by someone else. In some cases, he was a large estate owner. Such non-cultivating owners were found in Syria and Egypt. On the other land, there were owners who had very small tracts of land but could not till them for some reason. The people of Arabia living in cities and soldiers, who had been awarded fiefs, represented this class. The owner shared the produce on the basis of legal right, usually without contributing anything to the process of production. This class of owner was not equivalent to the present absentee-landlord, because such big estates were not allowed by Ḥadrat-'Umar.

Non-Owner Cultivator.

This class represented occupying tenants of private landlords. Both freemen and slaves, belonging to this class, were found in all parts of the empire.

Owner Cultivator.

An owner cultivator, also called a peasant-proprietor, had all the proprietary rights in land he possessed and cultivated. He differed from the big landlord only in the matter of the size of his holding. A holder having occupancy rights in land like the one cultivating the state-owned land was included in this class.

APPENDIX (B)

Some *Fatwās* (rulings) on Family Planning (reproduced from Birthright, Special Number)

(1) *Fatwā: The Legality of Contraception*
by His Excellency Ayatollah Hajji Sheikh Bahaeddin Mahallati
of Iran

Question:

Would you permit and is it religiously lawful that a physician temporarily prescribes drugs or contraceptive devices for excessive human reproduction?

Answer:

In the name of God: From the standpoint of the divine law, the utilisation of drugs or contraceptive devices, especially if it is temporary, to control human fertility does not seem illegal if this practice does not lead to damaging the female's fecundity and making her barren.

Source: Bahaeddin Mahallati, response to question from Dr. Mohammad Sarram in a latter dated Nov. 12, 1964.

(2) *Fatwā: Law number 81, Register 43*
Sheikh Abdul Majid Salim, the Mufti of Egypt

Question:

The married man has a child. He fears if he gets many children that he may be embarrassed by becoming unable to bring them up and take care of them, or that he may suffer ill-health and a nervous breakdown from the inability to fulfil his duties and responsibilities towards them; or that his wife's health may be affected from repeated pregnancies and deliveries without having intervals for her to rest and regain her strength and compensate for what her body lost during pregnancy.

Does he or his wife have the right to take some scientific measures according to a doctor's advice which lengthen the intervals between pregnancies, so that the mother can have rest and regain her health, and the father not be in ill health, or under economic or social stress?

Answer:

It is permitted to take some measures to prevent pregnancy under the circumstances cited in the question, either by ejaculating outside the vagina, or by the woman inserting something to shut off the opening of the uterus to prevent entrance of the seminal fluid.

The principle is that it is not the right of the man to ejaculate outside the vagina except with the permission of his wife and that it is not the right of the woman to shut off the opening of her uterus except with the permission of the husband.

But it may be allowed for the man to ejaculate outside the vagina without permission of the wife if he is afraid of having aberrant offspring, e.g. due to a bad living environment, or due to the man being away travelling and being afraid about the child.

By analogy, it may be allowed for the woman to shut off the opening of her uterus without the permission of her husband if she has reasons for it.

To sum up: either husband or wife, with the permission of the partner, is allowed to take measures to prevent entrance of the seminal fluid into the uterus as a method of birth control: and either of them may take such measures without permission of the partner if there are reasons such as those cited or similar ones.

Is it permissible to carry out a therapeutic abortion? According to the great authorities in Islam, it is permissible for a pregnant woman to terminate pregnancy in the early months before foetal movements occur, if the health of the mother is endangered.

Source: Abdul Majid Salim, *Fatwā* issued from Dar el Efta, No. 81, register 43, 12th Dhi al Qaada 1355 (January 25, 1937), in *Journal of the Egyptian Medical Association*, vol. 20, No. 7, July 1937, pp. 54–66.

(3) Fatwā: Azhar University
Mohd Abdul Fattah el Enani, Chairman, *Fatwā* Committee,
Azhar University, United Arab Republic

Question:

A married man has a child. He fears if he gets many children that he may be embarrassed by becoming unable to bring them up and take care of them; or that he may suffer ill-health and a nervous breakdown from the inability to fulfil his duties and responsibilities towards them; or that his wife's health may be affected from repeated pregnancies and deliveries without having intervals for her to rest and regain her strength and compensate for what her body lost during pregnancy.

Does he or his wife have the right to take some scientific measures according to a doctor's advice which lengthen the intervals between pregnancies, so that the mother can have rest and regain her health, and the father not be in ill health, or under economic or social stress?

Answer:

The use of medicine to prevent pregnancy temporarily is not forbidden by religion, especially if repeated pregnancies weaken the woman due to insufficient intervals for her to rest and regain her health. The Koran says: ". . . Allah desireth for you ease. He desireth not hardship for you . . ." 2/185); ". . . And hath not laid upon you in religion any hardship . . ." (22/78). But the use of medicine to prevent pregnancy absolutely and permanently is forbidden by religion.

Source: Abdul Fattah el Enani, *Fatwā* Committee, Azhar University, Response to Question No. 6746 by Dr. Muhammad Kamel Abdul Razzak, March 10, 1953.

(4) Fatwā: On Birth Control
Advisory Council on Religious Affairs in Turkey

We received the inquiry from the General Directorate of Health Affairs (No. 10456 dated 13-12-60), asking whether measures for birth control were legitimate according to the Muslim religion; this inquiry was forwarded to us by the Ministry of Health (No. 35739, dated 13-12-60) and our council has examined the matter.

Although coitus interruptus which could be considered as a means of birth control was condemned by certain of the Prophet's disciples, and by those scholars who followed them, it was considered lawful by the scholars among the disciples (including sages such as Hazreti Ali, Sa'ad Ibni Ebi Vakkas. Zeyd Ibni Sabit, Ebd Ayyubu 'l-Ensaf Cabir, Ibni Abbas, Haorti Hasan Habbab Ibni Erett, Ebi Saidi' i Hudrf, Abdullah Ibni Mesud), and, in deference to their views, by all subsequent scholars.

We can go so far as to say that, while the woman's consent is normally a necessary condition, if the proper raising of children is made impossible by the conditions of the time, such as the State's being in a state of war or disorder or similar circumstances, then this condition will also not apply.

We have decided to submit these findings to the Ministry in answer to the above-mentioned inquiry.

Source: Advisory Council on Religious Affairs in Turkey, Decree, December 19, 1960.

(5) *Fatwā: Family Planning in Islam*
Sheikh Abdullah Al-Qalqili, the Grand Mufti of Jordan

In the name of God, The Merciful and The Compassionate, Fears of the world from the increase of population have assumed serious proportions everywhere, and experts have come to regard this as a portent of woe, ruination and dire consequences. In their consideration of how the world can be protected against towering evil and grave menace, they have been led to think that "restriction of procreation" is one of the greatest measures. They know, however, that most people do not follow this course unless the ruling of religion in this respect has been made clear to them. Therefore, Muslims have looked up to reliable religious divines to state to them the ruling of religion on the subject. Questions converged on us for this purpose, including questions from official sources. This is our Statement on this matter.

It is acknowledged that the liberal Islamic law accommodates itself to nature and to human conditions. God says: "Set thou thy face then, as a true convert, towards the faith—the nature made by God in which he has made men; there is no altering of God's creation."

One of the natural things inherent in human beings is marriage. But the purpose of marriage is procreation for the perpetuation of the species. The divine Koranic verse refers to that, and regards it as one of the blessings bestowed upon God's servants. God says; "God, too, has given you wives from among yourselves and has given you sons and grandsons from your wives, and supplied you with good things." Therefore, marriage has been one of the Islamic religious ways and procreation has been one of its desirable and gratifying aims. Even the law-giver views multiplicity with favour, for multiplicity implies power, influence and invulnerability. This is why, in one of the traditions of the Prophet, marriage with an affectionate prolific woman is strongly urged. The tradition says: "Marry the affectionate prolific women, for I shall be proud of you among the nations."

Nevertheless, the lawgiver made marriage with a prolific woman and marriage for procreation conditional upon the availability of means and the ability to bear the costs of marriage and to meet the expenses of child education and training so that children may not go to the bad and develop anti-social ways. And according to Islamic religious rule (laws change as conditions change), marriage should be disallowed if the would-be husband is incapable of meeting the expenses of married life. To this, reference is clear in the Koran and in the Traditions. The Koran says: "And let those who do not find a match live in continence until God makes them free from want out of his bounty." The tradition says: "O young men, whoever of you is capable financially let him marry, and whoever is not capable let him fast, for fasting is preventive." From the foregoing verse and the tradition, the definite inference is that "restriction of procreation" is legal *a fortiori*; because to stop procreation altogether is more serious than to limit it. It is a cause for much wonder that those who urge celibacy should at the same time hesitate to allow family planning.

Moreover, there are genuine traditions which allow methods for restricting procreation, such as coitus interruptus. For instance, in the two most reliable collections of traditions, Abu-Said is reported to have said that in one of the raids, he and others captured a number of women, and they used to practise coitus interruptus. He also said that they asked the Prophet about that and the Prophet said: "Indeed, do that," and repeated it three times, and continued: "No creature to be created from now till the Day of Judgment will not be created". Another report has it that a man said to the Prophet: "I have a young wife, I hate that she should be pregnant, and I want what men want; but the Jews claim that coitus interruptus is minor infanticide." The Prophet replied, "The Jews lie. If God wishes to create the child, you will not be able to divert him from that." In the two reliable collections of traditions, it is stated that Muslims used to practise coitus interruptus during the life-time of the Prophet and during the period of the Koranic revelation. It is also reliably reported that Muslims used to practise coitus interruptus during the life-time of the Prophet; the Prophet knew of this, but he did not prohibit it.

In these genuine traditions there is definitely permission for the practice of coitus interruptus which is one of the ways of contraception or for restricting procreation even without excuse. Permission for this practice was reported by a number of the Prophet's Companions and Companions of the Companions, as laid down in the Four Orthodox Ways. A corollary of this is the dispensation for the use of medicine for contraception, or even for abortion before the embryo or the foetus is animated. The Hanafie allow that, if for an excuse.

The jurists gave examples to illustrate the meaning of the excuse for abortion, as in Ibu Abidin who says: "Like the mother who has a baby still unweaned and who becomes pregnant and thus her milk ceases, and the father is unable to hire a wet nurse to save the life of his baby."

The jurists also state that it is permissible to take medicine for abortion so long as the embryo is still unformed in the human shape. The period of this unformed state is given as 120 days. The jurists think that during this period the embryo or the foetus is not yet a human being. A report says that Omar (The Second Caliph) does not regard abortion as infanticide unless the foetus is already past the limit.

Milik, the founder of the Miliki Orthodox Way, says that the husband should not practise coitus interruptus with his wife unless she permits it. Al-Zarqani, in his comment on this, says that the practice is lawful if the wife allows it. Permission or prohibition of coitus interruptus may serve as a guide in deciding the question of abortion before the foetus is animated.

All this shows that there is agreement among the founders of the four Orthodox Ways that coitus interruptus is allowed as a means of contraception. Religious savants inferred from this that contraceptives might be used, and even medicines might be used for abortion.

Accordingly, we hereby give our judgment with confidence in favour of family planning.

Source: Abdullah Al-Qalqili, "Family Planning in Islam." Statement, December, 1964, mimeo issued by the International Planned Parenthood Federation.

(6) *Fatwā: Ruling for Birth Control.*
Al-Syyid Yusof bin Ali Al-Zawawi Mufti of Trengganu, Malaysia.
"Bismilla-hirrahma-nirrahim Al-hamdulilla-hi wabihi-nasta'inu."

The formation of bodies and associations for the purpose of family planning is an act demanded of Muslims by the religious laws of Islam. Muslims past and present have thought deeply about this subject and books of hadith (sayings of the Prophet) and jurisprudence in all schools have carried on a long controversy without coming to a definite conclusion. During the time of the Companions the act of preventing conception was called "al-'azl", which means preventing the male semen from entering the female womb. The Prophet was asked his opinion on the nature of this act. His answer was, approximately, "It is best that you do not practise such acts. Every soul that God has seen fit to create even to the Day of Judgment must be born nevertheless." (From this saying it should be understood that the Prophet did not forbid the practice of birth-control but He nevertheless advised the Companions not to indulge in it habitually).

Muslim theologians speculating upon the position of children have wondered whether by right a child belongs to its parents or to just one of them or whether by right a child belongs to both parents and to society in general. Opinions differ according to times and situations. Islam is a religion that urges its adherents towards unity whether in faith, economics or health. The teachings of Islam do not contradict medical science in the least where laws of health are concerned. About this all Muslim theologians are unanimous.

The Holy Qur'ān itself has often stated facts concerning health and physical welfare as in the following words of Allah, "*Walwa-lida-to yurdhi'na aula-dahunna haulaini ka-milain liman are-da an yutimma radha-'ah wa'alal mauluudi lahuu sizquhunna wa kis watuhunna bil ma'ruf bu-tukallafu nafsun ilbe wus'ahai 'tudha-va wa-lidatun biwala diha waq-mauluudun lahuu biwalidihy,*" which means mothers who wish to breastfeed their infants usually do so for about two years (the *Qur'ān* urges mothers to breastfeed their babies, for, as proved by medical science, a mother's milk contains all the foodstuff necessary to give strength to nurture her child). To the fathers is entrusted the responsibility of clothing and feeding their families in a decent and suitable manner. Every person is given responsibility to the degree of his ability. Therefore let not a mother harm her child nor should a father do likewise. (This statement is to be taken to mean that the mother who is breastfeeding her infant should take care not to conceive again so soon for it might harm the little one at her breast. From this statement we can also see that the Qur'ān certainly does encourage the practice of family-planning).

It has been told by Asma' binte Yazid Al-Sakan that she once overheard the Prophet saying "*La-taqtuluu aulu-dakum sirran fa'innal ghil yudrikul fa-risa fayudo'thiruhu min farasihi*" which means, "Do not kill your children in secret for 'al-ghil (intercourse with a woman while she is breastfeeding her infant) is like a horse-rider in a fight who shall be thrown off the horse and trampled" (this is to show that an infant conceived while its mother is breast-feeding another is weak in constitution).

Theologians of jurisprudence have concluded that birth control is 'makruh' (frowned upon because of religious reasons) for they regard children as belonging to the community as a whole and this conclusion they based upon the words of Syydina Abu Bakr, Umar and Ibn Masuud. Birth-control will result in the decrease of descendants. Where husbands and wives are concerned, it is ruled that it is forbidden for the husband to prevent his semen from entering the wife's womb without her consent unless there are imperative reasons compatible with the rulings of Muslim laws. Examples when incomplete intercourse is permissible occur when the couple are living in a country at war in the cause of Allah and pregnancy, along with the difficulties of travel and war, might further weaken the woman, for then the necessary rest and safeguard of health may not be possible. Among those who concur with such an opinion is Al-Sheikh al-Hijrah Musaffiguddin ibnu Auda-ma Al-Hambali who died in the year 630. And according to the opinion of Al-Imām al Nawawi (died in the year 676 al-Hijrah) recorded in his book "Sharh Saluh Muslim" his conclusion is:

The act of 'al-'azl, or the prevention of the male semen from entering the female womb is to be disapproved of on any ground irrespective of the wife's consent for it means cutting off the future generation and this the saying of the Prophet is called 'al-wa' dul Khafij' (secret burial of children). It cuts off life just as effectively as murdering a child by burying it alive.

In brief, I incline to see that there are three aspects to this problem. (*i*) If prevention of conception is necessary for health reasons, whether of the wife, the husband, or the child-to-be, there are absolutely no religious laws against it, as stated in the sentence "*al-tudha-ra wa-lidatun biwa-hadiha wala maulu-dun lahu biwaladihi.*" This also means that it applies to a definite and specific length of time and for special circumstances. (*ii*) After conception theologians of jurisprudence differ in their thinking on whether incomplete intercourse is permissible before the foetus has acquired a life of its own (this is usually four months after conception). But after four months they are unanimous in agreeing that it is "*haram*" or forbidden. Should the foetus be expelled through voluntary abortion, those responsible for the act, the doctors, midwives etc., have to pay blood-money to the parents should it come out alive, but should it be dead they are to pay the price of a slave to the parents, and the parents, who agreed to the abortion, are to pay a fine to the religious authorities. (*iii*) The total prevention of pregnancy or sterilization without reasons sanctionable by religion, although done voluntarily, is absolutely forbidden.

For the above explanation it could be seen what stand Islam takes upon this question of family-planning. The bodies and associations to be set up in connection with ths question must therefore work in accordance with what is permissible by the laws of Islam as explained in the ruling given by His Honour Al-Sheikh 'Abdul Fattah Al-'Inani.

Birth-control practised from no health reasons or merely for the sake of preserving the beauty of the figure or as a means of escape from the responsibility of bringing up children is unanimously judged to be "*haram*" or forbidden. A Muslim should not agree to the practice. Allah has shown His blessings on us in His words: "*Wulluhu ja'ala lakum mim anfusikum azwajan waja'ala min azwjikum bani-na waha-fadatan waraza-qakum minathaiy-ibat,*" which means "Allah has created you and given you your wives and from your wives offsprings and descendants and to you are also given gifts of goodly things."

Indeed birth-control practised because of poverty and because of health reasons is not accepted by the laws of Islam because both government and society are required to look after the propagation of their members in order that the society should become strong, powerful and great in the eyes of other nations.

In brief the ruling of religious laws upon this question depends very much upon the position of both husband and wife. I therefore strongly suggest that the government elect a body of genuinely responsible individuals with conscience toward God and men to see that the purpose of such associations is honestly carried out to the advantage of a nation which badly needs fine descendants to take over the responsibilities of the future. Such a body of men and women of integrity would ensure that the associations will work with inner discipline and in accordance with the strictest laws of Islam.

It is the purpose of such associations to give words of advice, wise and sensible, to husbands and wives, so that they might safeguard domestic harmony and family health. This is indeed a very worthy venture and it should be given full and every encouragement.

CHAPTER 7

Distribution of Income and Wealth in Islam

"In order that it (wealth) may not (merely) make a circuit between the wealthy among you."

Al-Qur'ān, (*Sūrah* LIX. 7)

"The wages of a labourer must be paid to him before the sweat dries upon his body."

Prophet Muhammad (peace be upon him)

7.1 Introduction

It is on the issue of the distribution of national income that the widest and bitterest controversy has been and is still going on between different sections of the people of every democratic country of the present-day world, since the economic welfare of the masses depends vitally upon the manner in which the total national income is distributed among the people. Common sense suggests that the theory of distribution should deal with the problem of distribution of national income among different classes of people. In particular, it should be in a position to explain the phenomenon that a few are very rich, while the great many are poor. Unfortunately, the tradition among modern economists is to treat the distribution problem not as a problem of personal distribution but as a problem of functional distribution. "The modern economic theory of distribution is a theory of pricing of productive service. It seeks to find out the value of the service of different factors of production. In this respect, the distribution theory is but an extension of the general theory of pricing. The problem of personal distribution can, perhaps, best be solved as soon as we investigate the problem of ownership of factors of production. The theory of factorial or functional distribution helps us to determine the prices of the services rendered by the different factors of production, such as land, labour, capital and organisation." But under a capitalist economy a person may get rent. As a labourer, he may get wages. As a capitalist, he may earn interest. As an enterpreneur, he may also be the recipient of profit. Now is the time to examine how a person gets income from various sources and in various capacities under the Islamic system of economics. Let us now analyze first the earnings of land (i.e. rent) and labour (i.e. wages).

7.2 Rent and Wages in Islam

Rent

As far as I know, there is no evidence on record that the concept of rent in the modern sense of the term was developed during the lifetime of the Prophet. Possibly at that time there was no scarcity of land as such. But the need for a lasting and permanent land system was felt during the Caliphate of 'Umar the Great, as a result of the conquest of Iraq, Syria, Iran and Egypt. To my mind, the concept of rent in its crude form developed not only from 'Umar's revolutionary step of prohibiting the purchase of land by Muslims in the conquered territories but also from his stopping the practice of distributing conquered lands among the Muslims, thereby allowing the original tillers to cultivate their lands on payment of *Kharāj* and *Jizyah*.

But the basic question which is agitating the minds of many Muslim and non-Muslim scholars is not whether the concept of rent developed during the Caliphate of 'Umar or at some subsequent stage of Muslim history, but whether the fixed rate of rent which appears to be synonymous with a fixed rate of interest is allowed in Islam. Before answering this question I want to discuss the modern concept of economic rent very briefly. According to Ricardo, rent is that part of the produce of the soil which is paid to the landlord for the use of the original and indestructible properties of the soil. Rent, according to Ricardo, is a differential surplus. It is the difference between the produce of superior land and that of inferior land. Rent may also emerge due to the scarcity of land in relation to demand. Thus Professor Marshall has rightly observed that the distinction between "differential rent" and "scarcity rent" is one of approach only. The rent enjoyed by a piece of land may be looked upon as a differential rent, if we compare its yield with that of an inferior or marginal piece of land, when both the pieces of land are worked upon with similar appliances. On the other hand, the rent enjoyed by the same piece of land may be looked upon as "scarcity rent", which emerges because of the scarcity of the total supply relative to the demand for this type of land. Superior lands get high "scarcity" rents because of the limitation of the total supply of such lands relative to the total demand for them. Alternatively, superior lands earn high "differential" rents because of the great difference between their produce and the produce of the inferior land. "In fact, the essence of the concept of rent is the concept of a 'surplus' earned by a particular unit of a factor of production over and above the minimum earnings necessary to induce it to do its work. Historically and verbally, this concept is closely associated with the idea of 'free gifts of nature' which economists designate by the term 'land'. Since land does not owe its existence to human efforts, the whole of the earnings of land may be designated as 'rent' in the economists' sense, since the free gifts of Nature do not require to be paid in order that they might be induced to exist.

"But there is no reason to suppose that rent is associated with land alone. Particular units of the other factors of production (e.g. labour, capital and entrepreneurship) may also earn rent whenever their remuneration happens to be in excess of the minimum amount necessary to keep that factor in its present occupation."

Rent and Interest.

Coming back to the question of the difference between rent and interest, it can be said that since there is no clear tradition as regards payment of rent, all questions pertaining to rent will have to be x-rayed through the application of the dynamics of Islamic Law. Viewed from the standpoint of Islamic Law, payment of rent does not seem to be inconsistent with the economic ethics of Islam because of the wide difference between rent and interest. But superficially both rent and interest appear to be one and the same, because it is said that rent is on land, or property, interest is on capital, which has the potential to be converted to any property or asset. So it is argued that the right of "ownership of land does not presuppose the unrestricted right to let out such land on rent just as the right to own money does not imply the right to practise usury".

In spite of the superficial similarity, the transaction and the returns in both cases are widely different in several ways. Firstly, rent is the result of initiative, enterprise and efficiency. It results after a definite value-creating process, because the owner of the property or asset remains involved in and concerned with its use by the user throughout. But it is not so with interest, because the lender becomes unconcerned with the use of the loan after his loan is secured and interest thereon guaranteed. Secondly, it follows that in the case of rent productive effort is very necessary in the process of creating value, because economic endeavour is made by the owner of the capital by converting it into property or asset. Thus the element of entrepreneurship remains as much patent and alive as in producing any goods and services whereas interest may even retard the value-creating process. Since the lender remains unconcerned with the use of the loan, the element of the entrepreneur is altogether missing.

Thirdly, in the case of rent the owner of capital himself determines the pattern, size and utility of the product. Therefore, it is restricted to definite and purposeful use, whereas in the case of interest the real owner does not seem to be interested in the economic use of his capital; therefore, capital is rendered liable to abuse.

Fourthly, in a sense rent does not enter into price. "Corn is not high because a rent is paid but rent is paid because corn is high." But interest does enter into price, retards the process of production and poor consumers are hard hit.

Fifthly, since the element of loss is very much present in the case of rent, the use of capital by the owner for earning rent does not create any idle class in the society whereas the element of loss is missing altogether in the case of interest which can make the rich richer and the poor poorer.

Finally, it is true that "capital is converted and has the potentiality to be converted into any property or asset, but this potentiality of capital is left to the discretion of the user, i.e. the means of production are vested in the borrower; whereas in the case of interest the capital remains vested in the owner and not in the user. The fact of the matter is that rent on a property or hire on an asset is more synonymous with wages and salary, or with the margin of gross profit determined by the manufacturer or trader on his good, or with 'remuneration' charged by any profession; it is strictly unlike interest on capital."

Wages in Islam.

Let us now turn to the question of wages in Islam. What are wages? Wages refer to the earning of labour. We can look at wages from two points of view, the monetary and the non-monetary. The quantity of money earned by a worker during a period of time, say, a month or a week or a day, refers to the nominal wages of labour. The real wages of labour, which depend on various factors like the amount of money wages, the purchasing power of money, etc., may be said to consist in the quantity of necessities of life which a worker actually earns by his work: "The labourer is rich or poor, is well or ill-rewarded, in proportion to the real, not to the nominal, price of his labour" (Adam Smith).

The generally accepted theory of wages is the Marginal Product Theory, according to which wages are determined by the equilibrium between the forces of demand and supply. Assuming the supply of labour to be constant in a greater period of time, the demand for labour, under a capitalist framework of society, comes from the employer who employs labour and other factors of production for making profits out of his business. As long as the net product of the labour is greater than the rate of the wages, the employer will continue to employ more and more units of labour. He will naturally stop employing the additional labourers at the point at which the cost of employing a labourer just equals (in fact it is a little less than) the addition made by him to the value of the total net product. "The individual employer, like the individual consumer, hires as many labourers as will equate the marginal product of labour to the prevailing rates of wages. It is the demand of all employers taken in the aggregate in relation to the given supply that determines the marginal product of labour as a whole and the rate of wages in the market."

Even if the Marginal Product Theory of wages, which has been subjected to various criticisms, is taken for granted, it will remain valid only under conditions of perfect competition. In the actual world, however, competition is never perfect. There may be lack of competition among the employers. Labour, we know, is the most perishable of all commodities. On the other hand, the employer as such is in an advantageous position. "For it must be remembered," says Professor Marshall, "that a man who employs a thousand others is in himself an absolutely rigid combination to the extent of one thousand units among buyers in the labour market." Due to their weakness in bargaining, the labourers, under capitalism, are likely to get wages much lower than their marginal product.

This exploitation of labour by employers is foreign to the Islamic faith. Here it is heartening to quote the Holy Prophet's (peace be upon him) observation: "Man has no right in his share in which God has no right. God's share is His command to give everyone his due and not to encroach on what belongs to another." The Prophet (peace be upon him) is also reported to have said: "The wages of a labourer must be paid to him before the sweat dries upon his body." Again, it is related on the authority of Ibn Mājah that the Prophet (peace be upon him) said: "It is the duty of the employers to take only such works from their employees which they can easily do. They should not be made to labour so that their health is told upon." The fact is that in the scheme of an Islamic society, a decent wage is not a concession, but a fundamental right, enforceable with all the might of the state. Once this reorientation of state attitude has been accomplished, the actual fixation of wage and productivity formulae will be a matter of correct adjudication. In all the Muslim states of the world, there is a supreme need for reaffirmation of the progressive ideals that should govern labour laws and for acceptance of the principle of universally recognized labour rights such as the right to strike, the right to a fair wage, to social security, to a share in the profits, etc. The acceptance of these rights does not mean that workers will have unrestricted freedom to do anything and everything. Islam has condemned misappropriation or the dishonest taking of any part of the master's property. The Prophet (peace be upon him) is reported to have said that "the best earning is that of the labourer provided he does his job with care and regard for his employer". The Islamic state is competent to curb any anti-social activity of the worker. In fact, Islam stands for the balanced growth of society for which a compromise between labour and capital is considered to be an essential precondition. I believe that if labourers and employers are imbued with the values of Islam, prohibition of strikes and lockouts will be unnecessary and relatively unimportant. Now, the fundamental problem before the Muslim States is not how to prohibit or restrict strikes but how to inject Islamic values of life into the existing labour-capital relationship.

Differences in Wages.

At this stage, it would seem necessary to analyze whether differences in wages are recognized by Islam. So far it has been tacitly assumed that all workers will be paid the same rate of wages. But in life, we come across a good deal of differences in wages. There are various factors which are responsible for these differences in wages. Cairnes has referred to the existence of a non-competing group among workers. There is a broad distinction between intellectual and manual workers, skilled and un-skilled workers. There is very little mobility of labour between the two classes of work. It follows that the equilibrium level of wages for each of the non-competing groups will be determined by the supply schedule and the demand schedule of each group.

Wage differences may also arise due to differences in non-monetary advantages. Some kinds of work are more pleasant, or at least less disagreeable than others. Differences in cost of training often account for differences in wages. Wage differences may also be due to sheer ignorance and immobility. However, in a sense, Islam has recognized these wage differences among different grades of workers, because the diversity of capacities and talents resulting in the diversity in earnings and material rewards has been recognized by the Holy *Qur'ān* (*Sūrah* IV. 32). Islam does not believe in dead-level equality in the distribution of wealth, because any social progress in the real sense of the term calls for the fullest opportunities for the growth of talents, which, in their turn, demand the recognition of the principle of differences in wages. This *Qur'ānic* approach in respect of the determination of wages, tempered by consideration of ability and talents, is one of the most significant contributions towards the progress of human civilization. The basic conditions as laid down, in this connection, both in the *Qur'ān* and the

Sunnah are that employers shall pay workers fully for the service rendered and that workers shall do their work faithfully and to the best of their ability. Any failure to fulfil these conditions will be treated as moral failure on the part of both employers and workers, for which they will be answerable to God. But under capitalist society employers and workers are answerable to none. Here once again, Islam establishes its superiority over secularism in handling the affairs of the state.

7.3 *Ribā*, Interest and Profit

The Qur'ānic prohibition of taking "*al-Ribā*" is clear and categorical. To my knowledge, nobody disputes this. But the controversy arises over the distinction between *al-Ribā* and interest. One school of thought believes that what Islam has prohibited is *al-Ribā*, not interest. Another school of thought feels that there is virtually no distinction between *Ribā* and interest. Therefore, the first question which is to be answered is whether there is any distinction between *al-Ribā* of the *Qur'ān* and interest in the capitalist world. Secondly, even if they are one and the same, is it possible to have an interest-free society? The last but not least question requiring careful attention is the difference between interest and normal profit.

Ribā and Interest.

In order to give an answer as to whether *al-Ribā* and interest are one and the same, one has to understand the meaning of *al-Ribā* in its correct historical perspective. The liberal meaning of the term which means increase or growth is not helpful for the purpose of our analysis, because any increase like that accruing from trade or manufacture is not prohibited. But the use in the *Qur'ān* of the definite article "*al*" before "*Ribā*" is indicative of the fact that *al-Ribā* refers to that practice of taking in excess of the amount due from a debtor which was prevalent amongst the Arabs and which was familiar to them at the time of the revelation of the *Qur'ān*. Obviously, it should be so, because a prohibition which concerns the day-to-day affairs of the people should be expressed in familiar language. Consequently, the '*Ulamā*', generally, have accepted it. Now we are to see what type of *Ribā* was actually current among the Arabs at that time. A number of jurists of great repute tried to define *al-Ribā* of the *Jāhilīyyah*. According to Mujāhid (d. 104 AH.) "*Ribā* of the *Jāhilīyyah*, which God has forbidden, was that if a person owed a loan to another person he would say to him, 'I would give you so much if you granted me extension of time.'" Imām Mālik (d. 119 AH.) says: "In the *Jāhilīyyah*, the *Ribā* was that when a person gave a loan for a specified period and that period expired, the lender would ask the debtor whether he would return the debt or increase the amount? If he made the payment it would be accepted, otherwise the amount of the debt would be increased and the debtor allowed an extension." Ibn Jarīr Ṭabarī (d. 310 AH.), commenting on the verse appearing in *Sūrah* II, says: "A debtor is called '*Murb*' because he doubles the amount of the debt." Commenting on the verse in *Sūrah* III prohibiting the charging of double or fourfold interest, he says, on the authority of Mujāhid, that this was the *Ribā* of the *Jāhilīyyah*. Almost similar sentiments were expressed by Imām Rāzī (d. 606 AH.) and Baiḍāvī (d. 685 AH). "The people of the *Jāhilīyyah*," according to Imām Rāzī, "used to advance their money and recover *Ribā* monthly without affecting the sum advanced. When the time for settlement came, the principal amount lent was demanded and if the debtor was unable to pay, the lender increased the amount in his own favour and granted extension of time." This was how the Arabs of the *Jāhilīyyah* used to transact their lending operations. Lastly, Baiḍāvī says: "If a person was due a debt after a specified time, then he would go on increasing it until the entire property of the debtor was absorbed against a small (original) loan". From all these observations of these learned jurists of different ages, it can safely be said that the *Ribā* which was prevalent in the pre-Islamic era consisted in extending the time limit and increasing the amount due, so much so that the borrower would at the end of the period of the loan return to the lender double or even more of the principal sum. Thus, judged by any standard of socio-economic ethics, the rate of *Ribā* was excessively high. Thus the *Qur'ān*'s prohibition of *Ribā* came in the following way:

"Those who devour usury
Will not stand except
As stands one whom
The Evil One by his touch
Hath driven to madness.
That is, because they say
'Trade is like usury.'
But God hath permitted trade
And forbidden usury.
Those, who after receiving
Direction from their Lord,
Desist, shall be pardoned
For the past; their case
Is for God (to judge);
But those who repeat
(The offence) are Companions
Of the Fire; they will
Abide therein (for ever)."

Sūrah II. 275

Let us now talk of interest. Haberler, in his *Prosperity and Depression,* has rightly observed that "the explanation and determination of the interest rate still gives rise to more disagreement amongst economists than any other branch of general theory." We shall later see that all theories of interest fail to answer the question as to why interest is paid.

But the consensus of opinion is that interest is the fixed addition to borrowed capital. It is argued that this fixed addition is a reasonable charge for the use of money employed in a productive process, whereas *Ribā* refers to usury on unproductive loans, which prevailed in pre-Islamic days when people were not used to productive loans and their influence on economic growth. But to me, if there is any difference between *al-Ribā* of the *Qur'ān* and interest in capitalist society, it is one of degree, not of kind, because both *Ribā* and interest represent excess over capital borrowed. True, *Ribā* was considered unsophisticated in comparison to interest. But calling *Ribā* or usury by the name of interest will not change its character. The fact of the matter is that the term "excess" must be taken in a relative sense, because what is a reasonable "excess' today may be considered to be an exorbitant or usurious rate tomorrow. Many co-operative societies of the Indo-Pakistan subcontinent used to charge 12 per cent to 15 per cent interest and at that time it was regarded as reasonable, whereas today it is considered excessive. Therefore, the prohibition of *Ribā* means prohibition of all types of excesses over borrowed capital whether we call it usury, interest or earning of the capital. In fact, capital invested in trade may bring an excess called profit, which is variable and implies the possibility of loss also. But capital invested in banking brings interest which is fixed and does not imply any loss whatsoever.

Again, it is not correct to say that in pre-Islamic days loans were not granted for productive purposes. We have records to show that the Jews of Madinah advanced money not only for consumption purposes, but also for trade. The mere existence then of "*Muḍarabah*" or sleeping partnership among the Arabs was not indicative of the fact that productive interest was not in vogue among them. The fact is that the difference between productive and unproductive loans is a difference of degree. If interest on consumption loans is harmful, then interest on productive loans must be harmful, because it enters into the cost of production and consequently into the price. It is the consumers who have to bear the burden of higher prices. Therefore, in the ultimate analysis, at *Ribā* of the *Qur'ān* and the interest of modern banking are the obverse and the reverse of the same coin. Now the preliminary question which has got to be answered is why interest is paid.

Why Interest is Paid

There is no clear-cut answer to the question of why interest is paid. We find a wide difference of opinion among economists regarding the theory of interest. Many great thinkers regarded payment of interest as unjust. In his *Politics*, Aristotle compared money to a barren hen which laid no eggs. According to him, a piece of money cannot beget another piece. In his *Laws*, Plato condemned interest. The Roman Empire was against the charging of interest in its early stages. Though interest appeared with the rise of the capitalist class, severe restrictions were imposed by the Romans by enforcing laws on rates of interest. In the Middle Ages, the Christian Church prohibited the practice of usury and the charging of interest was against the principles of common laws. Many early Mercantilists advocated a low rate of interest but did not explain why interest is paid at all.

The classical economists like Adam Smith, Ricardo and others treated interest as the compensation which the borrower paid to the lender for the profit the former would make by the use of the latter's money. Ricardo observes, "Whenever a great deal can be made by the use of it, a great deal can be given by the use of it." But the classical economists did not explain how to relate variable profits to fixed interest.

Again, the classical argument about the interest rate's inducement to savings was sharply criticized by economists like Keynes. He held the view that it is the level of income rather than the rate of interest that ensures equality between savings and investment. Savings do not depend so much on interest as on the level of investment and employment. It is the entrepreneurs, not the savers, who disturb the equilibrium and bring dynamism into economic growth. This is how one can explain the enormous increase in savings during the present century in spite of a steep fall in the rates of interest.

Another set of classical writers have tried to consider the above question from the view of supply. It was Senior who first pointed out that the supply of capital or savings involves a sacrifice or abstinence. But the idea of abstinence was widely criticized on the ground that it suggested positive discomfort, while many rich people save without the least inconvenience. A socialist writer, Lasalle, ridiculed Senior by saying that "the profit of capital is the wage of abstinence". It is mainly because of these criticisms that Marshall substituted the term "waiting" for "abstinence". According to him, when a person saves, he does not refrain from consumption for all time; he merely postpones present consumption to a future date. Some inducement is needed just to encourage such a postponement or waiting and that inducement is interest.

But all postponements to present consumption or waiting do not need the inducement of interest; secondly, it is impossible to evolve a uniform criterion to judge the price of "waiting". Furthermore, this explanation neglects the demand side and is, therefore, partial and incomplete. Even the productivity theory has failed to justify interest. The advocates of this theory regard productivity as an inherent property of capital just as land is productive of crops. They hold that interest exists because capital leads to greater production than would be the case without capital. Nobody can challenge that capital is productive. But it does not explain why a particular rate of interest is paid. If interest is paid because of the productivity of capital, then it should be variable, for productivity itself tends to vary from one industry to another in the same country in a given period. Further, if capital helps labour to produce more, how much of this extra production is due to capital and how much to labour, since capital without labour produces nothing? Again, consumption loans are not generally treated as productive, yet interest has to be paid on them all the same. It is not clear why a fixed interest rate is to be paid for a consumption loan which may be used for different kinds of consumption. A rich man may use the loan for the purchase of a car while a poor person may go for the necessities of life. In fact, all productivity theories of interest, including the most accepted version, the marginal productivity theory of interest, lack dimension. These theories have apparently ignored the fact that the economic system is dynamic. A new equilibrium situation is always disturbed with changes in tastes, population, savings and investment patterns and with changes in values and living standards. In economic activity, these variables have a tendency to operate in a cumulative and circular way, acting and reacting upon each other in a complex pattern. To ignore the mobility of these variables is to disregard the basic facts about changes in the economic system.

Again, the Austrian school of economists like Böhm-Bawerk bring in the idea of "time preference" in the explanation of why interest is paid. According to him, interest arises because men prefer present goods to future goods, and because future satisfaction, when judged from the standpoint of the present, undergoes a discount, and interest is this discount. Böhm-Bawerk gave three reasons as to why people prefer present satisfaction to future satisfaction. They are (*a*) "the perspective underestimate of the future," (*b*) "the relative scarcity of present goods compared to future goods," (*c*) "technical superiority over future goods".

The American economist Irving Fisher accepts the first two propositions of Böhm-Bawerk but denies the validity of the third. According to him, "time preference" is the central fact in the theory of interest. It is the preference that an individual has for present income over future income. As Fisher has observed, the "technical superiority" of present goods is a delusion and is in reality a *distinctive* form of productivity theory; as such it is vitiated by the fallacy of *petitio principii*. If resources are diverted more and more from present to future uses, there will be relative overprovision for the future and relative underprovision for the present. Present goods will become scarce and will be valued more than future goods, apart from the perspective underestimate of the future. The late Lord Keynes criticized this orthodox theory on the ground that reward need not be paid to anyone for an act of saving. People save, according to him, whenever their income and standard of living allow them to do so or they save for the rainy day, in total disregard of the reward they are expected to get on savings. Savings, in other words, represent an involuntary act and as such they do not require the payment of any reward or inducement. This explains why the theory of Böhm-Bawerk and the time preference theory of Fisher are inapplicable in the case of corporate savings, which form the bulk of savings in advanced countries irrespective of the rate of interest.

The neo-classical theory of interest which is fundamentally based on the Böhm-Bawerkian theory of interest is not free from this Keynesian criticism. It regards the rate of interest as the factor which brings the demand for investment and the willingness to save into equilibrium with one another. Just as the price of a commodity is necessarily fixed at that point where the demand for it is equal to supply, so the rate of interest is necessarily fixed at that point where the amount of investment of that rate of interest is equal to the amount of saving at that rate. The rate of interest, then, is, according to the neo-classical theory, determined by the supply of and demand for loanable funds. All monetary theories of interest, including the loanable funds theory, appear to have confused the problem of exchange and the problem of distribution. While the theory of price refers to a problem of exchange, the theory of interest refers to a problem of distribution.

The last but not least contribution to the theory of interest was made by Lord Keynes. While there is general agreement that the concept of liquidity preference introduces a welcome new variable to the classical theory of interest, there is a general reluctance to accept his claim that the new theory replaces the traditional interest theory. Although Keynes's theory ignores altogether the twin influences of the ideas of "thrift" and "productivity," yet his theory is to some extent analogous to Böhm-Bawerk's theory of interest. What Böhm-Bawerk calls "the perspective underestimate of the future" and Fisher calls "time preference," Keynes calls "propensity to consume". Both, in effect, are based on a subjective prototype—the preference for present over future goods. One theory regards interest as a premium on present goods, the other as a reward for parting with liquidity. In substance, they are one and the same thing.

From the above brief survey of all theories of interest, it appears that economists have failed to discover a clear and categorical answer to the question of why interest is paid. Instead, some of them only explain how it is determined, without taking note of the fact that fixation of the rate of interest in advance curbs the innate mobility of production and growth.

Islamic Theory of Capital.

Islam does recognize capital and its role in the process of production. Islam recognizes its share in national wealth only to the extent of its contribution, to be determined as a variable percentage of the profits earned rather than a fixed percentage of the wealth itself. In a restricted sense, the Islamic theory of capital recognizes not only the classical ideas of thrift and productivity but also the Keynesian ideas of liquidity preference because, in Islam, capital is productive in the sense that labour assisted by capital produces more than without capital. Again, profits which are allowed by Islam are the result of investments in production which is a time-consuming process. It is the profit motive which induces an individual to save and invest and thereby postpone present consumption to a future date.

The Islamic theory of capital is more realistic, more comprehensive and more ethical than the modern theories of capital. It is realistic, because the productivity of capital, which is subject to change, is related to the actualities of production, which is supposed to be mobile in the dynamic setting of growth; it is comprehensive, because it takes note of all variables like currency, population, inventions, habits, tastes, living standards, time-lag and so on; it is ethical, because the variable share of capital in an Islamic state must be just and equitable and must be free of the exploitation of other agents of production, which contribute to the creation of national wealth. Therefore, in the Islamic social framework, fixed interest on capital is not allowed to exercise its harmful effects on the economy. In other words, Islam believes in an interest-free economy. Now the question arises: Is it possible? I shall now try to frame an answer to this important question.

Possibility of an Interest-Free Economy

It is true that the economic values of Islam have not been given any fair trial by the modern Muslim world. But they have lost none of their cogency with the passage of time, because Islam is timeless. Thus while the fundamentals of Islamic economic values will remain valid for all ages, the details may change through the exercise of *Ijtihād*. Therefore, it is my conviction that even today it is quite possible to have an interest-free economic set-up, a set-up which will, I am sure, be a definite improvement over so-called capitalist and socialist economic systems. By retaining the incentive to work through the profit motive, the interest-free economy of Islam will, on the one hand, ensure maximum production and thus preserve one of the basic features of the capitalist system. By prohibiting fixed interest on capital and disallowing the growth of the capitalist class in the economy, it will, on the other hand, ensure the equitable distribution of national income for which the socialist system stands. This is not a mere compromise; the interest-free economy as propounded by Islam is more than a compromise in the sense that it regards man as a complete socio-moral creature, not merely as an "economic creature," and provides a system so co-ordinated as to enable man to accomplish both his spiritual and temporal values.

It is because of the determination and dedication of people that we have capitalist and socialist economies co-existing despite being diametrically opposed to each other. Again, it is because of the same determination and sacrifice of the people that Pakistanis belied the apprehensions of all by converting a so-called "uneconomic entity" like Pakistan into an economic entity envied by many. Lastly, it is because of an utter lack of the same determination and dedication that no Muslim state has ever tried to set up an interest-free economic system.

That many Muslim countries have given legal sanction to the payment of interest is indicative of the fact that they are still under the vicious influence of capitalism in some way or another. The fact is that an interest-free economy will be successful only when it comes from the conviction of society, not from the imposition of the system from outside. Therefore, sincere and honest efforts must be made to educate the people in the values of Islam, because every institution of a system reflects the ideas of men which are current in a given period of time. So it would be a mistake for any Muslim state to start implementing the principles of an interest-free economic system through the existing institutions without imbuing the people with the spirit of Islam. It would be just like constructing a huge university building without making any provision for teachers. Once a Muslim state is in a position to inculcate the Islamic spirit and its life-philosophy, it may go ahead with the implementation of the scheme of an interest-free economic system.

At this stage, it is necessary to explain why an interest-free economy would be better than an economy with interest. I propose to discuss this issue under the following headings: (*a*) Interest and Capitalism; (*b*) Interest and the Saving-Investment Relationship; (*c*) Interest and Unemployment; (*d*) Interest and Depression; (*e*) Interest and Scarcity of Resources; (*f*) Interest and the Debt-servicing Problem; (*g*) Interest and Underdeveloped Countries; and (*h*) Interest and World Peace.

(a) Interest and Capitalism.

It is interest which, in the ultimate analysis, is responsible for the growth of capitalists in society. In a socialist economy, there can be no question of payment of interest, because all savings are collective savings made by the state before the income is distributed among labourers. But in a planless capitalist economy, through the temptations of security and interest, savings are generally mobilized for capital formation on an individual, corporate and governmental basis. The rise of these groups seems to have its origin largely in the historical accident that some economic activities are first started by those who meet with success, and who in their turn, have a tendency to operate in a cumulative and circular way acting and reacting upon each other in a complex pattern of economic growth. When this powerful class of capitalists invest their own capital along with the capital of other people, they ensure the lion's share of production for themselves. "Having satisfied the real contributors of capital with security and a meagre amount of interest, the capitalist becomes free to regulate its employment and pocket the entire return he gets out of it, often at the cost of the direct return of those very factors of production which placed their capital in his hands.

In this process of production, the capitalist class becomes so powerful that it dominates all possible spheres of life. It vitiates society by making man selfish and self-conceited, because every activity is motivated by money alone. It vitiates economic life, because by holding the "means" of production in their hands the capitalists, in order to earn maximum profits, not only create unnatural demands for extremely harmful goods like alcohol, cigarettes, etc., but also form monopolies and cartels. When politicians, under dire popular pressure, try to cut capitalists down to size through various measures including progressive taxation, they are flouted through the evasion of taxes, hoarding, blackmarketing, smuggling, and the adulteration of products including even the necessities of life. Lastly, the capitalists vitiate the political life of a nation through their dictatorship in the economic life of the community. In modern capitalist countries we find that contesting for the office of president is a hugely expensive affair. In spite of popular pressure politicians must play to the tunes of and work in collaboration with the capitalists. In such a system only a capitalist or a person supported by him could dare contest for and capture political office. Therefore, the less fortunate and poorer masses of society learn to live in inhuman misery and are left completely at the mercy of the capitalists.

An interest-free economy, as advocated by Islam, is the only solution to mitigate the sufferings of the degraded humanity of the capitalist economic system. Under an Islamic economic system a great part of the economy will be under state control and a great part of savings will be collective savings made by the state for the exclusive welfare of the people, and the share of capital will be recognized only through normal profit. This is how the artificial class of capitalists is eliminated; social, economic and political life is purified through the spirit of co-operation and goodwill.

(b) Interest and the Saving-Investment Relationship

It is argued that in the absence of interest, savings could not be mobilized for capital formation and, therefore, the need for interest-bearing capital actually arose with the development of large-scale industry and commerce. The most scathing attacks on this contention have come from Keynes, who has denied that savings as such require any inducement in the shape of interest. He states that most savings are involuntary in character and as such they do not require any special reward by way of interest. Even if it is admitted that the rate of interest has some influence on marginal savings, the neo-classical contention is undermined by the assumption of constant income. Keynes has tried to prove that savings and investment are always and necessarily equal, their equality being brought about by changes in the level of income resulting from investment.

Even in the absence of inducement by interest, there are likely to be more savings and more investments and consequently more incomes, partly because of the charm of a higher margin of profit and partly because of a lesser risk of loss. It is due to the direct participation of the people in the process of production that the return from investment is likely to be proper and just without the lion's share thereof being exploited by the capitalist. Again, the decisions of policy-making being so broadbased and widely-shared, the chances of unwise and hazardous investment would be reduced, thereby reducing the risk of loss to the minimum. Moreover, production of goods and services, keeping in view the social utility under proper state planning based on the co-operation of the people, would certainly be better than uncontrolled production of wasteful goods and services under capitalism.

(c) Interest and Unemployment

It may sound strange to many modern thinkers obsessed by capitalistic ideas that interest stands in the way of fuller utilization of resources, thereby creating unemployment in society. It creates unemployment from the standpoints of both supply of and demand for investment funds. Even if it is admitted that the positive rate of interest (say, five per cent) induces the marginal savers to save, this means that this class of savers will not participate in any acitivity which is likely to yield a return less than the current rate of interest (say, five per cent). In a capitalistic economy, it is not possible to utilize the services of this class of savers who are not supposed to participate in the productive process.

Similarly, the demand for capital is governed by the profitability of investment relating to the rate of interest. Having regard to his own means, each entrepreneur will push the investment of capital until it appears, in his judgment, that the margin of profitability is reached; and that margin is not a fixed point but "a boundary-line cutting one after another every possible line of investment, and moving irregularly outwards in all directions whenever there is a fall in the rate of interest at which extra capital can be obtained." It follows that interest holds back investment in production, and the marginal efficiency of capital itself is pulled down by the rate of interest. In his *General Theory of Employment, Interest and Money*, Keynes has rightly observed: "It seems that the rate of interest on money plays a peculiar part in setting a limit to the level of employment, since it sets a standard to which marginal efficiency of a capital asset must attain if it is to be newly produced" (p. 235).

(d) Interest and Depression.

Without making any active contribution of its own to production, the capitalist class thrives and prospers through interest not only at the cost of other factors of production but also at the cost of poor consumers. Interest is a blatant means of unearned income; it is resented by the worker who considers that he is thereby deprived of a part of the fruits of his labour; consumers are also exploited, because interest enters into the cost of production and thereby delays recovery when depression attacks trade, commerce and industry. While giving account of Veblen's teachings, W. C. Mitchell has ably explained how interest plays a vital part in bringing about crisis under capitalism.

He observed: "When times are good, prices rise, profits are high business men borrow freely and enlarge their output. But such prosperity works its own undoing. The substantial security behind the loans is prospective net earnings capitalized at the current rate of interest. When the rate of interest rises, as it does during prosperity, the capitalized value of a given net income declines, and the loans become less safe. More than that, net earnings in many cases prove less than had been expected in the optimistic days of the nascent boom. Prices cannot be pushed up indefinitely; the costs of doing business rise and encroach upon profits;

bank reserves fall and it becomes difficult to get additional profit. When fading profits are added to high interest, creditors become nervous. In such a strained situation the embarrassment of a few conspicuous concerns will bring down the unstable structure which had seemed so imposing, a demand for liquidation starts and spreads rapidly, for the enterprisers, pressed for payment, put pressure on their debtors to pay up. So prosperity ends in a crisis followed by depression."

(e) Interest and Scarcity of Resources.

It is argued that the need for the payment of interest arises from scarcity of resources, because if capital resources are used for production of one particular assortment of goods and services, they have to be withdrawn from another assortment. It is, therefore, said that the concept of the rate of interest is not altogether useless even in a socialist State. The whole argument is fallacious, because Islam does recognize the share of capital in the productive process. What Islam does not view with favour is the fixed return for capital irrespective of its contribution. Since resources are not numerous, the Islamic state will have to allocate its total resources among different avenues in descending order of their relative profitability.

Those projects which are likely to yield the maximum returns will be taken up first. The surplus resources will be devoted to projects which stand next in their order of profitability, and it is practically certain that all resources will be exhausted before all conceivable projects are fulfilled. In such an economy there is every possibility of the maximum utilization of resources and the maximum level of employment will be reached. The fact is that if a community grows richer due to the fullest exploitation of her resources, and if it is accompanied by constant or declining growth in population, its propensity to consume is likely to decline. The proportion of income spent on consumption tends to diminish and the proportion that is saved tends to increase as the total income increases. This is likely to depress present consumption demand as well as the demand for investment funds. Hence the rate of interest is likely to fall to zero in a perfectly organized community. In such an economy there is ample scope for earning money by enterprise. As Keynes observed: "Though the rentier would disappear, there would still be room, nevertheless, for enterprise and skill in the estimation of prospective yields about which opinions could differ. For the above relates primarily to the pure rate of interest apart from any allowance for risk and the like and not to the gross yield of assets including the return in respect of risk. Thus unless the pure rate of interest were to be held at negative figure, there would still be a positive yield to skilled investment in individual assets having a doubtful prospective yield provided there was some measurable unwillingness to undertake risk; there would also be a positive net yield from the aggregate of such assets over a period of time. But it is not unlikely that in such circumstances, the eagerness to obtain a yield from doubtful investments might be such that would show in the aggregate a negative net yield." We have already mentioned that in the interest-free society of Islam, the possibility of such "a negative net yield" is likely to be reduced to the minimum because of the joint and co-operative efforts of all the sectors of the economy.

(f) Interest and the Debt-servicing Problem.

It is not difficult to show that the rate of interest acts as a hindrance to the better development of the world. The debt-servicing problem is a standing puzzle for almost all developing states like Pakistan, Indonesia, India, etc. It is universally recognized that foreign loans and aid play a very significant part in the economic development of all underdeveloped countries. But, in the ultimate analysis, loans require an export of resources from the borrower countries in an amount equivalent to the sum of principal plus interest, if the loans are interest-bearing. Foreign creditors consequently raise questions about the capacity of the borrower countries to export to those countries and earn vital foreign exchange. This is not the end of the story. A higher rate of interest also means a higher price of loans. Borrowing nations have started to find that higher interest rates swallow up most of all of any new finance they are able to obtain. Pakistan, for instance, paid an amount of $109 million to consortium members by way of interest and amortization, which constituted over one fourth of the disbursements from the consortium sources in 1967–8. India, with a large overseas debt, could be in danger of taxing her borrowing powers to the limit merely to service existing debts. She would be pedalling hard to stay in the same place. The Middle Eastern and African countries increased their debts by nearly 90 %, to a total of $ 4.9 million in 1958 and so on.

The debt-servicing problem is thus of great concern to all developing countries such as Pakistan, which depend on a large measure of international aid. Development loans without interest are likely to bring about a definite improvement in the existing pattern of world trade, world production and world co-operation. Consequently a significant improvement is likely to occur in the economic position of the less developed countries, because all reconstruction or development loans without interest will, in the long run, enlarge the production base and export potential of the receiving countries which, in turn, will improve their competitive position in world markets. The new pattern of foreign trade and investment through co-operation, which will then be registered in the balance of payments accounts, will modify the pattern for later periods, not only in aid-receiving countries but also in aid-giving as well as other countries. Thus humanity as a whole will be getting the maximum advantage out of the most efficient use of the human and natural resources God has given to mankind.

(g) Interest and Underdeveloped Countries.

All underdeveloped countries in general and Muslim countries in particular may switch to an interest-free economy in well-planned stages, since they do not already have a well-knit, integrated and developed system of financial institutions. It is a recognized fact that the quantitative flow of funds into channels compatible with a planned investment programme requires the existence and proper development of financial institutions through which that task is to be accomplished. Thus the limited role of the interest rate policy in underdeveloped Muslim countries can be understood from the fact that conditions necessary for the effectiveness of a flexible rate of interest, such as a developed bill market and a general discount market, the rationalized and highly sensitive assets structure of banks and the high chance of the development of capital markets, etc, are in most of these countries either totally unobtainable or only insignificantly present. In the advanced system of monetary management, a small increase in consumption expenditure stimulates a relatively large increase in investment expenditure. It suggests a degree of sensitivity in the latter which should give the monetary authority, through indirect control over the rate of interest, a guiding role in the direction and tempo of income movements, but in an underdeveloped system such sensitivity is utterly lacking and, therefore, interest rate policy is worthless as an instrument of control. So what is needed is a more direct control of the entire commodity market all the way from production to distribution so that price stability is achieved and prospective entrepreneurs are able to secure the necessary finances for potential investment. Without "slavish imitation" of advanced countries, underdeveloped Muslim countries shall have to go deep into their socio-economic problems so that they can evolve systems of their own, based on the economic philosophy of Islam, and can give the world a better solution to all the economic ills of humanity.

(h) Interest and World Peace.

So far I have discussed the ineffectiveness of the interest rate policy in accelerating the process of growth from a purely economic standpoint. Now I would like to discuss how interest rates on loans can stand in the way of creating a better world to live in. Fundamentally, the necessity for loans arises from the needs of the poor. Only a society of "haves" can afford to advance loans to a society of "have-nots". Therefore, the charging of interest in any form on loans is a negation of the universal principle of brotherhood of man and co-operation. It is a naked exploitation of the brother's needs. It appears as if the whole of humanity has been lost in the sea of materialism. Interest uproots the very foundation of humanity, mutual help and sympathy, and creates selfishness in man. All the persons in such a society have a tendency to indulge in a constant tussle motivated by "money" alone. What is applicable at the national level is equally applicable at the international level. Today, we find how a creditor nation holds a debtor nation in bondage through usurious loans. It is not a theory but a verdict of history that "since the First Great War, international loans, directly or indirectly controlled by the Loans Committee of the League of Nations, were similarly floated in the Danubian States and Balkan countries. The payments of interest on these debts brought added misery to these countries during a period of unparalleled international deflation, and most, if not all, of them, were in partial or total default." In spite of this, investigations conducted by the late League of Nations resulted in suggestions for reorganizing the internal economy and increased taxation in the debtor countries; so that "service" on these loans could be facilitated. Was it not an economic exploitation by the "haves" of the "have-nots". My answer is in the affirmative. Thus this type of exploitation, either in the domestic or in the international sphere, inevitably leads to domination by the exploiters, and develops into a potential threat to peace.

So far we have analyzed the harmful effects of interest on the existing scheme of society. Taken all in all, we can safely say that if interest is abolished, we can conceive of a nearly-ideal if not ideal socio-economic order.

Profit and Interest.

With this section, we are now entering into the final phase of our discussion relating to the difference between profit and interest. Before I take up the point at issue I would like to say a few words about the type of profit Islam has allowed. Islam has recognized the acceptance of profit only in a restricted sense, because the unrestricted and abnormal profit which a capitalist earns is a clear exploitation of society. This type of profit is generally the result of monopolies and cartels which become the main feature of a capitalist economy. But monopolies, the cornering of commodities, the holding back of produce from the market in expectation of a rise in prices, are prohibited in Islam, because they are all a negation of beneficence. Therefore, Islam is for normal profit which refers to that level of profit at which there is apparently no tendency for new firms to enter a given trade nor for old firms to disappear out of it. This tendency is not enough. The fundamental principle which should be kept in view is that no section of society should be deprived of its legitimate share in the process of production.

While Islam has recognized normal profit, it has prohibited interest. On scrutiny it would be seen that the transactions and returns in both cases are different in nature. In the case of interest, the lender becomes unconcerned with the use of the loan after the loan is secured and interest thereon guaranteed. In the case of profit, the owner of the firm remains involved in and concerned with the use by the user throughout. It follows that interest is not the result of any productive effort whereas profit is. Since in the case of interest, productive effort is not made at all by the lender, the element of the enterpreneur is absent altogether, whereas in the case of profit, that element remains alive throughout the process of production and marketing. Thus in the case of interest, the real owner of capital is generally missing from the productive process, whereas for profit, the real owner does determine the economic use of his capital; the entrepreneur adopts new inventions and tries to create new fashions in order to increase his profits. Thus profit is the reward of progress. Finally, in the case of interest, the element of the risk of loss is altogether missing, because the interest is fixed and certain, whereas profit is a payment for the assumption of risks by the entrepreneur. It is the entrepreneur's income which is uncertain and unknown. It is uncertain, because it is residual in nature. Since the assumption of risk is a disutility, it is to be paid for in the form of profit. It is unknown, because superior entrepreneurs can earn higher profit by virtue of their organizing ability or other mental and physical capacities compared with their inferior counterparts. Because of these vast differences, Islam has allowed profit and condemned interest. Surely, "Allah hath permitted trade and forbidden usury." It follows that in an Islamic economy, a given distribution of income and wealth will be acceptable when society is in a position to provide a guarantee of a minimum level of living to each of its members as defined in accordance with the *Sharī'ah* and with socio-economic realities, as well as when there are sustained efforts to defuse the concentration in a few people's hands of the ownership of the means of production and wealth, thereby reducing both relative and absolute disparities in income and wealth.

Distributive Measures

A number of operational policy packages which have far-reaching implications to reduce disparities of income and wealth may be evolved through the implementation of the Islamically-justified obligatory and voluntary distributive measures which include:
1. payment of "*Zakāt*" and "'*Ushr*";
2. prohibition of "*Ribā*" on both consumption and productive loans;
3. entitlement to pure economic rent (i.e. income earned without any special effort by anyone) of all members of the community or of the state;
4. implementation of laws of inheritance to ensure the equitable intergenerational transfer of property;
5. encouragement to give benevolent loans free of interest (i.e. *Qarḍ-i-Ḥasanah*);
6. discouragement of the depletion of exhaustible resources by the present generation to the disadvantage of all future generations;
7. encouragement of the payment of "*Sadaqah*" to the poor by those who have "surplus" funds beyond their needs;
8. encouragement of the organization of co-operative insurance;
9. encouragement of the setting-up of philanthropic trusts (i.e. *Awqāf*) for providing social goods, as well as private goods to deserving individuals);
10. encouragement of the lending of productive assets *without* charge to those who are in need of them, the recipients being expected to return

them to their original owners after accomplishing the objective for which they were borrowed (i.e. *Maa'un*);

11. legal measures against the public treasury to enforce the guaranteed minimum level of living, once defined by an Islamic state in accordance with the *Sharī'ah* as well as socio-economic realities;

12. provisioning for additional "taxes" beyond *Zakāt* and *'Ushr* by an Islamic state to ensure distributive justice.

7.4 The Islamic Law of Inheritance and Its Economic Significance

The Islamic law of inheritance has brought about a silent revolution in the whole philosophy of the distribution of wealth and introduced the new technique, unheard of before, of increasing national wealth through the participation of women in economic activities. But first the question arises: What is inheritance? According to the *Encyclopædia of Social Sciences*, "Inheritance is the entry of living persons into the possession of dead persons' property and exists in some form wherever the institution of private property is recognized as the basis of the social and economic system. But the actual forms of inheritance and the laws and customs governing it differ very greatly from country to country and from time to time. Changed ways of owning and using property will always bring with them in the long run alteration in the laws and practices relating to the inheritance of wealth."

The Islamic law of inheritance is, however, assumed to be founded on certain passages of the Holy *Qur'ān*, the inadequacy of which is indicative of the fact that the role of reason is recognized in Islam. Shorn of sectarian differences and the hair-splitting of jurists, the Islamic law of inheritance is at the present day a fixed, scientific and beautifully harmonious system. Without going into every detail, I propose to illustrate below a few generally accepted rules derived from the *Qur'ān* and the *Ḥadīth*.

(*i*) A son of a deceased person will get the share of two daughters. It follows that every brother of the deceased man will get double the share of his sister. But in all cases, the widow of the deceased will be getting one-eighth of the total share. For example:

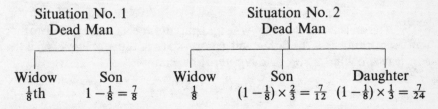

Situation No. 1
Dead Man

Widow	Son
$\frac{1}{8}$th	$1 - \frac{1}{8} = \frac{7}{8}$

Situation No. 2
Dead Man

Widow	Son	Daughter
$\frac{1}{8}$	$(1 - \frac{1}{8}) \times \frac{2}{3} = \frac{7}{12}$	$(1 - \frac{1}{8}) \times \frac{1}{3} = \frac{7}{24}$

(*ii*) If a man dies leaving behind a daughter and a widow, the daughter will get half of the property; if he leaves behind more than one daughter, together they will be getting two thirds of the property of the deceased.

For example:

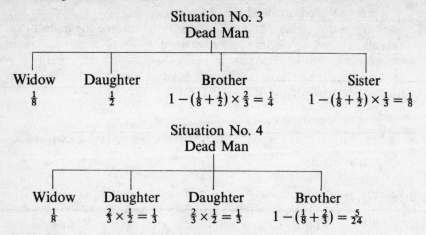

Situation No. 3
Dead Man

Widow	Daughter	Brother	Sister
$\frac{1}{8}$	$\frac{1}{2}$	$1-(\frac{1}{8}+\frac{1}{2})\times\frac{2}{3}=\frac{1}{4}$	$1-(\frac{1}{8}+\frac{1}{2})\times\frac{1}{3}=\frac{1}{8}$

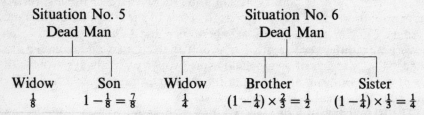

Situation No. 4
Dead Man

Widow	Daughter	Daughter	Brother
$\frac{1}{8}$	$\frac{2}{3}\times\frac{1}{2}=\frac{1}{3}$	$\frac{2}{3}\times\frac{1}{2}=\frac{1}{3}$	$1-(\frac{1}{8}+\frac{2}{3})=\frac{5}{24}$

(*iii*) We have seen that normally a widow will get one eighth of the property of the deceased husband. But if he leaves behind a widow only, she will get one quarter of the property. For example:

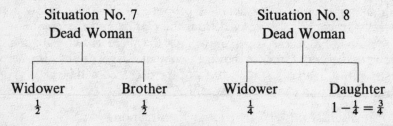

Situation No. 5
Dead Man

Widow	Son
$\frac{1}{8}$	$1-\frac{1}{8}=\frac{7}{8}$

Situation No. 6
Dead Man

Widow	Brother	Sister
$\frac{1}{4}$	$(1-\frac{1}{4})\times\frac{2}{3}=\frac{1}{2}$	$(1-\frac{1}{4})\times\frac{1}{3}=\frac{1}{4}$

(*iv*) If a wife possessing property dies and leaves behind her husband only and no children, the husband will get half of the property. But if she leaves behind any issue, the husband will get one quarter of the property. For example:

Situation No. 7
Dead Woman

Widower	Brother
$\frac{1}{2}$	$\frac{1}{2}$

Situation No. 8
Dead Woman

Widower	Daughter
$\frac{1}{4}$	$1-\frac{1}{4}=\frac{3}{4}$

(*v*) If a son leaves behind his wife and parents and a brother, the brother will get nothing. But the father will get one-sixth of the property even if the son leaves behind a son or daughter. For example:

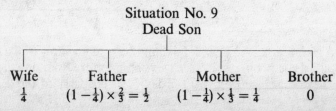

Situation No. 9
Dead Son

Wife	Father	Mother	Brother
$\frac{1}{4}$	$(1-\frac{1}{4})\times\frac{2}{3}=\frac{1}{2}$	$(1-\frac{1}{4})\times\frac{1}{3}=\frac{1}{4}$	0

(*vi*) If a man leaves behind only a mother and a brother, the mother will get one-third of the property; If not, she will get one-sixth of the property in any case. For example:

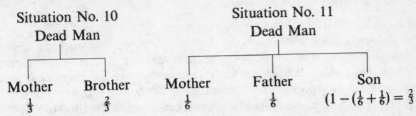

Situation No. 10
Dead Man

Mother $\frac{1}{3}$ Brother $\frac{2}{3}$

Situation No. 11
Dead Man

Mother $\frac{1}{6}$ Father $\frac{1}{6}$ Son $(1 - (\frac{1}{6} + \frac{1}{6}) = \frac{2}{3}$

(*vii*) If a man leaves behind a wife and son, his brother and sister will get nothing. For example:

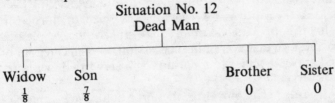

Situation No. 12
Dead Man

Widow $\frac{1}{8}$ Son $\frac{7}{8}$ Brother 0   Sister 0

(*viii*) If a man leaves behind only a wife and no near relations, then distant relations will get the share. For example:

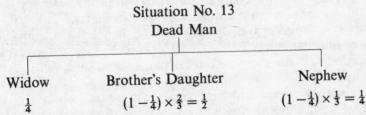

Situation No. 13
Dead Man

Widow $\frac{1}{4}$ Brother's Daughter $(1 - \frac{1}{4}) \times \frac{2}{3} = \frac{1}{2}$ Nephew $(1 - \frac{1}{4}) \times \frac{1}{3} = \frac{1}{4}$

(*ix*) If a son dies before the death of his father, his grandson/grand-daughter will get nothing. For instance:

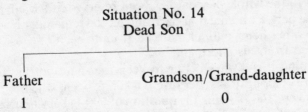

Situation No. 14
Dead Son

Father 1   Grandson/Grand-daughter 0

(*x*) If a woman leaves behind her a son or daughter, her step-son/daughter will get nothing. For instance:

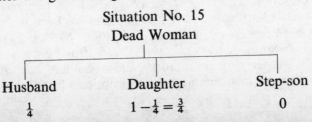

Situation No. 15
Dead Woman

Husband $\frac{1}{4}$ Daughter $1 - \frac{1}{4} = \frac{3}{4}$ Step-son 0

The rules explained above are not at all exhaustive; there may be many other situations.

Basic Principle

The reader should observe that the word "heir" is confined to those entitled to shares and residuary legatees; it does not include distant kindred. The basic principle concerning succession is that he is preferred in succession who is the nearest to the deceased, as the daughter's daughter is preferred to the daughter of the son's daughter, and if the claimants are equal in degree then the child of an heir is preferred to the child of a distant relation. This principle is to be kept in view in determining succession. Here brief reference may be made to how the question of succession may be determined on (a) hermaphrodites, (b) pregnancy, (c) lost persons, (d) apostates, (e) captives, (f) persons drowned or burned. Professor Rumsey, in his book *Mahommedan Law of Inheritance*, explained in some detail the question of ascertaining succession on each category of persons mentioned above. I prefer to mention them very briefly without entering into controversy.

(a) As regards hermaphrodites there is a controversy among jurists as to the size of their share in inheritance. Many of them are inclined to give hermaphrodites the greater of the respective shares of son and daughter. But, according to Abū Ḥanifah, a hermaphrodite whose sex is quite doubtful may be allotted the smaller of the two shares. That is, if a man leaves a son, a daughter and a hermaphrodite, then the hermaphrodite has the share of a daughter. This view appears to be reasonable, because a hermaphrodite is not supposed to discharge social obligations like sons and daughters.

(b) "The chief rule in arranging cases on pregnancy is that the case be arranged by two suppositions, we mean, by supposing that the child in the womb is male and by supposing that it is female, then, we are required to compare the arrangements of both cases. Thus when the child appears, if it be entitled to the whole of what has been reserved, it is well; but, if it be entitled to a part, let it take that part, and let the remainder be distributed among the other heirs, and let there be given to each of those heirs what was reserved from his allotment."

To my mind it is always better to keep the share on the high side to avoid future complications, because if a son is born, when the share of a daughter is kept, then solving the question of taking back a certain portion of the already distributed shares is not always an easy task. Again, among the learned jurists there is a great controversy in respect of determining the period of gestation. The longest period varies from two years to seven years while the shortest time for it is six months. I am not inclined to accept any of the periods of gestation determined by fanciful notions; we should, rather, be guided by medical experience. But the system of keeping a portion of property for an unborn child is just and scientific.

(c) The principle in arranging cases concerning a lost person is that the case be arranged on the supposition of his being alive, and then arranged on the supposition of his being dead; and the rest of the operation may be worked out. Here also there is no uniformity with regard to the presumption of the death of a lost person. Thus the period allowed before presuming a person dead varies from ninety years to one hundred and twenty-five years among jurists. This presumption appears to be unrealistic to me. We feel that after a reasonable period of time, say, ten years, anything which would accrue to a lost person may be distributed among his heirs according to the established practice, subject to the condition that property so distributed may be returned if the lost person reappears even after ten years. In England, presumption of death usually arises when a person has not been heard of for seven years. This rule was substantially adopted by Anglo-Indian legislation of 1872 (the Indian Evidence Act, 1872).

(*d*) As regards an apostate, we may say in the words of Professor Rumsey: "When an apostate from the faith has died naturally, or been killed, or passed into a hostile country, and the Kadi has given judgment on his passage thither, then what he had acquired of the time of his being a believer goes to his heirs who are believers; and what he has gained since the time of apostasy is placed in the public treasury, according to Abū Hanifah, but, according to the two lawyers [Abū Yūsuf and Muhammad] both the acquisitions go to his believing heirs; and, according to al-Shāfii both the acquisitions are placed in the public treasury; and what he gained after his arrival in the hostile country, that is confiscated by the general consent; and all the property of a female apostate goes to her heirs who are believers, without diversity of opinion among our masters to whom God be merciful! But an apostate shall not inherit from anyone, neither from a believer nor from an apostate like himself, and so a female apostate shall not inherit from anyone, except when the people of a whole district become apostates altogether, for then they inherit reciprocally."

According to natural justice, the state should not confiscate any aquisitions of an apostate. I am inclined to accept the view that all the acquisitions should go to his believing heirs, because if the State confiscates any portion of his property depriving his believing heirs, this may act as an inducement on the part of the heirs to apostatize.

(*e*) The rule concerning a captive is like the rule of other believers in regard to inheritance, as long as he has not departed from the faith; but, if he has departed from the faith, then the rule concerning him is the rule concerning an apostate; but, if his apostasy be not known nor is it known whether he is alive or dead, then the rule concerning him is the rule concerning a lost person.

(*f*) Supposing a man is possessed of property and one of his sons dies in an accident, and the deceased son has left a son. According to the "approved opinion," the property of the father of the deceased son will go to the "heirs who are living," that is, to the surviving sons; and "some of the deceased shall not inherit from others," so that the deceased son will not be deemed to have become entitled to anything, and, therefore, his son will get nothing. But Ḥaḍrat 'Ali and Ibn Mas'ūd say, according to one of the traditions from them, that some of them shall inherit from others, except in what each of them has inherited from the companion of his fate. Natural justice demands that the deceased son would be deemed to have been entitled to his portion as a residuary, provided he leaves behind wife, sons or daughters, because the question of this entitlement is very much linked up with the survival of the dependants of the deceased.

Economic Significance

The Islamic law of inheritance is anticapitalist in outlook. Under this system a person may not dispose of more than one third of his property by testamentary directions. While he is in the enjoyment of normal health he may dispose of his property freely, subject, of course, to moral obligations, but neither by will nor by gift, once he enters upon a stage of illness which terminates in death. By such disposition he may provide legacies for friends, for servants, and for charity.

The rest of the inheritance must be divided among the prescribed heirs in specified shares. No part of the one third is permitted to be disposed of by will so that it may be used to augment the share of one or more heirs to the prejudice of the remaining heirs. Each heir can take only his or her prescribed share and no more; nor can any heir be deprived of the whole or any part of his or her share. There is a wide circle of heirs. The Islamic system of inheritance operates to distribute wealth so that a large number of people may have sufficiency or, at least, a little, rather than that one or a few should have a large share and the rest nothing.

There are some critics who hold that the working of this law reduces agricultural land to uneconomic holdings. But this difficulty can be easily overcome by co-operative farming vital for the agricultural development of Muslim countries. Therefore, I find no harm in an Islamic state fixing the limit of economic holdings. We must realize the full implications of that famous *Ḥadith* of the Holy Prophet in which he declared: "The land belongs to him who enlivens the dead earth."

In fact, modern forms of economic organization are a very powerful solvent of the group notion of property, for they tend to make claims to income arising out of property divisible without the need for dividing the property itself. Thus, when property comes to consist largely of stocks and shares, the arguments against division have far less force.

In public companies and corporations the parcelling out of the shares among a large number of holders has little effect upon management; even in the case of family businesses charges can be made on the net earnings for different members of the family and where such a business is turned into a private company, actual shares can be issued and the business still carried on without change of policy. It can be urged that the setting up of charges on business or the diffusion of the ownership of shares makes the accumulation of capital out of reserved profits harder than it would be if the whole business were inherited by a single owner. But this is only one aspect of the wider argument that great inequalities of wealth and income are necessary for the adequate accumulation of capital in modern societies. In general there is no doubt that the institution of shareholding in joint-stock concerns as the outstanding form of property ownership has made far easier and less open to economic objection the diffusion of estates at their owner's death.

In modern industrialized societies, where the concept of property has become highly individual and the family survives as a social rather than an economic institution, the tendency has been to leave inheritance as free as possible from regulation by the state and, therefore, to extend continuously the right of unfettered bequest. Thus in most English-speaking countries people are left their very wide personal discretion—practically complete freedom—to carry out their wishes in wills. But under the Islamic law of inheritance, one is not allowed to make a will for an amount exceeding one third of the whole estate. The reason is that dependants of the deceased may be given a start in life from the bequests decreed by Islamic inheritance law. This may help solve the problem of unemployment and underdevelopment.

Before Mill the question of inheritance was considered, except by the socialists, almost solely in relation to the accumulation of capital and the efficient use of productive resources, hardly at all as a problem of social justice. In Mill the two points of view are in conflict; and from his time the question has always been considered from both standpoints. On the one hand, inheritance and freedom of bequest are defended as a necessary incentive to saving and as a means to the more effective use of capital; for, given freedom of bequest, it is held, men will tend to leave their capital in such ways as to promote its effective use. On the other hand, inheritance is attacked as one of the greatest sources of social and economic inequality and proposals are made to limit or even abolish it in order to secure a better distribution of income. But Islam considers the law of inheritance as a tool of social justice. That is why Islam tries to impress upon the Muslims possessing wealth that they can make no bequest of property which will enlarge the share of one of their heirs, even by a penny, against the others' shares—shares which are to be divided among a wide circle of prescribed heirs.

While giving emphasis to social justice, the Islamic law of inheritance cannot create economic inequality. Therefore, Islam has condemned any move for the abolition of inheritance. In fact, it can hardly be urged as a self-contained and sufficient reform for the state at its owner's death, and that is what abolition involves; the state will have either to make use of it for production under collective control or to let it out to individuals who seem best qualified to use it. The former is the complete socialist solution, the latter deprives its rightful heirs. Islam follows a middle path; it condemns extreme socialism because it is the negation of the principles of human freedom and liberty. While allowing the rightful heirs to enjoy property, Islam imposes a great moral responsibility on the shoulders of the persons enjoying it. The Islamic state has every right to deprive a person of ownership of property, if it is used to the detriment of society. Moreover, the abolition of inheritance, which involves a radical change in the economic as well as the social system, is connected with the basic problem of incentives.

Inheritance Tax

Short of abolition, the rights of bequest and inheritance can, of course, be drastically restricted by introducing some form of inheritance taxation. Such taxation has taken many forms in different countries, but it usually involves some degree of graduation according to the total value of the estate and the like. The obligatory nature of making some provision in one's property for charitable objects can be made use of by an Islamic state. If there are exigencies, there can be no objection on the score of making compulsory and fixed what has been left by Islam flexible although compulsory enough. The Muslims, as vicegerents of God on Earth, have every right to pass any legislation which would further "the cause of Allah". They can fix any ratio of death duty for themselves so long as it does not exceed one third, beyond which the Prophet forbids them to go.

We must not forget that the need for the private accumulation of capital does exist to a considerable degree in modern societies and inheritance will continue to find defenders on the ground that it promotes this end. Admitted, however, that any severe restriction on the right of inheritance would, unless the Islamic state used the proceeds as capital, reduce the rate of capital accumulation; the question is how far severe taxation of inheritance would react on the individual's will to accumulate. This question will have to be kept in view by the Islamic state while fixing the rate of death duty or inheritance tax. It is, moreover, highly relevant to point out that among the richest members of a modern community saving is largely automatic in that it represents surplus income beyond the desire to spend. Clearly, saving of this sort will not be affected by modern inheritance taxation except to the extent to which gifts and charitable donations may be stimulated. But this problem of the modern states can be handled in a better way by the Islamic state, which would make use of one's property intended for charitable purposes.

Participation of Women

Another significant contribution of the Islamic law of inheritance is that it recognizes the participation of women in economic activity. They can now own, possess, enter professions and services, join industry or trade and enter into contracts in their own name.

The difference between the normal share of female heirs and male heirs of the same relationship to the deceased is not, in fact, discriminatory to the prejudice of the female heirs. Under the Islamic system, the obligation of maintaining the family always rests upon the husband, even when, as is often the case, the wife's personal income may be larger than the husband's. To enable the male to discharge his obligations toward the family, his share in inheritance is twice that of a female in the same degree of relationship as himself. Far from operating to the prejudice of the female heir, this actually places her in a favourable position as compared with the male heir because she does not have financial obligations to the family.

What is important here from the economic point of view is that in Islam woman has an identity of her own. She can spare her time and can enter into any profession or trade and thus increase the national wealth. Thus the whole man and woman power is harnessed to produce value, increase national wealth and add to human happiness.

Subject to the injunctions of the *Qur'ān* and the *Sunnah*, the future of inheritance appears to depend, on the one hand, on the growth in modern Muslim communities of collective methods of capital accumulation and of the control of business resources and, on the other hand, on the pressure of the popular movement towards a less unequal distribution of the income; for this movement, ethical as well as economic in its driving force, results in forms of inheritance taxation which limit saving and impinge on profits, and thus it leads to the necessity of alternative methods of saving and of ensuring adequate production.

7.5 Summary and Conclusion

In this chapter I have discussed the rationale of the distribution of income among the various factors of production. In the first instance, the payment of rent, which generally refers to the concept of "surplus" earned by a particular unit of a factor of production in excess of the minimum amount necessary to keep that factor in its present occupation, does not seem to be inconsistent with the spirit of Islam. It is explained that rent and interest are widely different.

Secondly, wage differences resulting from differences in talents and capacities have been recognized by Islam. The fundamental conditions are that employers shall not exploit their labourers and must pay their "dues" and the workers shall not exploit their employers through trade unions and must do their job faithfully, sincerely and honestly.

Thirdly, there is a controversy over the differences between "*al Ribā*" and "*interest*". But if the meaning of *Ribā* is viewed in its correct historical perspective, there appears to be no difference between *Ribā* and interest. A brief survey of all modern theories of interest has revealed that economists have failed to discover a clear answer as to why interest is paid. On the other hand, the Islamic theory of capital does recognize the share of capital in national wealth only to the extent of its contribution, to be determined as a variable percentage of profits rather than a fixed percentage of capital itself. The author is confident enough that if sincere attempts are made by the leaders of the Muslim world, it is quite possible to have an interest-free economy. It is established that interest is responsible for the growth of capitalism with all its attendant evils in society: it creates the problem of unemployment; it retards the process of recovery from depression: it causes the debt-servicing problems of the underdeveloped countries: finally, it uproots the basic principles of co-operation and mutual help and creates in man selfishness.

Fourthly, Islam permits normal profit—not monopoly profit or profit arising from speculation.

Finally, we have illustrated a few generally accepted principles of the Islamic law of inheritance which is at present a fixed, scientific and beautifully harmonious system. The most positive contribution of the Islamic law of inheritance is that it recognizes the participation of women in the complex process of economic activity.

7.6 Selected Further Reading

Al-Araby, Muhammad Abdullah, "Private Property and its limits in Islam", Al-Azhar Academy for Islamic Research, First Conference, 1964.

Alan, Hashmat, "Distribution Theory under Islamic Law", Ph.D. Thesis, George Town University, 1953.

Huq, Ataul, "Distribution of Wealth and Income in Islam vis-a-vis other Economic Systems", Islamic Economic Research Bureau, 1980.

Ishaque, Kahlid M. "Private Property and its Role in Islamic Social Order" in *Economic System of Islam*, Karachi, 1980.

Kannun, Abdullah, "Private Property in Islam", in *The Islamic Review and Arab Affairs*, vol. 58, September, London, 1970.

Sharif, M. Raihan, "Problems of Distribution in an Islamic Society", in *Thoughts on Islamic Economics*, Islamic Economic Research Bureau, 1980.

Yusuf, S. M. "Land Agriculture and Rent in Islam" in *Islamic Culture*, Pakistan, 1957.

PART III

The Micro and Macro Economic Setting of an Islamic Economy

CHAPTER 14

The Principles of Trade and Commerce in Islam.

CHAPTER 15

Islamic Co-operative Insurance: Theory and Practice.

CHAPTER 8

Towards a Price Theory in an Islamic State

8.1 Introduction.

8.2 The Basis of the Islamic Price Theory.

8.3 The Islamic Market and Company Behaviour.

8.4 Prices in an Islamic State.

    (a) Monopoly Prices

    (b) Real Rises in Price

    (c) Artificial Rises in Price

    (d) Rises in Prices of the Necessities of Life

8.5 Suggestions and Conclusion

8.6 Suggested Further Reading

"Whoever withholds cereals that they may become scarce and dear is a sinner."

Prophet Muhammad (peace be upon him)

"Islam has created a society more free from widespread cruelty and social oppression than any society had ever been in the world before."

H. G. Wells, *The Outline of History*

8.1 Introduction

Imbued with so-called capitalist and socialist ideas even some Muslim scholars have started arguing that Islam does not have any economic system of its own. This conception, which is rather a misconception, arises out of a lack of proper appreciation of Islamic values and life philosophy. The fact is that Islam is the only religion which has enunciated the basic principles covering all aspects of human life, not to speak of economic values only. Since these principles are universal and fundamental, valid for all ages, an economic system based on these principles cannot simply lay everything down to the shape of the demand curve or lay down the policy of the daily meat or fish market. Islam has laid down a broad framework based on equality of economic opportunity and justice for its followers to guide them in the course of their normal economic life. The derivation of microconcepts through the exercise of *Ijtihād* from within this broad framework has been permitted. This provision for the application of *Ijtihād* is indicative of Islamic dynamism in the economic sphere of life. Therefore, we need not be surprised to know that Islam has provided us with a number of broad principles of pricing. If they are properly implemented, many of the present-day difficulties in handling the problem of pricing will disappear.

In a free economy, demand for and supply of commodities determine the normal price, which measures the effective demand being determined by the degree of the scarcity of the supply. An increase in demand for a commodity tends to raise its price and induce the producer to produce more of it. The problem of pricing arises because of the maladjustment between demand and supply. This maladjustment is mainly due to the existence of imperfect competition in the market. Competition is imperfect if the number of sellers is limited or if there is product differentiation. The basic point to note is that the producer cannot accept the ruling price as a datum. Perfect competition which assumes a perfect market in which the customers, who make up the market, will react in the same way to differences in the prices charged by different sellers, is merely a theoretical tool of price analysis. This is because under perfect competition the industry in full equilibrium will consist of a number of optimum-sized firms, and price will be equal to marginal cost as well as to average cost at the point at which the average cost is at its minimum. Both perfect competition and pure monopoly are rare phenomena. In actual life, we come across imperfect competition in most cases. Under imperfect competition the output of the individual firm will be determined at the point of intersection between the marginal cost curve and the marginal revenue.

8.2 The Basis of the Islamic Price Theory

With these general observations, let us pass on to the basis of the Islamic theory of prices. Whether unsocial trends of price changes, which are to the disadvantage of the mass of people in the community, should be controlled or regulated is not, perhaps, controversial either from the purely analytical viewpoint or from the Islamic point of view. To me, the basic difference arises from the fact that in an Islamic State, the urge for such control or regulation should come from "within" the community—a community which has already been imbued with the values of Islam. Therefore, its effect is lasting and decisive, whereas in the so-called capitalist and socialist States, these regulations are imposed upon the community and the community may or may not accept them in a desirable and effective way.

However, theoretically, it would perhaps be possible to conceive of an ideal Islamic state free of imperfections. But this is not an attainable goal, just because man is not, and cannot be, perfect. Even assuming these imperfections of society we cannot endorse the part played by the "marginal concept" in determining prices under a capitalist economy. In monopolistic competition we are used to giving undue emphasis to the doctrine of the "marginal concept" thereby underestimating the role of infra-marginal units of production. In Islamic theory, we are more inclined to accept the concept of "average" rather than that of "margin".

Since it is impossible to remove variety of ability, equity demands that returns must be related to effort. The Holy *Qur'an* says: "That man can have nothing, But what he strives for:" (*Surah* LIII. 39).

The fact is that in the Islamic scheme of society, fair price is not a concession but a fundamental right enforceable by the law of the state. Once this reorientation of state attitude has been accomplished, the actual fixation of price would be a matter of correct adjudication because the fundamental basis of the Islamic theory of price is the principle of co-operation and healthy competition instead of monopolistic competition as under a capitalist economy. Here, by healthy competition, I do not mean perfect competition in the modern sense of the term but a competition free of speculation, hoarding, smuggling, etc. However, once the normal price is determined through consensus of opinion the question of state control arises only in relation to that "norm". In order to create conditions for proper co-operation between producers and consumers in the long run, what is needed is to inject into them the spirit of Islamic values and code of business conduct through systematic education. But in the short run, it seems necessary to ensure that the state must encourage the formation of consumers' associations somewhat on lines similar to the producers' associations that already exist in our society. An Islamic state will have to assure them that their complaints would be heard in the proper quarters. If need be, the consumers' power to recommend the revocation of business licences has to be recognized. Simultaneously, the government should also encourage the formation of consumers' co-operatives and branch out into more fields where prices are manipulated by profiteers and monopolists.

8.3 The Islamic Market and Company Behaviour

In my paper entitled: "Islamic Perspectives on Market Prices and Allocation" (published by the International Centre for Research in Islamic Economics, Jeddah, Saudi Arabia, 1982), I argued that a free market mechanism based on effective demand, working through impersonal and invisible forces of demand and supply, is linked to the affluence-making resources available to those who can buy them and not necessarily to those who need them, and that the market is either inefficient or ineffective or indifferent in providing all aspects of the basic needs with which an Islamic market is concerned.

Thus, prices offered by the secular market are not seen as a guide to social welfare, particularly in the context of an Islamic economy, where social concern is so great as to treat distribution as a key to productive activities. The competition implicit in the market mechanism needs to be supplemented by conscious control, supervision and co-operation. Therefore, this author did not support the view that the poor might be allowed to enter into the market only through direct transfer payments, thereby allowing the market to operate freely.

Resource allocation cannot be left to the discretion of the individual when the question of collective welfare is involved. What is needed is necessary correction to all price-signals and economic incentive packages, coupled with vital institutional reform and delivery systems which can allocate resources directly to the poor, with a view to increasing on a permanent basis their real income through greater productivity.

Islamic reluctance to accept market price as a true guide to social welfare makes the function of conventional price elasticity of demand and supply limited in scope. The reaction of "need" to changes in "income" is also considered to be of far more importance than "price" in an Islamic economy. The main analytical task of an Islamic economy is, then, to analyze the factors or underlying forces that influence the *origins* of demand and supply.

However, pricing options such as non-price competition, rationing and co-operative prices as suggested offer a limited scope for a market mechanism, although the task of determining pricing policy in Islam will remain much more complicated than in a market or command economy.

Behaviour of the Company

The behaviour of the Islamic company or firm cannot be guided by a single objective. As a result, a company in an Islamic state may frequently have to give up the attempt to maximize anything, profits or sales or anything else.

While the behaviour of a firm in an Islamic state must conform to the principles of the *Sharī'ah*, every firm must ask: what contribution the output of the firm is going to make? Put differently: Who are the beneficiaries of the value-added component of the product of the firm? It is this emphasis which makes the Islamic firm distinctive.

This emphasis is based on the assumption that in an Islamic economy, the behaviour of the company needs to be guided, by among others, altruistic considerations – concern for others to be shown as a principle of action. This principle has its roots in the *Qur'ān* and the tradition of the Prophet. This assumption seems to imply that an individual company must display co-operative or collective economic behaviour with regard to redistribution and resource allocation. This is not to suggest that in an Islamic economy there is no scope for competitive markets, although competitive equilibrium requires no collective action. In an important sense, an Islamic economy preserves competitive markets as an allocative mechanism even when Islamic considerations for the poor and needy, coupled with consumption and production externalities, are present. This concern for others needs to be internalized within the behaviour of the firm. It does, of course, bring out a real problem: how are we to know when the behaviour of companies is altruistic and when it is not?

Unlike other social sciences, economics offers a better chance of finding a way out of this difficulty. It is customary in economics to take as axiomatic that the bundle of goods and services going to any one individual can be defined objectively. Thus, as long as the prior question of the definition of the bundle has been settled, the rest is straightforward.

Similarly, whether company behaviour is altruistic or not can be determined from its output and pricing decisions. Altruistic considerations may require the firm to produce goods and services which may not enable the firm to maximize profits or sales. The same consideration may require the firm to produce goods and services especially geared to the needs of the masses.

The behaviour of the company is to be guided by an overriding concern for public interest (as viewed by the principles of the *Sharī'ah*) which is relative to social needs. It is neither the profit-maximizing nor sales-maximizing behaviour of the firm that matters most. What matters is the structure of the decision-making institutional process that affects the substance of the decisions, so that different decisions will result from different kinds of organization, even if all else is unchanged. In such situations we may reasonably expect the firm's goal to be not maximizing profits or sales but attaining a target level, a rate of profit, a certain level of sales, a zero profit level (revenues equal to opportunity cost) or achieving an assigned social profit target. This means that the company could come to rest in a large number of situations rather than in one unique equilibrium situation. The main hypothesis is that in an Islamic economic analysis, equilibrium may *not* be unique, as different theories may yield different predictions. For example, a sales maximizing theory which predicts larger output and lower prices than a profit-maximizing theory in a particular situation have different implications for the elasticity of demand at the firm's market price. Again, under the "satisfying" theory, a firm may be content with a level of profit even when it is in a position to increase its profit due to the excess demand with regard to public interest. There is then a need for the active participation of the state in co-ordinating and initiating the multiple objectives of the firm within an Islamic framework. The extent of state interference will however tend to vary in different socio-economic circumstances.

8.4 Prices in an Islamic State

Now I will discuss the pricing problem arising out of the imperfect competition of the present-day economy under the following headings: (*a*) Monopoly Price; (*b*) Real Rises in Prices; (*c*) Artificial Rises in Prices; and (*d*) Rises in Prices of the Necessities of Life.

(a) Monopoly Prices.

The pricing problem under imperfect competition may best be approached with the help of the monopoly analysis. In spite of the threat of potential competition, the possibility of the consumption of substitutes and the risk of state interference, the general presumption is that the monopoly price is higher than the competitive price, and the output produced by a monopolist is lower than that produced under competitive conditions with perfect competition. The demand curve facing each seller is perfectly elastic, and he goes on producing and selling additional output until marginal revenue is equal to price. But a monopolist has to face a comparatively inelastic demand curve and as he produces and sells the additional output, price declines in the market. Marginal revenue will then be less than price, and a monopolist will produce up to the point at which his marginal cost is equal to his marginal revenue. Hence monopoly output is in general less than competitive output and monopoly price is higher than competitive price.

Thus, when lesser output under monopoly is connected with the idea of underutilization of resources and the consequent creation of unemployment in society, higher prices charged by the monopolist obviously cut the real income of workers and poor masses in general. Both situations are not consistent with the spirit of the *Qur'ān* and the *Sunnah*, because they are anti-social and deprive the poor, nay, the community as a whole, of the beneficent and proper use of the "Bounty of Allah". I maintain that the Islamic state has every right to control and regulate monopoly price and profit. Maximum prices may be fixed. Efforts may also be made to introduce a new element of incentives in the process of production. These may be in the form of maximum rewards of factors of production, in a manner that conditions approximating to competition may be created so that it may no longer be to the advantage of the monopolist to limit his output and keep productive factors out of employment. The difficulty here is to arrive at correct levels of prices and rewards of factors. This, however, can be achieved, if proper machinery is established for the purpose and the method of trial and error is allowed to arrive at correct prices. If need be, the nationalization of monopolies may be resorted to as an extreme step, because, according to the Holy *Qur'ān*, a legal owner of a firm or property is not the only person entitled to its use. Those in need have rights to the property of those who are better off, inasmuch as all wealth is a bounty of God and is acquired through the use of resources which God has provided for the benefit of the whole of mankind (*Sūrah* LI. 20).

Many Muslim countries such as Pakistan, have already introduced laws against monopolies and restrictive trade practices. State recognition has been accorded to the fact that the existence of monopoly power in industry, concentration of wealth in the hands of giant firms, and their widespread business collusions have led to corrupt practices and the exploitation of consumers. But much will, indeed, depend on the actual operation of the new laws which must have fool-proof machinery to enforce their intents and purposes. It is, however, felt that there should be proper assessment of how many monopolistic combines and cartels will actually break up under the impact of the new ordinance; if it affects only a few, the upper limit of what constitutes a monopoly should be scaled down.

To do away with the evils of wealth concentration, it may also be necessary to amend drastically company laws, abolish the managing agency system and strengthen the public sector. That would help to harmonize the dictates of Islamic social justice with the demands of economic dynamism—the underlying objective of new regulations.

(b) Real Rises in Prices.

The causes of real rises in price are: (1) increasing money supply, (2) decreasing productivity, (3) increasing development activity and (4) various fiscal and monetary measures. True, expansion in money supply generates effective demand. But any money expansion in the face of a disappointing growth of output, causing grave imbalance between availability of goods and monetary demand, is bound to create inflationary pressure. Expansion in the money supply also encourages speculative activities on a wide scale looking for resources in the form of excessive holdings of inventory. Therefore, the monetary authorities of an Islamic state must know that in a growing economy there is always a point where there is scope for using deficit financing (i.e. money expansion through loans mainly from banks) even when the objective is price stability. Where exactly that point lies is, of course, a matter of practical judgment. The question of this arises out of the expansion in output and the rise in monetary requirements per unit of output owing to decreasing income velocity and increasing monetization, which are the normal features of a developing economy. While handling this problem of deficit financing another important factor which should be kept in view is that interest on loans will not be allowed to exercise its adverse effects on production, distribution and employment.

Secondly, if a rise in price is due to an inadequate increase in productivity resulting either from seasonal or cyclical or other factors, much can be done by an Islamic state to prevent the price rise either by changing fiscal or monetary policies, or by rationing essential consumer goods and by licensing new investments. The concern for the welfare of the people is the guiding principle of an Islamic state.

This brings us to a discussion of the role of the Islamic state in regard to rises in price resulting from increasing development activity. In a growing economy where major development programmes, implying a shift of resources away from traditional production techniques and activity, have been undertaken, prices increase partly because of the existing socio-economic institutions running on the traditional pattern, partly because of the country's dependence mainly on an agricultural type of economy where rapid adjustments are not possible as in industry, and partly because of growing uncertainties of foreign aid and loans, the cumulative effects of which put on pressure which monetary authorities find it difficult to overcome. In my view, whether this price increase will be approved by an Islamic state or not depends on the type of objectives a country wants to achieve through the implementation of development programmes. If the development activities of a country bring fortunes only to a few privileged persons to the neglect of the vast masses of the people, we are not prepared to accept that type of development in an Islamic state whatever justification it may have. Even price rises which are inevitable due to development may be justified if the development is for the people. An Islamic state must see that everybody gets his due. The *Qur'ān* directs that the kindred, the needy and the wayfarer must be paid their due (*Sūrah* XXX. 38), and, there is emphatic and repeated exhortation of this in the *Qur'ān*. Such giving should be in proportion to the need of the person to be helped and in accord with the means of the giver, and should not proceed from any expectation of receiving a return (*Sūrah* XVII. 29), (*Sūrah* XLVII. 37).

It is indeed the highest bounty of God that He should have endowed man with appropriate faculties and capacities and then subjected the universe to the beneficent service of man to enable him to achieve the fullest development of his faculties in every sphere of life. Therefore, an Islamic state must use Islam as a factor of development so that people are inspired to put their faculties to beneficent use in the service of their fellow-beings. If people motivated by this spirit carry on development activities which result in a price increase, we are prepared to accept such a situation in an Islamic state.

Lastly, let us talk of fiscal measures like taxes on manufactured goods, which may contribute to rises in price. In an Islamic state there is always room for additional taxation. The principle is that, while imposing taxes on goods and services, their impact and incidence on the poor and the needy must be kept in view. The excessive concern for raising revenue through indirect taxes cannot be supported because indirect taxes are generally imposed on the necessities of life and poor people are likely to be hard hit.

(c) Artificial Rises in Price.

The artificial scarcity of goods created by unscrupulous business men resulting in rises in price is due to (*i*) speculative business, (*ii*) hoarding, (*iii*) black marketing and smuggling. Both the Holy *Qur'ān* and the *Sunnah* have emphatically condemned all these activities. Speculation, which implies buying a commodity with a view to selling it at a higher price in future, results in an increase in price. Islam has severely condemned this type of artificial rise in price, because in actual life we generally find illegitimate speculation, for perfect speculation tends to destroy itself. If speculators are perfectly wise, they will make a correct forecast of future changes in prices, and as a result of their action these price fluctuations will be eliminated altogether, so in the end prices would cease to fluctuate. Unscrupulous business men will not tolerate this situation under the capitalist frame of society. They will deliberately create a false opinions as to the general conditions of demand and supply. Islam is not prepared to accept this unrestricted, speculative activity resulting in rises in price. Ma'mar reported the Prophet (peace be upon him) said: "He who accumulates stocks of grain during shortage of it (with a view to profiteering later), is a great sinner." (Muslim and *Mishkāt*). Again, it is related on the authority of Jābir who reported that the Messenger of Allah (peace be upon him) said: "May Allah have mercy on the man who is generous when he buys and when he sells and when he demands (his due)" (Bukhārī).

Apart from the speculative rise in prices in actual life, many traders and business men, instead of putting their faculties to beneficent use in the service of their fellow-beings, have a tendency to hoarding and black marketing, not realizing that even from a purely selfish point of view the greatest benefit is to be derived from free and fair dealings, not from the apparent rise in price due to hoarding. The Holy *Qur'ān* declares that there is a grievous punishment in store for those who encourage hoarding. Thus Allah commands:

"And there are those
Who bury gold and silver
And spend it not in the Way
Of God: announce unto them
A most grievous penalty"

(*Sūrah* IX. 34)

The principle is that one must not hoard just to derive a temporary benefit out of a higher price. Holding back actually renders a person progressively poorer in the true sense inasmuch as he stultifies his faculties, and by putting that which he possesses out of human consumption in the time of need deprives the community of its proper and legitimate use.

To my mind, the Islamic state is quite competent, as a last resort, to deprive speculative and anti-social business firms of ownership. The government of the Islamic state is quite justified in taking drastic measures against hoarding, smuggling and profiteering in order to check undue rises in price. When hoarded stocks are brought into the open indicating a fall in prices as a result of the deliberate policy of the state, it must make arrangements for the production of a replenished stock of hoarded goods.

It is not out of place to mention here that another cause for artificial increase in price lies in the unrestricted earning and spending inherent in the capitalist system. The result is social chaos. Thus wealthy people indulge in "conspicuous waste" motivated by a false sense of prestige and dignity. This conspicuous waste is bound to create the problem of scarcity of specific goods resulting in a rise in prices. Islam is very critical of this type of expenditure. The Holy Qur'ān says:

". . . eat and drink
But waste not by excess,
For God loveth not the wasters."

(*Surah* VII. 31)

Another significant verse is:

"Those who, when they spend,
Are not extravagant and not
Niggardly, but hold a just (balance)
Between those extremes."

(*Sūrah* XXV. 67)

Therefore, an Islamic state is morally bound to control the "conspicuous waste" of the rich, lest it should undermine morals and paralyze lawful economic activities and increase the miseries of the poor. Thus while discouraging the "conspicuous waste" of the rich, Islam does not favour the idea of self-denying practices by which a man deprives himself of certain kinds of lawful goods. The *Qur'ān* says:

"O ye who believe? Make not unlawful
The good things which God
Hath made lawful for you,
But commit no excess

(*Sūrah* V. 90)

(d) Rises in Prices of the Necessities of Life

A religion which regulates and controls even our menu with a view to making us pure cannot ignore the rise in price of foodgrains. Great stress is laid on the sale of cereals, because they are the prime need of the common man. They should, therefore, be sold in the market so that they may be had at the price which the producer obtained. The question of speculation in this prime need of every man—rich or poor—is totally ruled out in Islam. Ibn 'Umar reported: "They used to buy cereals from the camel-owners in the time of the Prophet (peace be upon him) and be used to forbid them selling it where they purchased it, until it was brought to the place where cereals were sold (Bukhārī)" We have already seen that the withholding of cereals to raise their price artificially is condemned.

8.5 Suggestions and Conclusion

Taken all in all, we must say that the Islamic theory of prices precludes any type of exploitation either from the producer's side or from the consumer's side. In a mixed economy like Pakistan's, producers are more or less organized, but consumers are not. Hence the necessity of educating them under state patronage and control with a view to harmonizing the dictates of Islamic social justice with the demand of producers' incentive. However, to keep the price level of the basic necessities of life within the reach of common man and the workers, an Islamic state must take a number of policy decisions which may include some short-term measures like: (a) the procurement of some cash and non-cash crops by the state so that farmers get the due price of their produce, (b) the rationing of food-grains and supply of subsidized essential consumer goods, (c) the holding of seminars/discussions between producers and consumers under state patronage with the clear objective of imbuing them with an Islamic code of transactions, and long-term measures like (a) the setting up of a high-powered fair price authority (I do not like to suggest the term "price control" from the producer's viewpoint) consisting of representatives of producers, consumers, government experts and Islamic jurists, (b) the creation of a network of consumers' co-operatives throughout the country under state patronage on a no-profit-no-loss basis, (c) comprehensive consumption planning within the framework of state planning. Needless to mention that none of these measures is, to the best of my knowledge, against the injunctions of Islam.

Lastly, I submit that the big question that awaits solution by an Islamic state is the derivation of a foolproof institutional arrangement based on Islamic principles which will automatically take care of all the economic ills of society. Any one injunction working in isolation will, I am sure, produce a lopsided state of affairs, as is the case now in almost all Muslim countries.

8.6 Selected Further Reading

Khan, M. A. "Inflation and Islamic Economy: A Closed Economy Model" in *Monetary and Fiscal Economics of Islam*, ed. by M. Ariff, International Centre for Research in Islamic Economics, (I.C.R.I.E.), King Abdulaziz University, Jeddah, Saudi Arabia, 1982.

Laliwala, Jaferhusen. I. "Inflation in an Islamic Economy" in *Monetary and Fiscal Economics of Islam*, L.I,C.R.I.E., ed. by M. Ariff, King Abdulaziz University, Jeddah, Saudi Arabia, 1982.

Majid, Abdul, "Islam, Christianity and Monopoly" in *Islamic Review*, London, 1940.

Mannan, M. A. *Islamic Perspectives on Market Prices and Allocation*, I.C.R.I.E., King Abdulaziz University, Jeddah, 1982.

Mannan, M. A. "Islamic Perspectives on Market Imperfections." in *The Making of Islamic Economic Society: Islamic Dimensions in Economic Analysis*, Chapter 10 (forthcoming).

Mannan, M. A. "The Behaviour of the Firm and its Objectives in an Islamic Framework", in *The Making of Islamic Economic Society: Islamic Dimensions in Economic Analysis*, Chapter 10 (forthcoming).

Wickers, G. M. "Al-Jarsifi on the Hisba" in *Islamic Quarterly*, London, 1956–57.

CHAPTER 9

Towards a Theory of Interest-Free Banking in Islam

9.1 Introduction: The Concept of Money and Banking.

    The Concept of Money and its Role.
    Money as a Medium of Non-Exchange.
    The Concept of Islamic Banking.

9.2 Usury, Interest and Islam.

9.3 Classical and Keynesian Views on Interest.

9.4 The Theory of *Zakāt*.

9.5 The Principles of *Mudārabah*, *Murābaha*, *Mushāraka*.

9.6 The Mechanism of Islamic Banking.

9.7 Short-term and Long-term Financing.

9.8 A System of Guarantee.

9.9 Islamic Banks and Consumption Loans.

9.10 Relations with Depositors.

9.11 Relations with Entrepreneurs.

9.12 The Practicability of Partnership between Business Men and Banks.

9.13 The Superiority of the Islamic Concept of Banking.

9.14 Islamic Banks and Non-Banking Services

9.15 Islamic Banks and Extra-Banking Activities.

9.16 Islamic Banks and International Relations.

9.17 *Bait-ul-Māl* and Modern Central Banks.

9.18 Summary and Conclusions.

9.19 Selected Further Reading.

APPENDIX:

A Case for the Establishment of a Muslim World Bank.

"Trade is like usury. But God hath permitted trade and forbidden usury; God will deprive usury of all blessings, but will give increase for deeds of charity."

al-Qur'ān, (*Sūrah* II. 275–276)

". . . I mean the doctrine that the rate of interest is not self-adjusting at a level best suited to the social advantage but constantly tends to rise too high, so that a wise government is concerned to curb it by statute and custom and even by invoking the sanction of the moral law."

Lord Keynes, *The General Theory of Employment, Interest and Money*

9.1 Introduction: The Concept of Money and Banking

Imbued with the ideas of Western civilization many a Muslim scholar has started finding serious weaknesses in our religious injunctions. It is a blunder on the part of any person to think that Islam is merely a religion, and that its principles are out of tune with the modern world. In fact, Islam is not a religion; it is a social system, a composite code, a civilization of which religion is a part. But the fundamental principles of Islam are challenged by different schools of thought like capitalism, communism, etc. As followers of Islam, Muslims have to face the situation with the reasons and arguments of their faith in keeping with the intellectual standards of the modern world. Here an attempt is being made to point out the differences between the Islamic and capitalist concepts of modern banking and to see if the former has anything better to offer than the latter.

At this stage it is perhaps desirable to throw some light on the concept of money, and banking in Islam.

The Concept of Money and Its Role

In Islam money is viewed as a medium of exchange, not a commodity. The widespread acceptance of this role of money is intended to eliminate the possibilities of injustice, unfairness and exploitation under the barter economy. Since injustices under the barter economy can, among others be classified as "*Ribā-al-Fazal*", which is prohibited in Islam, the role of money as a medium of exchange is justified. Therefore, in Islam money does not in itself produce anything. As such interest (*Ribā*) on money-lending and borrowing is prohibited.

Once the role of money as a medium of exchange is recognized, money can play its role as a unit of account and as a store of value in an Islamic economy. It can very well serve as a measure of opportunity cost (i.e. foregone income).

At a theoretical level, the abolition of interest and the imposition of a 2.5 per cent annual *Zakāt* levy on idle money are most likely to discourage speculative motives for holding cash, thereby contributing stability to the value of money. This is not to suggest that the stability of money depends only on the abolition of interest and the imposition of *Zakāt*. It depends on other endogenous factors such as the level of business activity, the level of expected profit, the commercial banks' ability to respond to economic incentives as well as exogenous factors such as the control of the central bank. Nevertheless, the absence of interest and the presence of a *Zakāt* levy puts an Islamic economy in a better position to handle the problem of unfair speculation and the hoarding of money, thereby enabling money to perform its other derivative functions in a relatively easier way. This does not mean that an Islamic economy does not need a sound monetary policy, because there is still a controversy as to whether central banks should have the sole authority of money creation in an Islamic economy, or whether commercial banks should also be allowed to create money by credit.

Money as a Medium of Non-Exchange.

In an Islamic economy money has a special social and religious role to play, because it provides the best measure for channelling purchasing power in the form of transfer payments to the poor. The transfer payments have special religious significance in an Islamic economy, because in Islam they are not merely a voluntary obligation on the part of Muslims but also a compulsory obligation, particularly in respect of the payment of *Zakāt* by the rich to the poor. The religious significance of the role of money lies in the fact that it enables us to calculate '*Niṣāb*' and to assess *exactly* the rates of *Zakāt*. Under a money economy, it is relatively easy to assess one's exact contribution in respect of one's intrafamily and community obligations, particularly where there is no end-product available for bartering. The point is that a scale of Islamically justified ways of channelling transfer payments can be laid down more effectively under a money economy. That is, money would enable each individual or community to determine a scale of preference so that those who are most deserving are near the top of the scale.

Money also performs another social function by containing or resisting the open exploitation implicit in any situation of endless haggling. Without money we should have to show all the relative values of goods and services available for scale.

If there are 100 commodities on the market, this would entail 4950 rates of exchange. That is, nearly 5000 rates of exchange would have to be borne in mind, as is shown below:

$$\frac{n(n-1)}{2} = \frac{100\,(99)}{2} = 4950.$$

(Where n = number of commodities available in the market.)

Today there are not hundreds but thousands of commodities from which to choose in a modern supermarket. The use of money simplifies the procedure of settling terms, reduces the chances of exploitation in settling the terms of exchange in favour of the strong and the rich, in addition to eliminating the problem of double coincidence of wants.

Thus we see that when money performs its social and religious functions, essentially it acts as a medium of non-exchange.

It may, however, be asked what is "Islamic" about this non-exchange function of money, because in every society, money can perform this function. Although this phenomenon of non-exchange, either as a fact or as a possibility, does exist both in capitalist and traditional societies, the distinctiveness of the Islamic non-exchange phenomenon lies in the fact that it is seen as a part of "religious" duty. It is neither secularized nor is it "socialized" because in most western societies this phenomenon of non-exchange is seen as an attempt to escape the secular taxes. Most philanthropic and charitable organizations in the west do enjoy benefits of tax-exemption in varying degrees. Therefore non-exchange is secularized in a way. Again the exchange of gifts in most traditional societies, such as the Melanesian societies of the South Pacific, is viewed as an attempt to strengthen, the social bonds among kinship groups or tribes and is rooted very much in the principle of social reciprocity. This non-exchange phenomenon is then essentially a social affair. Thus it becomes clear that the social and religious function performed by money in an Islamic economy has a distinct character.

The Concept of Islamic Banking

Let me now say a few words on the concept of Islamic banking, which owes its origin to the Islamic concept of money. As noted earlier, in Islam money does not in itself produce interest or profit and is not viewed as a commodity. We have already seen that *Ribā'* (i.e. interest) is prohibited. The status of the Islamic bank in relation to its clients is that of partner, investor and trader, whereas in commercial banks in the West, the relationship is that of creditor or debtor.

In their actual operations Islamic banks use various techniques and methods of investment such as *Muḍārabah* contracts, under which a financier provides capital and the *Muḍāreb* (labour partner) provides his technical know-how and skill and the profit is shared between the partners according to an agreed percentage. Islamic banks are also involved in *Murābaha* (cost plus) contracts, under which banks purchase a certain commodity according to its clients' specifications and give delivery on the basis of sharing an agreed ratio of profit. Islamic banks are also involved in dealing with foreign exchange markets and other banking service operations such as letters of credit, and letters of guarantee. Islamic banks may also provide various non-banking services such as trust business, real estate, and consultancy services. The concept of Islamic banks and their operational techniques will be discussed in more detail later in this chapter and in Chapter 10.

9.2 Usury, Interest and Islam

The *Qur'ān* and the *Sunnah*—the two fundamental sources of Islamic Law—strictly forbid interest for its tyranny (*Sūrahs* LXXIII and II). Even some learned Muslims, blinded by the superficial charm of European civilization, say that what Islam prohibits is usury and not interest. They opine that interest paid on loans for investment in productive activities would not contravene the law of the *Qur'ān* for it refers only to usury on non-productive loans which prevailed in pre-Islamic times when people were not familiar with productive loans and their influence on economic development. In this the propounders of the theory of interest would appear to have overlooked that the *Qur'ān*, the last of the divine messages for human guidance, legislated for all ages, and that God's knowledge as embodied in it could not be substituted by the economic practice of interest on productive loans known to this or any other age. In fact, the difference between productive and so-called unproductive loans is a difference of degree, not of kind. Calling usury or *Ribā* by the name of "interest" will not change its character since interest is nothing but an addition to the borrowed capital, which is usury in both spirit and in the Islamic code of law. Again, *The Concise Oxford Dictionary* defines usury as follows: "Practice of lending money at exorbitant interest esp. at higher interest than is allowed by law." The same sentiment is also expressed by *Chambers Dictionary*.

But what is an exorbitant rate of interest? What is a reasonable rate of interest today will be an exorbitant rate of interest tomorrow. Again, what is reasonable to one country may be unreasonable to another country. In the nineteen-twenties many co-operative societies had been charging from twelve per cent to fifteen per cent interest and at that time it was considered reasonable. But today it is considered to be most excessive and exorbitant. Even the eight and a half per cent rate of interest which was considered by an expert body like the Financial Committee of the late League of Nations as reasonable is no longer relevant today. Moreover, even today there are instances where in some countries the legal rate of interest in one leading institution is exorbitant compared to the legal rate of interest of another institution in the same area for a similar type of loans. In the U.S.A., for example, during the nineteen-fifties and sixties a bank could not charge more than eight per cent as interest whereas a finance company could charge thirty per cent to thirty-six per cent rate of interest per annum for a similar loan. Again, for a personal loan a private money-lender charges twenty-four per cent to a hundred per cent per annum, and it is still not against the law.

As a matter of fact, there is no difference between interest and usury or *Ribā*. Islam definitely prohibits all forms of interest whatever high-sounding and persuasive names we may give them. But in our capitalist economy interest is the centre round which the banking system revolves. Without interest, it is argued, the banking system will become lifeless and the whole economy will be paralyzed. But Islam is a dynamic and progressive force, and it is quite possible to prove that the Islamic concept of an interest-free banking system is superior to modern banking. At this stage an attempt may be made to establish that the rate of interest has nothing to do with influencing the volume of saving. In this connection the classical and Keynesian views on interest may be recorded.

9.3 Classical and Keynesian Views on Interest

Classical economists like Alfred Marshall are of the opinion that the rate of interest and savings are interlinked. Since the rate of interest is one of the most important factors which govern the volume of savings, the higher the rate of interest, the larger the reward for saving, the higher the propensity to save and *vice versa*. Thus according to them any increase in the volume of saving means an increase in investment, which results in development of trade, commerce and industry.

The classical analysis is refuted by a world-famous capitalist economist, Lord Keynes. Keynes has cast serious doubt on the efficacy of the rate of interest in influencing the volume of saving. He boldly declares that the volume of savings, to all intents and purposes, depends on the volume of investment. A high rate of interest will damp down the volume of investment made by the business public. As a result, trade, commerce and industry as a whole will be adversely affected. Owing to this direct blow on the economic system the aggregate money income will shrink. But we are fully aware of the fact that savings depend on the level of the money incomes of the people. As the *per capita* income of people shrinks, automatically the volume of savings will be reduced.

Though Keynes, being the victim of his environment, regards three per cent as a reasonable rate of interest, yet in the middle of his famous book, *The General Theory of Employment, Interest and Money*, writing under the heading "Observations on Nature of Capital," he clearly admits the Islamic concept of banking and asks the people to earn money by enterprise. "A properly run community," observes Lord Keynes, "equipped with modern technical resources, of which the population is not increasing rapidly, ought to be able to bring down the marginal efficiency of capital to zero, within a single generation, so that we should attain the condition of a quasi-stationary community where change and progress would result only from changes in technique, taste, population and institutions with the products of capital selling at a price proportioned on just the same principles as govern the prices of consumption goods in which capital charges enter in an insignificant degree."

Keynes is fully conscious of the drawbacks of capitalism which can be got rid of if interest is abolished. Thus he said, "If I am right in supposing the capital goods so abundant that marginal efficiency of capital is zero, this may be the most sensible way of getting rid of many of the objectionable features of capitalism." In this connection, it is interesting to note that Crowther, in his book, *An Outline of Money* (1958 edn.) observed: "a gradual and imperceptible fall in the value of money is necessary to enable the world to slip out of its self-imposed claims of usury" (p. 98). He attributes the rise of prices in every succeeding century to this fall in the value of money, which is necessary "to keep the steadily mounting money from becoming a burden" (p. 178).

In fact, it has been found by modern research that, as Keynes suggested, interest has nothing to do with influencing the volume of saving. Practically, it is the rate of investment that determines the rate of saving. Islam prohibits interest but encourages investment. Here, one may argue that if no interest is paid on deposits, then the people may be tempted to keep their deposits idle and in hoarded form. It is here, we think, that *Zakāt* plays a very significant role. Islam penalizes those who keep their money idle.

9.4 The Theory of *Zakāt*

Zakāt is the strong blow at the root of capitalism. Unfortunately, *Zakāt* has been widely misunderstood. Some have taken it to be a voluntary private charity, whereas it is a compulsory tax on savings and property, at a rate varying from two and a half per cent to twenty per cent. Here I should not like to discuss the question of whether it is right in modern times that the categories of property defined in the early days of Islam on which *Zakāt* was imposed should be accepted as final and relevant. But the jurists are agreed that where *Zakāt* is due, and is not paid, enforcement measures can be taken against the defaulters. The history of Islam records many incidents where the state took severe steps to enforce payment of *Zakāt* as we find in the case of Caliph Abū Bakr al-Siddīq, the first Caliph of Islam.

    Zakāt is the uncompromising enemy of hoarding. It checks the tendency to hoard idle cash resources and provides a powerful stimulus for investing these idle stocks. This stimulus gets momentum from the fact that Islam allows profits and sleeping partnerships in which profits as well as loss are shared.

9.5 The Principles of *Muḍārabah*, *Murābaḥa*, and *Mushāraka*

Islamic banking will be based on the universally recognized principles of *Shirākah* (partnership). That is, the whole system of banking in which the shareholders, the depositors, the investors and the borrowers will participate on a partnership basis. This will, we are sure, work through the application of the eternal principle of *Muḍārabah*, where labour and capital can be combined together as partners for work. This is not merely a partnership in the modern sense of the term. It is something more than this, because Islam has provided a code of economic ethics combining the material and spiritual values for the conduct of its economic system. This code of economic ethics, has to be reflected when the principle of *Muḍārabah* is put into practice. The Islamic banking system can help establish certain institutions on the basis of *Muḍārabah* and thereby solve the age-old conflict between labour and capital. Industrial, commercial and agricultural enterprises can be worked out on the principle of *Muḍārabah* combining the various units of production. The income resulting from such enterprises can be shared proportionately among the various units of production after deducting all the legitimate expenses of the entrepreneurs during the year.

    It is indeed gratifying to note that Islamic-banks are actually involved in dealing with *Muḍarabah* contracts, under which banks provide the capital and the clients their expertise and the profits are shared according to an agreed ratio. It has been suggested that the *Muḍārabah* principle can be invoked in the case of self-liquidating short-term operations, and as a result the demand for short-term loans can be reduced substantially, because in an Islamic economy short-term loans on interest from the traditional commercial banks or discount houses will be not available.

Under *Murābaha* operations, the clients ask the banks to purchase a certain commodity according to certain specifications and require the bank to deliver them on the basis of a certain mark-up according to the initial agreement between the two parties.

Under *Mushāraka*, both the banks and the clients enter into partnership by contributing capital in varying degrees and agree upon a ratio of profit in advance for a *limited period of time*.

We shall discuss these principles in more detail in Chapter 10.

9.6 The Mechanism of Islamic Banking

The mechanism of Islamic banking, which is based on the principle of partnership, is free of interest. Therefore, the question of paying interest to depositors or charging any interest from clients does not arise.

Under the Islamic scheme of banking, there may be two types of depositors. The first type of depositors, who can deposit their surplus funds, may be allowed to withdraw their funds at any time without any notice. This type of deposit is for safe-depositing only, not for investment in any productive activity where risk is involved. In the case of such deposits, the bank may recover *Zakāt* and service charges from Muslim and non-Muslim depositors respectively. This taxation on idle funds is justified, because it checks the tendency to hoard cash in idle form and provides a stimulus for investing in productive activities.

The second type of depositors will not be in a position to withdraw their funds without notice. Their surplus funds may be invested in productive affairs on a short-term basis. The bank will not charge anything from these depositors; rather, they will be allowed to share the profit or loss of the bank proportionately at the end of the financial year in a form similar to that of dividends. The Islamic bank, however, can raise funds, if need be, by inviting investment for a period from one year to five years or more. Even in Western countries some of the banks issue investment certificates or investment bonds on a fixed rate of interest. But in an Islamic state these investment certificate-holders will be eligible to share the profits of the bank proportionately in the form of dividends which may be worked out at the end of the financial year. Obviously, the Islamic bank cannot issue debentures for fund-raising, as it involves the paying of a fixed rate of interest.

9.7 Short term and Long-term Financing

The short-term financing of industry, trade and agriculture can be made by the Islamic bank on a partnership basis. In this respect, the Islamic bank makes itself directly liable both to those who keep their funds with it and to those who borrow funds from it. An even more important function of the Islamic commercial bank is that it can create credit. Islam has prohibited the charging of usury or interest. This does not mean that Islam does not allow the financing of trade or industry on credit. Though there is a tendency for the banks to expand credit far beyond the limits of their reserves at times of prosperity and *vice versa*, yet business management contract allowed under the Islamic code will be able to check the factors that shake economic stability and set successive economic crises in motion.

Loans provided by ordinary deposit banks are often given on a short-term basis not exceeding two years. Since most of their borrowed funds are payable on demand or at short notice, they dare not lock them up in long-term loans and investments. This type of bank has a special liquidity problem which governs its choice of investments. Thus assets should not be chosen merely according to the principles of profitability and security. Even more important is the timing of the liquidity of the assets with respect to the time structure of the liabilities. Therefore, it is recommended that specialized credit institutions like industrial or agricultural development banks and the like may be developed for long-term financing of trade, industry or agriculture, as the case may be, on a partnership basis. The bank and the other party may work out the ratio of the profit and loss based on the amount of funds and on the length of period advanced in accordance with local practice and the Islamic code.

9.8 A System of Guarantee

Probably, an Islamic bank can evolve a system of guarantee of loans for industries, for working capital as well as for equipment. This guarantee may induce private capital to move into Muslim countries, because the flow of private capital in Muslim countries has always been inadequate in relation to the trends towards external assistance. The bank's guarantee may help the industrialists of small scale industries in providing tools and equipment. The foreign exchange thus saved, however small in amount it may be, may be directed to other productive purposes. It is only in the development of small-scale industry that private initiative and enterprise can find full scope for development and the economic base of democracy is thereby strengthened, because it creates opportunities for employment for both unemployed and underemployed in an economy like Pakistan's. In the absence of any growth of cottage and small-scale industries in rural and semi-urban areas, the agricultural economy of Muslim countries cannot offer employment to their labour force throughout the year. Therefore, there should not be two opinions on the question of financing development projects on a large dimension in the dynamic setting of the growth of Muslim countries. Now as to the question of ways and means it is a matter of detail and may be examined in the light of rapidly changing circumstances.

9.9 Islamic Banks and Consumption Loans

The requirements of daily life are becoming more and more complex. Therefore, the importance of consumption loans for the genuine requirements of individuals can hardly be over-estimated. Consumption loans are more or less unproductive in nature, though their influence on the productivity of the community has indirect bearing in so far as it stimulates production and supply. But as they do not produce any direct income, therefore, it may not be possible for Islamic banks to lend money for such loans on a partnership basis. It is recommended that such loans be made either by people's co-operative societies or by some government credit agency. Loans must, of course, be granted against a deposit or evidence of fixed assets owned by the borrowers. The establishment charges of these banks will be borne by the state like the charges of hospitals, orphanages and other public utility institutions. So in the Islamic social set-up the state is forced to tax all deposits and credit balances to meet its charges. People will not find it difficult to bear this burden of taxation since, on account of free service, trade, commerce and industry will flourish. As a result, economic resources will be exploited, the problem of unemployment will be solved and the national income will increase in an Islamic state.

It is interesting to note that a peculiar kind of loan existed—and still does exist in all the Muslim countries—which was called *Qarḍ-i-Ḥasanah*—a loan without interest. A debtor had to clear all his debts before his death, otherwise he would be a sinner. The lender, in some cases, not to subject his fellow-men to this sin, would advance "*Qarḍ-i-Ḥasanah*" the repayment of which was not imperative.

9.10 Relations with Depositors

Depositors as a whole, and not as individuals, shall be deemed to be the capitalist and the bank the absolute operator in the sense that it will be entitled to appoint agents for the investment of its deposit money. Some of these investments may achieve great success, others turn out to be moderately successful, and others, of course, prove a failure. It follows that in allotting funds the banks have to judge whether the particular type of trade or industry would be worth taking on or not, and can judge their customers and thereby provide a check on expansion of those types of trades and industries which are likely to be uneconomic in the long run and undesirable from the social point of view or involve too much risk which cannot be calculated with reasonable accuracy. The Islamic bank, by putting a check on undesirable investment, can render and does render a great service in fostering economic development on the most sure and sound lines. The need for this direction of investment arises from the fact that in all Muslim countries resources are very limited compared to the need for carrying out vast development programmes.

9.11 Relations with Entrepreneurs

Islamic banks in each financial year would compile a balance sheet of all profits and losses, and the ultimate balance remaining after the banks' general expenses are met, including salaries, wages and reserves, will be shared between the banks and the depositors in line with the relevant agreements. The banks' own share will then be distributed to the shareholders in proportion to their respective shares. In a recent article the Egyptian scholar, Dr M. A. al-'Arabī, has rightly pointed out:

"A bank in relation to depositors has been considered the operator or business manager, and the depositors deemed as capitalists. In relation to the entrepreneurs, however, the bank will be taken to be the capitalist and the latter the operators. In this case the conditions governing the rights and obligations of the capitalists and operators shall apply. Any profits realised by the entrepreneur—the operator in this case—shall be shared with the bank as capitalist, in the agreed proportions." (*The Pakistan Times*, 30 December 1966).

However, "If no profit or loss is suffered, the capital shall be restored to the bank intact, but in the case of a losing business, the loss shall be exclusively borne by the bank; should an entrepreneur (operator) be guilty of detrimental acts that damaged part of the capital, he shall be held responsible for damages."

Apart from this basic need for the direction of investment, banks must be aware of the fact that real security for the deposits is the quality of the advances and adequate liquidity. If the quality of the advances is high and liquidity is adequate, augmentation of capital structure would have little significance except perhaps in terms of advances which, I am afraid, are not yet a feature of banking in Muslim countries. In an Islamic banking system we find a fusion between investment, experience and financial experience. The greatest advantage which we can reasonably expect from harmony between the investment experience of the investors and the financial experience of the bank is the maximum guarantee for sounder investment through the best possible utilization of the limited resources the Muslim countries have.

9.12 The Practicability of Partnership between Businessmen and Banks

It may be argued that business men might refuse to take the bank as a partner in an interest-free loan system. As an Islamic economy is the fusion of capitalism and socialism, small business men, who do not want any loan from the bank for carrying out their internal or interregional trade, might be left free and they might not be allowed to become partners with the bank. But in the case of international trade and commerce, business men cannot refuse to take banks as partners, because comprehensive economic planning for the exploitation of economic resources is allowed under Islamic socialism and the entire commercial policy, which influences both exports and imports, will be dictated and guided by the state. No doubt, under the Islamic scheme of society, there is not much room for the capitalist trinity—the sovereignty of the consumer, the tyranny of the price system, and the quest for huge profits. Here, the economic architects generally would determine what use is to be made of limited resources and, therefore, to some extent impair the sovereignty of consumers. So the question of investing money in a joint-stock company by depositors directly instead of depositing money in the bank does not arise at all. The Islamic economy is a good substitute for that allocation of economic resources, which in a capitalist system is determined by prices and incomes, and related in turn to consumers' sovereignty and decisions made by innumerable business men who are responsible for either overproduction or underproduction. In these circumstances, business men would be tempted to co-operate with the banks to get the free banking services and to reap the benefits of the keen business outlook and financial experience of the banks. So the practicability and feasibility of partnership between business men and banks can hardly be challenged.

It is interesting to note that in the semi-socialist environment of the United Arab Republic, an experiment in interest-free banking was launched on a modest scale which has now flowered into a flourishing institution. The first bank (with 1000 savings depositors) was opened on 25 July 1963 in the town of Mit-Ghamr, with a population of 40,000, the centre of a province of another 200,000 people living in fifty-three villages along the Nile, about half-way between Cairo and the sea.

This scheme of interest-free banking is aimed at effecting a massive change in the fundamental attitude of villages in the heart of the Nile Delta towards saving and investment. The instrument of change is an ingenious savings bank project and the goal is to begin industrialization of the villages without state interference. Dr Ahmed El Naggar was the head of the project. "Deposits of such banks are of three kinds: (*a*) Savings accounts are opened with a minimum deposit of five piasters. The sum is withdrawable on demand and does not yield interest. (*b*) A social service fund is composed of charitable gifts held as trust by the bank. These are used as disaster insurance for savings depositors. (*c*) Investment accounts are opened with a minimum deposit of one Egyptian pound. The deposits are withdrawable once a year and yield the depositor a share in bank profits according to the size and terms of the deposit.

To date, the bank has not had one loan not repaid in good time. Dr El Naggar attributes this record to the community pressures built into the operations of the banks. By continually emphasizing that the banks belong to the people, and by building representation of the local people into bank management, the project creates a climate in which the people can exercise their own social controls over anyone who tries to cheat or harm the banks. This social control is practicable because exploitation in

Egypt is curbed and individual profit is subordinated to the collective good.

9.13 The Superiority of the Islamic Concept of Banking

The fact that modern banks are the creditors of industry adversely affects the economic health of the country. Naturally banks place their own interests above the interests of industry as they have no real share in them. It may be argued that modern banks collect idle savings and channel them for productive purposes for a low rate of interest and thereby offer a great service to humanity. So one may say that there is nothing wrong in the working of a modern bank in an Islamic polity. But, unfortunately, modern banks think only in terms of their own interests as they are guided by the profit-hunting motive. Business men who take loans from the bank will be sued civilly and prosecuted criminally if they fail to pay interest even by incurring loss in their business. So the banks of our capitalist economy encourage unhealthy investment during booms and depression is the logical outcome of unhealthy investment. Consequently, depression will be chronic. But banks in an Islamic state, being partners in industry, can never encourage unhealthy investment. So there is much less possibility of depression under an Islamic system. If depression takes place owing to some other reason, Islamic banks are in a better position to face the situation than the capitalistic banks because the fixed rate of interest which retards recovery from depression will not be allowed to exercise its tyrannical influence during the period of depression.

Banks being partners will share the loss and profit. But one point to be noted here is that there is little chance of loss in the Islamic system. For healthy investment, "keen business outlook and experience of the management of funds" will come in contact with industry. As a result of the happy marriage between finance and industry, the onward march of economic progress will continue. Industry will flourish and national income will increase. In his book *Islam and the Theory of Interest*, the same sentiment is expressed by Dr A.I. Qureshi, when he writes: "It must be borne in mind that if the country is to develop industrially, the finance must be made to co-operate wholeheartedly on an equal basis with industry. It must be on the basis of partnership with industry and not on mere payment of fixed interest. If the financier is a partner in industry his keen business outlook and experience of the management of funds is likely to stand in good stead and would lead to a better development of the industry."

Again, by maintaining the system of interest the modern bank is aggravating indirectly the problem of unemployment. A little reflection will enable us to understand this point. The capitalist or the businessman will be reluctant to invest when the rate of return from investment is less than the current rate of interest. For instance, if the current rate of interest is four per cent and money is invested, say, in irrigation works which indirectly yield only three per cent, then, according to the capitalist view, irrigation is unproductive. Money will not, therefore, be invested in irrigation works, however useful these may be for society. The result is that the resources will remain unexploited. Consequently, the avenues of employment will be smaller. Thus Keynes clearly admits that the rate of interest plays a peculiar part in setting a unit to the level of employment, since the marginal efficiency of capital itself is pulled down by the rate of interest. "The money rate of interest," he writes, "by setting the pace for all other commodity rates of interest, holds back investment in the production of these other commodities without being capable of stimulating investment for the production of money, which by hypothesis cannot be produced." Again, Lawrence R. Klein, in his book, *The Keynesian Revolution* (1950 edn.), even doubts the existence of a positive rate of interest at the full employment stage in the following words:

"A loanable-funds theory of interest should imply that regardless of the levels of other variables influencing savings and investment there should always exist a rate of interest which will equate savings and investment. The Keynesian theory shows that there do exist levels of other variables, namely, full employment, such that no positive rate will equate savings and investment."

But in the Islamic concept of banking there is no predetermined notion of fixed interest, so it is expected that resources will be exploited to the best possible extent to cure unemployment.

Thus when Islam encourages partnership, it has allowed profit. Then what justification is there for not allowing interest on business loans? We should bear in mind that if there is any difference between shareholders and bondholders in a joint-stock company, there is certainly a fundamental difference between profit and interest. This needs no further elaboration.

Islam prohibits interest because interest has nothing to do with influencing the volume of saving because it makes depression chronic, because it aggravates the problem of unemployment, and finally, because it encourages unequal distribution of wealth. The modern banks charge interest regardless of any loss or profit to business men. It would, therefore, be seen that under a capitalist economy an organized attempt is being made to further the interests of the rich, thereby eliminating the possibility of establishing economic equilibrium in society. As against this Islam has tried to bring about economic equality in the state by imposing *Zakāt* on surplus funds.

The institution of *Zakāt* is an element in Islamic socialism. *Zakāt* is, in fact, a tax which the rich have to pay towards the common welfare of the nation as a whole. It intends "to take wealth from the rich and to return it to the poor". In the light of such an explicit objective, Professor Pigou's cry of welfare economics on the basis of transference of wealth from the rich to the poor has nothing original in it. During Caliphate days, *Zakāt* was so comprehensive and broadbased that it not only produced socialist redistribution of wealth but also tended to create a healthy non-capitalist frame of mind and an *esprit de corps*.

In short, banks are regarded by Islam as one of the boldest means for the economic prosperity of a nation. Thus one has to conclude that Islamic banks are superior to the capitalistic concept of banking. It can also be explained with the help of the following two circles of economic activity.

(I = Investment: Y = Total Income; C = Consumption; S = Saving.)

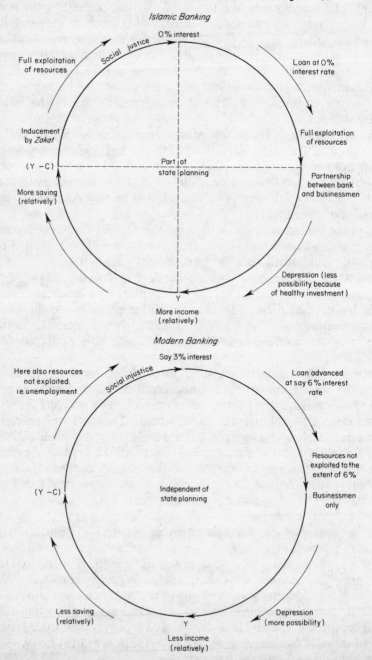

9.14 Islamic Banks and Non-Banking Services

A banker, besides having the primary functions of receiving deposits and lending money, performs many other functions of considerable import-ance to economic development. These services—both agency and general utility services—were originally undertaken to facilitate the clients, but being profitable have now been adopted by bankers all over the world. "The agency services rendered by the modern bank mainly consist of buying and selling of stock exchange, securities, making and receiving payment for rents, subscriptions, dividends, college and school fees, and acting as trustees, executors and attorneys and serving as correspondents and respresentatives." The general utility services are of many varieties. Of these the most important are the receiving of valuables for safe custody, transacting the business of foreign exchange, underwriting of stocks and shares, acting as referees and so on.

The social utility of these services lies in the fact that the banker saves the customer's valuable time and energy by under-taking these functions and bankers not only enable their customers to have knowledge of the trends of business situations but enable them to make deals with other parties with dependable knowledge about the general standing of these contracting parties. The economic significance of these non-banking services lies in the fact that they can contribute both directly and indirectly to the process of growth, especially in under-developed countries—directly because the gains the bank earns in the form of commission and the funds which it gets in the performance of such services may be utilized for financing development programmes, and indirectly because by these services, specially by transacting the business of foreign exchange, banks facilitate international trade and thereby help the fresh flow of capital from one place to another which, in turn, creates better conditions for investment.

These non-banking services, though so common in almost all the advanced countries like the U.S.A., the U.K., are still not very popular in Muslim countries. I think there is vast scope for expansion of these services in Muslim countries. The need for a systematic attempt by Islamic banks to undertake these services, arises from their obvious contribution to the process of growth.

9.15 Islamic Banks and Extra-Banking Activities

It may sound strange if I propose that Islamic banks can contribute to economic development by extra-banking activities. By extra-banking activities I mean the participation of banks in the process of economic growth by investing a modest proportion of their resources (say five per cent of their profits) in education and other social institutions for which the banks may not get immediate returns. This is no doubt an unorthodox approach to the whole theory of banking. But the importance of this approach of thinking can hardly be overestimated.

I believe that an Islamic bank is a vital social institution, so it must have a responsibility towards social development. Education is a major component of social development and a process by which economic growth is achieved. Investment in education for the development of human resources and in other social institutions will go a long way to creating automatism in economic growth. It may be that banks may not get any immediate returns but their contributions could well be decisive and lasting. Let us suppose that in a particular rural area where most of the people engaged in agriculture are illiterate a bank is set up. Naturally, in such an area the development of the bank is really a difficult task. Once a bank successfully invests a portion of its resources in schooling, in due course the invisible return which banks expect would be found in a change in the outlook of the people towards their standard of living and a consequent desire for growth. Increased productivity and development of banking habits are subordinate to the desire for growth. This is exactly what happended in the U.S.S.R. immediately after the socialist revolution.

9.16 Islamic Banks and International Relations

Some Muslims who talk of philosophy, not of facts, and have no knowledge regarding the nature of international economics are of the opinion that Islamic banking is impracticable, because it would isolate an Islamic state from the rest of the world, causing great loss in her international trade. But if it is possible for different nations of the world having different political and economic principles to live side by side, if it is possible for the U.S.A. and Yugoslavia or for the U.S.S.R. and Arab countries to conclude trade treaties, I find no reason why the Islamic state should be isolated from the rest of the world. If, for example, a Muslim country accepts the principles of an Islamic banking system, it would just be a matter of internal reorganization of her economy, just as in a federation the component units are given regional autonomy to solve their problems in accordance with their wishes without affecting the ultimate nature of the federation.

Secondly, far from causing loss in the international trade, Islamic banking would promote its volume. This is because modern banks finance foreign trade by accepting and collecting bills of exchange drawn up by customers, and by transacting other foreign exchange business on receiving some commission as remuneration for their services. But under the Islamic system banks would offer all these services without any remuneration because of their partnership with businessmen. Moreover, banks, being the partners of trade and commerce, would help businessmen to avoid uneconomic speculation so that the demand for and supply of a commodity could be adjusted to bring economic prosperity to a country and even the world as a whole.

Lastly, Islamic banking principles are quite consistent with international banking principles simply because the modern world, consciously or unconsciously, is drifting towards the economic philosophy of Islamic banking. This trend in world financial aid was recognized by the establishment of the International Development Association (I.D.A.) on 24 September 1960 as an affiliate of the International Bank for Reconstruction and Development (I.B.R.D.) or the World Bank. It has separate policies and separate financial resources from those of I.B.R.D. but its work is carried out by the secretariat of the I.B.R.D. The I.D.A. will start as a dispersing fund since it will provide loans even at a zero rate of interest in exceptional cases, depending upon the political and economic factors in each recipient country.

It should be noted here that for financing her planning a Muslim country must invite foreign capital on a partnership basis. In case of her failure to secure foreign capital on a partnership basis, she may take loans from abroad on the payment of interest. With regard to my second point I am definitely entering into a controversy. One may differ with me but the fact remains that Muslims cannot impose their religious injunctions on non-Muslims, and this is obviously against the spirit of Islam. So if foreign exchange becomes absolutely essential, Muslims may take loans from abroad on payment of interest on a reciprocal basis. This is simply for the sake of survival in this world of conflict and competition. We think it is permissible for an Islamic state to have interest transactions with non-Muslim states on the analogy of the action of the Caliph 'Umar, who permitted the levying of customs duties and tolls on the articles of trade of a non-Muslim neighbouring state in reprisal for and to the same extent as were levied by the latter. For the proper handling of these matters, a special account of the banks may be opened or a separate agency may be established. As a matter of fact, Islamic banking is not an obstacle to our international relations.

9.17 Bait-ul-Māl and Modern Central Banks

The present discussion will remain incomplete without reference to *Bait-ul-Māl*: therefore, before analyzing the role of the central bank in an Islamic state, an attempt may be made to discuss the functions of the *Bait-ul-Māl* as found in the history of early Islam. There is evidence to indicate that all the property belonging to the Muslims constituted a part of the *Bait-ul-Māl* regardless of its physical location. The *Bait-ul-Māl* was a very broad concept and was based on the faith that all suzerainty, inclusive of the right to property over the universe, belonged to Allah, man being His agent on the earth and possessing these things only temporarily.

The *Bait-ul-Māls* were of three types:
  (*a*) *Bait-ul-Māl al-Khās*.
  (*b*) *Bait-ul-Māl*.
  (*c*) *Bait-ul-Māl al-Muslimīn*.

(a) Bait-ul-Māl al-Khās.

This was the "royal treasury" or the privy purse, with its own sources of income and items of expenditure. It would cover the personal expenses of the Caliph, his palaces, harem, pensions of the members of the royal family, palace guards and gifts from the Caliphs to foreign princes.

(b) Bait-ul-Māl.

Bait-ul-Māl was a sort of a state bank for the Empire. This does not mean that it had all the functions of the present day central banks, but that whichever of these functions did exist in their primitive forms were performed by it.

Because the Islamic Empire was highly centralized, both at the provincial and the central levels, administration of *Bait-ul-Māl* was always in the hands of one person. At the provincial level, the supreme head of the *Bait-ul-Māl* was the governor of the province. He was in charge of collection and administration of the revenue. These *Bait-ul-Māls* were situated at provincial headquarters.

The central *Bait-ul-Māl* was situated at the capital of the Empire so that it could be under the direct control of the Caliph.

(c) Bait-ul-Māl al-Muslimīn.

The second public treasury was called *Bait-ul-Māl al-Muslimīn* or the treasury of all the Muslims. In fact, it was not for the Muslims alone; its functions included the welfare of all the citizens of the Islamic Empire regardless of their caste, colour or creed. The functions of this *Bait-ul-Māl* consisted of maintaining public works, roads, bridges, mosques, churches and the welfare and provision of the poor.

The Bait-ul-Māl was situated at the chief mosque and was administered by the Chief *Qāḍī* of the country at the central level and by the counterparts of this *Qāḍī* at the provincial level.

The following revenue items were to be deposited in the *Bait-ul-Māl*: (1) The *Ṣadaqah* or *Zakāt* revenue; (2) *Ghanīmah*, i.e. war-booty; (3) *Fai'*, i.e. *Kharāj* and Jizyah.

It was the duty of the Caliph to keep all these revenues apart from one another in the treasury because each had its own peculiarities and was to be administered according to its own set of rules.

Liabilities.

The liabilities of the public treasury were of two kinds: (*i*) liabilities incurred from property kept in the treasury for safe-keeping, (*ii*) The second type of liabilities were incurred with respect to revenues which were the treasury's own assets: (*a*) one part of these liabilities was incurred for value received, e.g. by way of compensation for the pay of the soldiers or price of arms and horses; (*b*) the other part consisted of the liabilities which had been incurred for the general interest or by way of assistance.

The *Bait-ul-Māl*, as we have seen, was the central bank. Apart from this, there were no commercial banks in the modern sense of the term. Most of the trade was carried on by individuals or in partnership but no evidence has been found to indicate the existence of large trading companies.

It appears that the *Bait-ul-Māl* used to meet all the needs and requirements of society. As a matter of fact the *Bait-ul-Māl* used to perform almost exactly similar functions to those which the present-day central banks are performing except the issue of currency, the supply of credit and control of the interest rate. Issue of currency is a modern device and can easily be fitted into the functions of the *Bait-ul-Māl* for even in this function the rate of interest does not play any part.

Again, there is no record to prove that Islam does not allow the financing of trade or industry on credit. Therefore, the Islamic central bank will provide credit to its member banks by way of investment for the sharing of profit or loss instead of providing them loans on a fixed rate of interest.

It follows that the central banking system under an Islamic scheme of society will be simpler and easier than ever before because the Islamic central bank need not give too much emphasis to the quantitative control of credit, the control of credit by raising or lowering the bank rate, by engaging in open market operations and by varying the reserve ratios of member banks. The Islamic central bank will use all such means which do not involve the application of interest. In fact, experience has shown that quantitative control of credit cannot be effective in underdeveloped Muslim countries as their money markets are utterly imperfect. The Islamic central bank should give emphasis not merely to qualitative control of credit but also to moral persuasion. The aim of moral persuasion, viewed as a method of credit control, is to mitigate the unfavourable psychological reaction to the methods of direct control; of course, it can be successfully employed only in countries possessing a comparatively small number of big banks with which the central bank is likely to develop an intimate relationship. This healthy relationship between central banks and other banks and between central banks and the people would be quite possible in the Islamic scheme of society. Because the banking system as a whole will not act as a mere creditor of industry, trade and commerce, but also as an active partner in all possible types of economic activity. A central bank will, in such circumstances, be the people's bank and will act according to the best advantage of the community as a whole. This favourable psychological atmosphere will, I am sure, go a long way towards creating an environment where healthy investment will be possible and thereby reduce the possibilities of depression in the economy.

In modern states, the central bank generally acts as the bankers' bank. All other banks of the country keep, either by law or by custom, a certain amount of their balances with the central bank. The central bank is the ultimate holder of the reserves of the banking system and any bank can draw upon this pool to tide over temporary needs and difficulties by rediscounting first-class bills. These central banks not only act as the bankers of the government but also as the custodians of credit and currency.

I find no reason why an Islamic central bank will not be in a position to perform all these functions without the application of interest in the name of co-operation, partnership and the maximum welfare of the people.

The share capital of an Islamic central bank can be provided by the state, or subscribed by the government and the people jointly by floating shares. As the central bank has many important functions to perform, the control of the bank generally remains in the hands of the state or it can be managed by a board of directors jointly elected by the government and the people.

9.18 Summary and Conclusions

(1) The *Qur'ān* prohibits the taking of "*al-Ribā*" which literally means "increase". But all increases are not prohibited in Islam. The *Qur'ān* has allowed increase from trade but not from the loan given to a debtor. The '*Ulamā*', generally, have accepted that by *al-Ribā* is meant usury-interest which was in force in pre-Islamic Arabia. Some people still think that what Islam prohibits is usury and not interest. It is established beyond doubt that interest and usury are the obverse and reverse of the same coin.

(2) It has been found by modern research that interest has nothing to do with influencing the value of savings. Practically, it is the rate of investment that determines the rate of saving. Islam prohibits interest but encourages investment. Again, we have seen that *Zakāt* provides a powerful stimulus for investing idle funds. This stimulus gets momentum from the fact that Islam allows profit and sleeping partnerships in which profit as well as loss is shared.

(3) The Islamic banking system will be based on the principle of partnership. Therefore, this banking system, which is free of interest, can help establish certain institutions on the basis of *Mudārabah*, where capital and labour can be combined together as partners for work. Islam has tried to bring about a lasting compromise between labour and capital by giving the whole question of their relationship a moral bent and by imposing moral obligations on each partner as part of the faith. It is, therefore, quite possible to work out industrial, commercial and agricultural enterprises on the principle of *Mudārabah*, combining the various units of production.

(4) After analyzing the mechanism for Islamic banking, the problem of short-term and long-term financing was discussed. The short-term financing of industry, trade and agriculture can be made by Islamic banks on a partnership basis. Since the ordinary deposit bank has a special liquidity problem, it is recommended that specialized credit institutions like industrial or agricultual development banks may be developed for long-term financing. Moreover, Islamic banks may evolve the system of guarantee of loans for industries, for working capital as well as for equipment. This guarantee may induce private capital to move into Muslim countries.

(5) The importance of consumption loans is recognized, but it is recommended that such loans be made either by people's co-operative societies or by a government credit agency in the Islamic state against the deposit of evidence of fixed assets owned by the borrowers.

(6) As regards a bank's relations with depositors and entrepreneurs it may be said that "a bank in relation to depositors has been considered the operator or business manager and the depositors deemed capitalists. In relation to the entrepreneur, however, the bank may be taken to be the capitalist and the entrepreneurs the operators. In this case the conditions governing a capitalist's rights and an operator's obligations shall apply. Any profits realized by the entrepreneur, the operator in this case, shall be shared with the bank as the capitalist in the agreed proportions."

(7) The practicability of partnership between businessmen and a bank can hardly be challenged. This is evident from the actual operation of Islamic banks during the nineteen-seventies and eighties.

(8) The superiority of the Islamic concept of banking over modern banking lies in the fact that Islam has eliminated the tyranny of interest. Islam has prohibited interest, because it has nothing to do with influencing the volume of saving, because it makes depression chronic by retarding the process of recovery, because it aggravates the unemployment problem and, finally, because it encourages the unequal distribution of wealth.

(9) Besides performing other modern non-banking services like general utility services of various kinds, it is proposed that Islamic banks can contribute to economic development by extra-banking activities, by which we mean participation of banks in the process of economic growth by investing a modest proportion of their resources (say, five per cent of their profits) in education and other social institutions for which the banks may not get immediate returns. But this is highly significant from the social point of view.

(10) I have explained that the *Bait-ul-Māl* established by early Islam used to perform almost exactly similar functions to those which the present-day central banks are performing, except the issue of currency, the supply of credit and control of the interest rate. It is explained that the functions of an Islamic central bank can easily be fitted into the functions of the *Bait-ul-Māl* to meet the growing needs of Muslim countries. I am

confident that the Islamic central bank can work without the application of interest.

9.19 Selected Further Reading

Ahmad, Sheikh Mahmud, *Economics of Islam: A Comparative Study*, Sh. Muhammad Ashraf, Lahore, 1972.

Ahmad, Ziauddin, (ed.) et al., *Money and Banking in Islam*, International Centre for Research in Islamic Economics (I.C.R.I.E.) King Abdulaziz University, Jeddah and Institute of Policy Studies, Islamabad, Pakistan, 1983.

Al-Naggar, Ahmad A. "Islamic Banks: A Model and the challenge" in *The Challange of Islam*, ed. by Altar Gauhar, Islamic Council of Europe, London, 1978.

Ariff, M. "The Role of Monetary Policy in an Islamic Economy" in *Nature and Scope* ed. by M. Ariff, (I.C.R.I.E.), King Abdulaziz University, Jeddah, 1982.

Ariff, M. (ed.) *Monetary and Fiscal Economics of Islam*, (I.C.R.I.E.) King Abdulaziz University, Jeddah, 1982.

Chapra, U. *Monetary Policy in an Islamic–Economy in Money and Banking*, ed. by Ahmad Ziauddin (I.C.R.I.E.), Jeddah, 1983.

Government of Pakistan, Islamabad, *Report of the Council of Islamic Ideology on the Elimination of Interest from the Economy,* Council of Islamic Ideology, Islamabad, 1980.

Government of Pakistan, Islamabad, House Building Finance Corporation Regulations, 1979, (S. R. O. 762 (i)/79) 1979.

Haus, J. "Islamic Law and Western Monetary Thinking" in *The Islamic Review*, London, 1949.

Huq, A. (ed.) et al. *Readings in Islamic Banking*, Vol. I, Bangladesh Islamic Bankers' Association, Dhaka, 1982.

Imamuddin, S. M. "Baytul Mal and Banks in the Medieval World" *Islamic Culture*, vol. 35, No. 1, Decean, 1961.

Mannan, M. A. "Islamic perspectives on Islamic Banks. An analysis of nine unconventional role and operational strategies" in *Thoughts on Islamic Banking*, Islamic Economics Research Bureau, Dhaka, Bangladesh, 1980.

Mannan, M. A. "Credition of Credit and Islamic Banks" in *The Making of Islamic Economic Society, Islamic Dimensions in Economic Analysis*, Chapter 14 (forthcoming).

Qureshi, Anwar Iqbal, *Islam and The Theory of Interest with a New Chapter on Interest Free Banking*, 2nd edn., S. L. Muhammad Ashraf, Lahore, 1967 and 1974.

Rushdi, Ali Ahmad, "Interest Rate – A Redundant Instrument of Monetary Policy" in *Thoughts on Islamic Economics*, Islamic Economics Research Bureau, Dhaka, Bangladesh, 1980.

Rahman, Afzalur, *Economic Doctrines of Islam: Banking and Finance*, The Muslim Students Trust, London, 1979.

Siddiqi, M. N. *Banking without Interest*, Islamic Foundation, London, 1982.

Udovitch, A. L. "Credit as a Means of Investment in Medieval Islamic Trade", *Journal of American Oriental Society*, 1967.

Uzair, M. "Some Conceptual and Practical Aspects of Interest-free Banking", *Islamic Studies*, XV, No. 4, Islamabad, 1976, Reprinted: *Quarterly Economic Journal*, N. B. P., Karachi, October, 1972.

Uzair, M. *Interest free Banking*, Royal Book Company, Karachi, 1978.

APPENDIX

[Note: The author has been advocating the establishment of a Muslim World Bank in different forums since the mid-nineteen-sixties. His paper on the subject appeared in *Islamic Review and Arab Affairs*, (vol. 56, Nov./Dec., London, U. K., 1968 and vol. 57, January, London, 1969) and was reproduced in the first edition of this book published in 1970. An Islamic Development Bank consisting of 26 founding members was formally established in October 1975. The Present membership of the Islamic development Bank consists of 42 countries. This new edition of the book reproduces "A Case for the Establishment of a Muslim World Bank" from its 1970 edition for its historical value.

A. Case for the Establishment of a Muslim World Bank

Now is the time to examine the practicability and feasibility of founding a Muslim World Bank which is capable of pooling the resources of the world of Islam so as to foster large-scale development efforts throughout the Muslim countries. The following positive and negative factors may be advanced in support of the formation of the proposed bank.

Positive Factors

The era of economic growth and political change in the past two decades has brought a marked increase in the demand for development capital. We have records to establish that in all Muslim countries the need for and ability to make effective use of outside capital have been increasing faster than the ability to service conventional loans. Some Muslim countries have already drawn close to the limits of the debt they can prudently assume on conventional terms. It is awareness of this problem which may lead to the founding of a Muslim World Bank. The primary purpose underlying the establishment of this proposed bank would be to create a supplementary source of development capital for Muslim countries whose balance of payments prospects would not justify their incurring or continuing to incur external debts on entirely conventional terms.

Nowadays, for the exploitation of the vast natural resources of the Muslim states what is required is huge public expenditure for which deficit financing is a must. For such economic growth what is needed is co-operation among all the Muslim countries so that they may not be victims of the exploitation of richer countries. The easiest way of achieving this co-operation is the founding of a Muslim World Bank on the lines of the I.B.R.D. Not until the world of Islam has conquered poverty can we plan any manner of political homogeneity and social cohesion. All the Muslims, despite their numerical strength and geographical distribution all over the world, are today, by and large, a poverty-stricken people—people who are mostly subject to exploitation. From Morocco to Indonesia and from Mauritania to Malaysia without exception, all the countries possess vast natural resources and rank amongst the world's most important growers of primary commodities and producers of mineral wealth. For instance, eighty per cent of the world's jute grows in Bangladesh; Egypt is amongst the largest of the world's cotton growers. Three quarters of the world's supplies of oil come from the Arab world. Indonesia and Malaysia meet the world's major requirements of tin and rubber.

The one and perhaps the only institution which is capable of pooling the resources of the world of Islam is a Muslim World Bank.

Negative Factors

Pan-Islamism will for long remain only an ideal, a dream to fire the imagination of the ardent sons of the faith, so as to bring about, in the fulfilment of our destinies, a spirit of ceaseless endeavour toward a more fruitful experiment of Islamic socialism as prescribed by the Holy *Qur'ān*.

The various Muslim lands have for centuries been subjected to differing political ideologies inspired mostly by the creeds and cults of the Western powers who have for long dominated them. Some of these lands are still in a state of agitation and ferment.

"The differing and sometimes conflicting patterns of Islamic politics in different territorial demarcations have, however, been chiefly responsible for defeating some of the most earnest attempts made for a political unification of the Islamic countries in the nineteenth century. The most notable campaign in this field was that of the valiant crusader, Jamaluddin Afghani, whose mission, despite its failure in the larger context, succeeded in awakening the Muslims of the world to the necessity of attaining national sovereignty as a priority objective. In the post-Jamaluddin era were born some very notable torchbearers of Islamic renaissance and amongst these lustrous luminaries were Mufti Mohammad Abduhu of Egypt, the Ali brothers of the Indo-Pakistani Sub-Continent, Allama Iqbal and Quaid-e-Azam, and the great Mujahid Syed Mohammad Amin-ul-Hussaini, the well-known Grand Mufti of Palestine."

It is true that a daring experiment is now under way in the shape of the

R.C.D. Organisation. While this project is an excellent beginning it does not claim to attack the real and basic problems of the Muslim world as a whole, which today are largely economic.

Considering all these factors, it can safely be concluded that the formation of a Muslim World Bank is a practical proposal which does not involve many complications as are likely to be faced for achieving the goal of pan-Islamism or the formation of a Muslim Common Market. Once Muslim countries of the world are in a position to establish a bank like this, it would be treated as a distinct milestone on the road to full co-operation among the Muslim countries in the economic field. It would be, a tool for the orderly adjustment of exchange rates and for a two-way adjustment for any disequilibrium in the international balance of payments. At the end of the transitional period, this bank may promise to bring in an era of free multi-lateral convertibility of national currencies of the various Muslim countries of the world.

Objectives and Functions

We have already pointed out that the prime objective of this bank would be to supplement the need for development capital of those Muslim countries whose balance of payments would not justify the taking-on of external debts entirely on conventional terms. So far as this involves the use of the bank's own resources, it must be able to mobilize capital from a variety of capital-exporting countries. The main functions of the proposed bank would be:

(*a*) to assist in the development of Muslim countries by facilitating the investment of capital for productive purposes;

(*b*) to promote private foreign investment by means of guarantees of participation in loans and other investments made by private investors;

(*c*) to promote the long-range balanced growth of international trade and the maintenance of equilibrium in the balance of payments by encouraging international investments for the development of the productive resources of members:

(*d*) to arrange the loans guaranteed by, in relation to international loans, or through other channels so that the more useful and urgent projects can be dealt with first;

(*e*) to offer technical advice on matters relating to loan operations; to locate experts qualified to deal with specific technical problems, for instance, with sulphur processing in Iraq, port administration in Turkey, pulp and paper manufacture in Pakistan; and

(*f*) to lend its good offices in seeking the settlement of economic disputes among Muslim countries as we find in the case of the World Bank's settlement of a water dispute between India and Pakistan in 1960.

Any other functions may be assigned to this proposed bank according to need and the exigencies of time.

Membership and Resources

All the Muslim countries should be eligible for membership of this proposed bank. It is, perhaps, appropriate to suggest that the lead in this direction should come from Pakistan for the formation of such a bank and to enlist, in particular, the assistance and help of Iran, Iraq, Turkey, Kuwait, Jordan, Afghanistan, Saudi Arabia, Lebanon, Egypt, Tunisia, Sudan, Algeria, Malaysia, Indonesia, Tanzania, Somalia, to name only a few of the more influential members of the Muslim world. The resources for the proposed bank should initially come from the member countries according to their means and strength to be supplemented by grants, aids and loans from the I.B.R.D; the I.D.A., the Asian Development Bank and other friendly governments. Like I.B.R.D. the capital subscription of this bank may be divided into three parts. Firstly, a certain proportion of the subscription (say two to three per cent) of all members should be payable in gold or U.S. dollars so that they may be used freely by the bank in any of its operations. Secondly, fifteen per cent of such subscriptions may be payable in the currency of the subscribing member. Lastly, the remaining subscription may not be payable to the bank for lending but may be subject to call only if required by the bank to meet its obligations on borrowings or on loans guaranteed by it. This is just a broad principle subject to change according to the requirements of the time.

Let us now throw some light on its administration and management.

Administration and Management

The holy city of Makkah should be selected for the bank's headquarters for obvious spiritual and psychological reasons. A board of governors and one alternate governor might be appointed by each member. However, the organisational structure of this proposed bank may be developed on the lines of other international financial institutions. The development credits of this bank would be interest-free but a service charge of .75 per cent or one per cent per annum, payable on the withdrawn and outstanding, may be made to meet this bank's administrative costs like the I.D.A. It is not, however, intended that this Muslim World Bank Fund should be used to finance a project which could not satisfy the normal criteria of economic and financial viability. The bank must make a general appraisal of the merits and priorities of the project or programme.

Anyway, before making a loan, the bank would satisfy itself that the borrowers, whether it be a government, an autonomous agency or a private corporation, would be able to service the debt.

We are quite sure that the principle of partnership which is quite applicable to the internal banking system may be applicable quite profitably to international banking. It is time for the world of Islam to be awakened to the necessity of preparing to survive in this highly competitive world largely on the basis of self-help and mutual assistance. Support for this proposal could gather momentum if high-level conferences were held in the capitals of the principal Muslim countries to exchange views. This bank will, if established, help solve the urgent and pressing problem of economic development in the Muslim world.

Here it is really gratifying to note that the Muslim Foreign Ministers' Conference, which ended its three-day session at Jeddah on 26 March 1970, decided to establish a Secretariat with Jeddah as its provisional seat until the liberation of Jerusalem. The countries giving unqualified support to set up this Secretariat were Afghanistan, Guinea, Indonesia, Iran, Jordan, Kuwait, the Lebanon, Malaysia, Mauritania, Morocco, Niger, Saudi Arabia, Senegal, Somalia, Tunisia, and the Yemen. The functions of the Secretariat will be liaison between participating states and implementation of the decisions taken by the conference. The expenditure incurred on the management and functioning of the Secretariat will be borne by participating states. It was also decided to meet once a year for the purpose of discussing matters of common interest to make recommendations on common action, to review progress achieved, and to implement decisions. This is the first time in several hundred years that Muslim states have met in a conference and chalked out common plans for their problems. The Jeddah conference will, I am sure, lead to the formation of a force distinct from both the capitalist and communist *blocs*—a *bloc* of Islamic nations—and it is hoped that the proposed Secretariat will take some positive steps to establish a bank for the Islamic nations.

CHAPTER 10

Islamic Banks and Investment Companies in Operation

APPENDIX A

A Note on the Islamic International Monetary Fund. (I.I.M.F.)

APPENDIX B

Monetary Policy: An Overview

Policy Mix

"Those who swallow usury cannot rise up save as he ariseth whom the devil hath staggered by [his] touch. That is because they say: Trade is just like usury; And Allah has permitted trading and forbidden usury".

Al-Qur'ān, Sūrah II. 275

"And if the debtor is in strained circumstances, then (let there) be postponement to (the time of) ease, and if ye remit the debt as almsgiving it would be better for you if ye did but know".

Al-Qur'ān, Sūrah II. 281

10.1 Introduction[1]

The main objective of this section is to examine the trends of the operational strategies of the Islamic Development Bank (I.D.B.) in particular and other local Islamic banks in general as well as to introduce certain issues for consideration in the course of analysis.

The establishment of the I.D.B. and local Islamic banks in the nineteen-seventies is a significant economic event of our time. These pioneering banks have to assume a historical role in initiating and implementing Islamic reforms in the areas of Islamic economics, money and banking. While recognizing that the policy directions set out for these banks require a different gestation period in order to become effective and operationally viable, it is perhaps desirable to indicate very briefly the trends of their operations and issues evolved therefrom.

10.2 The Islamic Development Bank (I.D.B.): An Overview and Appraisal.

The Islamic Development Bank was established in pursuance of the Declaration of Intent issued by a conference of Finance Ministers of Muslim Countries held in Jeddah in *Dhūl-I-Qa'da*, 1393, (December, 1973). The Bank formally opened on 15th *Shawwal*, 1395, (20th October, 1975).

"The purpose of the Bank is to foster the economic development and social progress of member countries and Muslim communities individually as well as jointly in accordance with the principles of the *Sharī'ah*. The functions of the Bank are to participate in equity capital and grant loans for productive projects and enterprises besides providing financial assistance to member countries in other forms for economic and social development. The Bank is also required to establish and operate special funds for specific purposes including a fund for assistance to Muslim communities in non-member countries, in addition to setting up trust funds. The Bank is authorized to accept deposits and to raise funds in any other manner. It is also charged with the responsibility of assisting in the promotion of foreign trade, especially in capital goods, among member countries, providing technical assistance to member countries, extending training facilities for personnel engaged in development activities and undertaking research for enabling the economic, financial and banking activities in Muslim countries to conform to the *Sharī'ah*". (I.D.B. report 1979) The present membership of the Bank consists of 44 countries.

"The basic condition for membership is that the prospective member country should be a member of the Organization of the Islamic Conference and be willing to accept such terms and conditions as may be decided upon by the Board of Governors."

An Overview of the Operations: (1975–1985)

The Bank completed the first ten years of its operation in 1985. It is now relatively easy to indicate the trend of its operations. Unlike many international organizations, the Bank commenced its financing operations in the very first year of its establishment. Up to the end of 1984, the Bank allocated a sum of Islamic *Dinārs* 4970.78 million (US$5559.70 million) to its member countries in the form of 85 loans, 41 equity participations, 73 technical assistances, 55 leasings, 241 foreign trade financings and one profit sharing deal. (See Tenth Annual Report of I.D.B. 1985.) In terms of allocation, the Bank's major allocation was in the area of foreign trade financing which constituted 80 % of operation financing followed by loan leasing, equity assistance and profit-sharing respectively.

In terms of its sectoral distribution up to 1985 the Bank's major contribution was in the areas of industry and mining which constituted about 34 % of the total amount approved for project financing, followed by transport and communication (20 %), agriculture (16.35 %) utility (13.8 %) and social services (12.04 %) and others (1.2 %).

Functional Targets and Sectoral Priorities.

The Bank's documents on "Policies and Procedures for Financing Operations" (p. 34) shows the following functional targets:-

i) Investment in profit-sharing projects	40 – 45 %
ii) Equity Participation	30 – 40 %
iii) Loans to social and infrastructure projects	20 – 25 %

and the tentative percentages of sectoral financing are also indicated below:

i) Agriculture and related fields	30 – 40 %
ii) Industry and related fields	25 – 35 %
iii) Public utility	10 – 15 %
iv) Transportation and Communications	10 – 15 %
v) Social Sectors	10 – 15 %
vi) Others	5 – 10 %

The past ten year operational experience of the Bank suggests that the Bank has to make major adjustments in its policy direction to achieve the targets or sectoral priorities it has set itself. In respect of equity participation, the Bank made a substantial improvement over the years despite the fact that it is still below the target indicated above. The further expansion of loan operations as a percentage of the total financing policy needs to be contained. Furthermore, the Bank's investment in profit-sharing projects, its contributions to agriculture and the social sector need to be increased substantially.

What is needed is an intensive search to identify agricultural and agro-industry projects, bearing in mind the needs of the rural communities, which make up the bulk of the population. In the social sector the Bank's contribution also needs to be augmented because of its critical importance in economic and social progress. The need for assistance in these sectors is of supreme importance from the viewpoint of the distribution of income also. Herein lies a clear Islamic dimension of the Bank's operations.

The I.D.B.'s Overall contribution and the least developed member countries (L.D.M.C.)

The I.D.B.'s total financial contributions to member countries must be examined with reference to the Bank's policy on assistance to the sixteen least developed member countries. Despite an increase in assistance to the least developed countries, a preliminary study shows that the Bank's operations appear to be tilted towards the more developed member countries, obviously for the so-called greater "absorptive capacity" in these countries.

In terms of population, the least developed member countries represent about thirty per cent of the total population of all the member countries. It is to be examined whether the least developed countries received less than other developing member countries *per capita* of population, although their need for grants, aids and loans is far greater than can be measured from the size of their population, which is only one of the determinants of the need for development assistance. An attempt is to be made to increase the financial contribution of the Bank to the least developed member countries through an action programme requiring identification of projects, the implementation of which the Bank can help to improve through infrastructure and institution building.

Let us now discuss each of the Bank's operations in some detail.

(a) Loan Operations.

The loans are given by the Bank free of interest. The I.D.B., however, collects service fees to cover its relevant administrative expenses. This is permissible in Islam. The present loan operations of the Bank, which are concentrated mainly on socio-economic infrastructural projects, are a move in the right direction. It is important to ascertain who is getting direct benefit from these projects. What is also important is to make the "service charge" internationally competitive.

In view of their inadequate physical, administrative and social infrastructures, the magnitude of investment needed for development in the least-developed countries will remain for many years to come at a level far beyond the saving capacities of these countries. It is to be considered whether a zero service fee on loans can be introduced, reducing the maturity period of the loan, thereby increasing the frequency of recycling of the fund. It has to be acknowledged that in real terms project lending even with high service charges cannot be considered a profitable operation for the Bank, if the present inflation rate is added to the normal monetary rate of discount.

I maintain that there is scope for indexation in an Islamic economy, for money is seen as a medium of exchange to obviate the difficulties of the barter system and *not* as a commodity. As such it is, among other things, unlawful in Islam to pay a premium for money when a debt is paid. On the same analogy, it should be examined whether loan contracts can be expressed in real terms rather than in money terms. An index-linked loan contract, which can be related to a specific or general price index of goods and services, may be repaid in terms of the prevailing purchasing power that it has at the time of concluding the loan agreement. In other words, interest-free loans can be settled at a constant price under which neither the debtor nor creditor gains at the cost of the other. Once this idea is institutionalized the Bank should be able to expand its scope for loan operations despite difficulties in implementation.

Nevertheless, the lending operations of the Bank have to be restrictive. The Bank has to divert its resources to explore other avenues of investment opportunities, either in the form of equity participation or in the form of expanded foreign trade operations or other similar lines of investment. The discussion on loan operations cannot, however, be complete without having reference to programme lending.

Project Lending Versus Programme Lending:
It appears that project lending seems to be one of the dominant types of the I.D.B.'s current lending operations. Like other international financial institutions such as the World Bank and the Asian Development Bank, normal lending operations cannot be a major function of the I.D.B. for the simple reason that the Bank cannot charge any interest on its loan operations. Viewed from this perspective, programme lending should take precedence over project lending. Programme lending is usually undertaken to finance a programme of maintenance in order to maximize productivity so that an underutilized capacity is fully utilized or a bottleneck in the process of production is removed.

Subject to further review by the Bank, programme lending operations may be diverted to industries, other sectors, or activities which (a) augment the productivity of the rural sector, (b) manufacture essential agricultural materials and equipment, (c) produce critical consumption goods and services, (d) produce goods for export markets, and/or (e) produce capital goods components thereof, or producer durables which are essential to development.

Package Loans
The Bank may also consider the possibility of introducing a multi-project package loan for public sector projects. Such a multi-project loan may include both foreign exchange and local expenditure financing. The total financing proportionate for every such project should remain flexible and be fixed on a case by case basis. If this package loan is introduced, due care

should be taken to see that it is spent primarily on rural industrialization projects because it is here that the key to the problem of distribution of income lies.

Lastly, in respect of loan operations it is perhaps desirable to make a passing remark about the grant element in I.D.B.'s current loans.

The grant element in the I.D.B.'s loans.
For the purpose of a future policy guide, a study may be made to see if there is any correlation between the amount of grant in-aid provided and the level of per capita income of the member countries. The grant-in-aid or its equivalent in loan is generally calculated with the present value method, involving the use of the discounting procedures of investment analysis. The difference between the face value of the loan and the present value of future payments on the loan, when expressed as a percentage of the sales value of the loan, gives the grant-in-aid element of a loan concerned. On the basis of this calculation, a preliminary result shows that both the least developed and more developed members are placed on the same footing in providing grant-in-aid. In other words, the grant-in-aid element in I.D.B. loans is perhaps inclined in favour of the more developed members of the Bank. Further investigation in this matter is however required.

(b) Equity participation and Lines of equity.

Article 17 of the Articles of Agreement of the Bank deals with Equity Participation and the Bank's document on "Policies and Procedures of Financing Operations", which provides its main guidelines.

Equity participation comes fourth in terms of the total volume of financing, representing 12.6% of the total financing operations of the Bank during this period. It suggests that greater effort is needed to identify projects in the Bank's participation on equity lines. Furthermore, the guidelines for equity participation presuppose the existence of an adequate and sound physical and social infrastructure and administrative machinery capable of formulating and implementing policies in all sectors of the economy. Unfortunately, this supposition is not the reality in many developing countries, not to mention the least-developed member countries of the Bank. Therefore, the current guidelines need to be reviewed and require change and reorientation. Given the inadequacy of the present infrastructures in most of the member countries, it is perhaps not realistic if investment projects are judged by solely financial criteria. If purely financial criteria, as stipulated in the guidelines, are applied, very few projects can be justified in the public sector for the purpose of equity participation by the Bank. Besides, traditionally, the private sector is extremely weak and shy in all member countries without exception.

Lines of equity to National Development Banks.
Thus, "in order to extend assistance to small and medium industrial projects particularly in the private sector, the Bank has started a new

operation called lines of equity which have been extended to national development finance institutions in the member countries. The national development finance institutions act as the agencies of the Bank for the purposes of identifying, appraising and implementing local projects which are suitable for this type of financing by the Bank. In this manner the Bank can participate in smaller projects which it could not otherwise do". (I.D.B. Report, 1979, 1985.)

These small projects are worth considering both from the point of view of sound economic development and distribution. These are the projects which are generally located in rural areas. The Bank's participation in such small projects through package loans or equity lines tend to bring a minimum of change and differentiation to family activities; "it humanizes production as the worker can see the connection between machine, man and his environment; it permits the old societies to adopt new ideas and enterprises gradually without major social breakdown and disturbances, thereby reducing the problems of migration, unemployment and squatter settlement".

So what is needed is to mount research missions with the task of identifying equity projects. Emphasis should also be given to project preparation and implementation. A prior study of local investment laws, and company and taxation laws is also called for. In addition, preinvestment and investment surveys, to ascertain the national resource endowment of member countries, appear to be necessary.

"Shopping basket" lines of equity
In this connection, I feel that there is a further need for a shift in emphasis from lines of equity to "shopping basket" lines of equity by which I mean that the I.D.B. should place an amount of equity finance with guidelines and advice at the disposal of appropriate national institutions for financing very small types of projects. The main advantages of such lines of credit are that they would involve fewer administrative costs, reduce the volume of bureaucratic red tape and can be expected to be more efficient in identifying the specific local need of relatively small investors, particularly in remote rural areas. The preparation of guideline presupposes that the Bank must have first-hand knowledge of the economics concerned.

(c) Lease financing.

"The Islamic Development Bank has also introduced leasing operations in order to assist the member countries in the procurement of necessary equipments and machineries for the production of various intermediaries and capital goods in its member countries. Lease financing has also been used for the acquisition of ocean-going vessels towards the building-up of necessary transportation facilities, thereby augmenting foreign trade activities." (I.D.B. Report, 1979). During the past ten years, lease financing, which comes second in terms of the total volume of financing (representing about 35.24 percent of the total), has increased considerably.

It seems that this leasing operation of the Bank is a legitimate income-generating operation and its scope needs to the further expanded and examined to see that no *Ribā* element is involved in its dealings. The member countries of the Bank can derive immense benefit from the expanded leasing operations.

(d) Technical assistance.

Despite the fact that all the technical assistance is given to the L.D.M.C. of the Bank, the Bank's current technical assistance programme, which is 2.38 per cent of the total financing operation, appears to be very limited in its scope and needs major expansion. What is required is to determine the specific needs and priorities of each of the member countries through careful programming from the project preparation stage to the evaluation and implementation stage.

(e) Profit-sharing.

During the past ten years, the Bank has actually been involved in one profit-sharing activity in the area of real estate business. There is a considerable scope for the expansion of these operations in other sectors. There is a clear need for the identification of joint-venture projects in the Bank's member countries on a priority basis so that the Bank can start negotiating to participate in these projects on the basis of profit-sharing. According to the *Sharī'ah*, profit follows the conditions agreed upon; the loss follows the capital.

However, a whole range of issues concerning the economics of profit-sharing need to be studied in depth and appropriate guidelines for financing on the basis of profit-sharing must be evolved. They include issues connected with partnership and ownership rights, calculations of the rate of return before and after local taxes, methods of depreciation, the determination of break-even periods and so on. It is felt, however, that the Bank's participation should not be limited to financial aspects only; its participation should also cover the sharing of the management and supervisory services of the enterprise.

(g) Foreign trade operations.

"The Bank undertakes *foreign trade financing operations* as a fund placement operation with a view to assist member countries in meeting the procurement of necessary industrial raw materials, needed by domestic industries. This facility is short-term in nature and is currently being used by member countries for the procurement of urgently-needed industrial raw materials. The difference between the purchase and the resale price constitutes a source of income for the Bank.' (I.D.B. Report, 1979).

Foreign trade operations, which come first (about 80 per cent) in terms of the total volume of financing, have increased considerably over the years from their base of 16 per cent in 1398 AH (1977–78). These operations have been able to act as a middleman in terms of trade among member countries. The nine to ten years' experience of the Bank now needs to be consolidated. What we need now is a massive change in its orientation and a shift of emphasis from the Bank's role of mere financier to the role of foreign trade entrepreneur and manager.

In its current role as foreign trade financier, the Bank signs a purchase contract on behalf of a member country and sells the same simultaneously to the beneficiary on the basis of a mark-up which is said to be stated as a percentage of the total financing approved. The main advantage of this current practice is that the Bank can invest its liquid fund on a short-term basis and that profit is almost assured.

Within the framework of current trade operations it should be possible for the Bank to introduce different preferential policy measures in favour of the least-developed member countries, or explicit preference may be given to a trade operation among member countries. At this stage it is important to mention that it is not really necessary to restrict current operations to capital goods only. The Bank should have built-in flexibility, that is, emphasis should be given to trading in critically important consumption goods as well as capital goods.

Past experience should enable the Bank to become more actively involved in trade operations in terms of partnership arrangments. The Bank, keeping in view the needs of the member countries, the nature and elasticity of commodities, the national and international trade cycles of the commodities concerned, will be expected to make purchases and stockpiles in a member country for future distribution and marketing. It goes without saying that a proper institutional arrangement has to be made for the successful implementation of this policy, which has the following avantages:

i) It is likely to have a favourable impact on the balance of payments of all member countries;
ii) The preferential markup would ease the financial burden on the least developed member countries;
iii) It would enable the Bank to identify the industrial and agricultural projects for the Bank's eventual participation.

Furthermore, the Bank is also expected in due course to assume an entrepreneurial role in trade and industry, particularly in countries where the necessary infrastructure facilities are lacking. The Bank's involvement in joint-venture projects may not be based merely on equity participation and consequent profit-sharing, but also on the basis of the assumption of a controlling interest in the venture. It goes without saying that this type of venture is to be undertaken on the basis of comparative cost advantages and/or proper market research. It may require the Bank to change its current financial policy in which it is stated that "the Bank may *not* acquire a majority or controlling interest in the share of capital of the projects or enterprises in which it participates". The Bank may eventually relinquish the ownership of enterprises in favour of member countries, once the operation is placed on a proper footing and is generating income.

Involvement in this type of activity by the Bank may be seen in some quarters as economic interference with the member countries. The fact is that the I.D.B. symbolizes the joint authority of Muslim countries and member states can co-operate effectively to the extent that they may abandon part of their sovereignty to this joint authority. The problem of interdependence in the sphere of economic co-operation among Muslim countries needs to be clearly understood. Thus, when a venture is undertaken by the Bank in any of the L.D.M.C. it increases its so-called low absorptive capacity. The participation in joint venture activities should not be confused with the vested interests of the multi-national corporations operating in many member countries. This type of integrated trade operation may ultimately require the Bank to develop its own shipping lines and co-operative insurance business, which is permitted by the *Sharī'ah*. At this stage it will be useful to throw some light on some of the policies and procedures of the I.D.B.

Some Policies and Procedures of the I.D.B.: A Review.

Special fund resources.

Although special fund resources were primarily intended for assisting Muslim communities in non-member countries and for technical assistance to member countries, yet they can also, be utilized to support the development efforts of L.D.M.C. in the following six areas:
(a) to cover the risk of foreign exchange rate fluctuations;
(b) to support service fees;
(c) to cover the risk of guarantee facilities needed for obtaining loans from the outside capital market;
(d) to provide foreign exchange for local currency expenditure in respect of projects having high social and economic value and whose financial and foreign exchange earnings are relatively indirect;
(e) to finance projects involving standardization and quality control, especially for small-scale industries; and
(f) to provide emergency grants or subsidies for food imports in case of droughts, famines, floods, earthquakes, etc.

In addition to conventional economic indicators, such as per capita income and the debt service ratio, social indicators such as the literacy rate, infant mortality, life expectancy rate, etc., may also be used to determine the relative priority of access to the special fund resources.

In determining the criteria for the use of such resources, inflexibility should be guarded against but this does not mean an absence of guidelines. Any indicators used for this purpose must be interpreted with prudence and care.

Lending foreign exchange for local currency expenditure.

It is stipulated that the Bank "may provide financing of foreign exchange components of the total cost in suitable cases.

"An examination of the current operations of the Bank suggests that the I.D.B. should be more flexible in providing foreign exchange for local currency expenditure on projects in favour of the L.D.M.C. In determining the need and justification for local cost financing, primary emphasis should be placed on the countries' macroeconomic and project considerations, which should be evaluated not only in terms of their domestic efforts for the mobilization of resources but also in terms of their expected foreign exchange gap, saving gaps and the inadequacy of physical and administrative infrastructures".

To facilitate the implementation of this policy, it is necessary to set aside a portion of the funds, for that purpose, preferably 15% to 20% of the total annual lendings from the ordinary capital resources of the Bank. A case-by-case approach is considered appropriate in deciding on the provision of portions of local cost financing.

Domestic procurement preference policy.

It appears that the Bank currently follows uniform financing procedures for financing contracts, which are awarded under universal international competitive biddings. Despite their obvious benefits in terms of cost efficiency and cost effectiveness, due consideration must be given to whether the Bank should formulate guidelines for adopting a domestic preference scheme in international competitive bidding, under which the lowest bid price of all foreign bidders is adjusted by adding to it a certain percentage of the bid price—a percentage representing the margin of domestic preference. The adjusted bid price is then compared with the lowest bid submitted by local bidders, and the contract is awarded in favour of the lower of these two bid prices.

The justification for having such a domestic preference scheme is based on the infant industry argument for protection. It is also important to examine whether the I.D.B. can adopt domestic preference schemes as a means of encouraging selected industries in member countries.

Guarantees for Loans.

It is to be examined whether the problems of obtaining guarantees for loans given by the Bank can be further simplified and whether the Bank can provide guarantee facilities to support loans taken by its member countries in the international money markets. It is, however, presumed that the cost of supporting guarantee operations could be *less* than the cost of the Bank's supporting the same volume of loans itself.

Organization and Method.

During this period, the Bank has seen a considerable expansion in its Operation and Project Department. This has enabled the I.D.B. to get involved in a number of important projects. The Economic Policy Planning Department has also seen considerable expansion in recent years. However, the Bank has made remarkable progress in building up an organizational structure although more work is needed to spell out the staff and line functions including further delegations of authority, without which the implementation of any policy will remain inadequate. The question of introducing a performance audit system should also be examined.

It may be noted here that the success of the operations greatly depends on the quality of the personnel the Bank recruits and on their leadership and commitment to Islamic ideology. In an innovative task of development, the professionals must have ideological commitment. The present secularized form of application for employment needs to be supplemented with a set of criteria that determine the level of professional competence *plus* commitment to Islam.

Establishment of a Research and Training Institute.

In consideration of the unorthodox functions which the Bank is expected to perform in diverse socio-economic settings, the recent decision to establish a separate Research and Training Institute after seven years of operation is one of the most important of all policy decisions. This Institute should immediately undertake responsibility for formulating an action programme at each country level, thereby helping to formulate the economic policy and planning of the Bank.

An independent evaluation and implementation unit should be set up within the Research Department to follow up the implementation of special measures, and to monitor the results, in order to obtain better policy guidelines.

Mobile Training Assistance.

It is, however, felt that there is a need to set up a mobile training assistance section within the Research Department with executives co-ordinating and training in assistance functions. This new unit should be deputed basically to establish training targets for development banks and other financial institutions and agencies with whom the Bank has or is likely to have an operational relationship, either through credit lines or through technical assistance.

Conclusions

It can be seen that up to 1985, the Bank has made remarkable progress in its various operations. The establishment of the I.D.B. represents a significant milestone towards achieving the goals of an Islamic economy in member countries and the consequent establishment of a Muslim "*Ummah*" or people. The innovative nature of the operations with which the Bank is expected to deal represents a new dimension of experiment in the economic and social affairs of men. The Bank's activities call for more than the replacement of interest rates with profitsharing and equity participation.

If the Bank during its short existence has created an impact less than our expectations, it is mainly due to a lack of experience in these kinds of operations in diverse socioeconomic settings. If the Bank's activities are considered to be conservative, it is mainly due to awareness of the risk and uncertainty associated with its new ventures. But the fact is that the Bank cannot escape from its responsibility in initiating and influencing economic and social progress in Muslim societies in conformity with the *Sharī'ah*. The Bank's activities need built-in dynamism and initiative for further expansion.

In the final analysis, however, the ability of member countries to attain self-sustained economic growth will depend largely on the political will of their leadership, expressed in terms of the efforts made towards domestic mobilization of resources, and on their political imagination and vision, expressed in terms of perceiving and implementing the structural and institutional changes needed for development, and finally on the vision of the Muslim "*Ummah*", expressed in terms of the co-operation extended to the IDB in achieving its objectives. The failure to perceive change in these directions will constitute a main obstacle to change itself in conformity with the *Sharī'ah*.

10.3 Local Islamic Banks And Investment Companies An Overview and Appraisal.

During the nineteen-seventies and early eighties more than fifty Islamic Banks and investment companies were established, operating on an interest-free basis in various parts of the Muslim and Western world (i.e. Denmark, Switzerland, Luxembourg). While the Nasser Social Bank of Egypt was established in 1971, the majority of other local banks came into existence in the late 1970s and early 80s. Despite the fact that these banks are relatively new and working in different local conditions, there is a common pattern to their operations, which I shall now discuss:

It appears from the various reports of Islamic banks that the local banking operations are guided by three basic principles: (a) the elimination of interest in all forms of transactions, (b) the undertaking of all legitimate and lawful business and commercial trade and industrial enterprises and (c) the provision of social services (reflected in utilizing *Zakāt* funds for the benefit of the poor and needy).

As for their common functions, these banks are also involved in four kinds of activity: (a) providing normal commercial banking services like effecting domestic and international transfers, collection of bills, opening of letters of credit and issuing letters of guarantee, providing safe custody on the basis of small commission charges, etc., (b) providing facilities for open non-investment accounts (e.g. current accounts), (c) providing facilities to attract funds for investment in trade and business and lastly

(d) providing social services on a humanitarian basis by utilizing *Zakāt* funds, allowing overdrafts free of charge and benevolent loans in special cases.

Utilization of Investment Funds.

However, the main activities of these banks are primarily concentrated into the diverse kinds of investment participation and partnership allowed in the *Sharī'ah*. The first of these is *Mushāraka*—a system whereby the banks enter into partnership with the clients for a limited period on a project. Both the banks and the clients contribute to the capital in varying degrees and agree upon a ratio of profit fixed in advance. The system is also based on the principle of diminishing participation leading to final ownership by the client under which the bank gives the partner the right to pay back the bank's shares either at once or in instalments paid out of a part of the net income of the operations. The Islamic banks have adopted this method of participation particularly in real estate businesses. In some cases, they have also adopted hire-purchase methods in solving housing problems (El-Najjar, 1980).

The second method of partnership is *Mudāraba* which combines financial experience with business experience. Under this system, the banks provide the capital and the clients the expertise. Again the profit is shared according to some agreed-upon ratio. In the case of loss, the bank bears all financial risk and the client loses the value of his labour only, should this be the result of circumstances beyond the control of the client. The possible economics of co-operation can be derived from the *Mudāraba* contract if properly implemented. It has a definite economic role to play. As Udovitch[3] observed:

"Sarakhsī's summary of the commenda's economic function is as accurate and to the point as that made by any contemporary student of medieval economic institutions. It includes the most important functions of the commenda in trade which have been described as "the hiring of capital" and the "hiring of trading skill'. By pointing to its economic function, Sarakshī also provides an explanation for its widespread use in medieval trade. To paraphrase him, profit can be realized only by the combination of capital and trading activity, and in certain commercial contexts such as long-distance trade, the commenda becomes the ideal instrument to attain this profitable goal."

The third method of investment is *Murābaha* under which the bank purchases commodities for its clients and resells them at a fixed mark-up or rate of profit on the stated original cost. By basing the sale price on the original cost of the item to the seller, the customer is provided with a modicum of protection against unfair exploitation. The general rule is "that money expended directly on the goods or on services indispensable to their sale (e.g. brokerage fees) may be included, whereas the personal expenses of the merchant and other expenses not directly involved with the goods are not to be figured into the stated original cost on which the *Murābaha* transaction is based. As an additional protection to the customer, the lawyers insist that the seller avoid any misleading statements. He must be scrupulous in how he designates the sum serving as the basis of the *Murābaha*. If he includes various expenses in this sum, he may not, directly or indirectly, lead the buyer to believe that the *Murābaha* is based on the purchase price, but must use some expression indicating that this is what it cost him, and not that this is what he paid for it."

Review of Operations

It appears that the system of *"Murābaha sale"* is very popular among Islamic Banks. But due care has to be taken in determining the mark-up or rate of profit in transacting *Murābaha* sales. The fact is that the legitimacy of transacting a *Murābaha* sale on the basis of any sum that is not misleading or fraudulent does not preclude the possibility of fixing the sale price *far higher than the original cost*. Unfair and excessive profit constitutes an element of *Ribā*, which is prohibited in Islam. What is needed is to define as objectively as possible the limits of the participant's freedom of action in such transactions as purchase, sale, deposit profit rates, credit, etc. It is important for the bank to demonstrate that in such transactions there is a risk involved and that the amount of time spent by the bank in addition to providing finance for the proper execution of this investment plan justifies the rate of profit. However, "one can envisage other hypothetical conditions under which the use of the *Murābaha* could have been particularly effective. One is the tantalizing possibility that it served as a form of commission sale. This possibility is supported by the fact that one is allowed to acquire goods on credit and then resell them on a *Murābaha* basis, with surcharge of either a fixed sum or a fixed rate of profit based on the purchase price. The only limitation placed on the seller is that he informs the buyer that the goods in question were acquired on credit. Honesty and probity require that this information be given, according to Sarakhsī, since customarily goods sold on credit fetch a higher price than those sold for cash. Whether the possibilities of commission sales inherent in the *Murābaha* were realized in medieval Islamic commercial life is a problem concerning which we can, at this point, make no definitive judgment. Whatever its possibilities, and whatever economic functions it fulfilled, the commenda agent possessed the right to engage in this transaction under the same conditions as applied to any other trader"[5].

Tawliya and Wadī'a Sale.

In this connection it may be mentioned that, in addition to the *Murābaha* sale, Islamic law also discusses in great detail two other forms of sale which have as their starting point the cost of the sale's object to the seller. "These are: the *tawliya,* resale at the stated original cost with no profit or loss to the seller; and the *wadī'a,* resale, at a discount from the original cost". In a truly Islamic spirit, the trade operations of Islamic banks should be expanded and they should also involve *Tawliya* and *Wadī'a* sale operations in special cases, particularly when a Muslim community or region is faced with natural calamities such as droughts, famines or earthquakes.

Summary

It appears that the current operations of the local banks are mainly concerned with quick returns and self-liquidating projects. In view of the competition from interest based banks and limited experience, expertise and finance, it is quite clear why local Islamic banks need to be operationalized within the shortest possible time.

Although Islamic investment companies are also issuing Islamic bonds (*Al-Muqāraḍa* bonds) and Islamic securities (*Al-Muḍāraba* certificates) on the basis of profit-sharing and loan certificates on a no-profit and no-loss basis for the mobilization of resources to finance big projects, the operations of local Islamic banks are currently of a short-term nature. By the very nature of their operations, it would be difficult on their part to exert decisive influence on the productive capacity of a country and to change the current composition of demand and the direction of economic developments. Co-ordinated efforts need to be made to mobilize voluntary and non-voluntary resources and channel them into productive uses in order to alter the priorities of development by investing in non-self-liquidating and long gestation projects. Besides, banks need to diversify their activities to include the business of commodity markets, intermediate goods, export and import substitutions. Some banks are involved in co-operative insurance, business and there exists further scope for its expansion; insurance coverage may be extended to depositors of investment accounts, operated by the local Islamic banks. The Islamic investment company's launching of a *solidarity Mudāraba* (an Islamic alternative to life-insurance) in 1979 was an important step forward. Insurance business is expected to cover other areas such as children's education, accidents, fire, etc.

However, the use of loan certificates by investment companies needs further examination. It appears that this practice is based on the implicit assumption that money is a commodity. In an important sense it encourages institutionalized hoarding. Despite the fact that investors allow their money for use, investment activities under the loan certificate scheme have to be extremely conservative and restrictive, because the reimbursement of such loans in full is guaranteed regardless of loss and profit. It is true, though, that this is a second best alternative to actual hoarding. It must be ascertained whether the reimbursement of loans under the loan certificate scheme is made in terms of a constant price of a representative basket of goods and services prevailing at the time of purchase of loan certificates. It is, however, important to keep clients fully informed of the economic implications of such loan certificates in the real world of inflation and recession through systematic banking and investment education programmes.

While the Islamic banks have made laudable attempts to mobilize *Zakāt* and other voluntary funds of the community, the banks' activities in providing social services to the poor and needy through the utilization of these resources appear to be very limited. There is room for further expansion of such activities. Merely granting a few "benevolent loans" or allowing "overdrafts" free of charge or making transfer payments to the poor is not enough. Through systematic planning these voluntary resources, particularly *"Zakāt* funds", should be utilized for productive purposes whose benefits go *exclusively* to the poor members of the community—benefits which enable the poor to raise their productive capacity and consequently bring them away from the poverty line. The spill-over benefits of such investment will, of course, be enjoyed by the community as a whole in terms of higher productivity, greater social peace and harmony and more spiritual satisfaction. This is how Islamic banks can gather the grass-root support of the masses of the poor people in the Muslim world.

The Success of Local Islamic Banks

Despite the difficulties in operating in unfavourable economic settings, almost all the Islamic Banks have been able to show a profit rate on capital ranging from nine per cent to twenty-five per cent, which is not being achieved by the commercial banks based on interest. On investment deposits, profits have been paid at the rate of eight percent to over fifteen percent by different banks. If this momentum is maintained and Islamic banks succeed in mobilizing a larger part of savings, they can bring influence to bear on corporate management to issue securities acceptable to the *Sharī'ah*. This will have a long-term impact on the institutional reforms, needed for these banks.

It may be noted here that many Islamic banks and investment companies are conducting their business not only in their respective countries but also in international trade and finance on the principles of reciprocity. That is, neither the Islamic banks nor the foreign banks should receive interest on funds deposited or borrowed by Islamic banks. (El-Najjar: 1980, p 126). It may, however, be difficult to establish this principle of reciprocity in local Islamic banks operating in the least-developed Muslim countries which have foreign exchange control and constraints. This very fact indicates not only the need for greater co-ordination among Islamic banks but also the establishment of a Central Islamic Bank which can serve as a clearing house for local Islamic banks, particularly where local Islamic banks are operating in a country whose currency is not convertible or subject to exchange controls (e.g. Sudan, Bangladesh).

Areas of Co-operation.

It has been suggested that the Islamic Development Bank (I.D.B.) can easily take over the function of a central clearing house. Besides, further areas of co-operation between the I.D.B. and the local Islamic banks which may be explored and examined are as follows:
(a) establishing "shopping basket" lines of equity and extending loans, leasing, profit-sharing or technical assistance operations;
(b) developing markets for convertible securities;
(c) mobile training and project appraisal units;
(d) joint market research;
(e) utilization of the surplus funds on short-term investments;
(f) joint venture projects;
(g) joint consultancy services;
(h) regional co-operation and marketing workshops on special problems and sharing experiences of economics, finance, banking and so on.

The need for such co-operation and co-ordination is all the more important because it is mutually beneficial and less costly to have a co-ordinated approach in the fields of personnel training, marketing, local project identification, investment, and research in Islamic economics. Since Islamic banks are operating in unfamiliar and adverse economic settings, it is particularly important to minimize costs, avoid wastage and unnecessary duplication and to have dynamic managerial strategies, so that the profitability of those banks is sustained over a long time. In the interests of the minimization of costs it is to be examined whether, instead of having religious supervisory boards for each of the banks, a permanent committee under the Institute of Research can provide this consultancy service to each banks. The same can be applied in the case of project feasibility studies. This would enable the banks to have a common pool of competent professionals and *Sharī'ah* scholars. It would be less costly and more efficient, provided that the existing information services become more organized and prompt. This is not to suggest that the success of these banks is to be judged only by the level or rate of profit earned. Their real success lies in using their material gains to influence reform in the existing socio-economic institutions in a way acceptable to the *Sharī'ah*. To achieve this goal, it is important to ensure the equitable distribution of lines of equity, loans and other benefits among the people as far as practicable. So a study of the "profile of beneficiaries" of these banks needs to be undertaken.

In conclusion, it can safely be said that the successful operation of the Islamic banks, despite the difficulties of working in unfamiliar socio-economic settings, has constituted a significant breakthrough; the banks have introduced a number of innovations in the field of Islamic economics, money and banking. Even some Western European Banks convinced of the feasibility of the Islamic economic system, accepted to operate in line with the Islamic *Sharī'ah*. However, we need not be complacent; the challenge of tomorrow is greater than today.

10.4 Dar Al-Maal Al-Islami (D.M.I.): A Brief Review.

To date *Dar Al-Maal Al-Islami* (D.M.I.) is the largest Islamic investment company. D.M.I. was formed by indenture on July 27, 1981, under the laws of the Commonwealth of the Bahamas as a distinct legal entity, with an authorized capital of $1 billion. Under the terms of the indenture, all trust assets are held by the fiduciary custodian and investments are administered by the trust administrator, D.M.I., SA. Geneva, a wholly-owned Swiss subsidiary. Operations of the D.M.I. Group commenced on January 1, 1982, and its total issued capital at June 30, 1982, was $307, 622, 906.

D.M.I., a multi-national holding company sponsored by Prince Muhammad Al-Faisal, plans to set up a world-wide network of banks, insurance companies and investment firms operating in accordance with the principles of the *Sharī'ah*. During its five year plan, D.M.I. is expected to establish twenty-eight Faisal Islamic Banks, nine investment companies and five insurance firms in both Islamic and Western countries.

There are five types of accounts available at the Islamic Investment Company. The first type of account called the "Fourth *Mudāraba*" can be opened with as little as $500 of which three per cent is retained. This account yields profit in the neighbourhood of that given by conventional banks except that no interest is allowed in the Islamic economy.

The second type of account offered to investors is the "Institutional Account", which needs an initial deposit of nearly $90,000 of which only 0.1 per cent is retained. It also gives a better yield. The third type is the "Investment Account", a kind of separate investment portfolio to be opened with $500,000, of which 0.1 percent is retained. Such accounts could yield more than thirty per cent profit per year.

The fourth type of account is an Islamic current account in Europe which can be opened with $20,000 and which yields no profit. Its only advantage is that the investor is assured that his money is not invested in immoral activities. The fifth type of account is called the 'Seventh *Mudāraba*". It is an insurance, saving and investment account according to Islamic tenets[6].

It may be noted here that deposit accounts, lending and financing activities are also open to non-Muslims as well, provided they do not engage in economic activities contrary to the principles of the *Sharī'ah*.

D.M.I. is expected to issue US$200 million shares for public subscription in 1983. Most of the profit made by D.M.I. during 1981–1982 (US$8.5 million net profit) is expected to be ploughed back into the business until D.M.I.'s first five year plan is completed.

D.M.I. is involved in financing various types of project such as poultry farms, shopping centres, and road construction projects, by supplying a fleet of tractors, loaders, bulldozers, etc.

D.M.I. also helps businessmen by participating in the equity of their projects, or simply in the equity of their working capital, with participating phasing out year after year until D.M.I. completely withdraws.

Although it is too early to analyze the full impact of D.M.I.'s various investment activities world wide, yet it can safely be said that D.M.I. has made a significant breakthrough by drawing the serious attention of Western world to the Islamic concept of banking and investment in shares and securities. By starting its operations in the West, D.M.I. has had instant exposure to Western technical skill and know-how and has enhanced the possibilities of greater co-operation between the Islamic and the Western world. This has put D.M.I. in a relatively advantageous position compared to I.D.B., whose operations are mainly confined to the Muslim world. This instant exposure to superior technical know-how may however retard the process of the growth of indigenous technology. What is needed is cautious planning for the future expansion of a network of Islamic banks and greater allocation of funds for research and training. D.M.I.'s research programme appears weak.

It is indeed significant that during 1981–85, D.M.I. is expected to set up a network of twenty-eight Faisal Islamic Banks, nine investment companies and five insurance firms, but its operational strategy needs to be altered or modified when it comes to work in the least-developed Muslim countries such as Bangladesh and Chad, particularly in regard to the "minimum initial deposit rate" in various types of accounts available at the Islamic investment company. While this initial deposit rate in various accounts may not be on the high side in the case of capital surplus rich Islamic and Western countries, they appear to be high in the case of capital-starved poor Muslim countries. If these initial deposit rates remain intact irrespective of the country, it may attract the rich of the poor country to obtaining the benefits of D.M.I.'s operations. This is what is not expected of an Islamic investment company.

Finally, ways and means should be found to ensure greater co-operation between D.M.I., I.D.B. and the other Islamic banks, particularly in the areas of research, training and joint venture projects. Taken all in all, D.M.I. is expected to make a significant contribution towards the development of Islamic financial markets. Its direct involvement in various types of investment and business activities may encourage understanding of the complementary nature of the two different economies of the Islamic and Western worlds and consequently it may contribute towards the development of an Islamic common market. The Al-Bareaka Islamic investment group, under the leadership of Sheikh Saleh Kamil of Saudi Arabia, has also been able to establish a world-wide network of Islamic banks and investment companies in both Islamic and Western countries.

Notes

[1] The material for this chapter is heavily drawn from the author's recent book: *The Making of an Islamic Economic Society: Islamic dimensions in economic analysis* published by International Association of Islamic Banks, Cairo, and International Institute of Islamic Banking and Economics, Kibris (Turkish Cyprus).

[2] "Three Arabic terms used to designate the commenda: *qirād, muqārada,* and *mudāraba*; the terms are interchangeable with no essential difference in meaning or connotation among them. The divergence in terminology was probably originally due to geographical factors. The terms *qirād* and *muqārada* apparently originated in the Arabian peninsula, and the term *mudaraba* was of Iraqi provenance. Subsequently, the difference was perpetuated by the legal schools, the Malikīs and *Shāfi'* is adopting the term *qirad* and, to a lesser degree, *muqārada,* and the *Hanafis* the term *mudāraba.* I however, have preferred the first term (*mudāraba*) because it corresponds to that which is found in the book of God, may He be exalted. God, may He be exalted, said: "While others travel in the land (*yadribuna fillard)* in search of Allah's bounty", that is to say, travel for the purposes of trade". (Udovitch, *Partnerships* and Profit in Medieval Islam, Princeton, New York, 1970 pp. 174–175

[3] Udovitch, pp. 17–6.

[4] Udovitch, p. 220.

[5] Udovitch, p. 221–222.

[6] *Arab News,* 7th May 1983.

10.5 Selected Further Reading

Ahmad, Sheikh Mahmud, "Economics of Islam–A Comparative Study", Second revised and enlarged edition, Sh. Muhammad Ashraf, Lahore, 1947, Reported 1977.

Agabany, Fouad, "Faisal Islamic Bank (Sudan): A Promising experience in comprehensive Islamic Banking", *Proceedings of International Seminar on Monetary and Fiscal Economics of Islam,* Islamabad, 1981.

Al-Arabi, Muhammad Abdullah, "Contemporary Bank Transaction and Islam's view thereon" in *The Islamic Review, vol.* 54. London, May 1966.

Albach, Horst, "Risk, Capital, Business Investment and Economic Cooperation", Paper presented at the *International Symposium on Islamic Banks and Strategies of Economic Cooperation* the International Association of Islamic Banks, Baden Baden, 1981.

Ali, Salamat, "A Matter of Interest" (P.L.S. in Pakistan) in *Far Eastern Economic Reveiw,* vol. 112, No. 25, Hong Kong, June, 1981.

Bahrain Islamic Bank. *Annual Report, 1400 AH,* Bahrain Islamic Bank, Manama, Bahrain, 1981.

Chowdhury, A. B. M. Masudul Alam, "A Mathematical Formulation of *"Mudārabah* the Profit-Sharing System in Islam", *in Association of Muslim Social Scientists Proceedings,* Third *International Seminar,* Indiana, 1974.

Conference of Islamic Finance Ministers, Jeddah, "Islamic Development Bank Articles Establishing the IDB", 1974.

Dar-al-Maal Al-Islami Brochure (no bibliographical data) 1981.

Dubai Islamic Bank. *Banking Services offered by Dubai Islamic Bank,* Dubai Islamic Bank, Dubai, 1976.

Faisal Islamic Bank of Egypt. *Annual Report of the Board of Directors 1980 A. D./1400 AH,* Faisal Islamic Bank of Egypt, Cairo, 1980.

Ghanameh, Abdul Hadi, "The Interestless Economy" in *Contemporary Aspects of Economic and Social Thinking in Islam,* M. S. A. of U. S. A. and Canada, Indiana, 1973.

Hamidullah, Muhammad, "A Suggestion for an Interest Free Islamic Monetary Fund" in *Islamic Review,* London, 1955.

Al-Hawari, Sayid, "The Distinctive Nature of Islamic banks" Paper 7/4 for "First Advanced Course on Islamic Banks" International Institute of Islamic Banking and Economics Cairo, 1981.

Homoud, Sami, "How an Islamic Bank works on an International basis" Paper II/I for "First Advanced Course on Islamic Banks", International Institute of Islamic banking and Economics, Cairo, 1981.

Hughes, Margaret, "Funding the Islamic way (D.M.I.)" in *Far Eastern Economic Review,* vol. in 113, No. 32 (31 July) Hong Kong, 1981.

Islamic Development Bank. *The First, Second, Third, Fourth, Fifth, Sixth Seventh, Eighth, Ninth and Tenth Annual Reports from 1395/1396 AH (1975/1976) to 1402/1403 A H (1982/1983),* Islamic Development, Bank, Jeddah.

Jordan Islamic Bank for Finance and Investment, Jordan Islamic Bank for Finance and Investment, Law No. 13 of 1978, Second edn, Jordan Islamic Bank.

Khan, Fahim M. "Islamic Banking as practised now in the world" in *Money and Banking in Islam,* ed. by Z. Ahmad *et al.* International Centre for Research in Islamic Economics, King Abdulaziz University, Jeddah, and International Institute for Policy Studies, Islamabad, Pakistan, 1981.

Kuwait Fianance House. *Guide Book for Banking and Investment Based on Islamic (Sharia) Law,* Kuwait Finance House,? 1977.

Mannan, M. A. "Indexation in an Islamic Economy, Problems and Prospects" in *Journal of Development Studies.* vol. IV, N. W. F. P. Agricultural University, Peshawar, Pakistan, 1980.

Mannan, M. A. "Islamic Banks in Operation Trends and Issues", in *The Making of Islamic Economic Society, Islamic Dimensions in Economic Analysis,* Chapter 18, International Association of Islamic Banks, Cairo, 1984.

Mommoud, Sami, "The Theory and Practice of Islamic Banking in the Modern World", Paper Presented at a Conference of the Arab Bankers Association and Arab British Chamber of Commerce in London, 1980.

Nienhaus, Volker, "Islamic Economics of Profit-Sharing Comments". Bochum Institut für Entwicklungsforschung und Entwicklungspolitik, 1981.

Scharf, Traute Whlers, "Positive Recycling and the Productive Use of Petrocapital in the 1980s: Possible Cooperation Strategies for Islamic Banks", Paper Presented at the 1st International Symposium on Islamic Banks and Strategies for Economic Cooperation, in Baden Baden 1981.

Udovitch, Abraham L. "Partnerships and Profit in Medieval Islam", Varsity Press, Princeton New York, 1970.

APPENDIX (A)

A Note on the Islamic International Monetary Fund (I.I.M.F.)

The need for having an Islamic International Monetary Fund (I.I.M.F.) arises from both positive and negative factors. While the positive factors relate to the establishment of the Islamic Development Bank and other local Islamic banks and investment companies deriving from the seventies and early eighties, the negative factors arise from the disappointing failure of the North-South dialogue for a new international economic order. The breakdown became inevitable in the face of the Third World's challenge to the North's areas of global economic domination. The group of 77 (which now consists of 121 developing countries including all the Muslim states) wanted a structural reform of the present financial and monetary institutions such as the I.M.F., the World Bank and GATT. Because the world has changed vastly in the three decades since the Bretton Woods Conference, new structures are needed for international trade, finance and banking. Under the system of weighted voting in these specialized financial monetary institutions and given that some decisions require a majority of eighty-five per cent of the votes, the developed industrialized countries of the West would veto any attempt at structural reforms in the prevailing economic order. This, at present, works to their advantage and is often biased against the interests of the developing countries. The U.S. alone, for instance, has twenty-three per cent of the voting strength in the I.M.F. and the European Economic Community (E.E.C.) about 19 per cent.

The developed countries were insistent that issues can be discussed, but only within the framework of the existing financial and monetary institutions, which must be preserved. It would, however, be naive to presume that the industrially developed countries will be easily persuaded to give up the existing structures, which guarantee them global economic domination, in favour of measures which would benefit the Third World countries equitably.

What are the alternatives for the Muslim World? The Muslim World has no choice but to explore the potential of all aspects of economic co-operation and to cultivate individual and collective self-reliance among the Muslim countries themselves as a matter of priority. The complexity of the Muslim World's choice arises from the fact that the Third World solution (even if there is any) may not be desirable for the Muslim World, which insists on making all the socio-economic institutions confirm with the principles of *Sharī'ah*. The social and economic ethics of Islam in many cases run counter to the policies and practices of the secular institutions of many Third World countries too.

The establishment of the Islamic International Monetary Fund is expected to provide a framework within which the various economic relationships such as exports, imports, domestic output, employment, prices and income among nations operate. The current poor volume of trade between the Muslim countries can be explained in terms of the lack of a well functioning monetary system. The absence of an appropriate institutional arrangement to deal with monetary problems among Muslim countries is discouraging the development of trade and investment among Islamic nations. Furthermore, inadequate transport and payment difficulties along with constant exchange rate fluctuations and the lack of proper remittance facilities also stand in the way of effective co-operation.

So what is required is not just a refurbishing of the old framework of co-operation based on the past colonial and neo-colonial systems, but also a new set of relationships based upon mutual demand and mutual sharing of experience and knowledge between nations. It is important that in the monetary sphere this co-operation must be reflected through the establishment of the I.I.M.F., which is expected not only to promote exchange stability and to facilitate the settlement of international accounts but also to encourage the expansion and balanced growth of trade among Muslim countries, thereby assisting in the establishment of a multilateral system of payments. As a result the I.I.M.F. may provide a frame of reference to the system.

APPENDIX (B)

Let me now provide an overview of the monetary policy in an Islamic state on the assumption that fiscal and monetary measures can complement each other, although they differ in their impact.

Monetary Policy: An Overview

There is growing recognition of the fact that in an Islamic economy, monetary policy should pursue the goals of maintaining stability in the value of money, economic well-being, full employment, optimum economic growth and the promotion of distributive justice. It is thus widely believed that the central banking system in an Islamic state must control the supply of money and that the money supply must be adjusted to the needs of the economy in terms of both short-term stability, long-term growth and the allocation of bank resources to help realize the goal of social welfare.

Thus, despite the abolition of the interest rate and the non-availability of an open market policy, a number of monetary policy instruments such as a cash reserve ratio, a liquidity ratio, credit ceilings, a "profit-sharing ratio" in different sectors, financing and moral persuasion, which can be legitimately used in an Islamic economy as indispensable components of stabilization, distribution and growth policies. Besides, due to its effects on international capital movements, monetary policy will have a special advantage in securing balance of payments equilibrium.

As regards the power to create credit by commercial banks, there is some controversy. But the predominent view is that commercial banks should have the power to create credit provided its benefits do not go to only to big family businesses or to groups of interlocking directorates of firms or banks to the neglect of the larger interests of society. This has crucial policy implications particularly in the case of poor Muslim countries, where conscious policy measures are to be taken by the central banks to bring about more equitable distribution and allocation of the bank resources (in the form of rural credit) to help finance the agricultural sector, rural development and agro-based industries so that the benefits go to rural areas, where the bulk of the people live in most of Muslim countries today.

As noted earlier, in an Islamic economy, being essentially equity-based rather than loan-based, the ideal alternatives to interest are profit-and loss-sharing and *Quard-i-Ḥasanah* in the production and consumption areas respectively.

Policy Mix

An Islamic economy does provide scope for securing a policy mix of monetary and fiscal policies which will permit the achievement of more objectives than would be possible with the use of one policy instrument alone, supervise exchange rate fluctuations and eventually start fulfilling the role of a Muslim world central bank. The use of the Islamic *dinār* by the Islamic Development Bank is a move towards eventual monetary integration.

If the proposed I.I.M.F. is to play a dynamic role in the Muslim world, aiming at Islamic reconstruction, reform and expansion, it must not insist on mere expenditure-reducing policies as the major means of correcting the external deficits of the least developed Muslim countries in particular, and other Muslim countries in general, as this type of policy is poorly founded in economic analysis and is unrealistic from a policy point of view in the light of the existing socio-economic realities.

CHAPTER 11

Consumption and Non-Consumption Loans in Islam

11.1 Consumption Loans: Principles

11.2 The Mechanism of Consumption Loans

11.3 Financing the Purchase of Consumer Durables

11.4 Interest-free Housing Finance

11.5 Selected Further Reading

"Whoever contracts a debt intending to repay it, Allah will pay it on his behalf, and whoever contracts a debt intending to waste it, Allah will bring him to ruin."

Prophet Muḥammad (peace be upon him)

"Thou shalt not give him the money upon usury, or lend him thy victuals for increase."

Old Testament, Lev., 25:37

Consumption Loans: Their Principles

Public finance, it is argued, differs from private finance in one vital respect because, unlike the State, the private individual has very little control over the size of his income; he is under the obligation of adjusting his expenditure to his income and not the other way round. It is, of course, argued that the private individual can, within certain limits, adjust his income to his expenditure. So if more money is to be spent, more money can be found by lending and borrowing. Islam has recognized these as necessary conditions in human transactions with one difference. This difference arises partly because of the introduction of the element of morality in taking a consumption loan, partly because of the unique mechanisms an Islamic State should adopt for handling this type of loan.

If we carefully analyze the various injunctions of Islam we can easily derive the following four principles pertaining to consumption loans. They are (*a*) principle of genuineness, (*b*) principle to contract, (*c*) principle of payment, and (*d*) principle of help.

The principle of genuineness arises from the fact that taking a loan without any valid reason is discouraged by the Prophet who is reported to have sought refuge from being in debt as well as from sin. 'Ā'ishah said: The Messenger of Allah (peace be upon him) used to pray while saying prayers "O Allah! I seek refuge in Thee from sin and from being in debt." Someone asked him, "How often dost thou, O Messenger of Allah! seek refuge from being in debt?" He said: "When a man is in debt he speaks and tells lies and he promises and breaks the promise"(Bukhārī).

In fact, Islam recognizes consumption loans for meeting indispensable minimum wants, which are basically physiological in character. These wants arise from the fact that man is not self-sufficient in himself. He requires food, shelter and clothing for his barest subsistence and he has to secure them by means of effort. This barest physiological minimum is not uniform for all persons in all countries and at all times. The minimum food requirements vary from person to person. Subject to this variation, one can take a loan for meeting one's basic requirements. But in modern times, there is a tendency for physiological wants to be overshadowed by psychological factors like snobbish imitation and exhibitionist impulses which determine the present-day physiological wants of most modern men. Islam does not recognize any consumption loans required for meeting such artificial wants.

This brings us to a discussion of the second principle, that is, the principle of contract, which owes its origin to the Holy *Qur'ān* which says: "When you deal with each other in contracting a debt for a fixed time, write it down. . . . Let him who owes the debt dictate". (*Sūrah* II 282). That is, every act of lending and borrowing should be written down clearly without the disadvantage of the debtor. The creditor should see that no injustice is being done to the debtor. If a loan is taken on behalf of a minor, or of a person of unsound judgement, then his guardian or the persons representing his interest should dictate the terms of the contract.

When ye deal with each other,
In transactions involving
Future obligations
In a fixed period of time
Reduce them to writing

. . . .

So let him write
Let him who incurs
The liability dictate.

(*Sūrah* II 282)

The necessity of such contracts arises because of the fact that they are "more likely to keep out of doubts and avoid future disputes". This principle of contract is equally applicable to both consumption and productive loans. Islam has also made provision for granting loans against proper security. Thus the mortgaging of property as security for payment of debt is allowed and the mortgagee is allowed to derive benefit from it. Thus it is related on the authority of 'Ā'ishah that the Prophet (peace be upon him) bought food from a Jew for payment to be made at an appointed time, and he mortgaged for it an iron coat-of-mail" (Bukhārī).

Again, Abū Hurairah reported the Messenger of Allah (peace be upon him) to have said: "The mortgaged animal may be used for riding when it is mortgaged on account of what is spent on it, and the milk of a milch animal may be drunk when it is mortgaged, and the expenditure shall be borne by him who rides (the animal) and drinks (the milk)" (Bukhārī).

This *Ḥadith* shows that "when a person has to spend money on the thing mortgaged, he is entitled to derive benefit from it. Hence a house or land can be mortgaged subject to the condition that the possession shall be made over to the mortgagee who is entitled to live in the house or let it on hire, if he carries out the repairs, and to till the land and have the produce of it if he spends on it."

Now we can pass on to the third principle governing loans which is the principle of payment. It is gratifying to note that Islam always maintains a balance between opposite tendencies. While the creditor has been directed to guard against any injustice being done to the debtor, the debtor has also been directed to make every sincere effort to make repayment of a loan. It is related on the authority of Abū Hurairah that the Prophet (peace be upon him) said "Whoever contracts a debt intending to repay it, Allah will pay it on his behalf, and whoever contracts a debt intending to waste it, Allah will bring him ruin"(Bukhārī.)

In Islam, the importance of repayment of a loan can hardly be overestimated. Salāmat reported, "A bier was brought to the Prophet (peace be upon him) that he may say a funeral prayer over it. He said, 'Was he in debt?' They said, 'No.' So he said prayers over it. Another bier was brought to him and he said, 'Was he in debt?' They said 'Yes,' He said, 'Say prayers over your companion.' Abū Qatādah said, 'I will pay his debt, O Messenger of Allah!' So he said funeral prayers over it.'' The learned commentators are of the opinion that the Prophet (peace be upon him) did not forbid the saying of funeral prayers over the bier of a person who was in debt. By refusing to say prayers himself, he wanted only to discourage the habit of contracting debts which one had not the means to repay. As a matter of fact, Islam does not justify deferring payments without valid reason. Abū Hurairah reported: The Messenger of Allah (peace be upon him) said, "Delaying the payment of a debt by a well-to-do person is injustice" (Bukhāri). The Prophet is reported to have even said: "Deferring payment by one who has the means to pay legalizes his punishment and his honour." (Bukhāri.) But the Welfare State of Islam is required to undertake both the maintenance of uncared-for families and the payment of unpaid debts. It is related on the authority of Abū Hurairah that the Prophet said (peace be upon him), "Whoever leaves property, it is for his heirs, and whoever leaves a burden, it shall be our charge."

The fourth principle governing loan, irrespective of whether it is a productive or consumption loan, is the principle of help which owes its origin both to the Holy *Qur'ān* and the *Sunnah*. This principle of help must be understood in a comprehensive sense. Viewed positively, all types of loan in Islam are free of interest ("Allah has allowed trading and forbidden usury") (*Sūrah* II 275), because usury is anti-social and because it is a naked exploitation of a brother's need. That is why, it is laid down in the Holy *Qur'ān*:

> "God will deprive
> Usury of all blessing,
> But will give increase
> For deeds of charity"
>
> (*Sūrah* II 276)

Even today we find how a creditor nation holds a debtor nation in bondage through usurious loans. The debt-servicing problem which is going to be aggravated by the element of interest is bound to embitter international relations between developed and underdeveloped countries. We have records to prove that the huge loan negotiated between the USA and UK under the Brettonwoods Agreement is responsible for the deterioration of mutual relations, the cause being the interest charged by the creditor. Even the late Lord Keynes, the author of this agreement on behalf of England, expressed his deep regret over the USA's failure to grant an interest-free loan to the UK. Never was the wisdom of the prohibition of interest so loudly vindicated as in the Parliament of England when the Brettonwoods bill was under heavy fire. In Islam loans are to be in the nature of grants-in-aid and not commercial transactions. Jābir reported: The Messenger of Allah (peace be upon him) cursed the usurer and the man who pays usury and the writer of the transaction and the two witnesses thereof, and he said, "They are alike" (Muslim and *Mishkāt*).

In an Islamic State, it is presumed that the consumption loan shall be taken only to meet the genuine needs of the people. Therefore, if the debtor is in real difficulty, the repayment of a loan may be postponed; even remission of debt is recommended in special extraordinary circumstances. The Holy *Qur'ān* says:

"If the debtor is
In a difficulty,
Grant him time
Till it is easy
For him to repay.
But if ye remit it
By way of charity,
That is best for you
If ye only Knew."

(*Sūrah* II 280)

But Islam has recommended the taking of voluntary payment in excess of the principal sum of the loan, because this is not interest. Jābir said: "I came to the Prophet (peace be upon him) while he was in the mosque, so he said, "Say two rak'ahs of prayer." And he owed me a debt, so he paid it to me and gave me more (than was due)." (Bukhāri).

While recommending the remission of debt in special circumstances, the genuine *interest* of the creditor is safeguarded. The modern practice of *attaching* the property of the insolvent is recognized in Islam. Thus Abū Hurairah said: The Messenger of Allah (peace be upon him) said, "Whoever finds his property itself with a man who has become insolvent, he has a greater right to it than others" (Bukhāri). Following the tradition of the Prophet (peace be upon him), Hadrat 'Uthmān is reported to have decided that "whoever takes his due before a man becomes insolvent, it is his, and whoever recognizes his property itself with an insolvent has a greater right to it" (Bukhāri).

In brief, these are the principles governing consumption loans in Islam.

11.2 The Mechanism of Consumption Loans

Now we are coming to the more difficult part of our discussion, that is, the mechanism for consumption loans in an Islamic state, because principles will remain principles if they are not translated into action, or if they are not made workable.

True, a peculiar kind of loan, called "*Qard-i-Hasanah*", the repayment of which was not imperative, existed and still does exist in all the Muslim countries. The scope of this type of loan appears to be very limited because of its nature. But we have no evidence to indicate that there is a set mechanism for the implementation of the principles of consumption loans in an Islamic state. The fact is that the mechanism which may be applicable in one country may not be applicable in another country. Because the type of mechanism suited to a particular country depends upon the type of development that the country has achieved. The only condition is that the mechanism for the implementation of the principles of a consumption loan must not come into conflict with the expressed or implied injunctions of the Holy *Qur'ān* and the *Sunnah*. Within this framework, I feel that the Islamic state may adopt any of or all the following three courses of action pertaining to the handling of the various aspects of consumption loans:

(*a*) through the creation of a network of consumers' cooperatives under the patronage of the state;

(*b*) through the Islamic Bank; and/or

(*c*) through the establishment of a consumption credit fund by the Government.

(*a*) The best way of handling the problem of consumption loans is to establish a network of consumers' co-operatives on a no-profit-no-loss basis under the patronage of the state. The consumers' co-operatives will, after scrutinizing the credit-worthiness of the prospective borrowers, allow the consumers to purchase goods at the market rate on credit up to a certain limit mutually agreed upon. This sale would obviously include a normal profit so that the establishment charges are met from such sales. This approach to the problem of consumer loans stands justified from almost any angle of analysis. It is psychologically justified, because of the consumers' feeling that these co-operatives which are organized on a no-profit-no-loss basis are the result of their own co-operation. It is morally justified, because it enables the consumers to make purchases of essential commodities to live on a human plane of existence and this, in turn, has proportionate relevancy to social values. It is economically justified, because selective and carefully assessed consumer loans will stimulate productivity, not only in developed countries, but also in developing countries and thereby eliminate the modern element of interest in the process of consumption, production and distribution.

Coming to the money aspect, these co-operatives may extend loans in terms of money under special circumstances. A certain percentage of the reserve fund or contingency fund of such co-operatives may be set aside to meet special types of consumption loans, which may not be carried out on a massive basis in view of the obvious scarcity of resources of such co-operatives; such consumers' co-operatives are in a better position to implement this loan policy because they are very aware of the needs of the borrowers.

(*b*) The problem of consumption loans can also be handled through Islamic banks in at least two ways. Firstly, the bank may advance loans to consumers against proper securities out of a part of the reserve fund created mainly from the deposits of those depositors who do not like to take any portion of the profit on their deposits from the bank. These people will generally make deposits with the bank simply for security reasons just as the locker system is available at modern banks, where people keep their jewellery, important documents and the like on payment of a certain fee. Such transactions can be carried out on a no-profit-no-loss basis. It is, of course, understood that the bank must be entitled to recover establishment and administrative charges from the borrowers to meet the servicing expenses of the loans. These service charges will obviously vary from person to person and from locality to locality depending upon the nature and amount of the loans.

Secondly, since the bank in an Islamic state will have to act as an active partner in various agricultural and industrial projects, I find no harm if banks in Islamic states run a network of consumer stores which may be organized on commercial lines. From such stores prospective genuine borrowers may be allowed to purchase goods up to a certain limit on credit. Credit ration cards may be issued after proper investigation into the credit-worthiness of borrowers. Apart from the normal profits which a bank is expected to earn from a normal transaction, banks must be empowered to recover a percentage of the calculated service charges.

This suggestion may sound strange to persons who are used to the capitalist concept of banking. The type of bank we propose for an Islamic state may not find its counterpart in the capitalist framework of society. The fact is that the concept of banking in an Islamic state is altogether different from the present-day type of banking which is essentially a capitalist concept banking. If the Islamic concept of banking is translated into action in order to handle the problem of consumption loans, it may be one of the effective means of increasing the purchasing power of the consumers, which will, in its turn, stimulate production and supply, and they will provide more employment and productivity in the community. It may be noted here that in a developing Muslim country, a consumption loans policy must be selective and must not be haphazard.

(c) Finally, consumption loans may be granted by governments out of a Consumption Credit Fund created through a small government contribution (say two to two and a half per cent) from the revenue surplus which a government is expected to have after meeting all non-development expenditures. In respect of consumption loans the government must act as a lender of the last resort. This government loan may be of two types: one a tied consumption loan where prospective borrowers will be required to purchase goods from a predetermined list of home-produced goods. This policy of tied consumption loans can be related to the policy of protection of infant industry. The other type of loan can be an untied consumption loan where the prospective borrowers may be allowed to exercise their own reason and judgement in spending the loan. What type of consumption loans, tied or untied, an Islamic state would encourage depends on the nature of development and the availability of resources. It goes without saying that this credit policy can be carried out on payment of nominal service charges and can also be insured against the risk of default and non-payment with insurance companies.

Since the be-all and end-all of every Islamic state is to achieve the goal of a welfare state, we need not be surprised to see the creation of a Consumption Credit Fund by the Islamic Government. In fact, "it will prevent the people from going into the hands of loan sharks, and this will keep the society healthy and free from usurious evils." Even in a capitalist social framework, the Government provides many welfare facilities like social security schemes, old-age pensions, running charitable hospitals, awarding scholarships to poor and talented students and so on.

The conclusion that ideally emerges is that the consumption loans policy of an Islamic state must include all of the three measures already mentioned, because none of these complex mechanisms can be a substitute for the others or provide the maximum effect, if pursued alone. From the Islamic standpoint, the fundamental justification for all these measures lies in the fact that if these measures are properly implemented, they may go a long way towards furnishing a strong motive for mutual co-operation and help—a basic element of an Islamic social framework. The Holy *Qur'ān* says: "Help one another in righteousness and virtue but help not one another in sin and transgression." The Prophet (peace be upon him) is also reported to have said: "If a person occupies himself in helping his brother, God occupies Himself in helping him."

11.3 Financing the Purchase of Consumer Durables

So far we have mainly confined our discussion to consumption loans for food and other basic necessities of life. Here we deal with the purchase of durable consumer goods (i.e. televisions, cars, radios, refrigerators) that are bought only occasionally. At the very outset it is important to note that we are here concerned not with a single isolated purchase, but with a continuous flow of purchases, because the quantity demanded of consumer durables is viewed as a flow concept.

However, in a growing Islamic economy, the question of financing the purchase of consumer durables is extremely important for two reasons. Firstly, the reaction of demand to changes in income is important in any economy, because with an increase of income, people tend to increase their demand for all but inferior commodities. But the demand for food and basic clothing will generally not increase nearly as much as the demand for consumer durables. Put in more technical terms, at low levels of income the income elasticity demand for food is fairly high but as the level of income rises, it tends to fall well below unity, so that every little of any additional amount of income is spent on food. Now, almost all the Muslim countries are having development plans designed to increase the *per capita* income of their people so that the current low consumption level can be raised. So we may not be surprised to see an increased demand for consumer durables in Muslim countries during the coming decades.

Secondly, the rise in income levels is expected to be shared equitably by all households in an Islamic economy because of Islam's deep concern for social justice in development planning. The point we are making is that in a growing Islamic economy we can reasonably expect an increase in the demand not only for food and clothing but for consumer durables in the future. It is pertinent to mention here that increased spending on consumer durables is also expected due to the erosion in the value of money as a result of inflationary pressure, the abolition of interest in an Islamic economy, the imposition of *Zakāt* on hoarded money, and the "demonstration effect", resulting from increased contact with the West, which has been achieved through significant improvements in transport and communications and increased cultural co-operation in the fields of education, science and technology between the Islamic and non-Islamic world.

This brings us to the next important question of how to obtain loans for the purchase of consumer durables. In the Western countries many consumer durables are bought on credit at interest rates between fifteen and twenty per cent. Such purchases respond to the cost and availability of credit. Since interest is prohibited in Islam, there are at least three other distinct ways under which the purchase of consumer durables can be arranged on credit. They are as follows:—

(a) *Murābaha*
(b) Hire-purchase
(c) Operating leases

(a) *Murābaha*

The purchase of consumer durables may be financed under *Murābaha* arrangements on a restricted scale as permitted by the *Sharī'ah*. In Chapters 9 and 10 we discussed the working of *Murābaha* contracts. As defined earlier, *Murābaha* is a sale in which the margin of profit is mutually agreed upon between the buyers and sellers. The payment of the price, including the agreed mark-up, may be made immediately or in instalments. This arrangement could be of considerable use not only in financing the purchase of consumer durables but also in financing the input requirements of industry and agriculture due to the relative simplicity of its operation. Its indiscriminate and wide use may, however, introduce interest rates through the back-door. The range of mark-ups on purchase prices if not controlled, may lead to the emergence of a system of credit on interest under a different name.

(b) Hire-purchase

Under this system, Islamic banks may finance the purchase of consumer durables under a joint-ownership arrangement subject to the provision of surety. In such cases banks would be entitled to a share in the net rental value of the goods concerned, in addition to the repayment of the principal in instalments. The user of the equipment is to meet its maintanance expenses, although, if the item is insured, the cost of insurance may be shared between the bank and the user.

(c) Operating leases

We have already seen in Chapter 10 that leasing operations come to about twenty-nine per cent of the total project financing provided by the Islamic Development Bank from 1975–82. It is a relatively new type of long-term financing contract between the lessor and the lessee for the hire of a specific asset. While the lessor retains the ownership of the asset, the lessee keeps possession of it and uses it, whilst paying the specified rental over a period usually ranging from five to fifteen years depending on the lift of the asset. In some cases, the rental is sufficient to recover the capital outlay of the asset and provide an element of profit. In the case of a short-term operating lease, the rental is not sufficient to recover the capital outlay. The residual value is recovered through sale of the asset. The financing of the purchase of consumer durables may be arranged through the leasing operations of local Islamic Banks.

In this connection it is appropriate to note that although expenditure on consumer durables is classified as consumption expenditure in the national income accounts, it is more like investment expenditure.

11.4 Interest-free Housing Finance

Purchases of new housing are classified as investment expenditure in the national income accounts and are known to be very sensitive to changes in the mortgage interest rate in Western countries. In an Islamic economy, these purchases are likely to be sensitive to normal rates of return in alternative investment opportunities. Nevertheless, the financing of the construction of houses or the purchase of already constructed houses can be arranged on a joint-ownership basis on somewhat similar lines to leasing operations, under which rental, after a mutually agreed grace period, is fixed in a way so that it is sufficient to recover the capital outlay and provide an element of profit, particularly when leasing is used for long-term financing. It is pertinent to mention here that the Pakistan House Building Finance Corporation has already started financing house construction by individuals on a joint-ownership basis, as recommended by the Panel of Economists and Bankers of Pakistan in its interim report submitted to the Pakistan Council of Islamic Ideology.

The Panel recommends that financial institutions, if satisfied with the bonafides of an applicant and the feasibility of his plan, would enter into an agreement with him for provision of housing finance on a joint ownership basis. The terms of such an agreement, as suggested by the Panel are reproduced below:

"1. The respective financial contributions of either party would be specified. The value of land on which the house is to be constructed and any construction costs already incurred will be taken into account in determining a party's financial contribution.

2. The period of joint ownership will be specified in the agreement.

3. The schedule of instalment payments, after a mutually agreed grace period covering the actual construction of the house, will be set up. With the payment of successive instalments the share of the financing institution in the ownership of property would go on declining and would finally cease on payment of the last instalment.

4. The initial rental value of the house will be determined at the time of agreement (with the help of expert appraisers, if necessary) on the basis of quality of construction, accommodation, location and prevalent rents in the locality. The rental value will be reviewed and refixed after every three years.

5. The share of the financing institution in the rent would be on a pro rata basis and the amount payable to the financing institution by way of rent will go on declining with the successive payment of instalments. The calculated share in rent will allow for the usual rate of depreciation and payment of taxes and property dues.

6. In case the builder/purchaser of the house wishes to sell the house before the expiry of the agreement, he would be free to do so and any capital gain/loss would be shared between the two parties proportionately according to the respective outstanding shares.

7. The builder/purchaser of the house would also be free to terminate the joint ownership agreement by paying off the outstanding amount of investment of the financing institution at any time during the period of agreement.

8. The financing institution will have the right to terminate the agreement in case of fraud and to auction the property in the event of default in the payment of instalments and rent."[1]

It is estimated that the system suggested by the Panel would provide substantial relief to prospective house builders or purchasers. Although the Panel recognized the possibility of a rise in the demand for funds as well as in the prices of construction materials and the wages of construction labour, it did not come up with a precise definition of a "small house" in the context of Pakistan.

What is needed is to develop a built-in mechanism so that more builders/purchasers of small houses can get access to the facilities of interest-free housing finance rather than the builders/purchasers of larger houses. The abolition of interest in respect of housing finance is vital in an Islamic economy. But how one gets 'relief' from the elimination of interest should be of equal concern to policy-makers in an Islamic state.

Notes

[1] Panel of Economists and Bankers of Pakistan Report, pp. 111–113, 1980

11.5 Selected Further Reading

Mannan, M. A. "Consumption Function in Islam" in *The Making of Islamic Economic Society, Islamic Dimensions in Economic Analysis*, Chapter 13 (forthcoming).

Report of the Council of Islamic Ideology, Pakistan, *Elimination of Interest from the Economy*, Islamabad, Pakistan, 1980.

Udovitch, Abraham L. "Reflections on the Institutions of Credit and Banking in the Medieval Islamic Near East" in *Studia Islamica* vol. 41, Paris 1975.

Udovitch, Abraham L. "Bankers Without Banks-Commerce, Banking and Society in the Islamic World of the Middle Ages" in *The Dawn of Modern Banking, Yale University Press*, London, 1979.

Uzair, Muhammad, "Some Conceptual and Practical Aspects of Interest-Free Banking" in *Islamic Studies*, vol. 15, Islamabad, Pakistan, 1976.

CHAPTER 12

Fiscal Policy and Budgeting in Islam

12.1 Fiscal Policy

   (a) Its Meaning

   (b) Expenditure Policy

   (c) Revenue Policy

   (d) Revenue Policy towards Non-Muslims

12.2 Budgetary Policy

   (a) Budgeting in Early Islam

   (b) What a Modern Budget Means

   (c) The Islamic State and the Modern Budget

   (d) Deficit Budgeting and Deficit Financing

   (e) Internal Revenue

12.3 Modern Trends in Budgeting – The Concept of Programme and Performance Budgeting and Muslim Countries

12.4 Summary and Conclusion

12.5 Selected Further Reading

APPENDIX

Fiscal Functions and Policy: An Overview

"Establish worship, pay the poor due, and bow your heads with those who bow in worship."

Al-Qur'ān Sūrah II. 43

"It is conceivable that the spirit of Islam might be the timely reinforcement which would decide this issue (of ascending racialism and nationalism) in favour of tolerance and peace.'

Arnold Toynbee, *Civilization on Trial*

12.1 Fiscal Policy

(a) Its Meaning.

The Islamic principle of fiscal and budgeting policy aims at evolving a society based on balanced distribution of wealth by placing material and spiritual values on an equal footing. Of all the religious books of yore, to my knowledge, the *Qur'ān* is the only one which has laid down precise instructions as to the policy of the State regarding the expenditure of income. This statement reflects a new approach towards a study of the problem of fiscal policy, which "is concerned," in the words of Professor R. W. Lindholm, "with the determination of the type, the time and the procedure to be followed in making Government expenditure and in obtaining Government revenues." This is, of course, to achieve certain specific objectives. Fiscal policy is regarded as a tool to regulate and control human behaviour, which can be influenced through incentives or disincentives supplied by raising government revenues (through taxation or borrowing or securing government expenditure). No doubt, in theory, the system of taxation introduced by modern secular states proposes to be based on the socio-political and maximum social advantage theories which aim at the general welfare of the people. To the extent that these desirable ends are achieved, they conform to the Islamic principle. But J. S. Mill has rightly pointed out in his book *Representative Governments* that in practice legislature is a representative of a small minority which used to capture the power of the state either by their wealth or by their organizational capacity. In such a state of affairs, how can we expect that fiscal policy would be conceived and executed in the interests of the people?

The Islamic state is not a theocracy in the sense of priest-hood but is an ideological state which serves as a mechanism for the implementation of the laws of the *Qur'ān* and the *Sunnah*. The fiscal policy in an Islamic state must, therefore, conform to the principles of Islamic laws and values. The fundamental object of the religious laws of Islam is to achieve the welfare of mankind. This welfare of mankind can be achieved if the whole legal and economic system, not to speak of fiscal policy only, is consistent with the main Divine Attributes which are (*a*) Providence, (*b*) Beneficence, and (*c*) Compassion. Thus the expenditure-incurring and the revenue-drawing activities of the state must be used for the achievement of certain specific economic and social ends within the general framework of Islamic Laws as laid down in the *Qur'ān* and the *Sunnah*.

(b) Expenditure Policy.

The expenditure-incurring activities of the state have a definite impact on the socio-economic life of the society. Unlike other religious books, the Holy *Qur'ān* has laid down very precise orders as to the policy of the state regarding expenditure of state income. Obviously, these activities are neither left at the mercy of the head of the state nor at the so-called will of modern legislature. The *Zakāt* [i.e. tax coming from Muslims] is intended for nothing other than the Muslim poor (*fuqarā'*), the poor among the resident aliens (*masākīn*), for winning the hearts, for liberating the slaves and the prisoners of war, for aiding those heavily indebted, those in the Path of God, and for the wayfarer. This is an obligation from God and God is Knowing, As the *Qur'ān* Says:

"Alms are for the poor
And the needy, and those
Employed to administer the (funds);
For those whose hearts
Have been (recently) reconciled
(To Truth); for those in bondage
And in debt; in the cause of God;
And for the wayfarer:
(Thus is it) ordained by God,
And God is full of knowledge
And wisdom."

(*Sūrah* IX. 60)

A brief explanation of these certain items for expenditure of *Zakāt* may be of interest. The very high authority of Caliph 'Umar is there to support the view that the term "*masākīn*" means the poor among the non-Muslim inhabitants of the Islamic state. Semitic philology confirms this. Again, as regards expenditure for winning the hearts, the following quotation may be useful: "As to those whose hearts are won, they are of four kinds: firstly, there are those whose hearts are won in order to make them come to the aid of the Muslims; secondly, there are those whose hearts are won for making them abstain from doing harm to Muslims; thirdly, there are those whose hearts are won for their embracing Islam; fourthly, there are those whose winning of heart persuades their peoples and their clans (equally) to embrace Islam. So it is permissible that each and everyone (belonging to these kinds) should be the recipient of this item of *Zakāt*, be he a Muslim or a polytheist."

The point we are making here is that *Zakāt* may also be used for the welfare of non-Muslims. Even the term "Path of God" is also a comprehensive one. Spending money for mitigating the suffering of non-Muslims could well be included as an expenditure in the path of God. From the last item "wayfarer", *Zakāt* may go towards not only supplying free board and lodging but also to improving tourist conditions, hotels, means of transport, the security of roads, and the like, not only for Muslims but also for non-Muslims.

Therefore, "if we visualize the condition of Arabia in the time of the Holy Prophet, it is not difficult to see that the above-mentioned items practically exhausted all the needs and requirements of the budding State and nascent community of Islam; they went much beyond what was known in the neighbouring 'civilized' countries, Byzantium and Iran. In fact, the Prophet established a Welfare State. If we look to its spirit, there is not the least difficulty in concluding that the Islamic law of finance has great elasticity for further expansion to meeting the requirements of any age and any civilization."[2]

Apart from precise instructions with regard to the expenditure of state income, the *Qur'ān* has also laid down a broad policy of expenditure for the balanced distribution of wealth among the various sections of the community. Thus, instead of accumulating wealth, Islam pleads for more expenditure.

The *Qur'ān* says: "Spend whatever remains after your needs" *Sūrah* II. 219. This does not mean spend money on frivolous things. Islam not only discourages but condemns extravagance. The *Qūr'ān* says, "Do not squander. Allah does not love the extravagant." Hoarding is equally condemned because it keeps wealth out of circulation and deprives the user as well as the community of its beneficial use. Besides this, the fragmentation of property under the Islamic law of inheritance and operation of *Zakāt* are the chief principles which rationalize the Islamic economic system. In fact, the whole economic philosophy of the expenditure-incurring activities of the state is to bring surplus wealth into circulation, and to ensure, consistently with the natural rights of private property, the balanced distribution of wealth among all sections of the community, especially among the poor and the needy. Naturally, the taxation system in the Islamic state must be guided by the principle of benevolence and care for the poor.

(c) Revenue Policy.

There is no doubt that there is great elasticity in the Islamic system of public finance and taxation. This can be established partly from the silence of the *Qur'ān* as to the rates to be charged on different articles belonging to Muslims and partly from the early history of the financial administration of Islam. In so far as the financial aspect of the administration is concerned, we can see a gradual evolution, beginning with persuasion and recommendation and culminating in obligations and duties enforced with all the power that the society could command. Before the Hijrah we have no record to prove that there was any fixed rate of *Zakāt*. No attempt was made to collect and disburse *Zakāt* revenues by the central authority. But the conditions changed fundamentally when the Holy Prophet and the persecuted Muslims left Makkah and settled in Madinah. In the course of a few years, detailed rules of *Zakāt* revenues were framed. In fact, *Zakāt* and *Sadaqah* comprised the entire state income of the time of the Holy Prophet in so far as it was collected from the Muslim subjects. At the time of the Holy Prophet the *Zakāt* and the *Sadaqah* included not only tax on cash, but also the land revenue and the tax on domesticated animals (sheep, goats, camels and cows); it included tax on mines (particularly gold and silver), on treasure-trove and the like.

The Arabia of fourteen hundred years ago and the modern world reveal a fundamental change in the socio-political and socio-economic pattern of society. So there is no reason to believe that items taxed and rates charged were meant to be unchanged with the changing circumstances because the door of *Ijtihād* is never closed in Islam. In fact, Hadrat 'Umar brought about certain changes in so far as the details of *Zakāt* are concerned. He is also reported to have lowered the existing rate of import duty on consumer goods coming from Madinah from ten per cent to only five per cent.

The modern complex system of taxation can be justified because of the complexity of modern life. But the fundamental point which is to be borne in mind, in order better to appreciate the nature of taxation in Islam, is to understand the double sanction—spiritual and temporal—behind government taxation in the Islamic state. But these aspects are welded together to create an equilibrium in man with his complex nature. Thus, as I have already pointed out, the revenue-drawing activities of the state must be guided by the principle of benevolence and care for the have-nots. Judged by this standard the modern system of taxation, especially the method of revenue-drawing through indirect taxation, comes under heavy fire, because the greater burden of this indirect tax falls mainly on the shoulders of the poor, indirect taxes being generally imposed on the necessities of life.

Indirect taxes are often regressive in character, particularly if the taxed commodity happens to be a necessity of life. In fact, from the point of view of having a progressive tax structure, direct taxes are certainly much more desirable than indirect taxes. If a policy of full employment requires a high marginal propensity to consume, progressive taxation is apparently necessary for transferring wealth from the rich, who have a relatively low marginal propensity to consume, to the poor, who have a very high marginal propensity to consume.

The Islamic system of taxation must ensure that only the rich and the prosperous, who have enough to spare, bear the main brunt of taxation. It is probably, for this reason that incomes are not taxed at the source or as they accrue but it is only the savings or hoardings which are taxed.

(d) Revenue Policy towards Non-Muslims.

An Islamic state is, in fact, bound to treat Muslims and non-Muslims on different footings in so far as revenue-collection is concerned. If the *Zakāt* revenue is collected from Muslims and spent on the welfare of poor Muslims and non-Muslims, it can be argued that an Islamic state may collect a certain amount of revenue from non-Muslims. Herein lies the justification of collecting *Jizyah* and *Kharāj* tax during the financial administration of early Islam. Even in modern times this question of different revenue policy towards non-Muslims does not appear to be unworkable. If only Muslims are required to pay a certain amount of tax to the exclusion of the non-Muslim subjects of the state, there is a chance that wealth will be transferred from Muslims to non-Muslims, who may already have prosperous trade and commerce, to the cost of the Muslims. Judged by any standard of justice and equity, this may not, it is said, stand up to the universal principle of social justice.

At this stage, it must be clearly recognized that the *Zakāt* levy has a double sanction – spiritual and temporal and not a double nature – religious and secular. Now when *Zakāt* revenue is collected from Muslims and spent for the welfare of both poor Muslims and non-Muslims, Muslims are acting in accordance with the Qur'anic imperatives and thereby performing their religious duties. Now the question arises of whether a modern Islamic state should impose some kind of welfare tax on the non-Muslim minority: I would view with favour the imposition of such a welfare tax on non-Muslims only if it is *exclusively* spent for the welfare of the poor non-Muslim citizens of an Islamic state. The idea of *Zakāt* revenue has a divine sanctity and should not be related or linked to any secular tax which is subject to the whims of the policy-makers of the state.

12.2 Budgetary Policy

(a) Budgeting in Early Islam

Before making an attempt at formulating a budgetary policy for an Islamic state we may have a look at the budgetary system in early Islam. The budget of the time of the Holy Prophet was quite simple and not as complex as modern budgeting systems. This is partly because socio-economic conditions have changed fundamentally and partly because the Islamic state, founded and run by the Holy Prophet, began in the first year of the Hijrah within only a few streets of the small city of Madinah. Though, within a span of ten years until the Prophet breathed his last, the whole of Arabia and parts of Southern Palestine and Iraq were under his jurisdiction, yet budgets were not complex. The income of the State varied from year to year and even from day to day. Different parts of the State used to send certain amounts of their revenues after meeting their own administrative and other expenditures. For instance, the local authorities in Palestine (of Jarba and Adburah) had each engaged to pay annually 100 dīnārs (I bn Sa'd, and others). The port of Aylah, on the gulf of 'Aqabah, paid 300 dīnārs every year (Ibn Sa'd, Maqrīzī). The region of Najrān, in the Yemen, sent in 2000 garments every year (each garment worth one ounce of gold). But we possess greater details regarding later times, especially the 'Abbāsid Caliphate, for which even the budget notes for the whole empire have been published by Von Kremer in several of his German writings. These refer only to income, yet they are interesting in the sense that we know nothing about contemporary Europe or the Empire of Charlemagne, for instance, who is said to have exchanged embassies with Hārūn al-Rashīd.

As a matter of fact, the *Bait-ul-Māl* did not receive the gross income of the *Kharāj* lands and alms-tax from the provinces but only surplus remaining after the costs of all local services and the pay of the military had been deducted.

How the income of the *Bait-ul-Māl* was normally expended may be gathered from the budgetary estimates for the year 306, which have been preserved. The main items of public expenditure were as follows:

		Dīnārs
(a)	On the holy cities (Makkah and Madinah and pilgrim routes thereof)	315,461½
(b)	On the frontier parts	491,465
(c)	Stipends of *Qādīs* in the empire	56,599
(d)	Stipends of police officers and magistrates in the empire	34,439
(e)	Stipends of officers of the *barīd* (posts)	79,402

The total cost of these public undertakings and other expenditure was less than one million dīnārs, while the expenditure on the royal household, the minor officials in the Government, the *Dīwāns*, the security police at the capital, and other items accounted for over 14½ million dīnārs. In fact, the objects on which public money was spent, and with which the public treasury dealt, were comparatively few and they differed with time and circumstances.

From the above analysis at least two things are clear. (i) During early Islam the basis of budgeting was, probably, the revenue which determined the amount available for expenditure. This was, however, not true in the case of emergency budgets due to war or other natural calamities for which special financial imposts were levied or contributions invited. (ii) Budgetary policy was not growth-oriented as there was then no cry for economic growth in the modern sense of the term.

Now the question arises as to what type of budgetary policy a modern Islamic state should adopt.

No doubt, the concept of a balanced or surplus budget was, probably, the prevailing practice of early Islam. Even today it is one of the accepted canons of financial orthodoxy that the national budget should always be balanced. A budget is said to be balanced if governmental expenditure and revenue are equal. If revenue exceeds expenditure in a given period of time, the budget becomes a surplus one, and in the case of a deficit budget it is the expenditure which exceeds revenue.

(b) What a Modern Budget Means.

Not only in the early Islamic period, but also in the recent past, the scope of the budget was so narrow and limited that when the budgeted sums were spent, the authorities concerned considered their task complete. Today the emphasis is not placed on the mere act of spending money; it is found in the relationship between expenditure and the fulfilment of plans, because planning and budgeting are considered to be complementary operations. Thus the "modern budget is a complex mixture of plans and projects which have to be carried out in the near future with the twofold purpose of increasing and improving on the future management of public affairs as well as eliminating the existing difficulties and obstacles on the path of the country's economic growth."

But the modern concept of a multiple budget, including both the income budget and the capital budget, has raised a fundamental question—the question whether the capital budget should be balanced or not. The supposed virtues of a balanced budget in certain circumstances are no longer believed in and deficit financing has come to be accepted as one of the most potent instruments for fighting a depression, whether cyclical or chronic.

(c) The Islamic State and the Modern Budget.

Modern Islamic states will have to accept the modern concept of budgeting with fundamental contrast as regards the handling of budget deficits. The Islamic states of today must start with indispensable expenditure and proceed to find ways and means to achieve it either by rationalization of tax structures or by taking loans from the banking system or from abroad.

It is due to following reasons:

1. For various economic and historical reasons most of the Muslim countries (with exception of oil-rich capital surplus Muslim countries) are either least developed or developing. The domestic resources may not be sufficient to meet the requirements of these economies.
2. In many cases foreign capital is needed to exploit the vast resources of the Muslim countries.

(d) Deficit Budgeting and Deficit Financing.

It was noted earlier that if revenues fall short of expenditure, there is a budget deficit. But a government has a surplus budget, if revenues exceed expenditure, and if current revenue is equal to current expenditure, there is a balanced budget.

Now if a government raises its spending without raising its taxes, its extra expenditure may be said to be deficit-financed. The question is whether an Islamic state should resort to deficit financing. There appears to be a controversy among Muslim economists. Some argue that an Islamic state should not resort to deficit financing because it may eventually lead to borrowing by the government on interest. This increased expenditure may also lead to wasteful expenditure.

It is true that a deficit requires an increase in borrowing, for which there are three traditional sources available in the case of most Muslim countries: the central bank, the commercial bank and the public. Generally, a government borrows from these sources by selling treasury bills or bonds, which carry interest rates. It is also true that in many cases a government may spend unwisely or spend in favour of the rich and so on.

In an Islamic economy, it would be inappropriate to discourage deficit financing as a matter of rule. A case can be made for deficit financing in an Islamic state, because money spent by the government may represent a net addition to aggregate demand and because variations in government taxes and expenditure will have a major impact on the gross national product (G.N.P) and on total employment. Again, it is possible to demonstrate that variations will serve to reallocate expenditure in favour of the poor people or poor regions or among all sectors of the economy but will have little effect on the overall level of aggregate demand, G.N.P. and total employment.

Since it is possible to make a case for deficit financing, there are also mechanisms by which an Islamic state can resort to deficit financing. We have already discussed in Chapters 9 and 10 the mechanisms of *Muḍārabah*, *Mushāraka* and *Murābaḥa* under which Islamically-justified project financing can be arranged on the basis of profit-sharing and equity participation. Besides, Islamic governments can also raise funds by issuing investment certificates or bonds on the basis of profit and loss-sharing. It has been pointed out earlier that local Islamic banks and *Dar Al-Maal Al-Islami* have already started selling shares to the public and issuing various forms of investment certificates and bonds.

It must however be recognized that once the government resorts to deficit financing, its extra expenditure must be carefully planned and money spent by the government may not lead to an increase in the volume of G.N.P. only, regardless of its effects on the distribution of income among the poor. It should be ascertained who are the main beneficiaries of the governments' extra expenditure out of deficit financing. Herein lies the Islamic dimension of the problem.

(e) Internal Revenue.

As far as the mobilization of internal resources, including loans from the banking system, is concerned, the Muslim states are, I believe, masters of their own affairs. In the Islamic socio-economic set up, banks must act as partners in trade, commerce, industry and development plans. A happy fusion of the financial experience of the banks and the investors' knowledge of investment and business must be made in order to achieve true social justice and the universal brotherhood of man. We have already seen that during the early Islamic period *Zakāt* and *Ṣadaqah* revenues formed the principal source of income. Obviously, in modern times, these revenues cannot meet the requirements of modern growth-oriented budgets in an Islamic state. There is a clear necessity for imposing new taxes especially on the richer section of the community in the interests of progress and social justice. The Tradition is clear on it: "There is always due besides *Zakāt*." Thus the Holy Prophet (peace be upon him) commends and commands socially beneficial expenditure. He said,

"Riches should be taken from the rich and returned to the poor" (Bukhārī).

> "And there are those
> Who bury gold and silver
> And spend it not in the way
> Of God: announce unto them
> A most grievous penalty"

(Sūrah IX 34)

From the above verse it is clear that there is a grievous punishment in store for those who abuse their riches to the detriment of society. Islam views with disfavour the monopoly of resources by a few self-seeking millionaires. God enjoins upon the wealthy to keep wealth in a state of circulation, as the Holy *Qur'ān* says, "in order that it (wealth) may not merely make a circuit between the wealthy among you" (Sūrah LIX. 7). Hence the necessity of more and more progressive taxation and public expenditure, and this policy will have to be reflected in the budgetary policy of an Islamic state.

12.3 Modern Trends in Budgeting—The Concept of Programme and Performance Budgeting and Muslim Countries

In recent years, a number of new approaches to budgeting have been developed in an effort to help the developing countries in their capital expansion programmes. Some countries are preparing consolidated cash budgets as supplements to conventional budgets, which furnish useful information on money flow and a basis for short-run estimates of the effects of government's fiscal operations. Again, a number of countries, especially Scandinavian countries, have adopted two budget systems— the operating or current budget and the capital budget. This is an attempt at reconciling the apparent conflict between a balanced budget and the financing of large capital outlays by borrowings.

In the capital budget system, capital outlays are covered in the capital budget, where expenditures are on self-liquidating, return-yielding projects. The budget system in Pakistan also follows the distinction between a capital budget and a revenue budget. But what is needed is effective budget classification to make it more meaningful in economic terms and consequent adoption of an economic-cum-functional classification as developed by the United Nations. This is needed to establish a link between the budgeting system and fiscal policy.

Finally, in modernizing the budgetary system, the new concept of programme and performance budgeting is gaining popularity, especially in the United States. Traditional budgets placed emphasis on the objects of expenditure, programme budgeting on defining national purposes and achieving public objectives. In performance budgeting we find the shift in emphasis from means of accomplishment to accomplishment itself. Mr G. N. Jones in a recent article has observed: "Under a performance budget system, the work programme is developed according to functions and activities in terms of expected accomplishments. Under the traditional budget system, the work programme is developed according to 'objectives of expenditure,' such as personnel services, materials and supplies and equipment in the terms of the means of accomplishment. The most important characteristic of performance budgeting is the shift in emphasis from the means of accomplishment to the accomplishment itself.

"A performance budget system treats budgeting as a tool of management and not that of finance. The utilization of financial resources takes precedence over financial accountability. The budget is tied directly with the executive and becomes one of his principal tools for management."[3]

It is true that the Budgetary Reforms Committee of Pakistan has recommended the formulation of budgets on a programme and performance basis. Several attempts were and are being made to modernize accounting the budget procedures, training of personnel, etc. But we feel that Muslim countries in general, are not mature enough to formulate their budgets on a programme and performance basis. Although several developing nations like the Philippines and some Latin American countries have been receptive to this new budgetary reform, yet we have no conclusive proof to show that they have been a success.

Performance budgeting would make it necessary to evolve a system of work measurement and to calculate the unit cost of each type of governmental activity. But the work done in government departments is so complex and varied in nature that it is very difficult to work out a common measurement for all types of activities. Certain types of work may not even lend themselves to quantitative measurement at all.

Since work measurement and determination of unit costs are hightly technical jobs requiring a thorough knowledge of and experience in the techniques of work study, time-and-motion study, etc. a successful programme and performance budgeting system in Muslim countries can be installed only when there exists a solid administrative infrastructure with sufficient numbers of trained accountants, economists, planners and other technical persons. In Muslim States like Pakistan, Iran, Iraq, and Indonesia, there is an acute scarcity of such trained personnel and their administrative infrastructures are not that solid. I, therefore, do not feel encouraged to suggest that the budgets of Muslim countries should be formulated on a programme and performance basis in the short run. Of course, this type of budgeting may be introduced in well-planned stages, depending on the nature of economic development in respective Muslim countries.

12.4 Summary and Conclusion

(*a*) *Fiscal Policy.* Unlike other religious books, the Holy *Qurān* is probably the only one which has laid down very precise commandments as to the policy of the state regarding expenditure of state income. The *Qur'ān* lists the items on which *Zakāt* revenue can be spent. *Zakāt* revenue which is to be collected only from Muslims can be used for the welfare of non-Muslims also.

Instead of encouraging the accumulation of wealth in the hands of a few, Islam pleads for more and more expenditure. But Islam not only discourages but condemns extravagance. Hoarding is equally condemned, because it keeps wealth out of circulation. The Islamic law of inheritance is another step towards the diffusion of wealth among various sections of society. Obviously, the taxation system in an Islamic state must be guided by the principle of benevolence and care for the have-nots.

Judged by the principle of benevolence and care for the have-nots the modern method of revenue-drawing through indirect taxation comes under fire because the burden of this heavy tax falls mainly on the shoulders of the poor as indirect taxes are generally imposed on articles of the necessities of life. In this sense, they are often regressive in character.

I have also suggested that the idea of *Zakāt* should not be linked with any secular taxes or to any proposal of imposing separate taxes on non-Muslims.

The silence of the *Qur'ān* as to the rates of *Zakāt* to be charged on different articles belonging to Muslims may be interpreted as revealing the great elasticity of the Islamic system of public finance and taxation. As the socio-economic condition has changed fundamentally, there is no reason to believe that items taxed and rates charged were meant to be unchangeable with changing circumstances, since the door of *Ijtihād* is never closed in Islam. There is a need for the rationalization of the rules of *Zakāt* and, indeed, Hadrat 'Umar is reported to have brought about certain changes in the details of *Zakāt*.

In fact, if we look to the spirit of financial administration of the Holy Prophet there is not the least difficulty in concluding that the Islamic law of public finance has great elasticity for expansion to meet the requirements of the modern age.

(*b*) *Budgetary Policy.* Owing to the complexity of modern life resulting from the onward march of human civilization, there is a need for changing the emphasis from orthodox balanced budgetary policy to growth-oriented budgetary policy. In an Islamic state the basis of budgeting is no longer the revenue which would determine the amount available for expenditure. It is the indispensable expenditure which should form the basis of budgeting in the Islamic state.

There is a case for deficit financing in an Islamic economy. This can be arranged through *Muḍārabah*, *Mushāraka* and *Murābaḥa* contract.

Besides, Islamic governments can raise funds by issuing investment bonds and certificates to the public on the basis of profit and loss-sharing.

The Islamic budgetary system is different from the existing system followed in modern states both in its spirit and essence mainly for two reasons:

(i) Tyranny of interest is the least in the case of an Islamic budgetary system.

(ii) Objectives of the budgetary policy must be consistent with the injunctions of the Holy *Qur'ān* or the *Sunnah*. People are not at the mercy of the so-called financial wizards of the state.

(*c*) *Modern Trends in Budgeting*. In recent years, a number of new forms of budgeting have been developed, of which programme and performance budgeting is the most important. Since the performance budgeting system is exceedingly complicated and rests on the complicated system of cost accounting, a successful system of programme and performance budgeting in Muslim countries in general can be installed only when there exists a solid administrative infrastructure with a staff of trained accountants, economists, planners and other skilled hands. Programme and performance budgeting should, therefore, be introduced in Muslim countries in well-planned stages.

Notes

[1] Abū Ya'lā Al-farrā', Al Akkan Al-Saltāniyah, p. 116.
[2] *Progressive Islam*, Vol. II (September 1955), p. 6.
[3] *NIPP Journal*, March 1967.

12.5 Selected Further Reading

Aghnides, Nicholas P. *Mohammadan Theories of Finance*, Premier publication, Lahore, 1961.

Akkas, Ali, "Fiscal Policy in an Islamic State", in *Thoughts on Islamic Economics*, Islamic Research Bureau, Dhaka, Bangladesh, 1980.

Ansari, A. "An Institutional Framework for Capital Formation in an Islamic Economy", a paper presented at the Second International Conference on Islamic Economics: Development, Finance and Distribution in an Islamic Perspective, Islamic University, Islamabad, 19–23 March, 1983.

Ariff, M. *Monetary and Fiscal Economics of Islam*, (I.C.R.I.E), King Abdulaziz University, Jeddah, a paper presented at the Second International Conference on Islamic Economics: Development, Finance and Distribution in an Islamic Perspective, Islamic University, Islamabad, 19–23 March 1983.

Chapra, M. Umar, "Monetary Policy in an Islamic Economy" *Proceedings of International Seminar on Monetary and Fiscal Economics of Islam*, Islamabad, Pakistan, 1981.

Faridi, F. R. "A Theory of Fiscal Policy in an Islamic State", *Proceedings of International Seminar on Monetary and Fiscal Economics of Islam*, Islamabad, Pakistan, 1981.

Faridi, R. R. "Public Budgeting, Capital Accumulation and Economic Growth in an Islamic Frame-work" a paper presented at the Second International Conference on Islamic Economics: Development, Finance and Distribution in an Islamic Perspective, Islamic University, Islamabad, Pakistan, 19–23 March, 1983.

Hamidullah, Muhammad, "Budgeting and Taxation in the Time of Holy Prophet", *Journal of the Pakistan Historical Society*, 1955.

Jarhi, M. A. "A Monetary and Financial Structure for an Interest-Free Economy: Institutions, Mechanism and Policy", *Proceedings of International Seminar on Monetary and Fiscal Economics of Islam*, Islamabad, 1981.

Kahf, Monzer, "Taxation Policy in an Islamic Economy" *Proceedings of International Seminar on Monetary and Fiscal Economics of Islam*, Islamabad, 1981.

Metwally, M. M. "Fiscal Policy in an Islamic Economy", *Proceedings of International Seminar on Monetary and Fiscal Economics of Islam*, Islamabad, 1981.

Qureshi, D. M. "Budget in the Context of Islamic Economic System" (in Pakistan), in *Pakistan Economist*, vol. 20, No. 30, Karachi, Pakistan, 1980.

Salama, A. A. "Fiscal Policy of an Islamic State", *Proceedings of International Seminar on Monetary and Fiscal Economics of Islam*, Islamabad, 1981.

Siddiqi, S. A. "Public Finance in Islam", Sh. Muhammad Ashraf, Lahore, 1948.

Uzair, M. "Comments on Fiscal Policy in an Islamic State", *Proceedings of International Seminar on Monetary and Fiscal Economics of Islam*, Islamabad, 1981.

APPENDIX

Fiscal Functions and Policy: An Overview.

The way the fiscal policy is expected to perform the *allocation, distribution* and *stabilization* function in an Islamic state has its own distinctiveness arising out of value orientation and ethical and social dimensions in public income and expenditure. The fiscal policy in Islam ceases to be neutral, and is expected to explain circumstances not merely *as they are* but *as they ought to be*. Thus in an Islamic state, the process of allocating the use of resources between private and social goods, adjustments of the distribution of earnings and the redistribution of existing incomes and wealth and the use of budgetary policy as an instrument of price stability, high employment and growth must provide a clear manifestation of social and moral concern in addition to material welfare. This value-loaded Islamic bias based on the principles of benevolence and care for the poor should enable the Islamic state to solve the problems of the co-ordination or conflict of fiscal functions in a relatively easy way, as in the real world budget planning does not frequently permit evaluation of various objectives on their own merits, resulting in multiple conflicts between allocation and distribution, growth and distribution stabilization and allocation and so on.

This overriding humane bias in Islamic public finance, as well as for that matter in other areas of economics, is derived from the idea of *Zakāt*, which contains enormous potential for communal betterment in favour of the poor and disadvantaged members of the community. The *Qur'ān* lists the items on which *Zakāt* revenues can be spent. *Zakāt* which is to be collected only from Muslims can be used for the welfare of non-Muslims as well. But by payment of *Zakāt*, Muslims are performing their religious duties also. Thus the *Zakāt* levy has a double sanction, spiritual and temporal, not the double nature, religious and secular, as wrongly maintained by some Western scholars. This is true with regard to most of the taxes of the early Islamic state.

In spite of the simplicity of the system, there were a number of taxes prevalent in the early Islamic state. Generally speaking, they were: (a) *Zakāt* (b) *Jizya*, (c) *Kharāj* (or land tax) (d) Spoils of war (e) Taxes on mines and treasure trove (f) Customs duties and tolls. (See Chapter 13)

It is possible to demonstrate that the tax system of the early Islamic state was elastic and dynamic in nature. For example, the categories of property to which *Zakāt* is to be applied were not rigidly maintained even by *Hadrat* 'Umar himself who introduced a number of changes in the system of *Zakāt*, because it is a means to an end, not an end in itself.

The Basis of Budgeting.

Again a careful study of the *Sharī'ah* provides us with some interesting clues as to what should be the basis of budgeting in Islam (i.e. revenue versus expenditure).

In an Islamic state, the basis of budgeting is not merely the revenue which should determine the expenditure. It is the expenditure which should primarily serve as a basis for the mobilization of revenue. This stems from the Islamic requirement that a state should provide for the basic minimum needs of all its citizens. Therefore, if the *Zakāt* revenue and contribution of the voluntary sector, recognized by Islam, are not sufficient to meet the basic provisioning of the poor, there is always scope for additional taxation beyond *Zakāt* provided it is spent in a judicious manner. It is therefore implicit that a case for deficit financing can be made in an Islamic economy. This can be arranged through *Muḍāraba*, *Mushāraka* and *Murābaha* contract. Besides, an Islamic government can also raise funds by issuing investment bonds and certificates to the public on basis of profit and loss-sharing.

From the preceding discussion, it is clear that an Islamic state should be able to use various fiscal instruments or policies designed to have an Islamic "Social Welfare Function", which describes society's judgement on the question of the weight to be given to the welfare of various individuals and groups (i.e. the poor, the elderly, low-income groups, minorities, etc).

CHAPTER 13

Some Aspects of Public Finance in Islam

13.1 Tax Structure in Early Islam

    (a) *Zakāt*

    (b) *Jizyah*

    (c) *Kharāj* or Land-Tax

    (d) Spoils of War

    (e) Tax on Mines and Treasure-Trove

    (f) Customs Duties and Tolls

13.2 *Zakāt*

    (a) Its Meaning for Modern Man

    (b) *Zakāt* on Industrial Machinery etc.

    (c) *Zakāt* on Bank Notes, etc.

    (d) *Zakāt* on Rent, Profits, etc.

    (e) *Zakāt* and Inflation

    (f) *Zakāt* and Principles of Public Finance

    (g) *Zakāt* and Canons of Taxation

    (h) *Zakāt's* advantages

    (i) Social advantages of *Zakāt*

    (j) *Zakāt* and Modern Muslim States

13.3 Conclusion

13.4 Selected Further Reading

13.5 Appendix:

Zakāt in Practice:

Zakāt and *'Ushr'* ordinance, 1980, of Pakistan

"Alms are for the poor
And the needy, and those
Employed to administer the (funds);
For those whose hearts
Have been (recently) reconciled
(To truth); for those in bondage
And in debt; in the cause
Of God; and for the wayfarer:
(Thus is it) ordained by God,
And God is full of knowledge
And wisdom."

Al-Qur'ān, Sūrah IX. 60

"Riches (i.e.: *Zakāt*) should be taken from the rich and returned to the poor."

Prophet Muhammad (peace be upon him)

Public finance, according to the traditional definition of the subject, deals with the financial problems pertaining to revenues, expenditure and debts of public authorities, in contradistinction from private finance which deals with the income and expenditure of private individuals. In the words of Bastable, "Public finance deals with expenditure and income of public authorities or the State and their mutual relation, as also with the financial administration and control." Here we shall confine our analysis to public revenues as they existed in early Islam. In this connection we would also like to examine *Zakāt* in the context of contemporary thinking.

13.1 Tax Structure in Early Islam

It is not correct to say that the fiscal system in early Islam falls into two classes of religious and secular revenues as maintained wrongly by Nicolas P. Aghnides in his work *Mohammedan Theories of Finance*. The very fact that *Zakāt* is collected from Muslims and *Jizyah* from non-Muslims does not imply that *Zakāt* is a religious tax *and Jizyah* and *Kharāj* are secular taxes, because the Islamic state is not a secular state in the modern sense of the term. A state which recognizes the sovereignty of Allah can hardly make a clear-cut distinction between the religious and temporal affairs of life. Universal morality is combined with secularism in a manner that they are the obverse and the reverse of the same coin. This is also true in the case of collection of revenue in an Islamic state.

Secondly, unlike secular states an Islamic state does make religion a basis for imposing taxes on the public. Thus, like *Zakāt, Kharāj* and *Jizyah* also have the sanction of either *Qur'ānic* injunction or the Prophet's *Sunnah* behind them and thus the imposition of these taxes is evidently an act of religiousness from the point of view of an Islamic state.

Lastly, this difference in treatment in respect of collection of revenue is an artificial one in the sense that the purpose behind all taxes in an Islamic state is one and the same, that is, motivated by the welfare of the people; no matter whether they are Muslims or non-Muslims, the Islamic State can impose taxes on the public. The oppression of minorities in any form is condemned in Islam, because the minority is a sacred trust in an Islamic state. It is, therefore, a futile effort to make any distinction between religious and secular revenue in an Islamic State. This fact must be kept in view in understanding the tax structure of early Islam in its correct perspective.

With these few words I would like to pass on to the various sources of revenue of the early Islamic State.

(a) *Zakāt*

The prime source of revenue for the early Islamic State and any Islamic State is *Zakāt*, which is also one of the five basic tenets of Islam. Next to prayer it is the most important of the religious duties enjoined on the Muslims. Hence *Zakāt* assumes a religious sanctity which is not matched by any mode of public finance anywhere else, so much so that the first Pious Caliph made war upon those tribes who refused to pay it.

Zakāt affects the various kinds of possessions which are hoarded wealth, agricultural produce (tithe), tax on capital (animals), etc.

These things are liable to tax only when they reach a certain minimum value called *Niṣāb* which varies for each item. It is 40 *riyāls* in the case of cash money, in the case of silver the *Niṣāb* is 206 *dirhams* or $52\frac{1}{2}$ *tolas*. In the case of gold, it is 20 *mithqāls* or $7\frac{1}{2}$ *tolas*, etc.

Without going into every detail of *Zakāt* (I shall discuss it in greater detail later on) it becomes apparent that *Zakāt* in its various forms virtually constituted a general property tax as it exhausted all the kinds of property then existing. Unlike modern taxes, the rules of collecting *Zakāt* are so simple that no specialized knowledge is required. With respect to collection, the most important point to emphasize is the distinction between apparent and non-apparent property. While the *Zakāt* on apparent property, namely, animals and agricultural produce, is collected and disbursed by the state, the *Zakāt* on non-apparent property, namely, gold and silver and articles of trade, is disbursed to the beneficiaries of *Zakāt* directly by the owners themselves. The *Zakāt* on non-apparent property came under state control only in so far as the owners passed with it by the public collectors stationed on public roads ('*Ashirs*).

The operation of this ideal tax can wipe out the glaring inequalities of wealth and can bring about its gradual redistribution and also help considerably in curbing inflationary tendencies. Apart from the erratic increase of currency in the country, paucity of goods and velocity of money, the false and unequal distribution of wealth generates inflationary tendencies and makes the market uneasy. The correct handling of *Zakāt* tax can gradually bring about the required equilibrium.

(b) *Jizyah*

The next source for revenue was *Jizyah*—a tax which was imposed on non-Muslims in return for the guarantee extended to them by an Islamic state for the protection of their lives, properties, religious rites and for their exemption from military service. Such non-Muslims, whose lives and properties are guaranteed, are called "*Dhimmīs*". There is a lot of controversy over the imposition of *Jizyah* on non-Muslims. Some say that *Jizyah* levied on the *Dhimmīs* is a rental for residing in the Muslim state and some say that it is taken from the *Dhimmīs* as a punishment for their disbelief in order to humiliate them. Thus it is said that during the process of payment they were rebuked in these words: "Oh *Dhimmīs*," or "Oh enemies of God! pay the *Jizyah*."

But if we go deeper into the problem it can easily be established that all these criticisms are not valid. It is quite uncharitable to treat *Jizyah* as rental on the part of the *Dhimmīs* for residing in the Muslim state. Had it been so, it should also have been imposed upon the children, women, the insane and old people. But these were not liable to pay this tax. It follows that the welfare of the people is the basic consideration behind the imposing of *Jizyah* upon non-Muslims. Moreover, it was not a repressive tax. This is supported by Aghnides in *Mohammedan Theories of Finance* when he writes: "The *Jizyah* is imposed by the Imām upon the population of a district conquered by force of arms. The yearly rate for the rich is forty-eight *dirhams*, i.e. four *dirhams* per month, for the middle class half of this sum, and for the poor who can earn their living, one-fourth of this sum. The above is based on the precedents of the Caliph Omar, Othman and Ali, the other Companions having approved of their action. In other words, it is based on ijma. There is no Zahir-al-riwayah report concerning the meaning of the terms rich, middle class and poor, but in the commentary of al-Tahawi it is stated that the person who owns 10,000 *dirhams* and upwards is rich, the person owning from 200 upwards is middle class, and finally the person owning less than that is poor."

Again, it is incorrect to say that *Jizyah* was some sort of a punishment. No doubt, the collection of the *Jizyah* is based on the divine words:

*Fight those who believe not
In God nor the last Day,
Nor hold that forbidden
Which hath been forbidden
By God and His Apostle,
Nor acknowledge the Religion
Of truth, (even if they are)
Of the People of the Book
Until they pay the *Jizya*
With willing submission,
And feel themselves subdued."

(*Sūrah* IX. 29).

Here the *Qur'ānic* word *Ṣāghirūn* (humiliation) simply means "submission" for two reasons: firstly, old men, women and children were exempted from the payment of *Jizyah*, secondly, the use of force for imposing religious belief on others is clearly prohibited in the Holy Book. Therefore, I agree with al-Shāfi'ī who, "on the strength of the opinions held by a number of people of knowledge (ilm), concludes that the humiliation referred to in the *Qur'an* consists in the submission of the infidels to Muslim rule (hukm al-Islam), and that consequently people may not be admitted into the status of Zimmis except on condition of submission to Muslim law.

"According to the most extreme view quoted by al-Adawi, the humiliation of the Zimmis is necessary in order to demonstrate their inborn hatred of the Moslems, their refutation of the Prophet, and the fact that if they had the power they would exterminate the Moslems gradually."

However, the *Qur'ānic* reference to "humiliation" must not be understood in the sense used in the course of our ordinary business of life. The rashness in the treatment of the *Dhimmīs* during the process of collection is obviously against the spirit of Islam. The whole problem of imposition of *Jizyah* must be understood in its historical perspective. In the primitive socio-economic set-up the imposition of *Jizyah* was possibly the best choice, because it is consistent with the principles of natural justice. Every subject of the state must pay his due for the maintenance of internal security and prevention of invasion from outside, no matter whether he is a Muslim or a non-Muslim. In fact, the spirit of Islam is faithfully reflected in the imposition of *Jizyah* upon the *Dhimmīs*. Thus Caliph 'Umar's general Abū Ubaidah is reported to have ordered the Governor of Syria to refund the *Jizyah* as the Muslim army was not confident of defending the *Dhimmīs* of Syria against the Roman attack. Again, we have evidence to prove that in many cases the children of *Dhimmīs* were given monetary help from the treasury.

(c) *Kharāj* or Land-Tax

By *Kharāj* we mean a kind of tax imposed on lands mainly conquered by the force of arms, irrespective of whether the owner is a minor or an adult, free or slave, Muslim or infidel. The method of collecting *Kharāj* is divided into two kinds: proportional *Kharāj* (*Muqāsimah*) and the fixed *Kharāj* (*Wazifah*). Proportional *Kharāj* pertains to a portion of the produce like one-half or one-third of the same. On the contrary, fixed *Kharāj* is a specific charge on the land at so much of natural produce or money per unit area. The proportional *Kharāj* is generally collected after one single crop while the fixed *Kharāj* becomes due on the expiry of one year.

In the case of fixed *Kharāj*, the rates that were fixed by the Caliph 'Umar on the lands of Sawād are generally considered final, but if there is any point where the precedent of 'Umar is not available, the tax-bearing capacity will be the standard for imposing a tax. The maximum tax bearing capacity has been fixed at one half of the produce.

Al-Māwardī discusses as follows the factors which determine the tax-bearing capacity (*tāqah*) of land. The person who assesses the *Kharāj* on a piece of land should consider the capacity of the land, which varies according to three factors, each factor affecting the amount of *Kharāj* more or less. "One of these factors pertaining to the land itself is the quality of the land by virtue of which the crop grown on it is rich, or the defect which causes the produce to be small. The second factor relates to the kind of crop, since grains and fruits vary in price, some fetching a higher price than the others, and *kharāj* must, therefore, be assessed accordingly. The third factor pertains to the method of irrigation, for the crop that has been irrigated with water carried on the back of beasts or raised by water-wheel, cannot stand the same rate of *Kharāj* which could be charged on land watered by running water or rain."

So long as land continues to remain the same with regard to its method of irrigation and advantage, the tax is neither increased not decreased. If, however, disruption to the method of irrigation is due to a natural factor and is to the disadvantage of the cultivator, the state should undertake any repairs and no *Kharāj* is chargeable for the period the land remains uncultivable. Also, in the case of permanent change in the method of irrigation which results in an advantage to the land, the state may or may not increase the rate of *Kharāj*. No *Kharāj* is charged if the entire crop is destroyed by factors beyond the control of the owner. Even if one is unable to pay the tax, one is given time till one's finances improve. But if anyone has any *mala fide* intention not to pay the *Kharāj* he is also forced to pay the tax. Thus we see that *Kharāj* tax is not only progressive but also flexible in nature. It is quite consistent with the modern canons of taxation. The modern practice of granting exemption of tax in special and deserving cases and of seizing the property of the cultivator in the event of his failure to pay the taxes appears to have owed its origin to the actual administration of *Kharāj* tax.

(d) Spoils of War

The spoils of war were one of the diminishing sources of revenue of the Islamic State. This revenue went on increasing during the expansionist period of Islam, because, technically, it meant property taken by force from infidels during war. Before the advent of Islam the victorious army or tribal chiefs used to keep the entire booty obtained in a war. But Islam gradually brought about a change in the mental outlook of the Muslim army. Islam restricted the claims of the conquering army to four-fifths of the entire proceeds keeping one-fifth of the spoils for the benefit of the community. It is based on the *Qur'ānic* verse,

> "And know that out of
> All the body that ye
> May acquire (in war)
> And fifth share is assigned
> To god, – and to the Apostle,
> And to near relatives,
> Orphans, the needy,
> And the wayfarer,"

(Sūrah VIII. 41)

"This was followed in the lifetime of the Prophet. After his death the Caliph Abū Bakr and after him the Caliph 'Umar divided the one-fifth of the booty into three shares, namely, the parts for orphans, the indigent and the wayfarers. The later Caliphs also followed this practice, which implies that the share of the Prophet and his relatives lapsed on the death of the Prophet."

The relatives, however, are entitled to a share in so far as they belong to one of the classes mentioned above and in that case they are given precedence over the rest. This is the Hanafite view which is in accordance with and based on the Caliph 'Umar's practice. The great majority of Muslim jurists are not inclined to accept the Shāfi'īte view that the descendants of the Prophet should be gathered together to have their share divided among them. We are rather prepared to accept al-Shāfi'ī's contention that the share of the Prophet should go to the Imām in the amount the Prophet took in his lifetime in order to use it for the strengthening of Islam.

However, the dynamism of Islamic law and financial administration is amply illustrated by the momentous decision of the Caliph 'Umar regarding the restoration of the land of Sawād to the original owners. The Caliph 'Umar's letter to Sa'd bin Abī Waqqāṣ says: "You urge in your letter that whatever lands and other property God has given you in booty should be distributed. On receipt of my letter you should distribute all the chattels including animals among the army after deducting one-fifth provided the booty has been obtained after actual warfare, and allow the lands and the camels to remain in the hands of the original owners so that they may be used in support of the allowances of the Muslims. If you distribute (the latter) among the present generation, there would be nothing left for posterity."

The Shāfi'ites object to making a present of lands to the original owners when the lands have been conquered by force on the ground that, like chattels, they are a booty of war and consequently the property of the soldiers. The Hanafites reply that "the exercise of option by the Imām in this case is only in accordance with the interests of the Muslims, for if he distributed these lands among the soldiers they would settle down on them in order to cultivate them and so they would stay from the holy war and their enemy would then return to charge against the Muslims. Moreover, the Muslims are often ill-adapted to agriculture. Consequently, if the lands are returned to the unbelievers who are more familiar with this art, and are made subject to payment of *Kharāj*, the Muslims can devote their time to the holy war. Furthermore, there is no prejudice in this for the soldiers' interests, for, although, in the case of distribution, the benefits are more immediate, in the other case they are more persistent. Then, too, future generations also have a right in these lands, and should the lands be distributed among the victorious army, future Muslims would have been wronged."

The basic fact which can be derived from the above analysis is that, without changing the basic objectives of achieving social justice through taxation, details of Islamic law governing the tax system may be changed keeping in view the requirements of the age. Thus the modern method of confiscating the spoils of war by the state may be justified if they are spent for the benefit of the community. The circumstances which compelled the distribution of the spoils of war among the conquering Muslim army are no longer in existence. At present soldiers all over the Muslim world are provided with regular scales of pay and other connected modern amenities of life. Thus, for the proper understanding of the spirit of the *Qur'ānic* law, reason and judgment will have to play a crucial part in the future scheme of an Islamic social set-up. In my view, the keynote of future Islamic public finance would be dynamism and flexibility.

(e) Tax on Mines and Treasure-Trove

There is some disagreement on the nature of the tax imposed on mines and treasure-trove. According to the Shāfi'ites and Hanbalites, this tax is considered as *Zakāt* while the Hanafites regard it as a case of spoils. However, without entering into the controversy, we can discuss it as a source of revenue. If a mine which is solid and which may be melted and admit of imprint like gold, silver, iron, etc., and a treasure-trove are discovered in the land of the Muslims, they are bound to surrender one-fifth to the state to meet the needs of social justice. But today, in view of the importance of mines and treasure-trove, all mines are nationalized.

Now the basic question which we must answer is whether the modern trend toward the nationalization of mines is justified from the Islamic standpoint. The door of *Ijtihād* is never closed in Islam. Therefore, what was justified during the early period of Islam may not be so justified due to changes of time and circumstance. Mining, as a separate branch of human knowledge, is of recent origin. So is the growth of cartel types of business and joint-stock companies. The exploitation of mines has, therefore, become a very profitable proposition. If private individuals are allowed to enjoy its benefit, it will certainly lead to the accumulation of wealth in a few hands and the consequent exploitation of society by a few individuals. Since this is against the spirit of the *Qur'ānic* Law, the modern system of nationalization of mines and treasure-trove is justified, provided the earnings from the mines are spent for the benefit of the community as a whole. Here the following *Hadīth* is worth quoting: "It is reported by Abyad Ma'aribî that he went to the Prophet and requested the grant of the salt lake at Ma'arib. The Prophet granted the request but just then one of those present observed that it was a salt-treasure which was being granted to the man. On knowing the truth of the matter, the Prophet refused to grant it to Abyad."

Thus we see that the state has every right to exploit mineral resources for the benefit of society. During the early period of Islam the exploitation of mineral resources was confined to merely scratching the surface and was not a source of huge profit which might result in the creation of a multimillionaire class, and, therefore, individuals were allowed to work out the mines. But the situation has altogether changed in view of the circumstances already stated. But we are not prepared to accept complete nationalization of mineral resources to the utter neglect of individual rights. The Islamic State must make provision for proper and due compensation if mines are found in private lands. What is proper and due compensation is always relative to the needs of the community and is to be decided keeping in view the inconvenience and distress of the owners and inhabitants of the land.

(f) Customs Duties and Tolls

The concept of customs duties and tolls took a practical shape during the reign of the Caliph 'Umar who appointed *'Ashīrs* and instructed them to collect from Muslim traders, from *Dhimmīs* and from *Harbīs* of a non-Muslim neighbouring state to the same extent as were levied by the latter.

The difference between the rate of customs duties and tolls that were levied on Muslims and those levied on *Dhimmīs* was "owing to the fact that they need protection from robbers more than the Muslims. Unlike the Muslims, who must pay the *zakāt* of their trade articles whether or not they pass an *ashir* the Zimmis are subject to this toll of five per cent only, in so far as they come under the jurisdiction of an *ashir* by travelling for trade. This difference is due to the fact that while the tax collected by the ashir from Muslims consists in their *zakāt* dues, the one collected from the Zimmis is in reality only an octroi duty. Except for these two differences the Zimmis are treated like the Muslims in every respect."

The *Harbī* traders come under the existing taxing power of the Muslim state, because the *Harbīs* during their sojourn in Muslim territory enjoy the protection of the Muslim state. But with respect to the rate of the tax the principle of reprisal holds true only in a restricted sense. Because if the *Harbīs* are collecting as a tax from Muslim traders the whole of their property, the *'Ashir* does not collect the whole of the *Harbīs*' property but leaves with them enough to enable them to return home, because they will need it for food and satisfying other wants, and because the property, being little, does not need protection from robbers.

If, finally, the *Harbīs* collect no tax from Muslim traders, then likewise the *'Ashīr* does not collect a tax from the *Harbīs*, because of the fact that they have given up their oppression (i.e. collecting taxes from Muslims) while they have the power. This is, on their part, an expression of favour toward us, but we (i.e. Muslims) are more fit to be possessed with virtues than the *Harbīs*. The children and women of the *Harbīs* are exempt from tax on condition that similar treatment is accorded to Muslims by the *Harbīs*.

Now, the question arises as to whether the modern system of customs duties and tolls is consistent with the spirit of Islam, especially when they are, both in scope and objectives, vastly different from what prevailed during early Islam. From the standpoint of the universal brotherhood of Islam it may not be justified to have artificial barriers in the field of international trade, because basically Islam believes in one humanity and hence in free trade. But viewed from the standpoint of the survival of a poor but developing Muslim state, the modern system of customs duties and tariffs will stand up to reason. In my view, the Islamic state is perfectly within its rights to impose any amount of customs duties provided that these revenues are used for the benefit of the community as a whole and that any of its objectivities do not encourage the growth of a monopoly or the like.

The above-mentioned taxes were the major heads of revenue during the early period of Islam. Other taxes on the public sector are not of great importance. The tax on the public sector is that land becomes the property of the state if its owner dies intestate or the land or property is found unclaimed. Again, another source of income was the *Waqf* property which refers voluntary transfer by an individual of his ownership to the ownership of the state for the benefit of the community. The first *Waqf* of immovable property was executed by the Caliph 'Umar and the precedent has been followed generally throughout the ages by Muslims. The *Qur'ānic* verses: "Who will give loan to Allah, a good loan" and "You cannot attain to righteousness unless you spend what is dear to you" have been a great incentive for *Waqf*.

Even in modern times *Waqf* property is a source of revenue for many Muslim states. Since this revenue is a "loan to Allah", as such they should not be mixed up with the general revenue of the state spending, of which some may not be always justified. In my view, *Waqf* revenue should be spent on lines somewhat similar to the heads of expenditure of *Zakāt* revenue.

There were some other taxes which were imposed by Muslim rulers. Since they are mostly extra-*Shari'ah*, they could not become part of the Islamic financial system.

It is a verdict of history that the 'Abbāsid period saw the culmination of several taxes introduced during the time of the Prophet. The peace and economic prosperity that prevailed during this period of Islamic history is indicative of the fact that the financial system was quite sound and practical. The very fact that the tax structure of early Islam was elastic and dynamic is a great lesson for modern economic experts and financial wizards. The modern fiscal system has faced the great problem of evasion of taxes, which was practically absent during the early period of Muslim rule. What is needed is to imbue the Muslim community with Islamic teachings in a manner that they think of paying taxes as a religious and moral duty. This is a challenge which an Islamic state must accept. Merely paying lip-service to our great Islamic teachings is not an answer to our problems.

13.2 *Zakāt*

(a) Its Meaning for Modern Man

The word "*Zakāt*" means "that which purifies" and "that which fosters". "All original sources of wealth—the sun, the moon, the stars, the earth, the clouds that bring rain, the winds that drive the clouds and carry the pollen, all phenomena of Nature—are the gifts of God to the whole of mankind. Wealth is produced by the application of man's skill and labour to the resources which God has provided for man's subsistence and comfort and over part of which man enjoys proprietary rights, to the extent recognized by Islam. In the wealth that is produced, therefore, three parties are entitled to share: the workman, whether skilled or unskilled; the person who supplies the capital; and the community as representing mankind. The community's share in produced wealth is called the *Zakāt*. After this has been set aside for the benefit of the community, the rest is 'purified' and may be divided between the remaining parties that are entitled to share in it."

Zakāt is the pivot and hub of Islamic public finance. It covers the moral, social and economic spheres. In the moral sphere *Zakāt* washes away the greed and acquisitiveness of the rich. In the social sphere *Zakāt* acts as a unique measure vouchsafed by Islam to abolish poverty from the society by making the rich alive to the social responsibilities they have. In the economic sphere *Zakāt* prevents the morbid accumulation of wealth in a few hands and allows it to be diffused before it assumes threatening proportions in the hands of its possessors. It is a compulsory contribution of the Muslims to the state exchequer.

The term "*Zakāt*" has no malevolent connotations as all other secular taxes of today have. In at least twenty different places in the Holy *Qur'ān* there is an association of *Zakāt* with *Salāt* (prayers). Thus the *Qur'ān* categorically states that whoever wants to enter the brotherhood of Islam shall have to establish regular prayers and pay *Zakāt* regularly. Both the practices are equally fundamental in importance. *Zakāt* is barren if it does not spring from a prayerful mood when there is no trace or taint of selfishness; *Salāt* (prayer) is fruitless if it does not bring about a mood and temper of voluntary submission to the demands and dictates of genuine social welfare. This dynamic interplay of these two spiritual and temporal institutions in Islamic society is symbolic of the inner unity of religion and economics. As the moral fervour behind the *Zakāt* institution is derived from the perennial spiritual source of *Salāt*, its social and economic effects are wholesome and the social pattern that emerges is free from the hideous tyrannies of capitalism and the coercive standardization of communist society. It was this all-pervading social harmony that led H. G. Wells, in *The Outline of History*, to remark: "Islam has created a society more free from widespread cruelty and social oppression than any society had ever been in the world before."[2]

In fact, equal stress on *Zakāt* and *Salāt* signifies true progress in Islamic society. Dr R. R. Marett rightly observed, "Real progress is progress in charity, all other advances being secondary thereto." Aldous Huxley writes in the same vein: "Such is the world in which we find ourselves—a world which, judged by the only acceptable criterion of progress, is manifestly in regression. Technological advance is rapid. But without progress in charity, technological advance is useless. Indeed, it is worse than useless. Technological progress has merely provided us with more efficient means for going back on words." The importance of *Zakāt* can, therefore, hardly be overestimated.

Six Principles

If one carefully observes the rules and regulations governing *Zakāt* one may easily find out six principles of the *Sharī'ah* governing *Zakāt*. They are: (*a*) the principle of faith, (*b*) the principle of equity, (*c*) the principle of productivity or maturity, (*d*) the principle of reason, (*e*) the principle of convenience and (*f*) the principle of freedom.

The first principle governing *Zakāt* is the principle of faith in Islam, because the payment of *Zakāt* is an act of worship and as such only a true believer can perform it in its real sense and spirit. In several verses of the Holy *Qur'ān* Allah enjoins *Salāt* (prayer) and *Zakāt* on those who believe in Islam for their spiritual and secular advancement. For instance, the *Qur'ān* says:

"And establish regular Prayer
And give regular Charity;
And loan to God
A beautiful Loan."

(*Sūrah* LXXIII. 20)

Once Ḥaḍrat Abū Bakr in a public address on the obligatoriness of *Zakāt* and its inseparableness from *Salāt* went so far as to say: "By God, I will wage war against those who discriminate between *Salāt* and *Zakāt*."

The second principle of equity governing *Zakāt* is contained in the saying of the Prophet (peace be upon him): "In (the product of) land, watered by rain and springs or in what is watered by water running on the surface of the ground is one-tenth, and (in) what is watered by wells one-twentieth" (Bukhāri) *Zakāt* is one generic term applicable to all ordinary compulsory contributions and the share of the state in various kinds of income such as treasure-trove, booty obtained in religious warfare, land produce, etc., follow the principle of equity which states that the lesser the amount of labour and capital, the lesser the rate of the levy.[3]

The third principle is the principle of productivity or maturity. Thus Ibn 'Umar said: The Messenger of Allah (peace be upon him) reported, "Whoever acquires wealth, there is *Zakāt* on it until a year has passed over it" (Tirmidhī and *Mishkāt*). Thus *Zakāt* is paid annually after calculating *Nisāb*. *Nisāb* means annual minimum surplus of the value of 40 riyāls or the property equivalent in value to it over necessary expenditure. *Nisāb* becomes subject to *Zakāt* only when it is mature and productive. But the *Nisāb* will be dissolved on the date of the sale during a year and the first year must elapse before the amount realized becomes subject to *Zakāt*. The lapse of a period of twelve months is essential because time is indispensable for productivity to materialize. Obviously, *Zakāt* is not charged on things which are perishable and are meant for personal use and consumption (i.e. residential houses, clothes, etc.). It may be noted that the *Nisāb* is different with different kinds of property and is also reckoned differently. For instance, in the case of *Ṣawā'im* (animals) *Zakāt* attaches importance to their physical identity and not to their commercial value as in the case of merchandise. In the case of gold and silver, *Zakāt* is determined in terms of weight. But whether the property is apparent or non-apparent, *Zakāt* will not be charged if the *Nisāb* is destroyed accidentally after the lapse of the year but before the *Zakāt* is actually paid.

Zakāt lapses on death and apostasy. If the death of the property-owner occurred during a year, a year must pass before *Zakāt* is charged on the property.

The fourth principle is the principle of reason. That is, the person who is to pay *Zakāt* must be a man of reason and responsibility. Hence the view that minors and the insane are exempt from *Zakāt*, which is regarded as an act of worship and, therefore, incumbent only on those who are capable of exercising discretion. But, according to the Mālikites (especially in the case of cattle and crops) and also according to al-Shāfi'ī, minors and the insane are subject to *Zakāt*. The basis of their contention is that *Zakāt* is a tax on property. Hence it is realizable, though the property may belong to minors or the insane. In the writer's opinion, minors and the insane may be subject to *Zakāt* only when their properties are under the care of such guardians as are expected to utilize their property in the most reasonable way. Where there is a possibility of losing the minor's property through lack of care, it should not be subject to *Zakāt*. The Tradition is clear about it. The Prophet (peace be upon him) is reported to have said: "Beware! whoever is the guardian of an orphan who has property, should trade with it and should not have it (undeveloped), so that the *Zakāt* should consume it" (Tirmidhī).

The fifth principle of convenience of *Zakāt* is derived partly from the nature of collection of *Zakāt* and partly from the Islamic code of economic ethics. As regards collection of *Zakāt* there is nothing more convenient than what is paid at the end of a year. Besides this, the converted Muslims who are in a non-Muslim state are not held responsible for the payment of *Zakāt*. It is not unlikely that a man who gives up his own religion and embraces Islam should suddenly find himself deprived of all means of livelihood. This change may wreck his business and may even ruin his civic life. Thus he is free from the payment of *Zakāt*, rather his maintenance is a justifiable charge on the *Zakāt* fund.

The last principle of *Zakāt* is the principle of freedom. That is, one must be a free man before one is eligible for payment of *Zakāt*. Therefore, a slave or a captive is not required to pay *Zakāt* as he is not supposed to own any property. In fact, a slave is entitled to some pecuniary help from *Zakāt* money which he might use to secure emancipation. Nowadays when slavery is extinct, persons who undergo imprisonment may be placed in the category of those who are not considered to be free men and their innocent dependants may get *Zakāt* revenue.

All these principles governing payment of *Zakāt* should be reflected not only in its traditional basis of assessment but also in the modern basis of the assessment of *Zakāt*.

Traditional Basis

The doctors of conventional law generally divided property on which *Zakāt* was to be applicable into four categories.

The first category was gold and silver and the profits of trade. Here the *Zakāt* levied was 2½ per cent. The taxable limit is the possession by an individual, for a continuous period of one year, of 52½ tolas of silver or 7½ tolas of gold. As a matter of fact, after deducting *Nisāb* and debt, all idle wealth is taxed at the rate of 2½ per cent.

The second category of property was cattle and other domestic animals. The percentage of *Zakāt* was approximately the same as in the case of the first category.

The third category was agricultural and farming produce and the proportion of *Zakāt* was assessed at one-tenth in regard to land irrigated by natural means (e.g. rain) without any extra effort by the owner, and one-twentieth in the case of land irrigated by artificial means and requiring extra effort on the part of the owner.

The fourth category was mines and treasure-trove. If a mine or a treasure-trove is discovered in the land of a Muslim, one-fifth of it, irrespective of whether it is owned by individuals or by the state, should form *Zakāt* revenue to be spent exclusively on the items mentioned in the *Qur'ān*.

It must be noted here that property which is subjected to *Zakāt* must be that which is in excess of the basic needs of the owner and of what is required for his bare livelihood. Let us now discuss in some detail the modern basis of assessment of *Zakāt* revenue.

Modern Basis

The modern controversy in regard to *Zakāt* is on the meaning of the term "property" referred to in the verses of the *Qur'ān*. The *Qur'ān* says: "Take alms out of their property—thou wouldst cleanse them and purify them thereby— and pray for them. Surely the prayer is a relief to them. And God is Hearing, Knowing" *Sūrah* IX 103.

"The parable of those who spend their property in the way of God is as the parable of a grain growing seven years, in every year a hundred grains. And God multiples further for whom He pleases. And God is Giving, Knowing" (*Sūrah* II. 261).

The categories of property defined in the early days of Islam on which *Zakāt* is to be applicable should not, in the writer's opinion, be rigidly maintained. The modern basis of assessment of *Zakāt* has been carefully studied by a group of eminent Islamic jurists.

The Arab League held a seminar on this subject, and a comprehensive report on social solidarity in the Arab world was presented to a meeting held in Damascus in December 1962. The report was prepared by Shaikh Muhammad Abū Zahrah, Shaikh 'Abd al-Wahhāb Khallāf of the Faculty of the *Sharī'ah* at the University of Cairo, and Shaikh 'Abd al-Raḥmān Ḥasan of al-Azhar University.

In this report, to which frequent reference will be made, the view is held that *Zakāt* would now be due on all kinds of property not known in the early days of Islam. Such things as industrial machinery, bank notes, profits of professions and trades would now be subject to *Zakāt*.

(b) *Zakāt* on Industrial Machinery, etc.

On this subject, the report says: "The application of this distinction in our time leads us inevitably to add to the category of property liable to *Zakāt* property which is now considered productive and which was not known to be productive at the time when the jurists originally formulated their theories on the subject. Where property is a means of exploitation for its owner, or where the owner of a big factory employs labour to run it and utilises industrial machinery as the means of bringing about profit, the property would be considered productive for the purpose of *Zakāt* and a charge made upon it. Here the gain which the owner of the factory secures comes from the industrial machinery he uses, and this machinery is not in the same category as the tools of the blacksmith or the carpenter who alone uses the tools and without whom there would be no production from the tools. For this reason *Zakāt* should be levied on this kind of industrial property on the ground that it is productive property and not in the category of property needed for the basic requirements of the person owning the property. The jurists of old order did not impose *Zakāt* upon industrial implements because these implements were of a primitive nature and were not of themselves productive, as is the case at present. Production from industrial implements can be possible only through their use by the worker. Now, however, machines produce more or less by themselves, and can be considered in the category of productive goods for the purposes of *Zakāt*. Modern factories consider their industrial machinery as their growing asset. But it must be pointed out here that tools owned by a craftsman and used solely by him, such as the tools of a hairdresser who works alone, should be exempt from *Zakāt* because they would be the basic and essential requirements for the craftsman without which he cannot produce anything. And it cannot be said here that this view is contrary to the views of the old jurists, for the simple reason that the old jurists did not know of this problem and could not have made any reasonable pronouncement in regard to it. We are merely applying the basic theories which the old jurists have devised on the subject."

The report discussed the rate of the *Zakāt* to be levied on industrial machinery and similar property, and came to the conclusion that it would be ten per cent of its net produce, by analogy to the *Zakāt* levied on the produce of agricultural property.

So far as the imposition of *Zakāt* on industrial machinery and factory produce is concerned, I agree entirely with the views expressed in the report, but with regard to the rate of *Zakāt* on industrial machinery, etc., I cannot agree with it on the following grounds. Firstly, the analogy of agricultural produce is not altogether apt, because the rate of depreciation is greater in the case of industrial machinery than in that of agricultural land. The rate of *Zakāt* must thus be assessed after making due allowances for depreciation. Obviously, the rate of *Zakāt* will in this case be lower than that on agricultural produce. Secondly, here the question of the rate of *Zakāt* is linked with productivity which varies from industry to industry. It is, therefore, felt that the rate of *Zakāt* on industrial machinery and factory produce should be made flexible so that the element of progressivity may be introduced.

(c) *Zakāt* on Bank-notes, etc.

The report also dealt with the question of *Zakāt* in regard to bank-notes and other forms of currency and bills of exchange, such as stocks, shares and bonds. These, of course, were not known in the early days of Islam. The report says: "Stocks, shares and bonds, if acquired for the purpose of trade and gain, are dealt with as commodities liable to the payment of *Zakāt*. For this purpose the value of the stocks, shares and bonds is taken at the beginning of the year, and *Zakāt* charged on the profit or gain secured. The jurists of old would agree with this. And where the stocks, shares and bonds are acquired for investment, *Zakāt* would be payable on the profit or dividend obtained from the investment."

This view is subject to criticism on the ground that it has combined stocks and shares, on the one hand, and bonds, on the other, and devised the same rules to apply to all three. Stocks and shares give a dividend which varies from year to year, and this is a permissible profit according to the *Sharī'ah*, while bonds may be contrary to the *Sharī'ah* and more like usury and illicit profit.

(d) *Zakāt* on Rent, Profits, etc.

On the question of the rate of *Zakāt* on rent derived from houses and other accommodation, the report says: "The majority of the jurists are known not to have agreed that *Zakāt* is chargeable on houses. The reason is that houses at the time were not exploited for commercial purposes but were used primarily by the owner, and were thus essential and basic needs. Things are different now, and houses and other property are built for the purpose of investment and for letting to others and the return on houses is now higher than the return that can be expected upon land. With the changed situation, the public interest requires that *Zakāt* should be charged on houses in the same way as it was, in the past, charged on land. There is no difference in reality between the owner of land who lets it out to others to farm and then collects a return on it, and the owner of houses who lets them and collects a return. It would be utterly unreasonable to charge tax on land but not on houses in such a case, and this would also be in injustice to the owners of agricultural land. Another result of this would be that people would give up ownership of buildings. The *Sharī'ah* cannot be said to make such an illogical rule. The difference between us and the jurists of old is not a difference as regards theories but as regards the application of the theories. In their days buildings were not exploited for profit, as they are now."

Though the learned jurists are inclined to recommend that the rate of *Zakāt* on bank-notes as well as rents, etc., should be 2½ per cent, yet I am for flexibility in determining the rate of *Zakāt*. That is, in such cases the rate of *Zakāt* should be fixed but tempered by considerations of productivity and profitability.

(e) *Zakāt* and Inflation

Now I would draw *Zakāt* and the attention of the jurists to the modern problem of inflation and its impact on the rate of *Zakāt*. What is inflation? By inflation we mean a rise in the general level of prices usually on account of an increase in the supply of money, unaccompanied by a corresponding increase in demand. thus, according to Professor Pigou, "Inflation exists when money income is expanding more than in proportion to income-earning activity," resulting in a rise in prices. When prices rise due to increased gold supply, we speak of gold inflation, when due to currency notes, currency inflation, and when it is due to an overexpansion of credit, the term credit inflation is used. Mere inflation implies a general rise in prices due to some, any, or all of these causes. Deflation is the opposite of inflation. It should be noted that high or low prices as such are immaterial. If all prices including prices of services double or halve overnight, it makes no material change in the economic position of the people concerned. But this never happens. Actually, rising or falling prices influence the course of production and the distribution of wealth in different and often adverse ways.

In the modern Muslim world, almost everywhere we find the problem of rising price levels as a part of a rise in the price levels throughout the world. Without going into the details of its causes, it can be said that the purchasing power of *Zakāt* revenue diminishes during periods of rising prices; the poor who are entitled to receive the *Zakāt* money are thus hard hit. Therefore, there is no reason to believe that the items taxed and rates charged were meant to be unchangeable with changing circumstances, as the door of *Ijtihād* is never closed in Islam. One school of thought held the view that the rate of *Zakāt* cannot be changed as it has been fixed by the Apostle of Allah himself. But if we look to the spirit of *Zakāt*, there is not the least difficulty in concluding that in fixing the rate of *Zakāt* the Islamic state may introduce the element of elasticity to face the inflationary tendencies of the economy of almost all the Muslim countries of the world. By change in the rate of *Zakāt*, I mean change in its rate in money terms, not in real terms. Let us suppose that twenty years ago one could purchase ten seers of rice with 2½ *riyāls*. Now if one can purchase five seers of rice with the same amount, then what does it mean? This means depreciation in the value of money to the extent of 50 per cent, which justifies an increase in the rate of *Zakāt* to the extent of 50 per cent. If this is not allowed, the objectives for which *Zakāt* is collected will be defeated.

Money itself is not valuable; it is valuable for it has an exchange value. Therefore, if the exchange value of the existing rate of *Zakāt* is reduced to zero, *Zakāt* will lose its significance in bringing an element of socialism in to society.

In fact, Ḥaḍrat 'Umar himself introduced many changes in the system of *Zakāt*. He imposed *Zakāt* on horses, whereas before him horses were exempt from *Zakāt*. He helped the non-Muslim aged and the sick and the unemployed out of the proceeds of *Zakāt*. Therefore, it is not the manner or the rate of collection that matters. *Zakāt* is not an end in itself; it is a means to an end.

(f) *Zakāt* and Principles of Public Finance

Let us now discuss some aspects of *Zakāt* in the light of the principles of modern public finance. Firstly, an attempt may be made to distinguish between *Zakāt* and modern sources of public finance, although the religio-economic character of *Zakāt* makes it a difficult task to compare it with the modern materialist sources of public finance, which consist of taxes, fees, prices, special assessments, rates, etc. Though compulsion is the essence of both tax and *Zakāt*, yet *Zakāt* differs fundamentally from tax on the grounds that tax (i.e. income-tax) is generally imposed on income while *Zakāt* is comprehensive in the sense that it is charged not only on savings but also on property.

Again, *Zakāt* is neither a fee nor a price. Fees are a compulsory payment but are paid only by those who obtain definite services in return. In the case of *Zakāt* the question of "definite return" does not arise. Moreover, the main difference between *Zakāt* and prices lies in the fact that one can escape prices by not purchasing a service since price is the payment for a service of a business character, e.g. charges for travelling on railways, whilst *Zakāt* is an obligatory tax.

Finally, *Zakāt* is not a special assessment, neither is it rates, Special assessment, as defined by Professor Seligman, is "a compulsory contribution levied in proportion to the special benefit derived, to defray the cost of a specific improvement to property undertaken in the public interest." The "benefit theory of taxation" which is the basis of special assessment is not the main consideration of *Zakāt*. Moreover, *Zakāt* differs from rates partly because rates are levied on immovable property and partly because rates generally vary from locality to locality. *Zakāt*, which is guided by one uniform principle, is not leviable on instruments and residential houses.

(g) *Zakāt* and Canons of Taxation

Though there is a fundamental difference between *Zakāt* and the modern sources of public finance, yet *Zakāt* can be linked to Adam Smith's four canons of taxation— Equality, Certainty, Convenience and Economy. Firstly, according to the canon of equality, "the subjects of every State ought to contribute towards the support of the Government, as nearly as possible in proportion to their respective abilities, that is, in proportion to the revenue which they respectively enjoy under the protection of the State." By ability is meant equality of sacrifice and not of amount paid. Every person should contribute towards the maintenance of the state according to his ability. Thus the rich should pay more taxes than the poor. This is true under the modern system of taxation under which the levy of a tax is on the income of an individual. *Zakāt*, on the other hand, is levied on the accumulated savings at a uniform rate which ensures equal sacrifice. Moreover, *Zakāt* cannot be spent by the state in any way it likes. It is an express objective of *Zakāt* that it should be made available for the poor and be something from which the rich can have little or no direct benefit.

Secondly, according to the canon of certainty, "the tax which each individual is bound to pay ought to be certain and not arbitrary. The time of payment, the quantity to be paid, ought all to be clear and plain to the contributor and to every other person." The tax-payer should know what amount he is to pay so that he may adjust his expenditure to his income. The tax-payer should also know when he is to pay and why he is to pay. As regards the certainty of *Zakāt* there can be no comparison, because its basic rules are unalterably fixed by Divine Sanction. Like any other tax, the ordinary principles of assessment would enable the state to ascertain the amount of revenue to be derived from *Zakāt*.

Thirdly, the canon of convenience states that "every tax ought to be so contrived as both to take out and to keep out of the pockets of people as little as possible over and above what it brings into the public treasury of the State." As for the collection of *Zakāt*, the rules are so simple that no specialized knowledge is required and consequently the cost is definitely economic. Similarly, in at least twenty places in the *Qur'ān*, *Zakāt* is associated with *Salāt*. It is this importance which enrobes *Zakāt* with a religious sanctity of the highest order and thus makes the realization of this tax easy, inexpensive and voluntary.

It should be noted here that economists have recently added two more canons—the canon of productivity and the canon of elasticity. It goes without saying that *Zakāt* is quite consistent with the canon of productivity since the taxing of idle money in the form of *Zakāt* inevitably leads to its perforce employment in productive channels, which in turn increase the national wealth of a country. True it is that *Zakāt* does not appear to be elastic in the modern sense of the term. But the question of elasticity loses its force as, under the Islamic scheme of society, it is open to the head of the state to devise and impose new taxes according to changing circumstances.

In no country does each tax satisfy each of these canons. Even all modern taxes are bound to infringe some canons in one way or the other. *Zakāt* as a system of taxation satisfies, not only most of the principles of taxation, but also possesses certain definite advantages over modern taxes.

(h) *Zakāt's* Advantages.

In comparison with modern taxes, *Zakāt* possesses definite advantages over them in at least three respects. In the first place tax evasion is a serious problem for modern tax collection. It is quite well known to everybody that many people try to evade paying income-tax by presenting false accounts. The question of dishonest practices in the case of *Zakāt* is quite unexpected because of *Zakāt's* religio-economic character. Needless to say that *Zakāt* is one of the five pillars of the Islamic faith. In the economic sphere it is a voluntary submission to God's will.

Secondly, the main source of *Zakāt* being unused hoarded wealth, it serves a noble purpose. It is only through *Zakāt* that it is possible to unearth hoarded wealth and utilize it for the greater benefit of society. As *Zakāt* is a divine order, wholehearted co-operation of the individual concerned to bring out his hoarded wealth would be forthcoming. Under a modern taxation system this co-operation will not be easily forthcoming as nobody will willingly give out to the state the secrets of his hidden treasures. Actually, *Zakāt* checks the tendency to hoard money and provides a powerful stimulus to investment in productive purposes, since Islam allows profit and partnership.

Finally, the purpose of *Zakāt* and the heads of its expenditure have been well defined in the Holy *Qur'ān*. So the government is not permitted to spend the money collected through *Zakāt* in any way it likes. But the revenue collected from taxes can be spent whimsically by the modern state. Empirically viewed, income from taxes is not always spent on productive purposes. Moreover, *Zakāt* is not "felt" as much as income tax, the payment of *Zakāt* being a divine order the people will pay it willingly.

Social Security. Nowadays, in almost all advanced countries, there is a call for social security schemes. Regarding the meaning and scope of security, Professor F. Benham in his book, *Economics,* observes: "It is the duty of the State to provide a minimum economic security for all its citizens. The phrase commonly used for this minimum of economic security is social security. There is no clear-cut line, established by general usage, between social security measures and other measures which reduce inequality, such as free hospital treatment, medical advice and medicine; free education; and subsidies on food-stuffs and on working class houses. The general practice is perhaps to include under social security measures only schemes for providing money benefit to persons suffering economic hardship. Such schemes include insurance against unemployment and sickness; compensation to workers who have met with accidents in course of their employment; maternity benefits; family allowances for children; pensions to old people, widows, the blind, and those injured in war; and in the last resort national assistance."

However, if we examine the heads of expenditure of *Zakāt*, there is hardly any difficulty in concluding that there is nothing original in modern social security schemes.

The heads of expenditure of *Zakāt* money, which are eight, have been clearly mentioned in the *Qur'ān*, namely, disbursement (i) in aid of the poor, the destitute and the disabled, (ii) to help the converted Muslim, (iii) to help the needy, (iv) to help the debtor to repay his debts, (v) to free slaves, (vi) to help travellers in difficulties, (vii) to pay the salaries of the staff employed in collecting *Zakāt* and (viii) in the way of Allah. It is to be noted that out of the eight items as many six concern poverty. *Salāt* (prayer) arouses feelings of equality and brotherhood between the rich and the poor, the high and the low, and *Zakāt* puts that feeling of brotherhood on a firm footing by making the rich and the capitalists responsible for the maintenance of the poor and the needy. The spiritual and moral values of Islam inculcated by *Salāt* would lose their significance if men did nothing to eradicate poverty and bring about social justice. *Zakāt* is really a revoluntionary concept, because in the cause of the poor, definite portions are assigned from almost all sectors of the economy. Thus by a levy of $2\frac{1}{2}$ per cent on all idle wealth, one-tenth or one-twentieth on all agricultural produce, one-fifth on all mineral wealth, the tax on the entire capital of the whole nation has been set aside to meet the requirements of the poor and the needy. Therefore, some of W. C. Smith's observations on *Zakāt* as reflected in his *Modern Islam in India* (p. 100) are false and misleading. Having misunderstood *Zakāt,* it is surprising that Mr Smith concludes that "most States in the world have had something of the kind, though in modern States it is always something much more substantial." How misleading this statement is when we all know that *Zakāt* does not spare any form of national wealth and there is nothing original in the so-called "substantial" provision made for the poor by modern states.

As a matter of fact, the first conscious and organized effort to saddle the state with the onerous responsibility of relieving economic distress by means of a social insurance scheme has been made in our times by the U. S. S. R. Whether it is an unconscious plagiarism from the *Zakāt* plan or the outcome of independent thinking, it rebounds to the credit of Islam that fourteen hundred years ago it made ample provisions for such social security. When the West was wallowing in a quagmire of ignorance and its early thinkers were in mental twilight, Islam laid down as one of the primary functions of the state by way of *Zakāt* from the rich the collection of money and the organization of social insurance on a massive scale.

In Chapter 12, we have already given a brief explanation of certain items of expenditure of *Zakāt* with special reference to terms such as *Masakin*, Path of God" and "Way farer". It was shown that *Zakāt* funds can be utilised for mitigating the suffering of the mon-Muslim poor. It is implicit in the Quranic concern for humanity. As the Qur'ān said:

"O mankind! We created you from a single (pair) of male and female. And made you into nations and tribes, that ye may know each other (not that ye may despise each other). Verily, the most honoured of you in the sight of God is (he who is) the most righteous of you."

(*Sūrah* XLIX: 13)

(i) Social Advantages of *Zakāt*

According to modern economists, whether a particular tax system is good or bad depends on its effects on society. That tax system is best which secures maximum social advantage—a system in which the economic welfare of a community can be increased. In his book *Principles of Public Finance,* Dr Dalton observed: "The two chief conditions of an increase in the economic welfare of a community are, first, improvements in production and, second, improvements in the distribution of what is produced.

"Improvements in production resolve themselves into (1) increase of productive power so that a large product per worker shall be obtained with a smaller effort, (2) improvements in the organisation of production so as to reduce to a minimum the waste of economic resources through unemployment and other causes, and (3) improvements in the composition or pattern of production so as to serve the needs of the community.

"Improvements in distribution resolve themselves into (1) a reduction in the great inequality which is found in most civilised communities in the incomes of different individuals and families, and (2) a reduction in great fluctuations between different periods of time in the incomes of particular individuals and families, especially among the poorer sections of the community."

Zakāt improves the consumption, production and distribution pattern of an Islamic society. One of the greatest evils of capitalism is that the productive resources are controlled and owned by a few fortunate people to the utter neglect of a vast majority. This results in a serious disparity and inequality of income which in its ultimate analysis retards the growth of industries and commerce in the country. Because a monopoly dominated economic order always stands in the way of the full utilization of the economic resources of a country.

But *Zakāt* is an uncompromising enemy of hoarding and a killer of capitalism. As *Zakāt* is an obligatory tax on rich Muslims, the object of it is to remove the inequality of income and to return purchasing power to the poor people. According to the teachings of the Holy *Qur'ān*, there is no harm in earning money but it is the sacred duty of the Islamic state to see that not a single citizen in the state is deprived of the bare necessities of life.

This object can easily be achieved by proper distribution of *Zakāt* money among the poor and the needy. *Zakāt,* by giving them purchasing power, brings about a balance between demand for and supply of goods and thus facilitates the course of production in the country and smooths the path of national progress and prosperity. Now these people, having purchasing power in their hands, will demand more goods; entrepreneurs will try to produce more; the scope of employment in the country will increase, and with that the national income will also go up. *Zakāt* thus benefits both the rich and the poor—those who pay it and those who receive it as the *Qur'ān* says: "It (*Zakāt*) brings well being to both the person who pays it and the person who receives it."

Thus it may be repeated that *Zakāt* is not an end in itself; it is a means to an end. So the essence of *Zakāt* lies not in its detailed rules, but in the purposes and objects for which it was designed. But we must be aware that the greater the hold of Islam on the people, the greater the chance of smooth collection and distribution and the less chance of evasion. So sincere attempts must be made by the Muslim states to inculcate the spirit of Islam among Muslim members of the community.

(j) *Zakāt* and Modern Muslim States

We have already seen that the institution of *Zakāt* contains enormous potential for mitigating the sufferings of degraded humanity. The modern Muslim states must mobilize their domestic resources through *Zakāt* for financing various development programmes in the education, health, labour and social welfare sectors. Therefore, attempts should be made not only to collect *Zakāt* revenue by the state but also to examine thoroughly the institution of *Zakāt*. To start with, they can set up "People's *Zakāt* Welfare Trusts" to be administered by eminent jurists of Islamic Law and administrators of great integrity of character under the overall supervision of the states concerned. It should be examined whether it is possible to introduce an element of flexibility in fixing the rate of *Zakāt* keeping in view the inflationary pressure on the developing economy as well as the peoples' sentiments about it. In the first phase of implementation of a *Zakāt* scheme, its rate, as fixed by the Prophet, may not be disturbed. Without losing further time, an environment will have to be created where it is possible to introduce the scheme of *Zakāt* Saving Certificates" somewhat on the lines of the National Investment Trust (N. I. T.) Units of Pakistan. The proposed "Trust" may invest these saving certificates like N.I.T. of Pakistan. The dividend may be declared minus the amount of *Zakāt* which must be known to the persons concerned so that they can recommend the names of the "entitled" persons. The persons who will purchase these certificates may be given relief against income-tax, which will, I am sure, be sufficient incentive on the financial side. But the freedom to realize such non-transferable certificates after the prescribed maturity period must be ensured. The superiority of such a scheme lies in the fact that, unlike modern schemes, the person concerned will be gaining both tangible and intangible advantages—tangible advantages in the form of profits from the investments, and intangible advantages in the from the act of performing a supreme religious obligation. This is just a broad outline of the scheme; what is needed is a mass of detailed provisions, fresh thinking and planning.

13.3 Conclusion

Tax structure in early Islam does not fall into the two classes of religious and secular revenue, as wrongly maintained by many Western scholars.

In spite of the simplicity of the system, there were a number of taxes prevalent in the early Islamic State. Generally speaking, they are: (a) *Zakāt,* (b) *Jizyah,* (c) *Kharāj* or Land-Tax, (d) Spoils of War, (e) Tax on Mines and Treasure Trove, (f) Customs Duties and Tolls. It is found by analysis that the tax system of early Islam was elastic and dynamic in nature.

The author feels profoundly that the institution of *Zakāt* even today contains enormous potential for communal betterment which we should utilize in a systematic manner through government agency, for financing the social welfare and social security schemes of the modern state such as poor-houses, centres for free medical treatment, schools to provide elementary, secondary and technical education or the indigent, money relief for the unemployed, aged, widows and orphans, and a beginning might be made with the grant of relief to the innocent dependants of persons who are suffering imprisonment for crimes, etc.

The author, however, feels that the categories of property defined in the early days of Islam to which *Zakāt* is to be applicable should not be rigidly maintained. It is to be decided whether or not such things as industrial machinery, bank-notes, shares, stocks, etc., should be subject to *Zakāt.*

The author also feels that in fixing the rate of *Zakāt,* the Islamic state may introduce an element of elasticity to face the inflationary tendencies of the economy of almost all the Muslim countries of the world. During the periods of rising prices, the purchasing power of *Zakāt* revenue diminishes; the poor who are entitled to it are thus hard hit in real terms. Hadrat Umar introduced many changes in the system of *Zakāt,* because it is a means to an end, not an end in itself.

Notes

[1] N. P. Aghnides, p. 319.
[2] H. G. Wells, *The Outline of History,* p. 325
[3] S. A. Siddiqi, *Public Finance in Islam*

13.4 Selected Further Reading

Abdullah, S. M. "Zakat and Poverty Comment" in *Voice of Islam,* Vol. 24, no. 4, Karachi, 1974.

Ahmed, Ziauddin, "Ushr and 'Ushr Lands" in *Islamic Studies,* vol. XIX, no. 2. Islamabad, 1980.

Faridi, F. R. "Zakat and Fiscal Policy", in *Studies in Islamic Economics,* ed. by Khurshid Ahmed, Islamic Foundation, London, 1980.

Government of Pakistan, "Zakat and Ushr Ordinance, 1980", Ordinance No. XVIII of 1980, in Zakat and *Ushr by Muhammad Ziaul Haq Ministry of Information* and Broadcasting, Islamabad, 1980.

Hasanuzzaman, S. M. "Zakat, Taxes and Estate Duty", in *Islamic Literature,* vol. 17, Lahore, 1971.

Izadi, Ali M. "The Role of az-Zakat (An Institutionalised Charity) in the Islamic System of Economics in curing the Poverty Dilemma" in *Association of Muslim Social Scientists Proceedings Third National Seminar,* Indiana, USA, 1974.

Kahf, Monzer, The Calculation of Zakat for Muslims in North America, Association of Muslim Social Scientists, Indiana, U.S.A. 1978.

Kahf, Monzer. n.d. "The Islamic Economy – Analytical Study of the Functioning of the Islamic Economic System", *The Muslim Students Association of the United States and Canada,* Plainfield, 1978.

Mannan, M. A. "Zakat its Disbursement and Intra-poor *Disbursement* Equity", in *The Making of Islamic Economic Society: Islamic Dimensions in Economic Analysis,* Chapter 14 (forthcoming).

Salama A. A. "Fiscal Analysis of Zakat with Special Reference to Saudi Arabia's Experience in Zakat", in *Monetary and Fiscal Economics of Islam,* ed. by M. Ariff, (I. C. R. I. E), King Abdulaziz University, Jeddah, Saudi Arabia, 1982.

Shemesh, A. Ben, *Taxation in Islam,* (vols. I, II), E. J. Brill, Leiden, 1976.

APPENDIX

ZAKĀT in Practice

ZAKĀT AND USHR ORDINANCE, 1980* (of Pakistan)

ORDINANCE NO. XVIII OF 1980

AN

ORDINANCE

to make provisions relating to the assessment, collection and disbursement of Zakāt and Ushr

ZAKĀT

3. **Charge and collection of Zakāt.**—(1) Subject to the other provisions of this Ordinance, Zakāt in respect of assets mentioned in the First Schedule shall be charged and collected, on compulsory basis, for each Zakāt year, at the rates and in the manner specified therein, and as may be prescribed, from every person who is on the Valuation Date, and for the whole of the preceding Zakāt year been, *sahib-e-nisab*, and who owns or possesses such assets on the Valuation Date:

Provided that where an asset mentioned in the First Schedule has been assigned by the person owning or possessing it, in favour of another person, Zakāt in respect of that asset shall be charged and collected on compulsory basis as if the asset had not been so assigned:

Provided further that, if an asset was owned or possessed by a person on the Valuation Date but is owned or possessed by some other person on the Deduction Date, the Zakāt on such asset shall be charged and collected from such other person on behalf of the person owning or possessing it on the Valuation Date:

Provided further that, if a person proves in the prescribed manner to the satisfaction of the Local Committee of the locality where he ordinarily resides that he was not a *sahib-e-nisab* on the Valuation Date or was not in ownership or possession of assets of the value of *nisab* for the whole of the preceding Zakāt year, Zakāt shall not be so charged and collected from him, or if collected shall be refunded to him in the prescribed manner:

Provided further that no Zakāt shall be charged and collected from the assets of a person who died on or before the Deduction Date.

Provided further that no Zakāt shall be charged or collected on compulsory basis in respect of any of the assets mentioned in the First Schedule which—

(a) have been acquired against payment in foreign currency; or

(b) are maintained in foreign currency;

and the return on which and the value on encashment, redemption or withdrawal of which, is payable in foreign currency.

(2) In determining the amount to be collected as Zakāt on compulsory basis, the value of an asset on which Zakāt is deductible at source may be reduced, to the extent and in the manner prescribed, only on account of debts which have been—

(a) primarily secured by that asset;
(b) used for the creation of an asset on which Zakāt is deductible at source; and
(c) obtained from the Deducting Agency having custody of the asset securing the debt and of the asset created under clause (b).

(3) Where a person from whom Zakāt has been deducted at source—

(a) proves that—

    (i) he is not a Muslim, or

    (ii) he is not a citizen of Pakistan, or

    (iii) the amount deducted from him is more than what is due under this Ordinance, either

        on account of an error apparent from the record, or

        on account of reduction provided for in sub-section (2) not having been duly allowed to him, or

    (iv) he falls under any of the exclusions given in sub-clauses (a) to (n) of clause (xxiii) of section 2, or

(b) proves, as laid down in the third proviso to sub-section (1), that he is not a *sahib-e-nisab* or was not in ownership or possession of *nisab* for the whole of the preceding Zakāt year, or

(c) files a declaration, which has not been challenged in the Federal Shariat Court under sub-section (3A) of that section and claims refund,

the amount so deducted or, as the case may be, the amount so deducted in excess shall be refunded to him in the prescribed manner.

(4) Where the recovery of Zakāt deductible at source, in respect of any of the assets mentioned in the First Schedule, falls into arrears, the Administrator-General may forward to the Collector of the district concerned a duly signed certificate specifying the amount of arrears due and the particulars of the person from whom due, and the Collector shall, on receipt of such certificate, proceed to recover the amount so specified, as if it were an arrear of land revenue.

(5) A *sahib-e-nisab* may pay either to a Zakāt Fund or directly to those eligible under Shariah to receive Zakāt so much of the Zakāt due under *Shari'ah* as is not deductible at source under this Ordinance, for example, that due in respect of assets mentioned in the Second Schedule.

(6) Any amount deducted at source by the Deducting Agency from any person shall be treated as payment of Zakāt on behalf of such person or, in the case of a person referred to in sub-section (3) of section 1 as contribution to Zakāt Fund or *sadaqah* or *khairat* in the name of Allah, as the case may be, on the part of that person.

4. **Secrecy of information**.—Any information furnished or collected in

connection with the deduction of Zakāt at source under this Ordinance shall be treated as secret and shall not be used for any other purpose, including the assessment or collection of any tax.

USHR

5. **Charge and collection of Ushr.**—(1) Subject to the other provisions of this Ordinance, there shall be charged and collected, on compulsory basis, in such manner as is laid down in section 6, and as may be prescribed, from every land-owner, grantee, allottee, lessee, lease-holder or land-holder (other than a person excluded from the definition of *sahib-e-nisab*) Ushr at the rate of five per cent of his share of the produce, as on the Valuation Date:

Provided that if any plot of land is used principally for growing one crop and a small portion thereof, not exceeding one-fourth of an acre, is used for growing another crop, Ushr shall not be charged in respect of the produce of such small portion.

Explanation.—In this section and section 6, 'land-owner', 'grantee', 'allottee', 'lessee', 'lease-holder', and 'land-holder' shall have the same meaning as in the laws relating to land administration and 'land-holder' includes a person in possession of any plot of land who has grown a crop on such plot.

(2) An individual land-owner, grantee, allottee, lessee, lease-holder or land-holder shall be exempt from the compulsory levy of Ushr if—

(a) he is eligible under *Shari'ah* to receive Zakāt; or

(b) the produce from his land is less than five *wasqs* (= 948 kilograms) of wheat, or its equivalent in value in the case of other crops liable to Ushr.

(3) The currency equivalent of five *wasqs* of wheat in value shall be such as may be notified for each Zakāt year by the Administrator-General.

(4) Ushr shall be the first charge on the produce.

(5) Ushr shall be collected in cash:

Provided that, where the produce consists of wheat or paddy, Ushr, at the option of the Provincial Council, may be collected in kind.

(6) A *sahib-e-nisab* may pay either to the Local Zakāt Fund or directly to those eligible under *Shari'ah* to receive Zakāt, so much of the Ushr due under *Shari'ah* as is not compulsorily realizable under this Ordinance, for example, in respect of item 9 of the Second Schedule.

6. **Mode of assessment and collection of Ushr.**—(1) A Local Committee shall be supplied by the Revenue Department, and such other department or official agency or any other person as may be determined by the Chief Administrator, in respect of a land-owner, grantee, allottee, lessee, lease-holder or land holder in the locality, in the prescribed form and manner, with the record containing such information for a crop season as may be required for the purposes of this Ordinance.

(2) An assessee may compute his Ushr liability on self-assessment basis and communicate the same to the Local Committee in such form and manner as may be prescribed and, while so computing his Ushr liability, shall be entitled to reduce to allow for possible over-estimation in assessment, one third of the Ushr due in the case of produce from land irrigated by tubewells and one fourth of the Ushr due in other cases.

(3) If the Local Committee finds that an assessee's self-assessment of his Ushr liability is acceptable, it shall notify it to the assessee as the Ushr demand of that assessee.

(4) Where an assessee fails to communicate to the Local Committee his self-assessment of Ushr liability under sub-section (2), or a Local Committee does not find the self-assessment of the Ushr liability by an assessee acceptable under sub-section (3), the Local Committee shall, subject to such guidelines and instructions as may be given by the Provincial Council or, if so authorised by the Provincial Council, by the District Committee, after taking into consideration the information furnished to it under sub-section (1) and any other information that it may deem relevant, adopting such procedure as it may deem fit, and allowing the reduction provided for in sub-section (2), make in the prescribed form and manner, its own assessment of Ushr realizable on compulsory basis under this Ordinance, and notify the demand to the assessee.

(5) In the case of a lease in force immediately before the commencement of this Ordinance, the liability of the lessor and the lessee to pay Ushr shall be equitably apportioned between them by the Local Committee.

"(6) An assessee aggrieved by the assessment under sub-section (4), or, as the case may be, a lessor or lessee aggrieved by the apportionment under sub-section (5), may, within fifteen days of the Local Committee's announcing the assessment, or, as the case may be, apportionment, apply, in the prescribed form and manner to the Tehsil Committee, Taluqa Committee or Sub-divisional Committee within whose jurisdiction the locality for which the Local Committee is constituted is situated for a revision of the assessment or apportionment:

Provided that no such application shall be admitted unless the applicant has deposited into the Local Zakāt Fund not less than fifty per cent of his liability as assessed or apportioned by the Local Committee.

(6A) The Tehsil Committee, Taluqa Committee or Sub-divisional Committee within whose jurisdiction the locality for which a Local Committee is constituted is situated may, at any time, either of its own motion or on the application of an adult Muslim residing within the locality, make an order enhancing the liability assessed under sub-section (4), or apportioned under sub-section (5), by the Local Committee:

Provided that no such order shall be made unless the person affected has been given an opportunity of showing cause against it and of being heard."; and

(7) The Tehsil Committee, Taluqa Committee or Sub-divisional

Committee to which an application is made under sub-section (6) or sub-section (6A), or which takes up a matter under sub-section (6A) of its own motion, shall give its decision within a period not exceeding one month counted from the date on which it receives the application or, as the case may be, so takes up the matter; and such decision shall be final and shall not be questioned before any Court or other authority.

(8) The demand as determined under sub-section (3), or, as the case may be, under sub-section (4) or sub-section (7), shall be paid by the assessee and collected by the Local Committee in such manner as may be prescribed.

(9) Where the recovery of Ushr compulsorily realizable under this Ordinance falls into arrears, the Chairman of the Local Committee shall forward to the Collector of the district concerned, a duly signed certificate specifying the amount of arrears due and the particulars of the person from whom due, and the Collector shall, on receipt of such certificate, proceed to recover the amount so specified as if it were an arrear of land revenue.

ZAKĀT FUNDS

7. **Establishment of Zakāt Funds.**—There shall be established the following Zakāt Funds, namely,—

(a) a Central Zakāt Fund to which shall be credited—
   (i) the Zakāt deducted at source;
   (ii) the Zakāt paid into it voluntarily;
   (iii) the transfers, if any, from the Provincial Zakāt Funds; and
   (iv) the grants, *atiyyat* and any other receipts;

(b) a Provincial Zakāt Fund for each Province to which shall be credited—
   (i) the transfers to it from the Central Zakāt Fund;
   (ii) the Zakāt paid into it voluntarily;
   (iii) the transfers, if any, from the Local Zakāt Funds; and
   (iv) the grants, *atiyyat* and any other receipts; and

(c) a Local Zakāt Fund for each Local Committee to which shall be credited—
   (i) the proceeds of Ushr;
   (ii) the Zakāt paid into it voluntarily;
   (iii) the transfers to it from the Provincial Zakāt Fund; and
   (iv) the grants, *atiyyat* and any other receipts.

8. **Utilization of Zakāt Funds.**—The moneys in a Zakāt Fund shall be utilized for the following purposes, namely,—

(a) assistance to the needy, the indigent and the poor, particularly orphans and widows, the handicapped and the disabled, eligible to receive Zakāt under *Shari'ah*, for their subsistence or rehabilitation, either directly or indirectly through *deeni madaris* or vocational educational institutions or public hospitals, clinics, dispensaries or health laboratories:

Provided that the lists of the individual to be assisted directly, and of the institutions through which assistance is to be given, from a Local Zakāt Fund shall be prepared and maintained, according to prescribed basis and manner, by the Local Committee in whose jurisdiction the individuals ordinarily reside, or the institutions through which they are to be assisted are situated, as the case may be:

Provided further that the list of institutions through which assistance from a Provincial Zakāt Fund is to be given shall be prepared and maintained, according to prescribed basis and manner, by the Provincial Council in whose jurisdiction these are situated; and

(b) expenditure on the collection, disbursement and administration of Zakāt and Ushr:

Provided that the expenditure on the Central Zakāt Council and the administrative organisation of the Administrator-General shall be met by the Federal Government, that on a Provincial Zakāt Council and the administrative organisation of a Chief Administrator, and that on a District Committee, Tehsil Committee, Taluqa Committee or Sub-divisional Committee, by the Provincial Government concerned, and that on a Local Committee from the Local Zakāt Fund not exceeding ten per cent of the receipts in that Fund during the year:

Provided further that the banking services and the services connected with the assessment or collection of Zakāt or Ushr realizable on compulsory basis under this Ordinance shall be rendered free of charge, except that the Administrator-General, or a Chief Administrator in regard to Ushr, may authorise payment of remuneration for any specified services; and

(c) any other purpose permitted by *Shari'ah*.

9. **Disbursements from Zakāt Funds.**—(1) The Central Council may from the Central Zakāt Fund make disbursements, and transfer funds to a Provincial Zakāt Fund, in such form and manner as may be prescribed and as would help in ensuring satisfaction of the needs of the needy and the poor throughout the country, as far as possible, on a uniform basis.

(2) A Provincial Council may from the Provincial Zakāt Fund make disbursements, and transfer funds to a Local Zakāt Fund, in such form and manner as may be prescribed and as would help in ensuring satisfaction of the needs of the needy and the poor throughout its jurisdiction, as far as possible, on a uniform basis:

Provided that a Provincial Council may, in exceptional circumstances, transfer funds from the Provincial Zakāt Fund to the Central Zakāt Fund.

(3) A Local Committee shall disburse, or incur expenditure from, the Local Zakāt Fund, in the prescribed manner, for authorised purposes within the locality, particularly for the benefit of the individuals directly or indirectly under clause (a) of section 8:

Provided that a Local Committee may or, if so required by the Provincial Council, shall, transfer from the Local Zakāt Fund to the Provincial Zakāt Fund, funds surplus to its needs.

10. **Accounts.**—(1) The accounts of the Central Zakāt Fund, a Provincial Zakāt Fund and a Local Zakāt Fund shall be maintained and operated, respectively, by the Administrator-General, the Chief Administrator, and the Local Committee, in such form and manner as may be prescribed.

(2) The records of the accounts of the Zakāt Funds shall be preserved for such period, and shall be made available for audit or inspection to such persons or agencies, and in such manner, as may be prescribed.

11. **Audit.**—(1) To carry out audit of the Central Zakāt Fund annually or at shorter intervals, the Central Council, and to carry out audit of a Provincial Zakāt Fund annually or at shorter intervals the Provincial Council, shall appoint auditors, being persons who are chartered accountants within the meaning of the Chartered Accountants Ordinance, 1961 (X of 1961).

(2) To carry out audit of the Local Zakāt Funds within a district annually or at shorter intervals, the District Committee shall appoint auditors being persons who are, in its opinion, qualified for the purpose.

(3) The audit performed by auditors under sub-sections (1) and (2) shall include propriety audit.

(4) The annual report of the auditors on the Central Zakāt Fund shall be laid before the Parliament, that on a Provincial Zakāt Fund before the Provincial Assembly concerned, and that on Local Zakāt Fund before the District Council concerned established under the law relating to local government.

(5) Nothing in this section shall be deemed to prevent—

(a) the Auditor-General of Pakistan from auditing any of the Zakāt Funds;

(b) the Central Council from getting audited any of the Provincial or Local Zakāt Funds;

(c) the Provincial Council from getting audited any of the Local Zakāt Funds within its jurisdiction; or

(d) a Local Committee from getting its own Local Zakāt Fund audited.

FIRST SCHEDULE

(*See* sections 2 and 3)

ASSETS SUBJECT TO COMPULSORY LEVY OF ZAKAT THROUGH DEDUCTION-AT-SOURCE FOR CREDIT TO THE CENTRAL ZAKAT FUND

S. No.	Assets	Rate and basis for computing the amount to be deducted as Zakat.	The Deduction Date	The Deducting Agency.
1	2	4	5	6
1.	Savings Bank Accounts and similar accounts by whatever name described—with the banks operating in Pakistan, post offices, National Savings Centres and financial institutions keeping such accounts.	2.5% of the amount standing to the credit of an account at the commencement of the day on the Valuation Date. (No deduction shall be made in case the amount standing to the credit of an account does not exceed the amount notified by the Administrator-General).	As notified by the administrator-General for the Zakat year.	The bank, office Centre, or institution as the case may be, keeping the account.
2.	Notice Deposit Receipts and Accounts and similar receipts and accounts by whatever name described with the banks operating in Pakistan, post offices, National Savings Centres and financial institutions issuing such receipts and keeping such accounts.	2.5% of the face value of a receipt or the amount standing to the credit of an account, as the case may be, at the commencement of the day on the Valuation Date, in each Zakat year.	The date on which the first return is paid or the date of encashment/withdrawal, whichever be earlier in the Zakat year.	The bank, office, Centre or institution, as the case may be, issuing the receipt or keeping the account and responsible for paying the return or the amount encashed/withdrawn.
3.	Fixed Deposit Receipts and Accounts and similar receipts and accounts and certificates (*e.g.* Khas Deposit Certificates), by whatever name described, issued by the banks operating in Pakistan, post offices, National Savings Centres and financial institutions—on which return is receivable by the holder periodically or is received earlier than maturity or withdrawal.	2.5% of the face value of a receipt or a certificate, or the amount standing to the credit of an account, as the case may be, as at the commencement of the day on the Valuation Date, in each Zakat year.	The date on which the first return is paid, or the date of encashment/redemption/withdrawal, whichever be earlier in the Zakat year.	The bank, office, Centre or institution, as the case may be, issuing the receipt or certificate or keeping the account, and responsible for paying the return or encashment/redemption/withdrawal.

4. Savings/deposit certificates (*e.g.* Defence Savings Certificates, National Deposit Certificates), receipts and accounts by whatever name described, issued or kept by the banks operating in Pakistan, post offices, National Savings Centres, financial institutions, companies and statutory corporations—on which return is receivable and is received by the holder, only on maturity or encashment.	2.5% of the payable value of certificates or receipts or the amount standing to the credit of an account as the case may be, as on the Valuation Date.	The date on which the maturity value paid, or of encashment/withdrawal.	The bank, office, Centre, company, or corporation as the case may be, responsible for paying the return or the amount withdrawn, or redeeming encashing the certificates or receipts.
5. Units of the National Investment (Unit) Trust.	2.5% of the face value or repurchase value of the Units whichever be lower, as on the Valuation Date in each Zakat year.	The date on which the first return or the repurchase value is paid whichever be earlier in the Zakat year.	The Trustee of the National Investment (Unit) Trust or its authorised agent paying the return on, or the repurchase value of, the Units.
6. I.C.P. Mutual Fund Certificates.	2.5% of the face value, or the market value based on the closing rate at the Karachi Stock Exchange, whichever be lower as on the Valuation Date in each Zakat year.	The date on which the first return is paid in the Zakat year.	Investment Corporation of Pakistan.
7. Government securities (other than prize bonds and certificates mentioned at serial number 3 and 4) on which return is receivable by the holder periodically.	2.5% of the face value of the Government securities as on the Valuation Date in each Zakat year.	The date on which the first return is paid or the date of encashment/redemption, whichever be earlier in the Zakat year.	The bank, office or institution, as the case may be, responsible for paying the return or encashing/redeeming the security.
8. Securities including shares and debentures (other than those mentioned at serial number 5, 6 and 7 above), of companies and statutory corporations (excluding those held in the name of a company or a statutory corporation), on which return is payable periodically or otherwise, and is paid.	If listed on the stock exchange, 2.5% of the paid-up value or the market value based on the closing rate at the Karachi Stock Exchange, whichever be lower as on the Valuation Date, in each Zakat year. If not listed on the stock exchange 2.5% of the paid-up value on the Valuation Date, in each Zakat year.	The date on which the first return is paid, or the date of encashment/redemption whichever be earlier in the Zakat year.	The corporation, company or institution, as the case may be, responsible for paying the return or encashing/redeeming the security.

S. No.	Assets	Rate and basis for computing the amount to be deducted as Zakat.	The Deduction Date	The Deducting Agency.
1	2	3	5	6
9.	Annuities	2.5% of the amount of annuity benefit in each Zakat year and in case of surrender 2.5% of the surrender value, on the Valuation Date, as the case may be.	The date of payment of the annuity benefit, of the surrender value.	The insurer or the bank keeping and the amount in the form of an annuity.
10.	Life insurance policies.	2.5% of the surrender value as on the Valuation Date in the Zakat year in which the policy matures or its survival benefit or surrender value is paid, as the case may be.	The date of payment of maturity value or of survival benefit or of surrender value.	The insurer.
11.	Provident Funds	In case of non-refundable advance, 2.5% of the amount drawn or, in case of final settlement, 2.5% of the balance standing to the credit of the subscriber as on the Valuation Date, excluding in both cases the employer's contribution and the return accrued thereon.	The date of payment of the advance or of the balance.	The authority, officer or institution making payment of the advance or the balance.

Note.—1. Deduction at source exceeding two and one-half per cent of the value of an asset specified in this Schedule, shall not be made in respect of that asset within the same Zakat year.

1A. No Zakat shall be charged on the amount paid as premium of a life insurance policy of a person from his Provident Fund and, where the proceeds of a life insurance policy of a person are credited to his Provident Fund during a Zakat year, no Zakat shall be charged on the amount received or drawn during that year as final settlement of his account in the Provident Fund or as non-refundable advance, to the extent of the proceeds so credited.

2. If the amount to be deducted at source as Zakat, in a particular case, is less than a rupee, it shall not be charged, and, if it is more than a rupee but has a fraction of a rupee, fifty paisas and more shall be treated as the next higher rupee and less than fifty paisas shall not be charged. Where the entire amount of the return or balance is to be appropriated towards Zakat and the amount contains a fraction of a rupee, this fraction shall not be so appropriated.

3. The Deduction Date for serial number 1 shall be deemed to be a public holiday, for banks only, within the meaning of the Negotiable Instruments Act, 1881 (XXVI of 1881). Banks shall, however, remain open for their employees.

4. In case the amount of the first return on any of the assets specified at S. Nos. 2, 3 and 5 to 8 is less than the Zakat due, the entire amount of such return shall be appropriated towards Zakat and the unrealized balance shall be deducted from the subsequent returns paid during the same Zakat year or, as the case may be, from the encashment or surrender value.

SECOND SCHEDULE

[*See* sections 2, 3 (5) and (5)]

ITEMS NOT SUBJECT TO COMPULSORY LEVY OF ZAKAT BUT ON WHICH ZAKAT IS PAYABLE BY EVERY *SAHIB-E-NISAB* ACCORDING TO THE RELEVANT *NISAB* ON SELF-ASSESSMENT BASIS, EITHER TO A ZAKAT FUND OR TO ANY INDIVIDUAL OR INSTITUTION, ELIGIBLE, UNDER THE SHARIAH, TO RECEIVE ZAKAT

S. No.	Items	Rate and Basis for Self-assessment
1	2	3
1.	Gold and silver and manufactures thereof.	2.5% of the market value, as on the Valuation Date.
2.	Cash	2.5% of the amount, as on the Valuation Date.
3.	Prize bonds	2.5% of the face value, as on the Valuation Date.
4.	Current Accounts and foreign currency accounts and, to the extent not subject to compulsory levy of Zakat under the First Schedule, other accounts, certificates, receipts, Units of National Investment (Unit) Trust, ICP-Mutual Fund Certificates, Government securities, annuities, life insurance policies and Provident Funds.	2.5% of the value of the asset, as on the Valuation Date.
5.	Loans receivable, excepting loans receivable by banks, other financial institutions, statutory corporations and companies.	2.5% of the amount of loan receivable, as on the Valuation Date.
6.	Securities including shares and debentures, to the extent not subject to compulsory levy of Zakat under the First Schedule.	If listed on the stock exchanges 2.5% of the market value (*i.e.* the closing rate at the Karachi Stock Exchange) as on the Valuation Date.
		If not listed on the stock exchange, 2.5% of the paid-up value as on the Valuation Date.
7.	Stock-in trade of:—	
	(*a*) Commercial undertakings (including dealers in real estate).	(*a*) 2.5% of the book value, or, at the option of the *sahib-e-nisab*, the market value, as on the Valuation Date.
	(*b*) Industrial undertakings	(*b*) 2.5% of the book value, or, at the option of the *sahib-e-nisab*, the market value of raw materials and finished goods, as on the Valuation Date.
	(*c*) Precious metals and stones and manufacturers thereof	(*c*) 2.5% of the market Value as on the Valuation Date.
	(*d*) Fish and other catch/produce of the sea, except catches by indigenous techniques.	(*d*) 2.5% of the value as on the Valuation Date.

S. No.	Items	Rate and Basis for Self-assessment
1	2	3
9.	Agricultural (including horticultural and forest) produce:	
	(a) Tenant's share..................	(a) (i) 10% of the produce, as on the Valuation Date, in the barani area; and
		(ii) 5% of the produce, as on the Valuation Date, in the non-barani area.
	(b) Other than the tenant's share........	(b) (i) 5% over and above the compulsory 5% in the barani area, as on the Valuation Date; and
		(ii) One-fourth of the value of produce allowed as an allowance for expenses on production.
10.	Animals (fed free in pastures):	As on the Valuation Date:
	(a) Sheep or goats	(a) (i) For owners of one to 39 heads: nil;
		(ii) For owners of 40 to 120 heads: one sheep/goat;
		(iii) For owners of 121 to 200 heads: two sheep/goats;
		(iv) For owners of 201 to 399 heads: three sheep/goats; and
		(v) For owners of every complete additional hundred heads: one sheep/goat.
	(b) Bovine animals	(b) (i) For owners of one to 29 heads: nil;
		(ii) For owners of 30 to 39 heads: one calf between one year and two years old;
		(iii) For owners of 40 to 59 heads: one calf between two years and three years old;
		(iv) For owners of 60 to 69 heads: two calves between one year and two years old;
		(v) For owners of 70 to 79 heads: one calf between one year and two years old and one between two years and three years old;
		(vi) For owners of 80 to 89 heads: two calves between two years and three years old;
		(vii) For owners of 90 to 99 heads: three calves between one year and two years old; and
		(viii) For owners of 100 and above 100 heads: as in *Shari'ah*.

(c) Camels . . . .

   (c)

    (*i*) For owners of one to 4 heads: nil;

    (*ii*) For owners of 5 to 24 heads: one sheep/goat for every five heads;

    (*iii*) For owners of 25 to 35 heads: one she-camel between one year and two years old;

    (*iv*) For owners of 36 to 45 heads: one she-camel between two years and three years old;

    (*v*) For owners of 46 to 60 heads: one she-camel between three years and four years old;

    (*vi*) For owners of 61 to 75 heads: one she-camel between four years and five years old;

    (*vii*) For owners of 76 to 90 heads: two she-camels between two years and three years old;

    (*viii*) For owners of 91 to 120 heads: two she-camels between three years and four years old; and

    (*ix*) For owners of more than 120 heads: as in *Shari'ah*. As per *Shari'ah*.

12. Wealth and financial assets other than those listed in Schedules, on which Zakat is payable according to *Shari'ah*.

Source: Government of Pakistan, Islamabad, Pakistan.

CHAPTER 14

The Principles of Trade and Commerce in Islam

"Monopoly is unlawful in Islam."

Prophet Muhammad (peace be upon him)

"The Islamic State was based upon social relations entirely different from those of the old. Religion extolled industry, and encouraged a normal indulgence of nature. Trade was free, and as noble a profession as statecraft, war, letters and science."

M. N. Ray, *Historical Role of Islam*

In Islam salvation of the spirit lies not only in spiritual development but also in living a worldly life on the basis of justice and good conduct. Therefore, worldly occupations are recommended again and again both in the *Qur'ān* and the *Hadīth*. The *Qur'ān* says: "When the prayer is finished, then disperse ye through the land and seek the bounty of Allah (*Sūrah* X11.10).

The Prophet said: "Earning of lawful livelihood is a duty only next in importance to the duty (of prayer)." Again, he said: "When you finish your morning prayer do not sleep until you strive for your livelihood."

Therefore, Islam has recognized all the legitimate economic activities of man—activities which are consistent with the spirit of Islam. Trade, commercial partnership, co-operatives, joint-stock companies are all legitimate activities and operations (*Sūrah* II. 276). Islam does, however, lay down regulations with regard to commercial activities designed to ensure that they will be carried on honestly, faithfully, and beneficially. The Prophet said: "The truthful, honest merchant is with the prophets and the truthful ones and martyrs" (Tirmidhi).

14.1 Basic Principles

The basic principles which Islam has prescribed concerning trade and commerce are a high standard of straightforwardness, reliability and honesty. Many of the present-day market imperfections would have been eliminated if these principles had been adopted by the business communities of the civilized nations of the world. However, these principles of trade and commerce have been reflected in various injunctions of the *Qur'ān* and the *Sunnah,* with regard to resorting to false oaths, giving correct weight, and creating good-will in business transactions.

False Oaths. Nowadays traders generally try to convince prospective buyers by resorting to trade oaths partly because of the present-day imperfections of market economy and partly because of the indifference of the people towards the moral and spiritual values of life. Islam has condemned all business transactions where businessmen resort to false oaths. Abū Hurairah said: I heard the Messenger of Allah (peace be upon him) say "The taking of oaths makes the commodities sell, but it obliterates the blessing (therein)" (Bukhārī). Again, "It is related on the authority of Abū Dharr (may Allah be pleased with him) who narrates that the Prophet of Allah (peace be upon him) said: 'Allah will neither speak to, nor look at, nor absolve from the impurity of their sins three (types of) persons; they shall suffer a grave chastisement.' Abū Dharr (thereupon) ejaculated, 'Ruined and lost are they (indeed)! Who are those persons, O Prophet of Allah?' The Prophet replied, 'One who displays his affluence by letting his trousers fall below his ankles, who is ever conscious of his obligations done to others, and one who sells out his goods by means of false oaths'" (Muslim).

Correct Weights. Secondly, the value of proper and standard weights and measures in trade can hardly be overestimated. But Islam laid a great emphasis on the utility of giving correct weights and measures fourteen hundred years ago. There are stern injunctions both in the *Qur'ān* and the *Hadīth* with regard to giving full weight and measure. Thus the *Qur'ān* says:

"Those who, when they
  Have to receive by measure
From men, exact full measure,
But when they have to give by measure or weight to men,
Give less than due.
Do they not think
That they will be called
To account?
On a Mighty Day,
A Day when (all) mankind stand to the
The Lords of the Worlds? Nay!
Surely the Record of the Wicked is (preserved) in Sijjīn.

(*Sūrah* LXXXIII. 2–7).

Good-will. Lastly, Islam has laid emphasis not only on giving full weight and measure but also on creating good-will in business transactions since it is considered to be the very foundation of present-day business. Close observation has revealed the fact that bad relations in business transactions mainly arise on account of the failure of parties to put down in writing their terms of business clearly and fairly. On this problem, there are clear instructions in the Holy *Qur'ān*. With a view to establishing good relations in business, all contracts must be put down in writing, setting out all the terms thereof, as "this is more equitable in the sight of Allah, and makes testimony surer and is more likely to keep out doubts, and avoid disputes" (*Sūrah* II. 282–283). The writing should set out the terms agreed upon fairly, and as a further precaution it is laid down that the terms of the contract shall be dictated by the person who undertakes the liability. If the person on whose behalf the liability is undertaken is a minor or of unsound judgment, then his guardian or the person representing his interests should dictate the terms of the contract (*Sūrah* II. 282).

From the above analysis it is clear that trade and commerce in the Islamic state differ fundamentally from the modern conception of trade and commerce; while the former is linked up with the moral and ethical values of life, the latter is not. Therefore, all business transactions which are opposed to beneficence cannot be Islamic in character, and the Islamic state has every right to curb any transactions or practices which seek to take advantage of the need or distress of poor people.

So far we have discussed the main principles which Islam has prescribed concerning trade and commerce. Now, an attempt may be made to discuss in some detail some aspects of modern trade and commerce in the light of the spirit of Islam.

14.2 Barter Trade

Time was when barter trade was the current practice of the day. Although the volume of barter trade, after the introduction of a money economy, has to a great extent, been reduced yet the importance of barter trade even today can hardly be overestimated. Islam has also recognized barter trade subject to the injunctions in the *Qur'ān* and the *Sunnah*. In fact, Islam has tried to impress upon traders that defective and worthless goods or articles should not be given in exchange for good ones (*Surah* IV. 2). If there is a defect in the thing sold it must be made manifest to the purchaser. Thus Ḥakim ibn Ḥizam reported: The Messenger of Allah (peace be upon him) said, "The buyer and the seller have the option of cancelling the contract as long as they have not separated; then, if they both speak the truth and make manifest, their transaction shall be blessed, and if they conceal and tell lies, the blessing of their transaction shall be obliterated" (Bukhari).

Moreover, two kinds of sale prevalent before Islam, *Munābadhah* and *Mulāmasah,* in which the purchaser was deprived of the occasion to examine the thing purchased, were made unlawful (Bukhārī). In fact, goods and commodities for sale should go on to the open market, and the buyer or his agents must be aware of the state of the market before proposals are made for the purchase of goods or commodities in bulk. He should not be taken unawares lest advantage be taken of his ignorance of the state of the market and the prevailing prices. All this is very clearly laid down by the Prophet.

Again, trade in idols and in things which are forbidden as food such as wine, swine, and that which dies of itself, is disallowed (Bukhārī). Islam has come to exterminate idolatry and hence it could not allow trade in idols. As regards things forbidden as food, a Muslim has evidently nothing to do with them and he cannot be allowed to carry them to other people. But as there is an expressed direction that the skin of the dead animal should not be thrown away and advantage should be derived therefrom (Bukhārī). Trade or barter trade in it is obviously not prohibited and the same rule may be allowed in other things prohibited as food, such as the bones and fat of dead animals, etc.

14.3 Monopoly Business

Let us now pass on to the desirability of monopoly and speculative business in an Islamic state. The be-all and end-all of Islamic economics is to achieve the maximum social advantage. Therefore, any economic activity which is likely to stand in the way of achieving this objective cannot be styled as Islamic. Judged by the standards of benevolence and care for the poor we cannot encourage monopoly and speculative business in Islam.

Because the monopolist generally charges a higher price for his output, as monopoly suggests the idea of concentration of supply in one hand, the question of exploitation is very much connected with the idea of monopoly. The competitive producer maximizes his profit by equalizing marginal cost to price. Since the price is given, he would go on producing more and more until his marginal cost becomes equal to price. In the case of the monopolist, however, the marginal revenue is not equal to but is always less than the price. Since the demand for his product is less than perfectly elastic, the monopolist can hope to sell increasing output at lower and lower prices. His total revenue is increased if he produces more because the price of the additional unit will be added to his total revenue. On the other hand, however, his total revenue will decline because all the previous units of his output will have to be sold at a lower price. The marginal revenue may, therefore, be easily negative even though the price is positive. The price is known as average revenue (total revenue divided by total output). The marginal revenue is, therefore, less than the average revenue.

Since the most advantageous situation for the monopolist is represented by that volume of output at which marginal cost is equal to marginal revenue, the monopolist will find it profitable to stop the production of further output before the marginal revenue becomes negative. Since marginal revenue will remain lower than average (price), production of optimum output is not possible. This may ultimately lead to under-utilization of resources and creation of unemployment.

As a matter of fact, many of the theoretical virtues of the system of free enterprise depend on the implied assumption that there is free competition. But, unfortunately, the actual working of capitalism has increased the power and influence of gigantic trusts, cartels and monopolies. Poor consumers and workers and even society as a whole have come very badly out of such a monopoly-dominated economic order—an order which has exhibited a lack of harmony between private and social interest and between private and social good. The point we are making here is that a monopoly-dominated economic order is the negation of the principle of maximum social advantage which an Islamic state proposes to achieve. Therefore, an Islamic state must condemn this type of economic order and must control the monopoly either passing laws or by comprehensive economic planning. It is to be noted here that monopolies in some activities (i.e., public utilities) may not be inconsistent with the spirit of Islam, because competition may lead to wastage of resources.

14.4 Speculative Business

As in the case of monopoly, Islam has also condemned speculative business. I mean essentially the phenomenon of buying something cheap at one time and selling the same thing dear at another time. When the future price is expected to be higher than the present price speculative buyers purchase with a view to selling at a higher price in future. Similarly, if the future price is expected to be lower than the present, speculators will sell now in order to avoid selling at a lower price in future. Speculators, it is claimed, confer great benefit on consumers and manufacturers, since the effect of their activities is to smooth out all price differences and to raise present price to the level of future price.

In so far as speculation renders social service by helping production and controlling the sudden fluctuation of prices, it is in conformity with the spirit of Islam. But a close observation will reveal the fact that speculators are primarily interested in private gains regardless of the larger interests of society. Since perfect speculation tends to destroy itself, most speculators, by adopting unfair means, try to create artificial scarcity of goods and commodities and thereby create an inflationary pressure on the economy. The poor masses have to pay for it. From the view of beneficence Islam has condemned such speculative point of practices. Thus it is related on the authority of Ma'mar who reported that the Prophet (peace be upon him) said, "He who accumulates stocks of grain during the shortage of it (with a view to profiteering later) is a great sinner" (Muslim and *Mishkdt*). Again, 'Umar reported: The Prophet (peace be upon him) said, "One who imports grain from outside and sells at the market rate his maintenance is blessed, while he who withholds grain from sale in view of estimated dearness in future, he is thrown away from God's pleasure". Thus withholding of grains and other commodities to raise their price artificially, as well as *Najsh* or deceiving a purchaser through a third party offering a higher price is prohibited (Bukhārī). But auction or open sale to the highest bidder is allowed in Islam (Tirmidhi).

Islam has tried to discourage speculative business by giving the whole problem a moral slant. Even in capitalist society several attempts are being made to control speculative business. In his book, *Economics of Control* (p. 97), Professor Lerner has suggested that the evils of aggressive speculation can be best tackled by what he calls speculative business, controlled by "counter-speculation". Governments should set up an agency which should make an estimate of proper prices, and use its resources to bring actual prices to these levels. If need be, the Islamic state will have to evolve such a system, so that the poor people, nay, the society as a whole, may be saved from the exploitation of unscrupulous speculators. Since modern secular states are drifting towards materialism they have failed to solve this problem in spite of their best efforts. Possibly because of this, Professor Taussig tried to find the solution to this problem in the moral improvement of the people. According to him, "The most effective remedy would be a better moral standard for all the industry and arousal of public opinion against all kinds of gambling." In this respect Professor Taussig's approach towards this problem is very close to the Islamic viewpoint. In fact, the principles of economics of Islam stand for a happy blending of moral and material values.

Forward Transactions

Like speculative business, Islam does not give any encouragement to forward transactions. Islam regards all such transactions as harmful to society, as trade cycles, which cause great disruption in the present capitalist system, are the result of brisk activity of such forward transactions. Therefore, Islam has warned its followers against indulging in forward transactions. Ibn 'Umar reported: The Prophet (peace be upon him) said, "Whoever buys cereals he shall not sell them until he obtains their possession" (Bukhārī). Again, it is related on the authotiy of Hākim b. Hizām, who reported: The Prophet (peace be upon him) said, "Bargain not about that which is not with you."

14.5 International Trade and Dumping

So far I have discussed some aspects of internal and local trade and commerce from the Islamic point of view. Let us now discuss some broad principles of international trade from an Islamic standpoint.

It is not a theory but a verdict of history that Islam has encouraged international trade. If one studies the history of commercial law, one can see that enlightened Muslim Moors used to have extensive trade with the Levant from Barcelona and other places. There were factories and consuls on the Tunis and a great trade was maintained with Constantinople. It reached ports of India and China and extended along the African coast as far as Madagascar. It is interesting to note that in the middle of the eighth century when Europe was in the Dark Ages, enlightened Spanish Muslim Arabs such as 'Abdul Qāsim and others were writing treatises on the principles of trade and commercial laws and rates. In fact, Islam has encouraged international trade, not only for economic co-operation, but also for establishing universal brotherhood through the mutual exchange of ideas and knowledge. No doubt, different rates and techniques existed among the Muslim trade areas for an efficient working of mercantile and commercial transactions. These rates and techniques are bound to change with the changing circumstances and time.

Nowadays the question arises as to what type of trade policy, whether free trade policy or protection, an Islamic state should adopt. Classical economists favoured a policy of free trade and were opposed to a policy of protection because it stands in the way of the most efficient allocation of resources throughout the world. From the purely economic viewpoint I may prescribe a free-trade policy for an Islamic state, since the Islamic system stands for free trade and believes that each country will produce those goods for the production of which it is especially suited on account of its natural or acquired advantages, and produce more of them than it requires for its own needs, exchanging the surplus with other countries against goods which it is less suited to produce, or which it cannot produce at all. In other words, Islam believes in the eternal doctrine of comparative costs—the very basis of international trade. But if the present-day imperfect and unhealthy competition in the field of international trade as well as the greater national interests of all underdeveloped Muslim countries of the world are taken into consideration, I would support a policy of protection for an Islamic state. This is not un-Islamic.

In fact, "the introduction of customs duties and tolls owes its origin to the fact that during the reign of the Caliph 'Umar the neighbouring countries with which the Islamic State had commercial dealings persisted in levying duties on the Muslim traders. When Abū Mūsā Ash'arī reported this fact to the Caliph 'Umar, he ordered that, as a reciprocal measure, the *Harbīs* should be charged the same rate as was being collected from the Muslims, i.e. 10 %; where the duty levied by the *Harbīs* was not known, the same rate 10 % was prescribed."

This led to the institution of 'Ashīr and the tax was extended to *Muslims* and *Dhimmīs* also at the rate of $2\frac{1}{2}$ per cent and 5 per cent, respectively.

"The difference in the rate of customs duty and tolls between that levied on the Muslims and that charged against the Dhimmīs is due to the fact that the Muslims pay the Zakāt on their trade articles whether or not they pass an 'Ashīr, whereas the Dhimmīs are subject to this toll of 5 % only in so far as they come under the jurisdiction of an 'Ashīr by travelling for trade. The difference in rates thus places the Dhimmī and the Muslim trader on a par without giving advantages to one class over the other."[2]

Dumping. The present discussion on international trade will remain incomplete if we make no reference to dumping in the field of trade. What is dumping? It occurs when producers (usually monopolists) of one country sell their outputs in another country at prices below those charged from the consumers in the country of origin. The objectives of dumping may be (a) to dispose of an overstock produced due to a wrong judgment of demand, (b) to develop new trade connections by charging low prices, (c) to drive competitors out of the foreign market whether foreigners or native producers, and (d) to reap the economics of large-scale production. Whatever may be the considerations of dumping, the ultimate objective of it is to achieve a monopoly-dominated economic order by ousting native and foreign producers from both the national international fields and thereby exploiting the vast masses of the people. All this is opposed to beneficence and those who indulge in such practices seek to take advantage of the need or distress of their fellow beings and, therefore, dumping is against the spirit of Islam. The Islamic state cannot encourage dumping and is quite at liberty to raise high tariff walls against dumping, especially if it affects its own industries.

This is not the end of the story. The most inhuman aspect of dumping is the destruction of goods after they have been produced, just to prevent lowering their price. In his *Inside Latin America* (p. 315), John Gunther depicts the story of Brazilian coffee. One of the greatest difficulties which Brazil faced was how to destroy its four million sacks of surplus crop of coffee in 1914 just to prevent lowering its price. "Again in 1934, a million oranges were dumped into the sea in Liverpool harbour, to prevent the supply lowering the price of the orange in the market—orange which to the children of the Liverpool poor is an unobtainable luxury. Nearer home one finds orders being issued for the restriction of 121 million pounds of tea in India, Ceylon and Dutch India."[3] The facts are too eloquent to need a comment from the Islamic point of view. Just for the sake of earning a huge profit by not allowing a fall in prices, this type of trade can hardly be justified in Islam. Islam has condemned all sorts of wastage of resources—both human and material. Thus dumping must be discouraged by the Muslim countries of the world.

14.6 Trade and Interest

At this stage, an attempt may be made to make an inquiry into this reasons which actuated Islam's forbidding interest and permitting trade. The *Qur'ān* says: "Allah has allowed trade and prohibited usury" (*Sūrah* II. 275). But even today many enemies of Islam make a reference to the following verse of the Holy *Qur'ān,* which says: "Trade is just like usury" (*Sūrah* II. 275). They opine that if trade is lawful, why should interest transactions be declared unlawful in view of the fact that it also amounts to trading in capital. It is said that capital invested in trade brings an excess called profit, invested in banking it brings interest. God prohibits one excess and permits another. Then what is the difference between the two? This problem has been discussed at length by a number of leading jurists in their works, either from the legal or from the moral point of view. Here we shall mainly make an attempt to put toward arguments from the economic point of view.

(a) It is risk-taking which differentiates trade from interest. Risk-taking is the basis of normal trade which is allowed in Islam, while interest is fixed and does not fluctuate like profit.

(b) When capital invested in trade brings profit, it is the result of initiative, enterprise and efficiency. This is not true in the case of interest, because the creditor gets for himself a definite amount of money for his loan regardless of loss or profit to the debtors or investors.

(c) In trade the moment a commodity is exchanged for its price the transaction comes to an end. The purchaser does not give anything after that transaction to the vendor. But in interest dealings, the creditor does not cease to demand his interest (as long as the principal is not returned).

Therefore, there is a limit to the profit which one may expect from trade but there is no such limitation in the case of interest due to creditors.

(*d*) Since trade is productive and a person derives benefit after undergoing labour, hardship and skill, it creates the conditions of full employment and economic growth. The harmful effects of interest during the great Depression of 1929–33 was so deep that the economists of capitalist countries were forced to discard the classical economic theories and evolve new ones advocating the elimination of interest from their enconomic institutions. Thus in his famous work, *The General Theory of Employment, Interest and Money,* J. M. Keynes observed: "The money rate of interest, by setting the pace for all other commodity rates of interest, holds back investment in the production of these other commodities without being capable of stimulating investment for the production of money, which by hypothesis cannot be produced". Again, he writes: "It seems that the rate of interest on money plays a peculiar part in setting a limit to the level of employment, since it sets a standard to which the marginal efficiency of a capital asset must attain if it is to be newly produced"[5] In fact, "interest both initiates and aggravates crises" which trade does not.

(*e*) The last, but not the least, point is that trade may act as one of the dominant factors in the process of the building of civilization through co-operation and mutual exchange of ideas. But interest creates in man the undesirable weakness of miserliness, selfishness and lack of sympathy. Thus, from the economic and ethical standpoints, interest uproots the very foundations of humanity and mutual help and stands in the way of full employment and economic growth. But trade in an Islamic state is a boon to society.

14.7 Conclusion

The conclusion which emerges from the preceding discussion is that Islam has encouraged all legitimate activities which are consistent with the spirit of Islam. Thus, barter trade is allowed in a restricted way. But Islam has condemned all monopoly and speculative business because these activities stand in the way of the desired goal of Islamic Economics, which is the attainment of maximum social advantage. Basically Islam believes in free trade. Protective trade may be allowed in special cases. But dumping must be condemned in Islam. There is a fundamental difference between trade and interest. If Islamic principles of trade and commerce are adopted by the traders and industrialists of the world, the weaker groups of the community will be saved from the disastrous repercussions of trade cycles—a common feature of the modern economy.

14.8 Selected Further Reading

Ahmad, Sh. Mohammad, "Monetary Theory of Trade Cycle" in *Islamic Studies,* vol. XII, No.3, Islamabad, 1973.

Barkan, O. L. "Research on the Othman Fiscal Surveys" in *Studies in the Economic History of the Middle East,* ed. by M. A. Cook, Oxford University Press, London, 1970.

Faure, A. (1968) "Trade Guilds in Islamic Countries in the Middle Ages" in *Islamic Review,* vol. 56, No. 1, London, 1968.

Gibb and Bowen, "Taxation and Finance" in *Islamic Society and the West,* Royal Institute of International Affairs, London, 1950.

Goitem, S. D. "Mediterranean Trade in the Eleventh Century: Some Facts and Problems", in *Studies in the Economic History of the Middle-East,* ed. by M. A. Cook, Oxford University Press, London, 1971.

Hasanuzzaman, S. M. "The Liability of Partners in an Islamic Shirkah" in *Islamic Studies,* vol. 10, No. 4, Islamabad, 1971.

Mannan M. A. "Market imperfection in an Islamic Economy" in *The Making of Islamic Economic Society: Islamic Dimensions in Economic Analysis,* International Centre for Research in Islamic Economics, Cairo, 1984.

Somogyi, De Josheph, "State Intervention in Traae in Classical Arabic Literature in *Studies in Islam,* vol. 4, No. 3, New Delhi, 1967.

Udovitch, A. L. "Commercial Techniques in Early Medieval Islamic Trade" in *Islam and Trade of Asia* ed. by D. S. Richards, 1970.

Yalcintos, Nevzad, (1979) "Trade and Cooperation Among the Muslim Countries" in *The Muslim World and the Future Economic Order,* Islamic Council of Europe, London, 1979.

APPENDIX

A Note on an Islamic Common Market (I.C.M.).

Although the need for having an Islamic Common Market can be explained in terms of ideological, historical, political and economic factors, here we shall confine our discussion mainly to economic factors.

The establishment of the Islamic Development Bank as well as a large number of local Islamic banks and investment companies during the nineteen-seventies and early eighties can be seen as an important milestone towards the eventual establishment of an Islamic Common Market consisting of all forty-two members of the Islamic Development Bank. Once the fragmented, isolated and small markets of the different individual member states of the Islamic Development Bank are integrated, they could provide the basis for a very large market for trade creation rather than trade diversion. Although it is difficult, even impossible, to estimate the economic gains of an Islamic Common

Market, it can be said that trade creation tends to increase welfare, and if it primarily gives rise to trade diversions, it may lead to a lowering in the world's welfare particularly in the welfare of the Third World. The inflicting of this deliberate and conscious harm to others may have a doubtful validity in the *Sharī'ah*.

Generally speaking, economic analysis of the custom unions may very well be linked to the economics of the common market. As noted earlier, here the gains are primarily connected with trade creation, although trade diversion may lead to welfare provided substition in consumption takes place. But how are these gains and losses to be measured? By volume only? Here the heights of the tariffs come in as an important factor. "The higher the initial tariff between the union partners, the greater is the scope for an increase in welfare. The lower the tariff to the outside world, the smaller are the losses, on trade diversion. The larger the part of trade originally covered by trade between the union partners, the greater is the scope for gains from the union. If a union leads to realisation of dynamic effects such as reaping of economics of scale and enforced competition, it could be important and these effects will have to be added to the effects of a comparative static nature".[6]

In addition to this, the cost differentials between the countries of the Common Market in goods they both produce need to be explained along with potential complementaries between the economies of Muslim countries. Because the larger the cost differentials between the countries of the union in goods they both produce, the larger is the scope for gains.

The above analysis shows that there are various economic implications to the setting up of an Islamic Common Market.

The fact is that there exists tremendous scope for the expansion of the current narrow base of economic co-operation as reflected in the actual volume of trade among the Muslim countries. For instance, in 1978, the imports of Algeria, Indonesia, Iraq, Kuwait, Libya, Saudi Arabia and the U. A. E. from other member countries of the Islamic Development Bank were of the order of 0.40, 4.54, 5.44, 3.74, 3.51, 7.16 and 10.19 per cent respectively of their total imports. In the same year the imports of Pakistan, Bangladesh, Jordan, Lebanon, Sudan, Syria, Tunisa, Turkey and Chad from the other member countries constituted 18.8, 11.84, 19.91, 16.49, 12.92, 18.45, 7.26, 14.72 and 6.14 per cent respectively of their total imports. The relatively high percentages of their imports were mainly due to oil.

What is needed is to explore various form of co-operation with a programme of priority projects and investment schedules, which can serve several Muslim countries. This implies that efforts should be made to reap the benefits of trade creation, the unused economics of scale on the production side. It should however by clearly recognized that economic factors *cannot* alone decide the question of an Islamic Common Market. Ideological and political considerations must be given due weight in establishing such an institution.

Notes

[1] *Mabsūt.*, p. 108; Yūsuf, *Kitāb-ul-Kharāj.* p. 76
[2] S. A. Siddiqi, *Public Finance in Islam*, p. 86.
[3] H. M. Mukerjee, *Introduction to Socialism*, p. 16.
[4] J. M. Keynes, *The General Theory of Employment, Interest and Money*, p. 235
[5] J. M. Keynes, p. 222.
[6] See Bo Sodersyen, *International Economics*, 2nd edn., Martin's Press, U. S. A. 1980, p. 225.

CHAPTER 15

Islamic Co-operative Insurance: Theory and Practice

"The best among you is he who treats the members of his family best."

Prophet Muhammad (peace be upon him)

"Private charity has the advantage of being ineffective. The security arising from regular state insurance does actually guarantee to the citizens the minimum subsistence."

Robert Briffault, *Reasons of Anger*

15.1 Insurance in Islam

In a survey of the modern economic world, the business of insurance must have a prominent place. There is general agreement among most economic theories that the essence of insurance lies in the elimination of the uncertain risk of loss for the individual through the combination of a large number of similarly exposed individuals who contribute premium payments to a common fund, sufficient to make good the loss caused by any individual. Therefore, before insurance can be undertaken on a sound economic basis, not only the nature of an insurable risk but its probable occurrence and resulting loss must be determined. It is obvious that all risks are not equally subject to indemnification by means of insurance. The chance or the uncertainty as well as the measurability of various types of risk differ.

15.2 Is Insurance Un-Islamic?

There is a misconception among some Muslims that insurance is un-Islamic. It is tantamount, they believe, to denying Divine blessings. But Allah is responsible for providing us with reasonable means of livelihood. True, He took upon Himself the provision of reasonable livelihood to His creatures. This is embodied in the following verses of the Holy Book:

"There is no moving creature on earth but its sustenance dependeth on
4 God"

(*Sūrah* XI. 6)

"And who gives you sustenance
From heaven and earth?
(Can there be another) god
Besides God?"

(*Sūrah* XXVII. 64)

"And We have provided therein
Means of subsistence,—for you
And for those for whose sustenance
Ye are not responsible"

(*Sūrah* XV. 20)

For a proper understanding of these verses, we must go deeper into the matter. These verses do not mean that Allah will supply our food and clothing from heaven even if we sit idle. In fact, all these verses speak eloquently of the economic millennium as envisaged by Islam, and the Muslim state, which claims to be God's vicegerent on earth, can only vindicate its grand title if it realizes its immense implication in actual fact. It is His will that no individual should be bereft of reasonable means of existence and he should be immune against any and every encroachment. It is the supreme duty of an Islamic state to ensure this. Insurance helps in achieving this objective.

Moreover, Islam recognizes the family as a basic social unit. Rearing and bearing of each and every member of the family is always considered to be a duty in Islam. In other words, there is no provision in Islam preventing a man from providing for the maintenance of his dependants. The insurance companies, by covering the risk and uncertainty, ensure provision for a man's dependants, because insurance is a forced saving. The importance of this forced saving can hardly be overestimated in a society where a great part of society consists of the middle class – a class which cannot store enough provisions for its dependants.

At this stage, it may be pointed out that there is a group of persons who confuse insurance and gambling. They hold the view that insurance is like speculation. If a man dies early, his dependants get a good return for the little money the deceased had given as premium. This appears to be a sort of gambling. But the difference between insurance and gambling is fundamental because the basis of insurance is co-operation which is recognized in Islam.

The economic foundation of insurance is not the elimination of risk or loss—although insurance organisations may find it profitable to engage in this activity—but rather the substitution of a known small loss for an uncertain large loss. The implications of this foundation are not as negative as they at first appear. Society as a whole benefits through the accumulation of capital reserves which make good the loss resulting from the destruction of valuable assets; business costs are lowered to the degree that risk is eliminated and credit strengthened and the insured individual is enabled through mutual action to obviate poverty and destitution for himself and his dependants. The fact that the payments of all participants aid each participant in case of need is an essential characteristic of insurance. This principle of mutuality is not limited in the slightest degree to mutual companies but applies to all insurance organizations whatever their legal structure, to joint-stock companies, as well as to government insurance funds. The more numerous the individuals of each class who share the risk, the more exactly can it be estimated and the more cheaply can it be covered and protection administered. It is precisely because insurance is mutual that public opinion, even in countries predominantly capitalist, has almost universally caused the governments to abandon the theory of individual initiative in favour of compulsory insurance of risks such as health, workmen's compensation and fire.

Thus insurance teaches us the need for interdependence in society. This very spirit is very helpful for achieving the goal of universal brotherhood. But gambling is prohibited inasmuch as it promotes dissension and hatred, and tends to deter those who indulge in it from the remembrance of God and from prayer, thus occasioning a greater harm than the possible benefit that may be derived from it (*Sūrah* II. 219; *Sūrah* V. 94).

Again, insurance has been recognized as one of the most effective means for the mobilization of national savings for productive purposes. Pakistan, for instance, has long been aware of the importance of this vital sector of the economy and the insurance industry has continued to make rapid progress both in life and non-life fields, whereas gambling is prohibited in Pakistan, because it pollutes social life, arrests the moral and spiritual development of man, and encourages wastage. Therefore, it is a bar to economic growth. Thus we see that insurance is motivated by the principles of co-operation and maximum social advantage, and gambling is the negation of these principles. Therefore, insurance cannot be styled as un-Islamic.

15.3 Differences between Modern Insurance and Islamic Insurance

Now the question arises whether there is any difference between the modern insurance industry and the insurance industry which an Islamic state proposes to have. Islamic insurance differs fundamentally from modern insurance both from the point of view of form and nature. Let me say a few words about the evolution of modern insurance in the first instance. The history of insurance is as yet unwritten; only milestones of its evolution are known. Devices resembling insurance were not unknown in antiquity. In Imperial Rome, for example, there existed collegia, associations of artisans, which paid the surviving dependants of their members a funeral sum in return for the payment of monthly premiums.

In this general evolution, there can be distinguished three types of insurance operations, more or less independent, not successive but rather passing often and continuously from one type to another. These three types may be called co-operative, capitalist and government.

The organization of insurance on a co-operative basis is motivated by the same causes and follows essentially the same development in modern times as in antiquity. In my view, an Islamic state should encourage the formation of an insurance industry motivated by a co-operative spirit, because the idea of co-operation is recognized in Islam. The capitalist type of insurance, the insurance business proper born of marine insurance, which is of Roman origin, was founded for profit and based on commercial calculations. The highly differentiated economic life of the second half of the nineteenth century brought with it numerous cultural gains accompanied by new dangers and new requirements. The expansion of the insurance industry made necessary, in turn, the extension and spread of reinsurance. Owing to the successful stabilization of currencies after post-War inflation the present century is even more clearly characterized by the growth of insurance companies into enterprises operating on an international scale, by the founding of subsidiary companies and by the formation of cartel-like associations of entrepreneurs in all large countries and in all branches of insurance. Horizontal concentration to reduce competition has been especially characteristic of this period. But vertical concentration, for instance, in the form of the combination of insurance and reinsurance within the same concern, is not uncommon.

There is the point for consideration whether cartel-like associations of entrepreneurs in the field of the insurance industry are Islamic. We all know that a monopoly-dominated economic order cannot deliver goods to the society. Since the basic objective of such cartel-type insurance is to maximize profits irrespective of the ultimate welfare of the individual, this cannot be called Islamic. The Islamic state must come forward either to control or to supervise such an insurance industry. In fact, the increasing importance of the insurance industry everywhere has resulted in legislation leading to more effective state supervision of its conduct and policy forms. A number of countries like India have nationalized the insurance industry. For an Islamic state the point at issue is not whether the insurance industry should be nationalized, but the main consideration is whether it is organized in such a way that it may promote the total welfare of mankind keeping in view the injunctions of the Holy *Qur'ān* and the *Sunnah*.

Thus, insurance should be encouraged and extended on a national scale, in an Islamic state. Insurance against death may be left to private companies. Insurance against old age, unemployment, sickness and injury may be sponsored by the government on a national scale, so that the whole nation may be collectively responsible for providing for those who are sick or old or unprovided for or unemployed. Besides the premia, an Islamic government will have its *Zakāt* revenue to spend on this social welfare. It would be very similar to the National Insurance scheme in England which covers all economic risks of all persons from the cradle to the grave. The only difference would be that the liabilities would not be used in interest-bearing undertakings.

Moreover, insurance companies these days invest their funds in mortgage businesses and other interest-bearing undertakings. But Islamic insurance companies will have to provide capital loans on a partnership basis in business and industry instead. It is recommended that the Islamic insurance industry should make investment either directly or on the basis of *Muḍārabah* or in participation with Islamic banks and other credit institutions. Since the ultimate purpose of all the Islamic credit institutions is one and the same, i.e. welfare of the people, the feasibility and practicability of establishing an insurance department in Islamic banks may be examined by Muslim states. As Islam does not allow speculation and gambling, the Islamic insurance industry would cover only the genuine risks and it would be a self-liquidating process which would provide protection to the insured on the principle of mutual assistance and co-operation.

15.4 Islamic Insurance in Practice

It is indeed gratifying to note that the policy recommendation made by the earlier edition of this book (1970) for the organization of co-operative insurance by Islamic banks has now been put into practice. As mentioned earlier the *Sharī'ah* approves co-operative insurance.

Before we describe the actual working of an Islamic insurance scheme, it is perhaps pertinent to mention that while the Islamic Jurisprudence Council of the Muslim World League, Makkah, Saudi Arabia, considers all modern insurance transactions including life insurance and commercial as contrary to Islamic teachings, the Council, however, approved "co-operative insurance".

In this system, contributors to the insurance fund are donors, and their contributions are donations, with the aim being to share out the losses that befall any of the contributors among them all. The compensation given is relevant to the loss incurred and not a fixed sum which is agreed between the insurer and the insured at the time when the contract is made.

Insurance schemes made by the government are also approved since they are a form of fulfilling the state's duty to look after its citizens and alleviate the hardships that they encounter.

The only dissenting voice to these decisions was that of Shaikh Mustafa Al-Zarqa, Professor of Islamic Jurisprudence at the University of Jordan and a prominent figure in his field. He has made extensive studies of the problem of insurance and he is of the opinion that insurance, in most of its forms, is Islamically acceptable. It is safer, however, to take the opinion of the Islamic Jurisprudence Council since it is much weightier and enjoys the backing of a large number of scholars.[1]

The Faisal Islamic Bank of Sudan took the initiative in establishing the Islamic Insurance Company in 1979 on a co-operative basis. The company has made considerable progress within a span of five years and was able to establish several branches in Saudi Arabia. The company is underwriting the following classes of business with the exception of Life Insurance:

1. Marine Cargo Insurance.
2. Marine Hull.
3. Fire & Burglary.
4. Aviation.
5. Personal Accident.
6. Engineering.
7. Workmen's Compensation.

The company maintains two separate and distinct accounts: one a policy-holders' account and the other a shareholders' account. The policy-holders' accounts are credited with all their contributions in consideration of insurance protection plus profits received on the investment of their contributions, and debited with their proportion of service charges and claims. The surplus after the establishment of necessary reserves is distributed amongst the policyholders in proportion to their paid contributions. The shareholders of the company do not participate in any part of the surplus of the policyholders' accounts but income derived from investment of the share capital alone is credited to their account and the surplus, if any is left after meeting their share of expenses for the corresponding period, is distributed amongst them. The company is also providing Islamic reinsurance facilities.

Despite initial start-up expenses like any other company, the bank distributed five per cent profit among its policyholders during 1979, the very first year of its operation and expects to distribute eight to ten per cent during 1982–83.

As noted earlier in Chapter 10, *Dar Al-Maal Al-Islami* has an aggressive business style and has already gone into insurance business and intends to expand its operations in the area of co-operative insurance also during its first five years of existence ending in 1985–86.

15.5 Conclusion

(*a*) There is a feeling that insurance is un-Islamic, because it is said that it is nothing but gambling or speculation. But there is a fundamental difference between gambling and insurance. While gambling promotes dissension and hatred and tends to deter those who indulge in it from remembrance of Allah, insurance is based on co-operation and the insured individual is enabled through mutual action to obviate poverty for himself and his dependants. There is nothing in Islam which prevents anyone from making provision for his dependants. In fact, through insurance, society as a whole gets benefits from the accumulation of capital reserves.

(*b*) The difference between the modern insurance industry and an Islamic insurance industry lies not only in its form but also in the nature of its handling business. The present-day trend towards the formation of cartel like associations of entrepreneurs in the field of insurance and reinsurance is the negation of the Islamic values of life. We know that the modern insurance industry invest its funds in interest-bearing undertakings. But the Islamic insurance companies will provide capital loans instead, either directly on the basis of *Muḍārabah* or in participation with Islamic banks and others specialized credit institutions. The possibility of opening insurance departments in the Islamic banks also deserves active consideration.

(*c*) Islamic co-operative insurance has already been put into practice by the Faisal Islamic Bank of Sudan and *Dar Al-Maal Al-Islami*. Their initial success, is indeed encouraging and provides scope for further expansion.

Notes

[1] See *Arab News*, 1st April, 1983

15.6 Selected Further Reading

Faisal, Prince Mohammad, Al-Saud. "Banking and Insurance in Islam", International Institute for Islamic Banking and Economics, Paper 6/1 for "First Advanced Course on Islamic Banks", Cairo, 1981.

Hamidullah, M. "Islamic Insurance" in *Islamic Review*, vol. 39, no. 3–4, London, 1951.

Mohammed, Youssef Kamal, "Rationalisation of Contemporary Insurance", International Institute of Islamic Banking and Economics, Paper 12/1 for "First Advanced Course on Islamic Banks", Cairo, 1981.

Muslehuddin, Muhammad, "Insurance and Islamic Law", Islamic publications, Lahore, 1963.

Naggar, Ahmad El, "The Framework of Islamic Banks and Islamic Insurance Companies", International Institute of Islamic Banking and Economics, Paper 7/1 for "First Advanced Course on Islamic Banks", Cairo, 1981.

Naqvi, S. Nawab Haider, "Islamic Economic System: Fundamental Issues" in *Islamic Studies*, vol. XVI, no. 4, Islamabad, 1977.

Qureshi, Anwar Iqbal, "Islam's Concept of Life Regarding Economic Matters", in *Islamic Studies*, vol. II, Islamabad, 1972.

Rahman, Afzalur, "Banking and Insurance – Economic Doctrines of Islam" vol. 4, The Muslim Schools Trust, London, 1979.

Sakr, Muhammad Ahmad, "The Role of the State in the Economic System of Islam" in *Islam and a New International Economic Order – The Social Dimension*, International Institute for Labour Studies, Geneva, 1980.

PART IV

Comparative Economics and Development

CHAPTER 16

Islam and Other Economic Systems

16.1 Introduction

16.2 Capitalism

16.3 Socialism

16.4 Communism

16.5 Fascism

16.6 Islam and Other "Isms": A Comparative Analysis
in terms of:

(a) The *Qur'ānic* concept of history
(b) The Concept of Private Property
(c) The Concept of Brotherhood
(d) Co-existence
(e) Sovereignty

16.7 Selected Further Reading

"To Him belongs the dominion of the heavens and the earth:
and all affairs are
Referred back to God.

"He merges Night into Day,
And He merges Day into Night;
And He has full knowledge
of the secrets of (all) hearts.

"Believe in God
And His Apostle,
And spend (in charity)
Out of the (substance)
Whereof He has made you
Heirs. For, those of you
who believe and spend
(In charity) – for them
Is a great Reward."

Al Qur'ān (Sūrah LVII. 5–7)

"All men are equal in their human rights."

Prophet Muhammad (peace be upon him)

16.1 Introduction

The history of human civilization has witnessed the rise and fall of many systems. A programme for the improvement of society cannot ignore the fundamental institutions and the broad plan of organization which underlie our economic system as a whole. Several comprehensive plans of social organization have been proposed for such a foundation from time immemorial. These are anarchism, feudalism, capitalism, socialism, communism, fascism and Islam. Each presents a different scheme of social organization.

In comparison of economic systems, we are much interested in comparing performances. It is, therefore, impossible to reach an objectively valid conclusion, if by "objective' we mean a judgment that supporters of all economic systems can be logically forced to accept. But our comparison of performances can achieve only two things: it can point out where each system excels the other in meeting certain goals, and it may suggest the extent to which one purpose is sacrificed for another. Since the whole analysis is subjective, we need not be surprised to find that those whose goals are different or who give different weight to the same goals refuse to accept our point of view.

16.2 Capitalism

The concept of capitalism may be traced primarily to the writings of socialist theoreticians. The works of Sombart are the first in which the concept of capitalism has been definitely recognized as fundamental to the system of economic thought. Here it is demonstrated that "capitalism" designates an economic system significantly characterized by the predominance of "capital". Like any other economic system, capitalism also contains certain constituent elements which are the economic spirit or outlook—the sum total of the purposes, motives and principles. These motives and principles are dominated by three ideas: acquisition, competition and rationality.

The purpose of economic activity under capitalism is acquisition in terms of money. The idea of increasing the sum of money on hand is the exact opposite of the idea of earning a livelihood which dominated all pre-capitalist systems, particularly the feudal handicraft economy. While acquisition constitutes the purpose of economic activity, the attitudes displayed in the process of acquisition form the content of the idea of competition. These attitudes, which are logically inherent in acquisition, may be described as freedom of acquisition from the outside.

By reason of its freedom from regulation, capitalism rests essentially on the individual's assertion of his natural power. Economic activity is, therefore, closely associated with personal risk, but the economic agent is free to strive for economic success in any way he chooses provided he does not violate the penal code.

When the direction of economic affairs is oriented solely upon acquisition, it is inevitable that those modes of economic behaviour should be adopted which seem most rational, most systematic and best adapted to the purpose in hand. Economic rationality is, thus, the third dominating idea of the capitalist system.

In fact, capitalism, as we find it today, has come to signify a religion of money or dollar dictatorship. Thus H.G. Wells says, "Capitalism is something none of us know how to define, but we called it generally the Capitalist System—a complex of traditional usage, uncontrolled acquisitive energy and perverted opportunities, wasting life." Let us now turn to some of the salient features of capitalism.

Absence of Planning.

The absence of a central economic plan is one of the salient features of capitalism. The economies of the capitalist countries rest, in the main, on the independent (but interdependent) individual actions of millions of private economies. These actions are not co-ordinated by a central plan. Market prices, on which the decisions and calculations and producing units are based, are, as a rule, not set by the government; under competitive conditions they are the result of market forces. Absence of a central plan does not, of course, constitute a case of *laissez faire*. The government ought to establish healthy monetary and credit conditions, to maintain an aggregate demand which is neither too large nor too small, and to see to it that monopolist powers are kept in check.

Consumers' Sovereignty.

Absence of a central economic plan implies consumers' sovereignty in the capitalist economy. The very existence of centralized power endangers consumers' sovereignty, because those who have the duty and the power to plan are invariably tempted to substitute their (supposedly superior) decisions for the wishes of the consumers. The socialists claim that consumers' sovereignty has little meaning in capitalism, owing to the unequal income distribution. Thus if a defender of capitalism speaks of the dollar ballots which guide production, the socialist will answer that, considering the much larger number of votes the rich can cast, capitalism cannot be considered a true consumers' democracy. Capitalism does in fact imply producers' sovereignty.

Free Choice of Occupation.

Freedom of choice of occupation is always considered one of the most important features of capitalism. Thus, free choice of occupation implies that, in order to attract a sufficient supply of a special kind of labour to an industry, where this labour is more urgently needed than elsewhere, wages must be high enough to exert the needed entlicement. Free choice of occupation is, therefore, incompatible with equal income distribution.

Wage differentials and unequal income distribution have a tendency to perpetuate themselves to some degree. We must emphasize that a free choice of occupation does not imply a right to work. Free occupational choice may mean little in an economy suffering from prolonged mass unemployment. Karl Marx suggested that the labourer in the capitalist system is "free in the double sense, that as a free man he can dispose of his labour-power as his own commodity and that, on the other hand, he has no other commodity for sale, is short of everything necessary for the realisation of his labour power".

In fact, there is little chance that under a system of individual labour contracts the wage will be at the level of the perfectly competitive market; usually unionization of labour will be needed to bring the wages up to the level that corresponds to perfect competition. Although a labour union is formed by the collusion of sellers of labour and, therefore, has the outward marks of a monopoly, it is not certain that the union will achieve a monopoly price; there may be a case of countervailing power, which just restores the balance of the market. But there is no assurance either that this will be the situation. Marx, however, pointed out that, once the worker had sold his labour power, he was no longer free during the labour day but under the command of his capitalist employer. But a change-over from a market economy to a centrally planned economy would not alter the dependent status of most workers and it may still be better to work for a private firm (whose domination one may escape) than for the all-powerful state.

Free Enterprise.

Free enterprise is another feature of capitalism. This freedom of private enterprise necessitates private ownership of the material means of production. Without these property rights it would be next to impossible to have an unplanned economy, which implies freedom of individual initiative. Where the government does not co-ordinate the productive efforts of the citizens, such co-ordination must be the result of the activities of private enterprise. Thus we see that the institution of private property is regarded as part of the system of capitalism, for liberty is construed as implying freedom to acquire property by production, occupation, or exchange, and to dispose of it as one likes—as long as it is not wrested by force from someone else. Carver in his *Principles of National Economy* (1921, p. 140) said, "Property exists automatically and necessarily in any group where the individual is safeguarded against violence. If he is safeguarded against violence, he may hold anything in his possession until he sees it fit to give it up of his own free will. If anyone who tries to dispossess him by violence is promptly repressed by the group, that very act on the part of the group safeguards him in his possession—it transforms his possession into property."

Some have held that liberty involves the right to property, because property is necessary to the maintenance of personal independence. But this would require that everyone should own some wealth—a condition that is not realized under a system of liberty and free enterprise. Rather we see millionaires and poor men living side by side as master and servant. This would lead to a criticism of the institution of property as it now exists. The capitalists' defence of private property and free enterprise cannot be accepted without qualification.

When private property can no longer be justified as a natural right or as the product of the labour of its possessor, its position becomes very vulnerable. If its validity rests upon its social usefulness, the right can be restricted and ought to be in every case where no social welfare is promoted by it. The desirability of some private ownership as a general principle is not denied, but it cannot be regarded as an inviolable right.

The Freedom to Save and Invest.

In capitalism the right to save is supported and enhanced by the right to bequeath wealth. The right to bequeath (or to inherit) cannot be granted too readily in the economic systems which aim at government ownership of the material means of production. The freedom to save, to inherit, and to accumulate wealth is, therefore, a right which is even more peculiar to capitalism than is the free choice of consumption and of occupation. The freedom to invest is implied in the unplanned character of the capitalist economy. In a capitalist economy entrepreneurs who wish to take advantage of investment opportunities are bidding for the temporary use of the funds which individual savers have accumulated, offering to pay interest from the yield of their investments. In this way, a market rate of interest is established. Aside from its significance for individual savers and individual borrowers, according to capitalists, it satisfies the social need for a barrier to protect resources for the satisfaction of present consumption from being depleted for the sake of the future. But a discrepancy between saving and investment is possible in an unplanned economy. It is possible because of the freedom to consume, to save, and to invest, and because of the fact that those who save are, as a rule, a different group from those who invest. True, the market is supposed to bring saving and investment into balance, but under certain circumstances it may fail to do so. Then it is the task of the government to see to it that a sufficient amount of spending is maintained.

Competition and Monopoly.

The model of the capitalist economy is a competitive model; it has to be, because a sufficient amount of competition is indispensable if the whole production and distribution process is to be regulated by market forces. Capitalism is based on the belief that competition is necessary in a capitalist economy to keep initiative constantly on the alert, to protect the consumer against exploitation, and to maintain a sufficiently flexible price system. Capitalism further claims that competition leads to a process of natural selection, by which each individual will find his level in the position which he is best able to fill. Those who are capable of leadership and executive organization will become successful entrepreneurs, where they will be in the best position to exercise these qualities. The inefficient businessmen will be weeded out by the simple process of failure. Those who are best fitted for employment under the direction of somebody else will naturally become wage-earners. Employers compete with each other to secure the most efficient workers, so that each labourer will find that place in industry where he can contribute service of the greatest value. The relative wages paid in different employments will induce each labourer to do the highest type of work of which he is capable. Unfortunately, these arguments have been effectively disproved by the facts of history. Competition, when unrestricted by regulatory laws, does not protect the consumer from deception or extortion, the investor from swindling, nor the high-minded businessman from the unfair methods of his unscrupulous rivals. These things can be attained only by collective control.

One might suppose that such collective control need not be contrary to the principles of capitalism, for capitalists themselves suggest government interference as necessary to maintain free and fair competition. Under modern conditions, however, the measures necessary to achieve these ends involve such extensive regulating bodies that they are hardly compatible with the principles of free enterprise of capitalism. There are three reasons why competition fails to regulate business satisfactorily. In the first place, unscrupulous businessmen lack the ethical standards essential to fair competition. In the second place, free competition is not necessarily equal competition. Obviously, he who has capital to begin with is in a better position than he who has not. In other words, competition bestows its prizes upon the strong and lucky at the expense of the weak and unlucky. This destroys the connection between reward and service which is assumed to exist by the capitalist. The inventor may live in poverty, while some capitalist entrepreneur reaps a fortune from the marketing of his invention. In view of these things, it is by no means certain that competition selects those who are really most fit to contribute to social welfare. In the third place, competition is so distasteful to the competitors that, sooner or later, they seek to escape it by establishing a monopoly. Monopolist tendencies are an intrinsic feature of the capitalist economy.

Some Attacks on Capitalism.

Objective standards for the evaluation of a socio-economic system are impossible to find. Nevertheless, the attacks on capitalism in the words of Professor Halm are essentially four:

(1) The oldest attack aims at the unequal distribution of wealth and income and the fact is that such inequality leads to inequality in economic and political power as well.

(2) Capitalism is often considered less productive than collectivist systems which can consciously plan for development. In particular, it is

argued that profitability is not identical with productivity and that competition is often excessive.

(3) At the same time, capitalism is, in the opinion of many observers, not competitive enough. The profit motive and the competitive struggle, together with modern technology, lead to monopolist tendencies which seem to violate the very philosophy of capitalism. In this criticism socialists and the proponents of the free market economy join forces, though they disagree on the proper remedies.

(4) Capitalism does not always maintain a high level of employment. In a depression, productive resources are wasted and the national income is kept below a potential maximum. Apart from this loss in productivity, prolonged mass unemployment is one of the most dangerous social diseases to which an economic system can be exposed. Professor Laski, a noted British political scientist, observed:

"The present system of capitalistic production stands condemned from almost any angle of analysis. . . . It makes a part of the community parasite upon the rest, and it deprives most of the opportunity to live on a human plane of existence."

But in his book *Economic Systems* Professor Halm concluded by saying: "We must be particularly careful when capitalism's deficiencies are to be corrected at the price of the freedoms which are the most characteristic feature of the market economy. We ought not to forget that capitalism has proved its compatibility with political democracy, whereas all centrally planned systems, so far, have been totalitarian. Will it be possible to maintain economic and political freedom when we aim for goals which capitalism admittedly cannot reach?"

16.3 Socialism

Socialism, as defined in the *Encyclopaedia Britannica*, is that policy or theory which aims at securing, by the action of the central democratic authority, a better distribution and, in due subordination thereto, a better production of wealth than now prevails. According to Joad, the various measures which socialism recommends for the socialization of community life, are:

"(*i*) The abolition of the private ownership of the means of production. This would be substituted by public ownership and control of the major industries and services.

(*ii*) The nature and extent of industry and production to be subservient to social needs and not the profit motive.

(*iii*) In capitalism the motive force is private profit. This will be replaced by the motive of social service."

Presence of Planning.

We have seen that the economies of capitalist countries rest in the main on the independent individual actions of millions of private economies. But under socialism the decision as to what and how much to produce will no longer be decided by considerations of profit. These decisions will be reached on the basis of the usefulness of such things to the society. In the place of a blind working of the productive forces there will be central planning of the economic life of the country. The various branches of production will be developed harmoniously by a central planning authority to serve the best interests of the society as a whole. As the central planning authority has a greater knowledge about the supply and demand positions than a number of isolated enterpreneurs, the socialists believe that they can reach correct equilibrium prices more quickly than the latter.

Again, under capitalism the system of production is anarchic, and a periodic crisis is bound to occur. But taking a long-range view-point, the socialist economy can control the functions of the trade cycles much better than the present order through central planning. It will also tend to reduce those risks and uncertainties which exist in the capitalist society owing to unbridled competition. It would avoid the wastes of the competitive system. Capitalists would argue that the decisions of a central planning authority are bound to be arbitrary, and the economy may suffer from a wrong rate of capital accumulation in the long run. It is, however, true that a rate of interest as determined under a capitalist economy on the basis of the consumers' preferences for liquidity may not always prove superior, from the strict economic standpoint, to one determined by the planning authority. Moreover, the socialists argue that they do not necessarily propose to do away with pecuniary incentives entirely. Most socialists expect wages to vary with the productivity of the worker, so that there would be wage differentials to stimulate the people to develop skills and to exert themselves diligently. They believe also that, under socialism, a better spirit of co-operation and service will prevail; that with competition removed, new standards of morality and ethics will take their place. Only a trial of socialism would enable us to reach a satisfactory conclusion on this point.

Income Distribution.

We have seen that the capitalist distribution of wealth and income is quite unequal and that the possibilities for greater equality within the institutional framework of capitalism are limited. Private property in the material means of production, the connection of personal with functional distribution, private capital accumulation, and the importance of the profit motive—all these features make more equal personal distribution difficult and, in most instances, are capable of doing more harm than good. The socialists claim that their system will establish a more equal income distribution. This claim is based on the fact that public ownership of the material means of production eliminates the so-called unearned income of private persons. Interest, rent, and profit go to the government.

H. D. Dickinson points out that in a socialist system there is no essential connection between the value of labour and the payment of a sum of money to a labourer. In other words, wages might be used for accounting purposes only, while the national income would actually be divided up according to such principles as perfect equality or payment according to need. Dickinson's remark refers, however, to authoritarian rather than to liberal socialism. Free choice of occupation under capitalism makes it imperative that wage differences be used to guide workers into industries where their particular skills can be most productively used. Socialism does not believe in the principle of free choice of occupation. In socialism wage differences are, therefore, used for more than accounting purposes; they are essential if labour is to be allocated without compulsion to the production of commodities which consumers demand. Oskar Lange believes that these wage differentials would be negligible in view of the fact that the choice of an occupation offering a lower income, but also a smaller disutility, may be interpreted as the purchase of leisure, safety, agreeableness of work, etc., at a price equal to the difference between money earned in that particular occupation and in others. Probably a majority of socialists however, favour a system of wages determined by the efficiency, or productivity, of the worker. This is a frank recognition that an individual who is more able or willing to work than his fellows should be paid higher remuneration accordingly. This would permit some degree of inequality to exist. But by abolishing incomes from property and permitting only wages, socialists believe that such inequality of earnings as would be based upon differences in ability would be fair, and at the same time would stimulate each to his maximum endeavour. While perhaps ethically not as ideal as payment in accordance with need, this basis of wages is more expedient.

Public Enterprise.

Under socialism, industry, instead of being in the hands of individual enterprisers, would be controlled through some kind of common organization. Just what the organization would be is a matter of detail on which different socialist groups are not entirely agreed. Whatever the arrangement, its distinctive feature would be the absence of capitalistic proprietors, the ownership being vested, by one means or another, in the masses of the people.

This collective ownership, however, does not apply to all property which is now privately owned. It applies only to the basic (or, as some socialists put it, the "socially necessary") means of production. These include all large landholdings, forests and mineral deposits, railroads and other public utilities, and the more important factories. It is only in those industries upon which the public is peculiarly dependent, and in which the danger of exploitation of the working class by huge capitalists is most present, that the socialists insist upon the abolition of private enterprise. The socialists desire to see the control of industry actually in the hands of the working class for which they advocate the idea of industrial democracy. Democratic control of industry would be made possible, they believe, by placing political power much more truly in the hands of the people than at present. The socialists generally believe that collective ownership can be established by means of the ballot, after the voters have been won over to the idea by the educational and propaganda activities of a well-organized socialist party. In their emphasis upon democracy, the socialists are diametrically opposed to the communists, whose regime in the Soviet Union is one of ruthless dictatorship.

Competition and Socialism.

It is said that an obstacle to productive efficiency under socialism lies in the fact that without competition, the principle of natural selection in industry would be destroyed. Under socialism, every position in industry would be subject to the bickerings and baneful influence of political life. Collective enterprise, it is said, is notoriously wasteful and inefficient. Where it is not positively corrupt, it is deadened by bureaucracy and red tape. The opponents of socialism claim that, instead of increasing production and bringing about the ideal conditions expected by the socialists, it would actually result in colossal inefficiency and industrial stagnation. The socialists reply that competitive industry is much less efficient than its defenders believe. Influence and favouritism are by no means absent from private business.

Some economists have argued that the problem of pricing under socialism would present serious difficulties because socialism would be bound to interfere with the natural economy inherent in the competitive price system since land rents and interest, which at present enter into costs, would be largely done away with, and wages, presumably, would be limited by maximum and minimum rates, instead of being left solely to the play of supply and demand. It is true that some socialists, dominated by Marx's mistaken labour theory of value, have visualized the collective economy as one in which prices would be based only on the quantities of labour required to produce various goods to the neglect of the contribution of other factors. But a number of economists who have interested themselves in the theoretical aspects of this problem have in recent years reasoned that a socialist economy could use the principles of the present pricing process, and might even keep prices closer to their norms than they are under capitalism. Interest and rents would not go to private investors and landowners, but to the state, which could use the proceeds for various projects of social welfare, such as education, free medical care, scientific research, promotion of the arts, and so on. Thus the essential elements of the competitive pricing process could be retained.

Oskar Lange mentions among the advantages of socialism the comprehensiveness of the items entering into the price system. Following Pigou he shows that

"There is frequently a divergence between the private cost borne by an enterpreneur and the social cost of production. Into the cost account of the private entrepreneur only those items enter for which he has to pay a price, while such items as the maintenance of the unemployed created when he discharges workers, the provision for the victims of occupational diseases and industrial accidents, etc., do not enter, or as Professor J. M. Clark has shown, are diverted into social overhead costs. On the other side, there are the cases where private producers render services which are not included in the price of the product. . . . A socialist economy would be able to put all the alternatives into its economic accounting. Thus it would evaluate all the services rendered by production and take into the cost accounts all the alternatives sacrified; as a result it would also be able to convert its social overhead costs into prime costs. By so doing it would avoid much of the social waste connected with private enterprise."

Incentive and Socialism.

By eliminating the large property incomes and reducing differences in wages the socialists believe that they would establish a far greater measure of equality of incomes than now exists. No one would be very poor, and no one would be immensely rich. But one of the strongest criticisms which may be urged against a socialist programme is that it would remove the element of incentive which is present under capitalism.

Many socialists are, nevertheless, quite conscious of the problem of lacking incentives under bureaucratic management. Oskar Lange, for instance, asserts "that the real danger of socialism is that of a bureaucratization of economic life, and not the impossibility of coping with the problem of allocation of resources." But he makes this concession to the critics of socialism only because he believes that the same, or even greater, danger cannot be averted under monopolistic capitalism. "Officials subject to democratic control seem preferable to private corporation executives who practically are responsible to nobody."

Moreover, we have already seen that the socialists do not necessarily propose to do away with pecuniary incentives entirely. They believe also that, under socialism, a better spirit of co-operation and service will prevail.

Socialism and Family.

There is a popular misconception that socialism does not believe in family life. In fact, socialism is primarily an economic and political, rather than a complete sociological, programme, and any changes which might take place in the family would be only such as would naturally follow from the changed economic status of the working classes; socialists believe that happy and normal family life is largely interfered with today by our economic institutions. Economic pressure, they assert, brings about the subjection of women, while poverty interferes with the maintenance of the home. Whatever individual socialists may think about the ideal forms of family relationships, there is nothing inherent in the socialist organization of society which is incompatible with monogamy. Similarly, there is a similar popular misconception about the relationship between socialism and religion. It has frequently been alleged that socialists are atheists and that socialism would destroy religious institutions. But there is nothing in socialism, however, which is necessarily antagonistic to religion. Although it is true that socialists in some countries have grievances against the organized church, it is not fair to say that socialism is anti-religious.

Conclusion.

Socialism claims to reduce waste and eliminate depressions and un-employment through the central planning of the economy as a whole. It also would hope to eliminate unearned incomes and reduce inequality while promoting the welfare of the masses. On the other hand, it would lose some of the forces of individual initiative, its efficiency might be impaired by the stagnation and regimentation of bureaucracy, and it would reduce somewhat the scope of man's liberties both as consumer and producer.

Some socialists believe in the comprehensive planning of industry, and in directing the economy toward certain goals of social welfare. If the plans are to be made effective, say the critics, the central officials would have to have authority to put their plans into effect. Socialism would place great power, they think, in the hands of government officials. They fear that the latter will be intoxicated by this power, and will arrogate more and more authority to themselves. In this way, personal liberties will gradually diminish, and the regime will take on more and more the character of a dictatorship.

The socialists believe that these developments are hardly likely in a country where there is a long-established tradition of political democracy.

16.4 Communism

Concept of Communism.

The term "communism", which is derived from the Latin word "com-munis", does not occur before 1840, although the concept it embraces is as old as civilization itself. The name was coined in the secret revolution-ary societies of Paris between 1834 and 1839. Its general use is to describe the practice of or belief in the desirability of the social control of economic life, including the social ownership of property. It is distinguished in a technical sense from socialism, in that it generally includes ownership of some or all forms of consumer goods as well. In addition to this historical and general meaning of the term, "communism" came in the years 1840–72 to imply revolutionary action for the violent overthrow of capitalist society.

Underlying the general concept of communism are three basic doctrines. The first is that of the state of nature which in varying forms dominated the thought of antiquity and of the modern world from the Renaissance to the mid-nineteenth century. This doctrine is essentially Utopian, rationalist and pacific. The second doctrine is Manichæism, which considered human history as a ceaseless contest between two sovereign powers—good and evil, spirit and matter, light and darkness. The third doctrine is Marxism, or the economic theory concerning the rise and development of the productive forces of capitalist society, its inherent collectivist tendencies and antagonistic interests, with the class war as the human dynamic power of civilization. Communism formed an integral part of the ancient myth of the golden age, the idealization by civilized man of the primitive, "natural" tribal stage of human history. It was a reaction against the growing complications of ages of transition.

Modern communism has become, instead of a myth or the subject of literary romance, a practical goal and programme in the form of socialism agitated by international socialist groups and regarded by them as the inevitable next step in social development, to be brought about by a class whose self-interest drives it to such a type of economic and social organization.

Philosophy of Communism.

Communism is more extreme than socialism. To understand how the communists went about their task, it is necessary to know something of their theory of social evolution. Marxian communism believes in an economic or materialist interpretation of history, that is, economic events dominates in controlling the social and political life. Marx called the economic system of society the substructure (*unterbau*) and religion, laws, ethics and other institutions of society the superstructure (*oberbau*). According to Marx, the close analysis of any element of the superstructure would reveal the influence of the substructure as a determining factor. Religions and morals are concocted by dominant classes to fortify their own interests; therefore, all religion and ethics hitherto prevalent among mankind are suspect. The ideas of eternal truth and social justice have no place in reality; they were invented by the dominant classes to perpetuate their power. Marx's economic interpretation may briefly be summed up in five principles: the law of concentration, surplus value, the two-class struggle, the overproduction theory of depressions, and social revolution.

Marx saw the transition which had taken place from the domestic industry which preceded the Industrial Revolution to the large factories which followed it. This concentration of industry would go on until the small independent businessmen would be eliminated and forced to become employees of a few powerful capitalists. Thus society would be separated into two groups—the capitalists and the proletariat or wage-earning class.

Again, according to the doctrine of surplus value, all wealth is produced by labour. But the labourer is paid only enough to maintain him at a bare level of subsistence. Consequently, there is a surplus value created which the capitalist is able to take for himself. It is unearned by the capitalist because he did nt produce it. Profits are, therefore, the result of exploitation. Marx's 'Law of Concentration", coupled with his doctrine of surplus value, must lead to class war between the two groups. There can be no compromise, for the situation becomes progressively worse as society advances. Since the labourers who constitute the great mass of consumers are not given all the purchasing power which they produce, they are unable to buy back from the capitalists the extra wealth created by their additional production. The result will be general overproduction of goods. Industrial collapse follows. The capitalist system will destroy itself. When this catastrophe befalls, it is believed, a revolution will take place in which the proletariat, having become conscious of its own strength, will establish a new system of society in which the capitalists will be dispossessed of their property. There follows the stage known as dictatorship of the proletariat that is the intelligent minority—the communist party—must hold its power at any cost, and rule the country with an iron hand, until it has brought socialism into being, and educated the people to its ideals.

When the people are thus made ready for it, the stage of dictatorship will give way to the socialist society, which is regarded as the lower phase of communism. In this stage, all the means of production will be in the hands of the democratically governed state. But there will be considerable centralization of economic and political control. In short, this stage is simply one of state socialism as described in the preceding pages.

Finally, the socialist society will evolve into the communist society, which is the higher phase of communism, the ultimate goal of the communist party. When this stage is reached, the coercive authority of the state will no longer be needed. The state will "wither away", for society will now be "classless". Then the communist principle of "from each according to his ability, to each according to his need" will prevail. One of the powerful appeals of communism is directed to the human desire of bettering the situation of the poor and the weak. It takes the shape of an appeal for the universal brotherhood of man. Communist eschatology promises betterment, brotherhood, and complete happiness for all individuals; man is not considered as an end. The end is quite clearly the whole, the society. It is true that communists believe that even the individual man will be happy once the goal is achieved. But they are not interested in him, for collectivity is the only truly real factor in the human world.

It may be noted here that modern communism, which is exemplified by the Soviet Union, is very different from Utopian communism, for it proposes to apply communist principles on a national scale, achieving power for the Communist Party by violent revolution, if necessary.

Planning in Communism.

Communism is a complete substitute for that allocation of economic resources which, in a capitalist system, is determined by prices and incomes and related in turn to consumers' sovereignty and where decisions are made by innumerable businessmen. It has practically involved the liquidation of private enterprise and of private property; under the Russian system of communism there is not much room for the capitalist trinity—the sovereignty of the consumer, the tyranny of the price sysem and the quest for profits. There the economic architects generally determine what use is to be made of limited resources and, therefore, to some extent impair the sovereignty of consumers. The targets for production are set according to an objective determined by the State, e.g. producing for war or raising the mass standard of living, and thus do not allow price and income movements to regulate the productive process; and since these goals are selected by the general strategy, acting for the Party, the Government or the people, the planned economy supplants the entrepreneur, who is the human magnet in the capitalist machine.

Under communism, consumption as well as production would be collectively controlled, and money, prices, wages, and free exchange would be abolished. The collective organization would determine what was to be produced and in what quantities, distributing the product through a system of rationing, where it was believed that it would do the most good. The communist formula is "from each according to his ability; to each according to his need".

Social and Educational Programmes

Communism is more than an economic programme. It involves sweeping social reforms as well. It is interesting to note what the Soviet Government is doing in matters of this kind. The communist theory of evolution requires an intelligent working class. Therefore, the communists have resolutely set about the building up of a universal school system. Attention is also paid to art, music, drama, and other cultural needs. Religious marriages are not recognized, the only legal ceremony being a civil one. Family life is somewhat different from that to which we are accustomed. The home is not as important a factor in the lives of the people, partly because the housing shortage has been so acute that families are very crowded, and partly because the workers' lives have been so filled up with the new activities of clubs, political meetings, lectures, evening classes, theatres, concerts, etc. It is apparent that these features are going to make profound changes in the social life and institutions of the people. It is true that the communists have carried on anti-religious propaganda. While there is complete religious toleration (so long as the church does not become a centre for anti-revolutionary activity), the communists do not approve of religious organizations. In a sense, communism is itself a religion.

An Appraisal of Communism.

Communism is, both in its theory and in its practice, an incredible oversimplification leading to a distortion of reality. This oversimplification appears first in communist eschatology. Despite the tremendous complexity of human nature and human desires, the communists teach that one simple method, collectivization, will render man completely happy and satisfied. This they do either by completely disregarding some other human desires or by asserting that collectivization will cause other desires (e.g. the religious) to dissolve.

Communism, for example, teaches that all problems of labour can be solved by the nationalization of factories, or rather it seems to assert that only one such problem exists: private ownership of industry. This obviously contradicts everything we know about modern industrial life. Problems like wages, working conditions or personal relations inside the factory are obviously more important to the workers than the question of ownership. The communists disregard all of them and insist that everything will be right once the factories have been nationalized. This does not mean that nationalization must necessarily be considered bad. But to reduce the whole problem to a question of ownership is oversimplifying the situation greatly.

Again, historical materialism is the result of Marxian communism's oversimplification of human motives and human history. It got hold of only a fragment of truth and tried to convince humanity that it was the whole truth or the fundamental truth. It is a fact that within every human society there is always present a covert or an overt conflict of opposing tendencies. But Marxian communism simplifies the whole human situation by declaring that only two human classes exist, the exploiters and the exploited, the haves and the have-nots, and it is the conflict between these classes which creates and explains all history. Human motivation is not so simple.

If we take a realistic view of history, we shall have to admit that different epochs and different human groups have been actuated by a variety of motives. Take, for instance, the religious motive which is considered by the Marxists to be a reflection of economic motives and economic conflicts, but if we read the bloody history of religious conflicts, we shall be surprised to realize that competition between rival religions has been responsible for more wars than any single cause. Joad in his *Book Mark* (p. 110) observed:

"It is estimated that competition between rival religions has been responsible for more wars than any other single cause, and of these the most numerous and the fiercest have been waged between sects representing different versions of the religion of peace. Men have fought to maintain their right to turn to the East during the recital of the Apostles' Creed and have died in thousands over the question of whether the words "and the son" should or should not be inserted in the Nicene Creed. Unless, therefore, we are to suppose that the scope of the economic motive is to be extended to cover the expectation of pecuniary benefits in the next world, as well as in this one, the Marxian analysis of the causes of what are called religious wars breaks down. Personally, I think, it is doubtful whether Marx would have consented to any such extension; he did not believe in heaven, which he considered a bourgeois invention."

Besides religious conflicts, human society has suffered from countless dynastic wars and wars waged by the military, motivated by the instincts of glory and self-aggrandizement. The fact is that all attempts to interpret human history through economic determinants lead to the denial of the role of great men as shapers of human destiny. They assert that French or European history would have taken the same course, with or without Napoleon, or if Bonaparte had not sprung up from somewhere, someone else was dialectically bound to do the same job. But if religion is the opium of the people and it was invented by the exploiting class as a method of ensuring the subservience of the exploited, how would they explain Christ's philosophy who was neither a landlord nor a slave-owner nor a capitalist. It is ridiculous to assert that dialectical or historical materialism produced Muhammad (peace be upon him), and that the Prophet was the mouthpiece of economic class-conflicts. Arabia had remained unchanged for millenniums and would have continued indefinitely in its ancient ways, if a man of the genius of the Prophet had not canalized the energies of the people into entirely new channels. Muhammad (peace be upon him) found a good deal of exploitation and economic injustice about him and tried to remedy them radically: but it was ideology acting on economics and not changes in production or modes of exchange and distribution creating an ideology, as a rationalization or justification.

The same oversimplification occurs in moral questions. Everything that serves the party and its single goal is obviously considered good; everything opposed to it is branded as completely wicked. The communists act as if everything is either all black or all white. But human experience indicates that in life nothing is all good or all bad. Therefore, communism is explicitly monistic in its approach; it believes that there is only one absolute value, the victory of the party, while all others are relative.

The communists themselves claim that their doctrine is based on science. But in reality it is difficult to justify this claim. Because communism is not based on experience, but rather proposed as a sort of *a priori* dogma, it also rejects free criticism and forbids the expression of any opinion besides its own, believing itself to be eternal and unchanging.

Coming to the other side of the picture, we find that the labour theory of value on which Marx developed the theory of surplus value itself is quite unsatisfactory, because it is not possible to reduce all labour into one grade as Marx and others have tried to do. Moreover, commodities which require no labour to produce also possess value, provided they are scarce in relation to demand. Moreover, the theory ignores the demand side altogether. As regards surplus value, it is arbitrary to say that fixed capital produces no surplus value. In fact, observation shows that profits are highest where fixed capital is used in abandance, which is contrary to Marx's theory as he himself admits.

Again, the course of economic development in various capitalist countries, however, does not seem to have followed the path laid down for it by Marxian communists. True, the control of capital is more concentrated now through the development of the joint-stock principle than it was at the time when Marx wrote. But the ownership of capital is more scattered in the form of small shares held by a large number of people mostly belonging to the working classes. The relative importance of the middle class has increased rather than decreased. Moreover, an average working-class family in advanced capitalist societies is enjoying a living standard much above the level of bare subsistence. Techniques have been discovered for the control, if not elimination, of the wide swings of cyclical fluctuations. There is no sign that the capitalist system is moving towards its doom as Marx predicted. Capitalist societies have survived major calamities like the two World Wars and the Great Depression.

No doubt, totalitarian planning on the Soviet model can help to remove unemployment, maldistribution and many other shortcomings of capitalism. It is generally believed that the U.S.S.R. is not troubled by excessive salesmen and advertisers, while the factories are short of labour, and, unlike the British post-War experience, purchasing power is not shunted disproportionately to tobacco, alcohol and entertainment. The U.S.S.R. would not permit a student body of millions in higher institutions of learning since the market demand is not likely to absorb one half of this number.

The most serious doubts concerning economic planning revolve round the issue of incentives and that of personal liberty. Profits are certainly an effective incentive in the capitalist system. If profits are to go, is it possible to maintain an atmosphere of economic progress such as is secured under the competitive system? Russia's great achievements in the economic field completely belie all misgivings regarding the compatibility of a truly socialist economy with economic progress. Moreover, it is possible to provide incentives for managers and workers even in a collectivist state. The issue of personal liberty is certainly a much more intractable one than the problem of incentives. The Russian economy is based on regimentation and the compulsory direction of labour. Though the masses everywhere seem to prefer bread and housing to liberty, the best thing would, of course, be to combine, if possible, planning with individual liberty.

Sir William Beveridge stressed the compatibility of a planned society and the retention of fundamental freedoms. He, however, came to the conclusion that even democratic planning requires direction of labour as well as direction of investment. Dr Lange and Dr Lerner have on the whole supported collectivism. But their plans are based upon price calculations. The manager of a collectivist farm will have to equate marginal cost with price, if the optimum output is to be secured. Lerner formulated certain welfare equations which must be fulfilled, if the ideal output is to be evolved. Lange stressed the social aspects of cost determination. Only socialism can take into account the full social cost of production which can easily exceed the private costs incurred by entrepreneurs.

Professor Robbins, however, has expressed grave doubts as regards the working of the collectivist organization in a free and democratic society. Nationalization of the means of production would just mean the creation of gigantic state monopolies exhibiting in an even higher degree the rigidities of monopoly capitalism. The goal of progress, declares Professor Robbins, lies in a direction different from that of overall collectivism. He believes that the loose institutions of individualism offer scope for the development of a way of life, more congenial to what most of us desire in our hearts than the tight centralized controls which are necessary, if these institutions are greatly curtailed or suspended.

Finally, we take it for granted that the socio-economic systems which were designated as liberal are compatible with political democracy, while an authoritarian economy (whether communist or fascist) is the economic expression of a totalitarian political system.

16.5 Fascism

Viewed either negatively or positively, fascism has elements in common with other systems of social organization. If defined simply as a negation of liberalism and parliamentarianism, it is inadequately differentiated from communism and other ideologies which manifest an equal antipathy to the older democratic tenets. If, on the other hand, defined positively as an unlimited sovereignty of the state over all phases of national activity, it approximates nationalism.

It is only when viewed as a peculiarly Italian phenomenon that the essence of fascism becomes clearly delineated. In its philosophy, origin and development, political structure and cultural aspirations, it is an integral part of the Italian matrix. As a reaction to the spread of collectivism, fascism arose in Europe after the First World War. Its philosophy substitutes for democracy the totalitarian state, in which individual rights are replaced by duties. It advocates racial supremacy, nationalist expansion, self-sufficiency, military preparedness, and population growth. Beginning with Mussolini's march on Rome in 1922, fascism soon spread throughout Central Europe, and even made its influence felt in Central and South America.

Philosophy of Fascism.

Fascism is the product of peculiar post-War conditions, largely anti-intellectual, opportunistic in methods. In support of their opposition to democracy, fascists point to its hesitancy, partisan political bickerings, and time-consuming debates. For fascism has developed the idea of the totalitarian state. The state, to the fascists, is absolute. It is an end in itself. To them everything is for the State, nothing against the state, nothing outside the state. Thus it insists upon exerting its domination over educational, religious, scientific and artistic institutions. All national institutions and agencies exist for the service of the state alone. The highest obligation and duty of the individual is a contribution to the power and unity of the state and he loses his own identity completely in it. The only right which the individual as such possesses is the right to assist in the strengthening of the state. In other words, he has individual rights only in so far as they do not conflict with the needs of the sovereign state. The fascist party cuts through the horizontal layers of society, which, with the aid of the arbitrary state government, hold it together like a clamp. Just as in Soviet Russia the party seeks, through a host of auxiliary groups, associations of teachers, students, rail-road-men and the like—to extend to all spheres of modern life, fascism is for militant nationalism. Here is a clear contrast to the class internationalism of collectivism. Fascism stresses purely national virtues, in many cases developing likewise an acute racial consciousness, Fascism has nothing but contempt for pacifism. War and the pursuits of war are glorified. International relations rest not upon a basis of international law and morality, but upon the test of military powers. Strength alone gives a nation the right to possess territory. Thus the fascist philosophy leads its followers to seek that continuous national expansion which its conception of power politics serves to justify. The fascist school legislation has made religious education obligatory in state schools. Although the relationship of fascism to the Catholic Church is in many respects extremely complicated, it is unquestionably true that the two movements share in common many features as, for example, an antipathy to liberalism and a close contact with the middle classes, especially the agrarian middle classes.

Economic Philosophy of Fascism.

The economic philosophy of fascism is guided by the basic philosophy of state. Though it calls for the preservation of the institution of private property which communism threatens, yet in practice, however, traditional liberal, *laissez-faire* capitalism almost completely disappears under fascism. While private enterprise is stated to be the most effective method of production and distribution, the exercise of a considerable degree of state regulation is considered essential for the promotion of economic stability and the full utilization of productive resources. A unified and centrally directed economic programme is regarded as essential. Since everything is for the state, the private entrepreneur is held responsible to the state for the direction given to production. When private initiative is unequal to the task at hand, or is regarded as inefficient, state intervention is permitted.

The most thorough-going interventionism of the corporative state is in regard to the freedom of labour. A syndicalist structure incorporating the various vocations of the nation is designed to regulate all relationships involving labour. Although this is accompanied by a campaign of moral and national education among the members, the regulations are rigidly binding upon all. Consistent with the emphasis on the supremacy of the state is the effort to transcend the disastrous economic and political effects of class conflict by emphasizing the solidarity of capital and labour in the production process. Actually, of course, there is still a sharp division between labour associations and employers' associations, leaving the way open to a clash of interests. But since all strikes and lockouts are outlawed, such disputes are to be settled mostly by arbitration groups.

Not only in the field of production but also in the case of distribution the state has the power. Thus the state assumes the right to distribute the essential factors of production and to direct the flow of raw materials and credit. It assumes the right to fix wages, rents, interest rates, and, in certain cases, commodity prices. In these respects, fascism bears some resemblance to state socialism, but without either its democracy or its interest in the welfare of the workers. The question of exercising private initiative loses its significance when it is realised that the primary aim of economic activity under fascism is not the attainment of the highest possible standard of living, as presumably it is under both capitalism and collectivism, but a continuous increase in the military power of the state. With this as its objective, the fascist state operates always on the basis of a wartime economy. Huge resources are, therefore, wasted.

Again, it is a menace to human civilization, because it encourages the rapid growth of population for building up a large army. They often forget that the world is facing the problem of population explosion. A considerable proportion of the national income is devoted to the maintenance of a large army and the financing of imperialist adventures. Overpopulation, resulting from the encouragement given to a high birth-rate, aggravates the decline of production. The only incentive fascism has is its nationalist glorification of the state. The population is exhorted to choose bullets, the symbol of the power of the nation, in preference to bread, the symbol of mere individual well-being.

A Brief Review of Fascism

Fascism and communism are two symptoms of the same disease. They are frequently grouped together as totalitarian systems. They are alike in that their governments are one-party dictatorships. In both, the ruling party maintains its power with an iron hand; civil liberties are suppressed. The term "totalitarian" can perhaps be applied to them both, in that each sets up a philosophy and a policy that are regarded as supreme values that must command the complete allegiance of the people above their allegiances to their church, their fellow individuals, and even the members of their own families.

Yet the two systems' conceptions of the state are very different. To the fascists, the state is a superior entity, an end in itself. To the communists, the state is an organ of class oppression, eventually to wither away and disappear. For, the fascist idea is nationalist expansion through aggressive encroachment upon other nations, while the communists envisage themselves as the promoters of a world revolution. Those who believe in the importance and dignity of the individual will not readily sacrifice the democratic method of policy determination for the sake of so-called increased mechanical efficiency under fascism or communism. Under fascism, efficiency is secured by the sacrifice of individual rights. The fascist glorification of war forces dictatorships and democracies alike to dissipate a large portion of their productive resources in the manufacture of armaments, and thereby delay indefinitely the further progress of social legislation and reform. It reduces markedly the volume of international trade. The general breakdown of world trade for which these policies are partly responsible was leading cause of the Depression that prevailed everywhere during the two World Wars. The heavy expenditure on military preparations unbalanced the government budgets badly in both Italy and Germany.

The Government of fascist Italy represented the centralization of power carried to an extreme. Nominally a monarchy, the supreme governing body of the country was a cabinet composed of the heads of fourteen ministries. Fascist Italy's principal contribution in the economic field was the development of the corporative structure. Twenty-two corporations were set up in various industries, trades and public services. Although adopting the name National Socialism, the Nazi government of Germany possessed all the general characteristics of fascism. The defeat of the Axis powers put an end to fascism in Germany and Italy. Fascism is now a forgotten chapter of history. It cannot solve the conflicting problems of the day.

16.6 Islam and Other "Isms": A Comparative Analysis

To make a comparison between Islam and other "isms" like capitalism, socialism, communism and fascism is something more than merely putting old wine in a new bottle. The challenge of time Islam faces today points out to us the need for an analysis which can point out where Islam surpasses the others in meeting certain goals. Since the whole analysis is subjective, we need not be surprised to find that those whose goals are different or who give different weight to the same goals refuse to accept our point of view.

Rightly or wrongly, each of the social philosophies has got its basic objectives. Thus capitalism believes in the unrestricted private ownership of the means of production, the motive force of which is private profit. The capitalist's motto is "Everything for himself and the devil take the hindmost." Again, "from each according to his ability, to each according to his need" is the basic goal of communism. In realizing this objective, communism regimentalizes the means of production, crushes personal liberty, destroys family and religion. But socialism also aims at the abolition of private ownership of the means of production. The concept of private profit as exists in capitalism will be replaced by the motive of social service under socialism whose motto is "From each according to his worth, to each according to his work." Communism is more extreme than socialism. But fascism which is almost a forgotten chapter of history can be also grouped as a totalitarian system. The fascist ideal is nationalist expansion through aggressive encroachment upon other nations. "Everything for the state, nothing against the state and nothing outside the state' is the philosophy of fascism. In spite of certain differences, fascism and communism are two symptoms of the same disease.

But Islam aims at achieving a social system which is capitalist in broad outline restricted very largely by socialist institutions and ideas. That is, an Islamic concept of society is based on five principles. They are (*a*) the *Qur'ānic* concept of history, (*b*) the restricted private ownership of the means of production, (*c*) the universal brotherhood of man, (*d*) the eternal principle of co-existence and (*e*) the sovereignty of Almighty Allah. In our comparison of different economic systems, I would confine my discussion to comparing performances in respect of each of the principles just mentioned.

(a) Concept of History

Before developing the *Qur'ānic* concept of history I would prefer to take up the Marxian materialist interpretation of history according to which the economic event is dominant in controlling social and political life. True, in every human society there is always present a covert and overt conflict of opposing tendencies. But Marx tries to impress upon us that only two human classes exist: the exploiters and the exploited, the haves and the have-nots, and it is the conflict between these two classes which creates and explains all history. Marx believed that in the process of social evolution there has been slavery and serfdom, feudalism, capitalism and socialism from the standpoint of production and distribution. According to Marx, each stage is an advance on its predecessor. But the revolutionary struggle of Marx was actually directed against capitalism under which the labourer is, Marx believes, paid only enough to maintain himself on a bare level of subsistence. Consequently, there is a surplus value created which the capitalist is able to take for himself. The profits of the capitalists are nothing but exploitation. Marx's "Law of Concentration", coupled with his doctrine of "surplus value", must lead to class war between the two groups which will ultimately bring about the downfall of capitalism and establish the dictatorship of the proletariat.

This idea of the inevitability of the historical process leading to the fulfilment of a predestined end finds no counterpart in the *Qur'ān* in at least two ways. Firstly, the *Qur'ān* recognizes the existence of different classes of people in the society; it does recognize the differences in talents, differences in income among the different members of society for the progress and prosperity of the same (*Sūrah* IV. 32). This leads directly to a denial of the doctrine of proletarianism developed by Marx, namely, that the proletariat majority will shape the future course of history. The *Qur'ānic* concept of history is more practical and more realistic in the sense that the *Qur'ān* by recognizing the multiplicity of human motives and sentiments, takes into consideration the role of great men like Prophet Muhammad (peace be upon him), Jesus Christ, and others in shaping the future course of history and destiny of nations. But Marx is so obsessed with viewing economic relations as the sole determinant of human history in every direction that he denies categorically the part played by religious conflicts, countless dynastic wars and great men like the Quā'id-i-A'zam, Kemal Ataturk, Abraham Lincoln, and Napoleon Bonaparte as the shapers of human destiny. "The *Qur'ānic* concept in this respect approximates Toynbee's concept of creative minority, for it is only a minority of purposeful and thinking persons that form the leadership of any movement even of the proletariat movement under Communism. The vast majority of people merely follow the lead given by the minority."

Secondly, the inevitability of class conflict leading to the ultimate victory of the proletariat over the capitalist as propounded by Marx is not supported by the *Qur'ānic* concept of history. True, the *Qur'ān* has promised victory to the Prophet of Islam over his opponents as in the verse.

> "It is He Who has sent
> His Apostle with
> Guidance
> And the Religion of Truth,
> To proclaim it over all Religion: and enough
> Is God for a Witness."
>
> (*Sūrah* XLVIII. 28)

But there the victory promised is clearly the victory of Islam in Arabia over the polytheists, the Jews and the Christians, and the promise was fulfilled in the lifetime of the Prophet.

From the above-quoted verse we are not prepared to accept that the success of Islam is guaranteed by the process of history. If the Muslim community does not follow the path laid down by the Holy *Qur'ān* and the *Sunnah*, it might fail to secure the power and domination promised by the Holy *Qur'ān*.

The *Qur'ān* guarantees the victory of Islam on other grounds, and says.

> "Truth has (now)
> Arrived, and
> Falsehood Perished:
> For Falsehood is (by its nature)
> Bound to perish."
>
> (*Sūrah* XVII. 81)

Islam, being truth, is bound to prevail over untruth. Its victory, therefore, is a normal and not a historical necessity, except in so far as a moral necessity is bound to influence the historical process, which is largely governed by the moral nature of man.

This concept of universal morality is based on the *Qur'ānic* doctrine of *"Tawhīd"*, i.e. all life is one, therefore, no separate sphere can claim independence of another, since it is the moral and spiritual version of man that co-ordinates and harmonizes the economic, social, political, and biological activities of society. Thus "the *Qur'ān* does not propound any set of laws which may be said to govern the historical process. It only shows that certain traits of human nature express themselves in the history of all decaying societies, while other traits of human nature exhibit themselves in the history of growing societies. At the same time the *Qur'ān* tells us through the mouths of the Prophets what kind of moral teachings, beliefs and socio-economic values, tangibly incorporated in laws, can arrest the process of social decay and lead a community to material as well as spiritual power."

Thus, it is possible to explain the advent of Islam, the decline and fall of the Roman Empire, and the movement of Pakistan through the *Qur'ānic* concept of history which is based on a deep understanding of human nature. But I wonder how all these events of history can be explained through the materialist interpretation of Marxian communism.

This brings us to the discussion of the significance of "matter" in shaping human history. Marx started with the denial of Allah; if He does not exist, only the "matter" is left. Like all materialists he presumed the purposelessness of "matter" in the dynamic setting of human society. But borrowing the idea of Hegel he told us that "matter", though unconscious and unpurposive, somehow possesses the attribute of progressively creating the values of life, because mere class conflict as propounded by Marx is of no significance, if it does not create values of life. The *Qur'ān* teaches us that the entire creation is meaningful (*Sūrah*. XXXVIII. 27; *Sūrah*. XI. 15, 16) and, therefore, neither is "matter" purposeless. In fact, all physical life comes out of it and is reabsorbed by it. Matter, life and mind denote varieties and gradations of being and all that existed is real.

It is not out of place to mention here that neither capitalism nor fascism propounds any set of laws which may be said to govern historical progress. Unrestricted individual initiative and unhealthy competition between the rich and the poor are likely to determine the future socio-economic set-up under capitalism. Again, fascism, which is the product of peculiar post-War conditions, is largely anti-intellectual and opportunist in method. If there is any law, it is the militant nationalism which may be said to govern the future course of a bloody history under fascism.

Another significant aspect of the *Qur'ānic* concept of history is the part played by religion in the process of social evolution. Marxian communism does not recognize religion. To Marx, it is the opium of the people and was invented by the exploiting class as a method of ensuring the subservience of the exploited. True, Marx found a good deal of exploitation and economic injustice about him in the name of religion. But there is always a basic difference between religion and cult just as there is a difference between the eternal problem of housing and the method of handling this problem. The first is eternal and the second relative to the needs of the community just as the basic principles of religion are eternal and those of a cult subject to change. But Marx confused religion and cult, condemned religion and gave us a materialist interpretation of history. It is ridiculous to assert that historical materialism produced men like Prophet Muhammad, Jesus Christ, Gautama Buddha and others.

. Under fascism, religion has no part to play except in so far as religion is used to assist in the strengthening of the state. Like socialism, capitalism is not anti-religious; religion could flourish in such societies in its own way. But here also, religion is divorced from the social, political and economic activities of the society. In such a scheme of society religion is just a misnomer. The whole society is drifting towards materialism to the utter neglect of the role of morality and spirituality, which consist in harmonizing the conflicting requirements of material life.

But the *Qur'ānic* concept of religion is based on the oneness of God which is symbolic and significant in the sense that all life is one and wholesome and the religion of Islam provides for the entire gamut of activity—social, political, economic and biological, and brings about equilibrium in society. With these words, we may turn to the second part of our comparative analysis.

(b) The Concept of Private Property

As we have seen there are vast differences among social systems with regard to the concept of private property. "Islam maintains a balance between exaggerated opposites." Capitalism believes in free enterprise which necessitates private ownership of the material means of production. The freedom to save, to invest, to inherit and to accumulate is a right which is even more peculiar to capitalism than is the free choice of consumption and of occupation. In such a social system we find great inequalities of income. Some people are found living in palatial buildings and some in huts and tents. But communism wants a complete substitute for the allocation of economic resources which in a capitalist system is determined by price and incomes, and is related in turn to consumer sovereignty and decisions made by innumerable businessmen. Communism has practically involved the liquidation of private enterprise and private property. The regimentation and compulsory direction of labour under communism is too high a price for "mess of pottage". In fact, communism in this respect holds a more extreme view than socialism which also stands for the abolition of private ownership of the means of production. Here the nature and extent of industry and production are to be subservient to social needs and not the profit motive. Though it avoids the wastes of the competitive system, yet here also we find the same problem of incentives and individual liberty. Again, in theory, fascism calls for the preservation of private property but in practice liberal *laissez-faire* capitalism almost completely disappears under fascism. Since everything is for the state, the private entrepreneur is held responsible to the state for the direction given to production. It assumes the right to fix wages, rents, interest and, in certain cases, commodity prices. In these respects, fascism bears some resemblance to state socialism, but without either its democracy or its interest in the welfare of the workers. The question of exercising private initiative loses its significance when it is realised that the primary aim of economic activity under fascism is not the attainment of the highest possible standard of living, as presumably it is under both capitalism and collectivism, but a continuous increase in the military power of the State.

But in Islam absolute ownership of everything belongs to God.

"The dominion of the heavens
And the earth, and all.
This is between:
And unto Him.
Is the final goal (of all)."

(*Surah* V. 20 and elsewhere)

It follows that proprietorship of all the free gifts of Nature—land, water and their wealth—does not belong to any individual. Mankind holds them jointly in trust. The trust is conditional in the sense that men benefit themselves equally and not to the exclusion of anyone, not for enriching one's self or exploiting others or holding others in subjection. Thus Islam allows private ownership of property, but subjects the owner to restrictions preventing him from using property except to the common good. It encourages the acquisition of private property, but requires that this should be by means conducive to the good of the community as a whole. In brief, while Islam allows the individual to promote his own good it exhorts him not to forget that he is part of the group, and reminds him of the need to protect and promote the interest of his fellows. The moral injunctions about ownership are to create a sense of responsibility and a conscience.

Broadly speaking, the ethical injunctions—both positive and negative—on the owners of the property are the following:

    (*i*) to exploit property to the fullest extent without adversely affecting the interests of the community;

    (*ii*) to pay *Zakāt*;

    (*iii*) to spend "in the way of Allah";

    (*iv*) to abstain from taking interest;

    (*v*) to avoid fraud in business dealings, hoarding or monopoly.

From the above analysis, we can safely say that capitalism believes in an unplanned economy resulting in the occurrence of periodic crisis: communism in totalitarian planning with total damage to individual liberty; socialism in comprehensive planning with considerable harm to personal liberty; fascism in militant planning which aims at increasing the military power of the State to the utter disregard of the welfare of the people. But Islam provides a realisable synthesis between planning by inducement and planning by direction.

We may now pass on to the third part of our comparative analysis based on the principle of universal brotherhood.

(c) Concept of Brotherhood

The Islamic concept of brotherhood distinguishes Islam from other social systems in the moral, social and economic spheres of life. In the moral sphere, it is "*Ṣalāt*" (prayer) which plays a decisive role. Prayer in Islam finds expression in many ways. The most important is the one known as "*Ṣalāt*" which comprises five daily services. The service is led by one of the congregation preferably the one who possesses the best understanding of the *Qur'ān*. There is no priesthood or anything corresponding to ordination or the taking of Holy Orders in Islam. Every Muslim is, or should be, competent to lead a congregation in the service.

In other words, "*Ṣalāt*" places everybody—rich and poor, high and low, king and beggar—on an equal footing. In fact, "*Ṣalāt*" teaches us man's equality to man, his dignity and his value. This vision is a part of the Islamic faith. Because in the "*Ṣalāt*" the worshipper repeatedly returns to contemplation of the Majesty of God, imploring Him to guide and direct his life and effort along beneficent channels. This repeated effort made in the right spirit. humility and sincerity must leave its impress on the mind and soul of the worshipper and cleanse him thoroughly of all dross. The *Qur'ān* says that the "*Ṣalāt*" purifies a worshipper and washes him clean of all evil and misbehaviour (*Sūrah* XXIX. 45). The Prophet has said: "If a person has a stream of pure water running at his doorstep and washes himself thoroughly in it five times a day no impurity would even approach him. Remember, the *Ṣalāt* is such a stream."

Thus "*Ṣalāt*" is fruitless if it does not bring the mood and temper of voluntary submission to the demands and dictates of genuine social welfare. This contribution of Islam towards developing the concept of brotherhood from the moral standpoint is practically absent in communism, socialism, capitalism, and fascism, for some reason or other. It is absent in communism, because communism, which is anti-religious, stresses more material progress in life and uproots all feelings of brotherhood from the minds of the people. It is absent in capitalism, because capitalism like socialism limits the scope of religion and morality to within the four corners of the church. The dynamic interplay of spiritual and secular institutions is not found either in a capitalist or a socialist society. It is absent in fascism, because fascism glorifies only in the state, which is an end in itself and not a means to an end. Therefore, it banishes all feelings of fraternity from the minds of the individuals.

Secondly, in the social sphere the Islamic concept of brotherhood springs from spiritual renovation and not from social surgery, which is the sole weapon for ensuring social security under communism. The *Qur'ān* says that Allah has divided mankind into tribes and nations for greater facility of intercourse. The true source of honour in the sight of God is a righteous life for the individual irrespective of his membership of any race or tribe (*Sūrah* XLIX. 13). In his Farewell Address, the Prophet said: "You are all brothers and are all equal. None of you can claim any privilege or any superiority over any other. An Arab is not to be preferred to a non-Arab, nor is a non-Arab to be preferred to an Arab."

It is stressed that true brotherhood can be established only by virtue of men's relationships with one another through God. While stressing the showing of due kindness and proper affection towards children and other members of the family, the *Qur'ān* lays great stress on kindness toward neighbours (*Sūrah* IV. 37). The Prophet emphasized on many occasions the duty owed to a neighbour, saying: "So repeatedly and so much has God impressed upon me the duty owed to a neighbour that I began to think that a neighbour might perhaps be named an heir." In the same way, the needy and the wayfarer must be looked after (*Sūrah*. IV. 36). Orphans have been made the objects of particular care. The property of the orphan should not be dealt with to his prejudice by exchange or by being held in common with the property of the guardian (*Sūrah* IV. 2).

Thus it follows that all men, rich and poor alike, must aid one another materially and personally; the rules vary in details but they maintain the principle of universal mutual aid in the Muslim fraternity. This fraternity is absolute and comprises men of all colours and of all races: black, white, yellow, all are sons of Adam by the flesh and all carry in them a spark of the Divine Light. Everyone should do his best to see to it that this spark is not extinguished, rather developed to that full companionship on High which the Prophet saw clearly awaiting him on his death-bed. It is impossible in Islamic society to reduce man in the name of Islam to the kind of degradation to which we find whole races or castes condemned in many non-Islamic societies. There are no parallels in Islam to the programme which characterized the history of Europe in the Middle Ages. Nor will there be found in the chronicles of even the worst Muslim ruler any instance of the kind of bigotry and race hatred which has darkened the history of modern European imperialism. Islam can claim both in the light of the *Qur'ān* and the *Sunnah* as well as the practices of Muslim governments to have been able to solve the problem of race prejudice far more effectively than any system or philosophy, ancient, mediaeval or modern, known to man. That this is no mean achievement will be appreciated by those who are aware how even in the most advanced countries periodic outbursts of irrational racial hatred continue to menace human life.

Thus Islam aims at merging all sections of society into a single community so that all persons may feel themselves to be members of the same family. Thus Dr Dhalla in this book *Our Perfecting World*, says: "Muhammadanism alone, among the religions of the world, has remained free from colour bias . . . It welcomes all converts with open arms, whether they are negroes or pariahs. Without reserve it accords them their rights and privileges and receives them into its social circle as much as into its religion. It excludes all barriers of birth and colour and admits its convert within the community on the basis of complete social equality."

Again, in his book *Authors of History*, H. G. Wells observed: "The stress of creed and class and the practical domestic brotherhood of Muslims has made the faith one of the greatest forces of the civilized world today."

In the social sphere also, true brotherhood cannot be developed under communism, capitalism, socialism and fascism. Because communism stresses mere technological advance in social affairs through class conflicts, the basis of which is hatred and not love. The total erosion of all private initiative under communism has resolved the individual into an unprogressive social welfare. Karl Mannheim, in his *Diagnosis of Our Time*, says, "If there is a lesson to be learned from the experiments of the totalitarian states, it is this: that ruthless regimentation leads to the enslavement of the citizen and the mechanistic concept of equality defeats itself." We find the same regimentation in varying degrees both under socialism and fascism. In the first case it is in the name of the welfare of the masses and in the latter case it is in the name of the state. Therefore, these social systems cannot help to develop the true brotherhood of man. Again, in a capitalist society we find not only landlords and landless masses living side by side but also an obnoxious distinction between man and man on the basis of race and colour and creed. The racial conflict of the U.S.A. and the apartheid policy of South Africa are some of the living testimonies to this fact. I wonder how the concept of universal brotherhood can be developed in such societies.

In the economic sphere, the uniqueness of the Islamic concept of brotherhood lies in the fact that Islam abrogates all anti-social economic activities which are not conducive to communal welfare. Thus all monopoly and speculative businesses are prohibited, because all these are opposed to beneficence and take advantage of the need or distress of their fellow-beings. Hoarding is condemned, because it puts wealth out of circulation and deprives the owner as well as the rest of the community of its beneficent use. Again, by condemning interest, Islam has not only helped expand production and employment but also placed the culture of brotherhood on a firm footing, because human brotherhood and sympathy evaporate when interest is charged for loans of money. Positively, the payment of *Zakāt* has been made a vital part of the Islamic faith. The spiritual discipline inculcated by "*Ṣalāt*" would lose its practical significance if Muslims did not pay *Zakāt* to root out economic and social injustice. Moreover, in carrying out legitimate economic activities, it is stressed that all contracts, whether involving large or small amounts, must be put down in writing setting out all the terms agreed upon fairly and as a further precaution it is laid down that if the person on whose behalf the liability is undertaken is a minor or of unsound judgment, then his guardian or the persons representing his interest should dictate the terms of the contract (*Sūrah* II. 282–283).

The point is that in all economic activities permitted by Islam there should not be one iota of exploitation or unfair dealing which may ultimately stand in the way of true human brotherhood. Islam recognizes that absolute equality in economic terms is likely to remain a wholly unattainable object; what it has sought to prescribe is a system which, if followed strictly, reduces to a minimum the danger of one individual or group exploiting another and perpetuating the exploitation such as may be found in the case of capitalism. This is probably far more important that the setting-up of a system aiming apparently to enforce absolute economic equality but actually ending in the thwarting of basic human impulses as in the case of communism and socialism. Economic egalitarianism in many countries today has led to the development of cults in which one single individual is elevated to the rank of divinity. This results in the degradation of human dignity, the debasement of man's self-respect.

Thus in the economic sphere also, we cannot have true brotherhood of man under communism, capitalism, socialism or fascism. Man cannot have it under communism, because economic progress under communism is not only a record of class conflict and ruthless suppression of one group by another but also of the total erosion of individual freedom and liberty. The individual's feelings, his mental and moral faculties are submerged in his function as an economic tool. We cannot have brotherhood under capitalism, because capitalism is the climax of economic pursuits which are not subordinate to the ethical discipline of religion. Therefore, all anti-social economic activities like monopolies, speculative business hoarding etc., which are not prohibited under capitalism in the name of individual freedom, prevent the culture of brotherhood. Again, we cannot have brotherhood under fascism, because fascism charges the state with the task of social and economic planning. It favours the notion of forced conformity in the name of the state. When an individual is denied the reasonable exercise of his God-given faculties, when he cannot influence the policies or change the personnel sitting astride the executive machine, when he has perforce to fall in line with what the ruling oligarchy decides and prescribes, he ceases to be a rational being; the question of brotherhood of man does not, therefore, arise under fascism. In the economic sphere, if there is any similarity between Islam and other "isms," it is with socialism minus its ruthless curb on individual initiative and drive.

Now I shall make a comparative analysis of systems on the basis of the principle of co-existence.

(d) Co-existence.

Unlike any other "ism", the basic principle of co-existence owes its origin to the Holy *Qur'ān* and the *Sunnah*. While the Holy *Qur'ān* commanded the Muslims to work wholly for peace (*Sūrah* II. 209), the Prophet himself exhibited this principle of the *Qur'ān* through his action and deeds.

Thus the Muslim greeting in all parts of the world is: "Peace be on you, and the mercy of Allah and His blessings". Every pursuit and activity which has the tendency to disturb the peace is severely condemned. "Do not promote disorder in the earth after peace has been established" (*Sūrah* VII. 56–57); "Do not go about committing iniquity in the earth and causing disorder" (*Sūrah* VII. 75); XI. 86; XXIX. 37); "They seek to create disorder and Allah loves not those who create disorder" (*Sūrah* V. 65); "Seek not to create disorder in the earth. Verily, God loves not those who seek to create disorder" (*Sūrah* XXVIII. 78).

Thus all the possible factors which tend to disturb the peace and order of society are strongly condemned by Islam. Domination of one group by another in the domestic sphere or of one people by another in the international sphere or economic exploitation of any form which may develop into a threat to peace is strictly prohibited. The *Qur'ān* says: "Do not raise thine eyes covetously after that which We have bestowed on some groups, to enjoy for a period, of the ornaments of this life that We may try them thereby—the provision bestowed upon thee by thy Lord is better and more enduring" (*Sūrah* XX. 132).

Again, many an international conflict arises because of the divergence between proclaimed intentions and policies and actual practice and conduct.

A true Islamic state cannot behave in such a manner. The *Qur'ān* emphasises complete conformity of conduct with declarations and professions of intent. "O ye who believe! Why do you say what you do not: most displeasing is it in the sight of Allah that you say what you do not" (*Sūrah* LXI. 3–4). On the other hand, the *Qur'ān* warns against indulgence in undue suspicion of other people's motives and against seeking to discover pretexts for differences and disagreements, as this might result in much harm. Even hostility toward a people should not incite a Muslim of the Muslim community or the Muslim State to act unjustly or inequitably toward them. "O ye who believe! Be steadfast in the cause of Allah, and bear witness in equity, and let not a people's enmity toward you incite you to act otherwise than with justice. Be always just, that is, closest to righteousness. Fear Allah, Surely, Allah is aware of what you do" (*Sūrah* V. 9).

No doubt, Islam takes note of the diversity that exists among nations and peoples, but inasmuch as God's sovereignty extends over the whole universe, the ultimate ideal of a State in Islam is a universal federation, or confederation, of autonomous States, associated together for upholding freedom of conscience and for the maintenance of peace and co-operation in promoting human welfare throughout the world.

In fact, the Islamic attitude towards idolatry, in spite of its uncompromising stand on the unity of God, is indicative of the firm Islamic faith in the principle of co-existence. The principle is that even false doctrines and unsocial and destructive ideas, so long as they are believed in and adhered to, must be taken into account as having an appeal to those who entertain them; all conduct which is likely to cause provocation should be avoided (*Sūrah* VI. 109). This tolerance is a unique contribution of Islam in the domain of international relations. A Muslim does not differentiate the secular from the religious and he is required to allow others to follow the dictates of their conscience. Such is the seminal demand of Islam. Islam does not merely tolerate but fully recognises the co-existence of other faiths in the political State evolved by it. The manifestation of the principle of co-existence we find in Islam has no counterpart in any other existing "ism". It is absent in communism, because communism believes in world revolution through material progress and is virtually nationalist in practice. This undue emphasis on material welfare will, I am sure, increase human greed and destructive ambition. This greed at the national level means a clash of interests with other nations resulting in international chaos and conflict.

The principle of co-existence is conspicuously absent in capitalism, because capitalism, in its drive for unrestricted ownership of the means of production and private profit, ultimately leads to imperialism, which resulted from the need of markets for finished goods and raw materials for industry. This means naked exploitation of a poorer nation by a richer one. Under capitalism this exploitation is there either in the name of financing poor nations' development programmes or in the name of "enlightened self-interest". Whatever argument we offer for capitalism in this regard, the fact remains that this inevitability of imperialism is the negation of the principle of co-existence. Clearly, militant nationalism under fascism cannot give this world of conflicting ideologies a lesson for co-existence. Even under socialism we cannot have the principle of co-existence fully manifested because the motive force of socialism is social service to the utter neglect of the motive for private profit and incentive. On the face of it, this may appear to be an ideal but it is not workable and practical. I wonder how the principle of co-existence can find its fullest expression and manifestation under such social systems.

(e) Sovereignty

Islam differs fundamentally from all other systems with regard to the concept of sovereignty. In Islam, sovereignty in all matters belongs to Allah and to no one else. It does not belong to the monarchs or to the state or even to the people. The people are the trustees of that power, that is, sovereignty. They are sovereign in their own way as the capitalist and socialist systems hold. Like capitalism, communism does not believe in the sovereignty of God. The Western democracies of the capitalist societies believe in the so-called sovereignty of the people. Again, sovereignty under communism is the sovereignty of the proletariat to the neglect of the wishes of the non-proletariat. Lastly, fascism believes in the sovereignty of the state which is, to them, an end in itself, not a means to an end.

The Islamic concept of sovereignty is superior to all these existing systems in at least two ways: firstly, its superiority lies in its belief in God and its fear of violation of the moral code of life given by God in the Holy *Qur'ān*—a code which can also bring harmony among the conflicting requirements of material life. This fear of God is expected to keep the Islamic governments always within the borders of democracy and justice in the real senses of the terms. Because of the ultimate sovereignty of God, Islamic democracy is more than a people's democracy or a proletariat democracy. As physical (personal) charm decreases, a human ruler's mental hold on the people also starts slipping. As Allah is not to be seen, His hold remains firm for all time to come.

Secondly, the Islamic concept of sovereignty is clearer and more simple than the concept of any other system. The Western concept of sovereignty is unclear and vague, because there are scores of schools giving their own theories with regard to the nature, extent and location of sovereignty. Here the strife between monistic and pluralistic concepts of sovereignty is still going on. Again, their concept of sovereignty (i.e. sovereignty of the people) is also misleading partly because people cannot act as the sovereign power and partly because people's sovereignty cannot guarantee people's welfare, especially as under capitalism the will of the people is rarely the will of all the people. Again, sovereignty under communism is confusing, because in theory it means the sovereignty of the people but, in practice, it becomes the sovereignty of the proletariat suppressing the individual's freedom of thought and conscience. The fascists' concept of the sovereignty of the state was so abstract that the individuals for whom the state existed lost their identity.

But the Islamic concept of sovereignty, on the other hand, is very simple, clear, reasonable and convincing. It is in consonance with the nature of things, with the place of mankind in the universe, with the position of the individual in society and the aims of moral, economic and political life evolved by it.

In fact, the original polity of Islam was a republican democracy where the head of the state—*Khalīfah* or *Amīr*—was chosen by the consensus of the citizens. He was the first citizen of the state but with no special privileges, being subject to all the laws of the realm. He was a constitutional head of the state, not a dictator. He was to be obeyed as long as he followed the principles laid down in the Holy *Qur'ān* and the *Sunnah*.

The moment the head starts disregarding any principle of the Holy *Qur'ān* and the established *Sunnah* of the Prophet, the people have every right to disobey him. Herein lies the role of opposition in an Islamic state. In his first address Hadrat Abū Bakr said: "Obey me as long as I obey God and His Prophet. In case I disobey God and His Prophet, I have no right to obedience from you." This opposition, of course, has to be political, not ideological. In an Islamic state there cannot be "party loyalty" as such. If truth lies on the opposite side, one must acknowledge it. Therefore, parties in an Islamic state must be radically different from those we see in capitalism, communism and fascism. The Western democracy of the capitalist countries believes more in so-called "party loyalty" than in truth and justice. Thus if truth lies on the opposite side, the other party will not normally acknowledge it as such. This is true even in the case of the most highly-developed democracy of the United Kingdom. Like fascism, communism believes in what the Communist Party says. "My party—right or wrong" is the slogan of communism as well as of fascism.

Again, that all men are equal in the eye of Allah is a gift of Islam to humanity. There is nothing original in the modern theory of the "rule of law". By guaranteeing security to life and property, Islam taught all the modern constitutions a basic moral code. By rejecting the narrow concept of nationality, Islam attacks the very root of present-day conflicts, dissensions and strife, and shows the communists a way out in their present conflict within their body politic. The Western democracies recognize the individual and give him the right to frame laws for his own good, but that right is only "indirect". The Communist democracy prescribes some birthrights to the individual but controls his brain. The individual has the right to vote but the government can be changed only by revolution and not otherwise.

While communism calls Western democracy a plutocracy, where, directly or indirectly, capital governs and labour is exploited, Western capitalism calls communism or so-called socialism totalitarianism, where power capitalism and domination of one party have deprived the individual of fundamental rights. Islam is neither Nazism nor fascism, neither plutocracy nor totalitarianism. It is humanitarianism and inter-nationalism. It guarantees full liberties of speech and action to all its members belonging to different religions, races, colours, languages, classes and castes. Here any exasperated majority does not inflict persecution on its minorities in the name of national security. In an Islamic state neither capital governs nor is labour exploited, nor are individuals deprived of their basic human rights. It is a democracy only in the sense that all people irrespective of race and creed are regarded equal before the law. The ultimate aim is to reach the goals of social justice and public welfare.

Again, minorities are a sacred trust in the Islamic state; they are in a more advantageous position than the Muslims, because they enjoy the same privileges as Muslims without discharging the obligations enjoined upon Muslims. Moreover, in an Islamic state the minority is not at the mercy of the majority, because the majority is not empowered by the Holy *Qur'ān* to frame any and every law on conducive to the welfare of the entire population irrespective of their faith, colour and creed.

Under Western democracy we find that the fate of the minority is entirely dependent on the whims of the so-called majority who can make any laws excepting "making a man a woman and woman a man". Not only this, we find a gloomy picture of persecution and victimization of minorities on the basis of colour and race under the garb of Western democracy. John Strachey, in his book *Menace of Fascism*, said: "Freedom in capitalist society always remains just about the same as it was in the ancient Greek Republics, freedom for the slave-owners. The modern wage-slaves owing to the condition of capitalist exploitation are so crushed by want and poverty that democracy is nothing to them. Politics is nothing to them; that in the ordinary course of events, the majority of the population is debarred from participating in social and political life." The same victimization of minorities under communism is there in the name of ideology and class conflict. Again, in the name of glorification of the state we find persecution of minorities under fascism. In a sense communism and fascism are the obverse and reverse of the same coin. But Islam is not, because both communism and fascism are social titanism. Man is liquidated in society. He is made to devote himself to superpersonal ends for the greater glory of the communist society. But when man finally ceases to exist as an independent entity, the society he is out to build up will also come to an end. This is a deep contradiction in itself.

Considering all these points it is tempting to conclude that the Islamic principles of social system, in which the principle of pure religion plays a part, have an appeal to humanity of all ages. Many of the social malices of the present' world of conflicting ideologies are bound to disappear if we implement the universal principles of Islam in our socio-economic systems. Dennis Saraut in his *History of Religions* writes. "Mohammadanism is not unequipped for survival in the modern world. Its great principles are simple and rational." But the fundamental problem before the Muslim states is how to put these principles into practice in the existing social systems, which are based on exploitation in varying degrees.

16.7 Selected Further Reading

Abdul Hakim, Khalifa, *Islam and Communism*, Institute of Islamic culture; Lahore, 1953.

Abdur Rauf, M. "Islam and Contemporary Economic Systems" in *Contemporary Aspects of Economic and Social Thinking in Islam*. M. S. A. of U.S.A., and Canada, Indiana, U.S.A. 1973.

Ahmad, Abu Sulaiman Abdul Hamid Ahmad, "The Theory of Economics of Islam: The Economics of Tawhid and Brotherhood, Philosophy concept and Suggestions" in *Contemporary Aspects of Economic and Social Thinking in Islam*, M.S.A. of U.S.A. and Canada, Indiana, 1973.

Akbar Muradpuri, Muhammad, *Conflict between Socialism and Islam*, Sh. Muhammad Ashraf, Lahore, 1970.

Hamidullah, Muhammad, "The Economic System of Islam" in *Introduction to Islam*, I.I.F.S.O., 1970.

Jomo, K. S. "Islam and Weber Rodinson on the Implications of Religion for Capitalist Development" in *The Developing Economics*, vol. 15, Tokyo, 1977.

Khan, Mohammad Akram, "Economic Implications of Tawhid, Rashid, Risala and Akhira" in *The Criterion,* vol. 12, 6/7, Karachi, 1977.

Mahmud, Abu Saud. "The Economic Order within the General Conception of Islamic Way of Life" in *Islamic Review*, London, 1967.

Mannan, M. A. "The State in Market Command and Islamic Society: in analysis of their paradigms and roles" in *The Making of Islamic Economic Society: Islamic Dimensions in Economic Analysis.* Chapter 8, International Association of Islamic Banks, Cairo, 1984.

CHAPTER 17

Islamic Social Order

17.1 Introduction: Family, Intrafamily and Collective Responsibility

17.2 Islamic Social Order: Its Salient Features

17.3 The Concept of the Welfare State in Islam: Moral, Spiritual, Social, Political and Economic Values

17.4 Selected Further Reading

"O mankind! we created
you from a single (pair)
Of a male and a female,
And made you into
Nations and tribes. That
ye may know each other
(Not that ye may despise
Each other). Verily
The most honoured of you
In the sight of God
Is (he who is) The most
Righteous of you.
And God has full knowledge
And is well acquainted
(With all things)"

Al-Qur'ān (*Sūrah* XLIX. 13)

"No man hath believed perfectly until he wisheth for his brother that which he wisheth for himself."

Prophet Muḥammad (peace be upon him)

17.1 Introduction: Family, Intrafamily and Collective Responsibility

The family is the basic unit of Islamic society. The foundation of a family is laid through marriage. Although marriage is a civil contract, imparting mutual duties and obligations on both husband and wife, yet it is the responsibility of a husband to support his wife and children as a matter of rule. The Prophet (peace be upon him) is reported to have said that the best among men is he who treats the members of his family best. Thus while great stress is laid on the proper upbringing and training of children, Islam does not approve of undue indulgence.

In an Islamic society, this family responsibility is not seen as an end in itself, but as a means to an end, because an individual's social and financial responsibilities do not end after meeting his immediate family obligations. If a person has the means, he has to extend his help not only to his poor and needy relatives but also to the deserving members of his community and neighbours. The fact that begging is prohibited by Islam except in the case of extreme need implies that better-off individuals have a social and moral responsibility to help the poor in the community.

Both the *Qur'ān* and the *Sunnah* have also emphasized the duty owed to a neighbour. In the same way, the needy and the wayfarer must be looked after. Orphans have been made the objects of particular care by the *Qur'ān*. Thus Kahf, in his book *The Islamic Economy* (p. 48), has rightly mentioned that "in order to strengthen the social orientation of Muslims, Islam introduced the concept of collective obligations which carry individual responsibility and accountability. In Islamic jurisprudence, this is called Fard-al-Kifayah. The concept emphasizes the needs of society and encourages individual effort in meeting them. Since it holds every individual responsible as long as these needs are not met, Fard-al-Kifayah means that in relation to areas of endeavour or knowledge which are essential for the Muslim community's well-being, it is sufficient if they are undertaken by some members of the community, but until the task is actually being performed by specific persons, every person in the community is individually responsible and accountable before Allah for it." It must be recognized that this notion of collective responsibility is not inconsistent with the principle of individual responsibility. It is this collective obligation which helps an individual to perform his individual responsibilities more effectively and efficiently.

17.2 Islamic Social Order: Its Salient Features

Meaning and Scope. The social order conceived of by Islam is mainly based on the teachings of the Holy *Qur'ān* and the sayings and practices of the Holy Prophet. It is neither capitalist nor communist, but it stands on its own and combines all the good features of a healthy and balanced society. Both the capitalist and communist systems are making great efforts in improving themselves in such a way that communism seems to have started to lose its rigidity towards the ownership of personal property and capitalism is finding more ways and means for the equitable distribution of national wealth for the benefit of the common people. But Islam has already provided for these fundamentals in its economic system where free enterprise and ownership of private property are allowed and accumulation of wealth in a few hands and exploitation of the poor by the rich are prohibited. This Islamic economic system is called Islamic socialism or social order.

The fundamental basis of Islamic democracy or socialism is summed up in the following verses of the Holy *Qur'ān*:

"We have made you an Ummah justly balanced, and seek to pursue the middle course.

O people! be careful of (your duty to) your Lord Who created you from a single being.

All people are a single nation." (*Sūrah* XLIX: 13)

Thus we have:

(*i*) Our duty to God Almighty.

(*ii*) Our duty to our fellow man who is equally free and worthy. This establishes the unity of all humanity.

(*iii*) The injunction to follow the middle path in all matters, of course, it is not geometrically or exactly physically the middle, only proverbially so. The intention is to steer clear of the extreme.

The desire to avoid the extreme in politics and economics gave rise to the use of the terms "Islamic democracy" and "Islamic socialism," which are really interchangeable, for the Islamic variation offers the best of the two systems.

This fact was admitted even by many Western thinkers of repute. Professor Arnold Toynbee, commenting in his *Civilization on Trial* on the racialism and nationalism of the Western culture, sees salvation for the world in Islam. "We can, however, discern certain principles of Islam which, if brought to bear on the social life of the new cosmopolitan proletariat, might have important and salutary effects on the great society, in a near future. The extinction of race-consciousness as between Muslims, is one of the outstanding achievements of Islam; and in the contemporary world there is, as it happens, a crying need for the propagation of this Islamic virtue. It is conceivable that the spirit of Islam might be the timely reinforcement which would decide this issue (of ascending racialism and nationalism) in favour of tolerance and peace."

Professor H. A. R. Gibb, in *Whither Islam*, says: "Within the western world, Islam still maintains the balance between exaggerated opposites. It has not yet succumbed to (that) obsession with the economic side of life." Professor Massignon, another orientalist, pays tribute to Islam thus: "Islam has the merit of standing for a very equalitarian conception. It occupies an intermediate position between the doctrines of bourgeois capitalism and Bolshevist Communism."

Social Equality.

The distinguishing mark of Islam is its respect for the individual, and for absolute human equality, irrespective of any other considerations at all. All enjoy equal status—socially, politically and economically. The status of women, minorities and slaves in Islam is matchless and proverbial. The dignity of labour is an article of faith in Islam.

"The believers are but a single brotherhood," says the Holy *Qur'ān*. Equality in Islamic socialism is equality before the law, and equality of opportunities to all without any favour or consideration. The history of Islam records many incidents which bear ample testimony to the fact that Islam believes in equality before the law both in theory and practice. The following two incidents may be cited as instances:

(*a*) The Caliph Ḥaḍrat 'Ali had lost a shield. A servant told 'Alī that he had seen the shield in the possession of a Jew. So 'Ali filed an application in the court of the *Qāḍi* (Judge) for the restoration of his property. The Jew was summoned and asked to prove that the shield was his. He replied that the fact that it was in his possession was enough proof that it was his; it was up to the Caliph to prove that it was his. Ḥaḍrat 'Ali presented his son Ḥusain and his servant as witnesses. The Jew objected that the testimony could not be accepted in law because one was his son and the other his servant. Though the *Qāḍi* knew personally that neither 'Ali nor Ḥusain could tell lies he dismissed the petition of the Caliph saying that the evidence offered was not acceptable to law. And the Caliph also accepted the verdict. The Jew was moved at the respect for law that he witnessed; he came to the Caliph, gave him the shield and announced that he had also decided to become a Muslim.

(*b*) A Christian had filed a suit before Caliph 'Umar ibn 'Abdul 'Aziz against Prince Hishām ibn 'Abdul Malik, who was sitting as one of the courtiers. It was then the custom for the complainant and the defendant to stand shoulder to shoulder before the court. Caliph 'Umar ibn 'Abdul 'Aziz asked Prince Hishām to get up and stand in front, along with the complainant before he began the enquiry. Prince Hishām's face grew red and he did not move from his seat. The Caliph at once commanded him to get up and stand in front, and added: "In Islamic justice, a Muslim prince and a Christian civilian are both equal" (*Muslim World*, 24 February 1968).

Thus in his book *Authors of History*, H. G. Wells rightly writes: "The stress Islam lays on equality of all men without any distinction of creed and class and the practical domestic brotherhood of Muslims has made the faith one of the greatest forces of the civilized world today." By laying special stress on merit and virtue to the entire exclusion of all other conventional labels and badges of distinction, Islam has created what in modern phraseology may be termed as "balanced society" or "inter-mediate community" as the Holy *Qur'ān* calls it. It does not merely emphasize social equality, but also disallows all such attitudes and activities as are likely to disrupt social harmony in the long run.

Exploitation and Private Property

Islam conceives of a society immune from class distinctions and vested interests, and hence free from the various kinds of class conflict, which threaten modern countries, excepting Russia (and China), with deep-seated economic maladies. "Whatever form it may have assumed, the exploitation of one part of society by the other has been a fact common to all past ages. In proportion as the exploitation of one individual by another comes to an end, the exploitation of one nation by another will come to an end" (Karl Marx).

According to Islam, land belongs to none but God. Therefore it is state property under Divine decree. In industry there cannot be any exploitation of labour by capital under Islam. Legal ownership by the individual, that is to say, the right of possession, enjoyment and transfer of property, is recognized and safeguarded in Islam, but all ownership is, as we have seen, subject to the moral obligation that in all wealth all sections of society, and even animals, have a right to share (*Qur'ān*, *Sūrah* LI. 20). Part of this obligation is given legal form and is made effective through legal sanctions, but the greater part is secured by voluntary effort put forth through the desire to achieve the highest moral and spiritual benefits for all concerned. In fact, this supplementing of legal obligations, which secure the irreducible minimum, with moral obligations to be discharged through voluntary effort runs through every part of the Islamic system. The uniqueness of the Islamic concept of private property lies in the fact that in Islam the legitimacy of ownership depends on the moral sign attached to it. In short, Islam purges private property of its vicious potentialities and allows it to have beneficial growth. The right to property is confined to essentials and necessities. Beyond that, one's wealth is to be spent in the way of God, through various channels. "The son of man." says the Prophet, "has no other right (than) that he would have a house wherein he may live, and a piece of cloth wherewith he may hide his nakedness, and a chip of bread and some water" (Tirmidhī). Nothing could be more socialist than that.

Within the framework of the bourgeois system of production, freedom means free trade, free buying and selling. Certainly we are concerned to make an end of bourgeois individuality, and bourgeois independence and bourgeois freedom. "Communism does not deprive anyone of the power of appropriating social products. It only does away with the power of turning that appropriation to account as a means for the subjugation of another's labour" (Marx). In their awareness and condemnation of, and to guard against, the evils of private property, Islam and socialism are equally vehement. But theoretically socialism goes the whole way, while Islam's is the middle path, the golden mean. Socialism starts with the dispossession, even forceful dispossession, of all owners of property. It envisages a cataclysmic change at the outset. It sublimates violence into revolutionary legalism. Islam, like socialism, views the unsocial accumulation of wealth with scorn and contempt because of its disturbing repercussions on society, but it lays down a different course of action. It countenances socio-economic gradations which do not prejudice the welfare of society. The Holy *Qur'ān* says: "God doth enlarge, or grant by strict measure the sustenance which He giveth, to whomso He pleaseth" (*Sūrah* III. 26). It allows the earning of money and the possession of it. Private enterprise is not taboo in Islam. It is disfavoured only when it assumes an aggressive role and cuts deep into the livelihood of the people at large. Under Islam, all the avenues of such morbid developments in trade and business are closed.

Economic Activities

Islam not only allows its followers freely to engage themselves in everyday economic activities for worldly possessions but also induces them strongly to work for a livelihood.

> "And when the prayer
> Is finished, then disperse
> Ye through the land
> And seek the bounty of God"
>
> (*Sūrah* LXII. 10)

Trade, commercial partnerships, co-operatives, joint-stock companies are all legitimate activities and operations (*Sūrah* II. 275). Islam does, however, lay down regulations with regard to commercial activities, designed to ensure that they are carried on honestly and beneficently. All contracts, whether involving large amounts or small, must be put down in writing, setting out all the terms thereof as this is"more equitable in the sight of Allah, and avoids disputes" (*Sūrah* II. 282). Monopolies and the cornering of commodities are prohibited; so also is the holding back of produce from the market in expectation of a rise in prices. All this is opposed to beneficence, and those who indulge in such practices seek to take advantage of the need or distress of their fellow beings. There are stern injunctions in the *Qur'ān* with regard to the giving of full weight and measure (*Sūrah* XXVI. 181–183).

Capitalism

The chief requisite for the existence and rule of the bourgeois is the accumulation of wealth in the hands of private individuals: the formation and increase of capital. The chief requisite for capital is wage labour. In bourgeois society, capital is independent and has individuality, whereas the living person is dependent and lacks individuality (Karl Marx).

Again, interest is the centre round which capitalism moves. Therefore, capitalism encourages hoarding of wealth. But Islam directs that wealth should not be hoarded. It should remain in circulation and should be invested to provide productivity in society.

"Who hoard their wealth
And enjoin avarice on others
And hide what Allah hath bestowed
Upon them of His bounty.
For disbelievers We prepare
A shameful doom."

(*Sūrah* IV. 37)

Again, the lending of money on interest or usury is strictly prohibited as it results in economic crises and makes the rich richer and the poor poorer. Islam has, therefore, allowed banking and financing on a partnership basis where the creditor and borrower should share the profit and loss of the enterprise equitably.

"But God has permitted trade
And forbidden usury"

(*Sūrah* II. 275)

The Prophet (peace be upon him) has condemned both the receiver and the giver of usury (Bukhārī).

The harmful effects of interest on the traditional capitalist countries were found to be so deep, especially during the Great Depression of 1929–33, that the economists of those countries were forced to discard the classical economic theories and evolve new ones advocating the elimination of interest from their economic institutions. John Maynard Keynes (1883–1946), the pioneer of the new economic theories, looking at the expanding money supply, predicted in his famous book, *The General Theory of Employment, Interest and Money,* published in 1936, that the rate of interest would approach zero in the next thirty years (p. 220).

Islamic Social Order

In fact, the workability of the economic principles of the elimination of interest as enunciated by the *Qur'ān* is manifested through the successful operations of over 30 Islamic Banks, established during the '70s. This experimentation could be the sine qua non for full employment and economic growth in Muslim Countries.

"In fact, the great economic principle of the elimination of interest, as enunciated by the *Qur'ān*, is found by modern research and experimentation to be the sine qua non for full employment and economic growth."

Again, Islam offers a blow to capitalism by condemning the concentration of wealth in a few hands; Islam does not allow that wealth should be concentrated in a few hands to disturb the equilibrium of the society, because it results in exploitation of the poor by the rich. The Qur'ān states that some of God's gifts belong to:

"The needy and the wayfarer;
In order that wealth may not
Make a circuit merely
Between the wealthy among you."

(*Sūrah* LIX. 7)

Planning

The modern concept of planning which refers to the utilization of the resources of the country to attain certain objectives is recognized in Islam. Economic planning in Islam is nothing but a synthesis of planning by inducement and planning by direction. Various injunctions of the Holy *Qur'ān* and sayings of the Prophet (peace be upon him) confirm it. Cooperation between public and private sectors is the basis of economic planning in Islam. The objectives of economic planning in Islam are relative to the needs of the community, and they can be changed with the changing circumstances subject to the injunctions of the Holy *Qur'ān* and the *Sunnah*. The soundness of its objectives can be judged by the principle of beneficence and care for the poor. The execution of planning will be made through the participation of both public and private sectors on a partnership basis, which will work through the application of the principle of *Mudārabah*. It is because of this that there will be fewer chances of loss and less possibility of economic depression under the Islamic system of planning.

Social Justice

The institution of *Zakāt* and the Islamic doctrine of inheritance are the pillars of the Islamic concept of social justice. Islam has provided the institution of *Zakāt* whereby well-off people have to contribute to a compulsory charity to provide relief to the poor and the distressed and thus to eradicate poverty from society. It also serves the purpose that wealth cannot be hoarded indefinitely by any one person.

"Establish worship, pay the poor-due (*Zakāt*)
And bow your heads with those who
Bow in worship"

(*Sūrah* II. 43)

The Islamic concept of taxation is so comprehensive and broadbased that it not only promotes socialist redistribution of wealth but also creates a healthy non-capitalist frame of mind and a collective spirit. Thus *Zakāt* generates and releases the positive forces of socialism. In order that wealth may not be concentrated in a few hands, Islam makes it obligatory to distribute the property of a deceased person among a large number of heirs under the Islamic law of inheritance. Under this law, the property is distributed among male as well as female heirs. One cannot make an extra legacy worth more than one third of the property. This law of inheritance also shows the active participation of women in economic activities allowed by Islam. There is a group of thinkers who hold the view that the Islamic law of inheritance has aggravated the problem of the subdivision and fragmentation of holdings. But it is not that great a problem. This can be prevented by legislation prescribing the size of a minimum holding and by paying off other heirs in convenient instalments. (Egypt has already passed such legislation and other Muslim countries are bound to follow suit during the course of agrarian reforms that are being rapidly effected in all Muslim lands. Muslim peasant-proprietors may be encouraged by the state to adopt a system of co-operative farming in the interests of increased production.)

Islam advocates the provision of basic needs because it believes in a society where the state should be responsible for providing a living wage to every inhabitant of the country. To ensure social justice for the people the state should also take responsibility for providing the basic needs of every citizen of the country for clothing, food and shelter. This will serve as a solution to the economic ills of the unequitable distribution of national wealth among the people of the country.

Perhaps we can sum up by saying that Islamic socialism condemns capitalism and exploitation in all forms; it is based on the eternal principle of social justice, equality and universal brotherhood of man. The crying need of the hour is to strike a balance between conflicting ideologies. We have the Quaid-i-Azam's wise choice and decision: "Pakistan should be based on sure foundations of social justice and Islamic Socialism (not any other 'ism)—which emphasizes the equality and brotherhood of man."

17.3 The Concept of a Welfare State in Islam

The concept of a welfare state is gradually gaining ground day by day in a number of modern states. This concept of the welfare state is based either on the Marxian interpretation of history or on the principles of welfare economics of Professor Pigou. In both cases emphasis is given to the material welfare of the people to the neglect of their spiritual and moral welfare. But the Islamic concept of the welfare state differs fundamentally from the prevailing notion of the same. Because its concept is so comprehensive in nature, the welfare state in Islam aims at achieving the total welfare of mankind, of which economic welfare is merely a part. Equal stress on *Zakāt* and *Salāt* in the *Qur'ān* is quite significant for a proper understanding of the true nature of the welfare state in Islam. Its social and economic effects are wholesome and the social pattern that emerges is free from the hideous tyrannies of capitalism and the coercive standardization of communist society. It was this all-pervading social harmony that led H. G. Wells to remark: "Islam has created a society more free from widespread cruelty and social oppression than any society had ever been in the world before."[1] As a matter of fact, the Islamic concept of the welfare state is based not only on the manifestation of economic values but also on the moral and spiritual, social and political values of Islam. Let us now discuss in some detail the nature of these values and the part a Muslim state can play in fostering those values.

Moral and Spiritual Values.

The basis of moral and spiritual values lies in their acceptance of life and its proper development. "Righteous living, making proper and balanced use of one's faculties and of the bounties provided by God, is the rule of life" (*Sūrah* XXIII. 51). "Say, 'Who has prohibited the use of the good and pure things which God has provided for His creatures?'" (*Sūrah* VII. 32).

Within this general concept, the *Qur'ān* lays down detailed instructions for the fostering of moral and spiritual values. The object is the beneficent and co-ordinated development of all faculties. Whatsoever God has bestowed upon man by way of inner faculties and external possessions must all be put to appropriate use. That use must be adjusted and regulated, otherwise it would cease to be a moral activity. Islam teaches that natural instincts and tendencies are converted into moral qualities through their proper regulation and adjustment by the exercise of reason and judgement. The *Qur'ān* classifies moral qualities from different points of view. There are those that relate to the mind and those that relate to the body. The *Qur'ān* directs: "Approach not evils and indecencies whether manifest or hidden". (*Sūrah* VI. 151).

Man is accountable in respect of two kinds of conduct: that which manifests itself in action and that which is contemplated and meditated but does not find expression. The *Qur'ān* places every person under an obligation to safeguard and promote the welfare of his own soul as well as the welfare of his fellow beings (*Sūrah* V. 108; III. 110, 114, 115). A penalty proportionate to the wrong committed is permissible, but it is better to forgive where forgiveness may be reasonably expected to help the offender improve himself—and it is even better to add benevolence to forgiveness. To endure wrong patiently and to forgive is described as a "matter of high resolve" (*Sūrah* III.186; *Sūrah* XXXI.17; (*Sūrah* XLII. 43).

The *Qur'ān* declares that the strongest and highest love of those who believe is for Allah, meaning that the love of God must come before everything else (*Sūrah* II.165). Here is a very clear gradation in the matter of the duty derived from love and affection: "Worship Allah and associate naught with Him, and conduct yourselves with beneficence toward parents, and toward kindred and orphans, and the needy, and toward the neighbour that is of the kindred, and the neighbour that is a stranger, and the companions by your side, and the wayfarer, and those who work for you. Surely, Allah loves not the proud and boastful who are niggardly and enjoin people to niggardliness" *Sūrah* IV.37–38). Love of children is not stressed, for it is a natural instinct. But the *Qur'ān* stresses the need for their proper upbringing and points out that love of children involves the duty of safeguarding their future, both here and in the hereafter (*Sūrah* LXVI.7).

The natural instinct opposed to love is hate, repugnance, or enmity. In the first place it is not a moral quality at all; it is a natural instinct. Its proper regulation converts it into a moral quality. One must hate evil; one must resent certain types of wrongdoing. Another natural instinct is the desire to outstrip one's fellow beings in the race for progress. The *Qur'ān* says that everyone has an urge toward the achievement of some purpose, but that the proper goal toward which to direct this urge is the progressive achievement of righteousness (*Sūrah* II.149). If this instinct is not properly regulated it might generate envy, fault-finding and lack of appreciation of the good qualities of others. It might make a man proud and boastful. In short, natural instincts are a bounty of God as much as mental and physical capacities. It is not their essential nature, but their proper or improper exercise that is good or evil. Indeed, the neglect of any capacity is itself evil inasmuch as it amounts to misuse of it. That is why Islam does not permit celibacy or monasticism as a way of life. It recognizes that the people who instituted these systems did so with a good motive, but inasmuch as the systems offended against the principle of the beneficent use of all faculties and capacities, they lent themselves to abuse and did harm (*Sūrah* LVII. 28).

The Islamic state must take the responsibility of converting natural instincts into moral qualities. To achieve this end there is an imperative need for a reorientation of the educational systems of the Muslim states. The syllabuses of schools, colleges and universities should be fashioned in such a manner that the future generation is imbued with the spirit of Islam.

Social Values. The Islamic concept of the welfare state is also concerned with the fostering of social values which are so comprehensive in nature that they regulate one's behaviour and code of conduct with regard to one's family life, one's servants, one's neighbours, one's management of orphans' property and so on. The object of all these instructions as laid down in the *Qur'ān* and the *Sunnah* is to set up a healthy society based on the lasting welfare of mankind.

The *Qur'ān* takes note of the diversities of race, colour, language, wealth, etc., which serve man's own useful purposes in the social scheme, and describes them as signs of God for those who hear and possess knowledge (*Sūrah* XXX. 22, 23). But none of these confers any privilege or imposes any disability. The *Qur'ān* says that God has divided mankind into tribes and nations for greater facility of intercourse. Neither membership of a tribe nor citizenship in a state confers any privilege, nor are they sources of honour. The true source of honour in the sight of God is a righteous life (*Sūrah* XLIX. 13). In his Farewell Address, the Prophet said: "You are all brothers and are all equal. None of you can claim any privilege or superiority over any other. An Arab is not to be preferred to a non-Arab, nor is a non-Arab to be preferred to an Arab."

It is only the consciousness that mankind are all equally creatures and servants of God and that they must all constantly seek the pleasure of God, that can bring about the realization of true brotherhood, which can stand the test of all the contingencies to which life is subject. "Hold fast, all together, by the rope of Allah, and be not divided: and remember the favour of Allah" (*Sūrah* III.103).

This sublime aspect of the Islamic teachings has evoked glowing tributes even from the enemies of Islam. Dr Dhalla, in his book *Our Perfecting World*, says: "Muhammadanism alone among the religions of the world has remained free from the colour bias. It welcomes all converts with open arms, whether they be negroes or pariahs. Without reserve it accords them their rights and privileges and receives them into its social circle as much as into its religion. It excludes all barriers of birth and colour and admits its converts within the community on the basis of complete social equality." Dr Dennison Ross says: "It was among the Arabs that the man was born who was to unite the whole known world of the East and the West. This unique concept of brotherhood of Muslims has made Islam one of the greatest forces of the civilized world today."

Political Values.

But the most important characteristic of the welfare state lies in its political values. Unlike modern Western democracy, sovereignty in the Islamic state belongs to Almighty Allah and equality of mankind in His eyes distinguishes the rule of law of the Islamic states from that of Western countries. In Western democracy, sovereignty belongs to the people. Thus, the head of the state with his so-called majority can make or interpret any law suited to his requirements. In such a state of affairs the so-called minority or rather the whole of mankind, is really at the mercy of the so-called majority.

The term used for governmental or political authority in Islam is the "*Khilāfat*" or Vicegerency. It speaks of man's vice-gerency. He is not an absolute sovereign. He is a deputy working with delegated powers—an agent working under the authority of the principal. Unlike Aristotle and Plato, or Hegel and Green, Islam does not consider the state to be an end itself. Nor does it consider the state to be the repository of absolute sovereignty. Islam is perhaps the first religion to put forward the philosophy of limited sovereignty, by using the word "vicegerent" in place of "ruler", "monarch" or "sovereign". This doctrine of limited sovereignty is the first thing that needs to be borne in mind for understanding the Islamic concept of the state. In Islam the state is a means to an end, the end being to "enjoin what is good and forbid evil" (*Sūrah* III.110) and make justice prevail in the world (*Sūrah* LVII.25). The beneficent and harmonious working of human society in accordance with the law and the will of the Creator is the end that is sought to be achieved through the state in Islam. The sovereignty of man, therefore, is limited by Divine Ordinances and by the principles on which they are based.

But a study of the Holy *Qur'ān* also reveals that the limited sovereignty or vicegerency is vested in the people and not in any individual. "Allah hath promised such of you as believe and do good works that He will surely make them successors in the earth" (*Sūrah* XXIV. 55). It is the society as a whole that has been promised succession or vicegerency and not one individual.

That is the second characteristic of the Islamic concept of the state. Similarly, "Allah commands you to make over the trusts to those entitled to them, and that, when you judge between men, you judge with justice" (*Sūrah* IV. 58). In this verse also it is the people as a whole who have been addressed and asked to make over the trust, that is, the political authority, to those who deserve.

The concept of the state that emerges is: (1) that real and absolute sovereignty belongs to Allah; (2) that man being His vicegerent has been vested with limited sovereignty. The rights and obligations of both man and state stem from the Divine Law and both of them are bound to submit to that law.

In the theory of Muslim Law, a "contract" is not a bilateral bond. It is really a trilateral one, God being the third party. "Who is a surety for the due performance of the obligations contracted for by those entering into a contract" (*Sūrah* XVI. 91). It is clear that the only kind of government recognized by Islam is a representative government. The word "trust" used in the verse also indicates that those who are elected to discharge the responsibilities of the state should return the "trust" to the real owners, that is, the people, and should not pass it over on a hereditary basis.

That being the nature of things, we have now to see whether political opposition is possible in such a state. The Holy *Qur'ān* has prescribed certain guiding principles for those in authority and has also given certain directions to the people. Those in authority have been enjoined to conduct themselves in accordance with the law of God and His Messenger and have been warned that "whoso judges not by that which Allah has sent down, these it is who are the disbelievers" (*Sūrah* V. 47) and "these it is who are wrongdoers" (*Sūrah* V. 48) and "whoso judge not by what Allah has revealed, these it is who are the rebellious" (*Sūrah* V. 50). They have also been directed to "take whatsoever the Messenger gives, and to abstain from whatsoever the Messenger forbids" (*Sūrah* LIX. 7). They have also been warned that they should not follow the evil inclinations turning away from the truth "that has come to thee" (*Sūrah* V. 51).

The people, on the other hand, have been asked to obey those in authority and not to disobey what is right" (*Sūrah* IV. 59) and "to help not one another in sin and transgression" (*Sūrah* V. 3) and "to yield not to anyone among them who is sinful" (*Sūrah* LXXVI. 24). These limitations of obedience indicate that the people have a right to disagree with those in authority when the clear law of God and the Prophet is being disregarded. Where obedience ends, disagreement and opposition start. The fact that there is a limitation to obedience is tantamount to saying that there is a point where opposition should step in. Thus in his first address Ḥaḍrat Abū Bakr said: "Obey me as long as I obey God and His

Prophet. In case I disobey God and His Prophet, I have no right to obedience from you". He also said: "Help me if I am in the right and set me right if I am in the wrong". Similarly, in one of his addresses, Ḥaḍrat 'Umar said that "nobody should be obeyed in disobedience to God". After becoming *Khalifah*, Ḥaḍrat 'Uthmān also reiterated the same principle. Ḥaḍrat Ali said: "As long as I obey God, you must obey all my commands whether you like them or not; if I disobey God, then none need be obeyed in defiance of Allah". All this suggests ample scope for opposition, at least on an individual level.

But whether there can be opposition on the basis of a party system, as exists in modern democracies, requires analysis. MacIver defines a political party as an association of individuals organized in support of some principle or policy which, by constitutional means, it endeavours to make the determinant of government. If the sole and primary purpose of a political party be to capture political power, such a party, in my view, would not be in keeping with the spirit of Islam. Islam insists on unity of faith and action and enjoins us to "hold fast, all together, by the rope of Allah and be not divided" (*Sūrah* III.103).

In an Islamic state, elections or expressions of popular will, in one way or the other, are likely to be a regular feature; in everyday matters also, people are likely to have divergent views. Islam being the greatest exponent of freedom of conscience, this divergence of views is to be welcomed. The opposition, of course, has to be political and not ideological. In an Islamic state loyalty is only to the constitution and to truth. There is no such thing as party loyalty. If truth lies on the opposite side one must acknowledge it as such. In my view political opposition is possible on the basis of party system, but parties in an Islamic state would be radically different from the ones we see in modern democracies. It is for the modern Muslim state to evolve a system that may reflect all the Islamic principles. Islam has nothing against a party that is based on the principle of helping one another in righteousness and piety. Hence there is little or no scope for exploitation of the minority by the majority. A welfare state in Islam must be based on the proper realization of this political value.

Economic Values.

The last, but not least of the values, are economic values, the proper manifestation of which is one of the basic aims of the welfare state in Islam. The basic economic values of Islam start with the fact that absolute ownership of everything belongs to Allah and the whole of mankind is His vicegerent on the earth and everybody has a share in its resources. Thus everybody has the right to participate in the process of production, and no section of society will be ignored in the process of distribution.

Legal ownership by the individual is recognized and safeguarded in Islam, but all ownership is subject to the moral obligation that in all wealth all sections of society, and even animals, have a right to share

(*Sūrah* LI. 19). In fact, this supplementing of legal obligations to be discharged through voluntary effort runs through every part of the Islamic system.

Islam has encouraged all types of economic activities subject to the injunctions of the *Qur'ān* and the *Sunnah*. Monopolies and speculative businesses are prohibited because they are opposed to beneficence.

Islam views with extreme disfavour the monopoly of resources by a few self-seeking millionaires. The Holy *Qur'an* says:

"In order that it (wealth) may not
(Merely) make a circuit
Between the wealthy among you."

(Sūrah LIX. 7)

The Holy Prophet (peace and blessings of God be upon him) commends and commands socially beneficial expenditure: "Riches (i.e. *Zakāt*) should be taken from the rich and returned to the poor" (Bukhārī).

There is a grievous punishment in store for those who abuse their riches to the detriment of society. God commands:

(The stern command will say:)
"Seize ye him,
And bind ye him,
And burn ye him,
In the Blazing Fire.
Further, make him march
In a chain, whereof
The length is seventy cubits"

(Sūrah LXIX. 30–32).

Islam, as the above-quoted verses prove, is all for the equitable distribution of wealth and does not countenance the idle hoarding of the Napoleons of finance and others of their ilk who profiteer at the cost of others. But, unlike communism, Islam does not hold rich men under a sentence of death. It permits the holding of what is known as functional property and encourages the productive and beneficial use of capital. The motive of the Islamic teachings in regard to the economic system is that they seek to discourage hoarding and stimulate spending, because wealth, whether in the hands of one or a few men, has a social destiny. The Holy Book says:

"Speak to My servants
Who have believed,
That they may establish
Regular prayers and spend
(In charity) out of the Sustenance

We have given them,
Secretly, and openly, before
The coming of a Day
In which there will be
Neither mutual bargaining
Nor befriending". (*Sūrah* XIV. 31)
"And spend (in charity)
Out of what We have provided
For them, secretly and openly.
Hope for Commerce
That will never fail.

(*Sūrah* XXXV. 29)

It is obvious that the stress is on socially beneficial spending only. Lest it should be misinterpreted, God warns against ostentatious extravagance and reckless spending. He commands:

"But waste not
By excess, for God loveth not wasters"

(*Sūrah* XIV. 14)

"Verily spendthrifts are brothers
Of the Evil Ones;
And the Evil One
Is to his Lord (Himself)
Ungrateful"

(*Sūrah* XVII. 27)

Thus we see that niggardliness is condemned as a negative and destructive quality. Wealth of misers, instead of bringing them any advantage, becomes a handicap and arrests their moral and spiritual development (*Sūrah* III. 180). The other extreme, extravagance, is equally condemned. Again, "hoarding is absolutely prohibited because it puts wealth out of circulation and deprives the owner as well as the rest of the community of its beneficent use" (*Sūrah* IX. 34).

Islam prohibits interest because interest has nothing to do with influencing the volume of saving, because it makes depression chronic, because it aggravates the unemployment problem and, finally, because it encourages unequal distribution of wealth. Modern banks charge interest regardless of any loss and profit to business men. It can, therefore, be seen that under a capitalistic economy an organized attempt is being made to further the interests of the rich and preclude the possibility of establishing economic equilibrium in society. As against this Islam has tried to bring economic equality in the state by imposing *Zakāt* on surplus funds.

The institution of *Zakāt* is an element in Islamic socialism. *Zakāt* is, in fact, a tax which the rich have to pay towards the common welfare of the nation as a whole. It intends to take wealth from the rich and to return it to the poor. In the light of such an explicit objective, Professor Pigou's cry for welfare economics on the basis of transference of wealth from the rich to the poor has nothing original in it. During Caliphate days *Zakāt* was so comprehensive and broadbased that it not only produced socialist redistribution of wealth but also tended to create a healthy noncapitalist frame of mind and a collective spirit.

Lastly, the Islamic law of inheritance runs counter to the concentration of wealth in a few hands and, by allowing women to take their share in the ownership of property, Islam encourages the participation of women in economic activities. The basic objective of all these economic values is to increase the total economic wealth, which must have the widest and most beneficent distribution among all sections of the community and should not become the monopoly of the rich. (*Sūrah* XIX. 7).

Thus the welfare state in Islam is based on the harmonious development and manifestation of all possible values of life—moral and spiritual, social, economic and political. However, there is hardly any Muslim country in our contemporary society which fulfils the conditions of an Islamic welfare state. We need not only functional changes but also basic structural reforms in many of the existing social and economic institutions of Muslim societies of today.

17.4 Selected Further Reading

Abdullah, Al-Araby Muhammad, *Economics in the Social Structure of Islam*, World Muslim League, Singapore, 1966.

Ahmad, Sh. Mahmud, *Social Justice in Islam*, Institute of Islamic culture, Lahore, 1975.

Ahmad, Ajmal, "Social Work in the Light of Islam", in *Voice of Islam*, vol. 12, Karachi, 1963/64.

Ali, Shaukat, *Administrative Ethics in a Muslim State*, Publishers United, Lahore, 1975.

Chapra, M. U. "The Islamic Welfare State and its Role in the Economy", in *Islamic perspectives*, ed. by Khurshid Ahmad, Zafar Ishaq Ansari. The Islamic Foundation, Leicester, 1979.

Goitein, S. D. "Commercial and Family Partnership in the Countries of Medieval Islam" in *Islamic Studies*, vol. III, no. 3, Islamabad, 1964.

Hasan, A. "Social Justice in Islam", *Islamic Studies*, vol. X, no. 3, Islamabad, 1971.

Hasanuzzaman, S. M. *The Function of the State in the Early Period of Islam*, International Publications, Karachi, Pakistan, 1982.

Irving, T. B. *Islam and Social Responsibility*, 2nd revised edition, The Islamic Foundation, Leicester, 1971.

Kotb, Syed, *Social Justice in Islam*, Octagon Books, New York *Reprinted from a 1953 edition of the American Council of Learned Societies.*

Mannan, M. A. "Nature and Scope of Individual Society-State Relationship and its Socio-Economic Significance" in *The Making of*

Islamic Economic Society: Islamic Dimensions in Economic Analysis. Chapter 6, International Association of Islamic Banks, Cairo, 1984.

Mannan, M. A. "The Structure of Social Justice in Islam: Perspectives on Social and Economic goals" in *The Making of Islamic Economic Society: Islamic dimensions in Economic Analysis*, Chapter 7, International Association of Islamic Banks, Cairo, 1984.

Mintiges, H. "Social Justice in Islam", Institute for the Study of Religion, Free University, Amsterdam, 1977.

Nazeer, Mian M. *The Islamic Economic System – A Few Highlights* (Pakistan Institute of Development Economics, Islamabad, 1981.

Nait-Belkacem, M. K. "The Concept of Social Justice in Islam" in, *The Challenge of Islam*, ed. by Altar Gauhar, Islamic Council of Europe, London, 1978.

Nowaihi, Muhammad, "Fundamentals of Economic Justice in Islam" in *Contemporary Aspects of Economic and Social Thinking in Islam*, M.S.A. of U.S.A. and Canada, Indiana U.S.A., 1973.

Qureshi, A. I. "*The Economic and Social System of Islam*, Islamic Book Service, Lahore, 1979.

Yousef, S. M. "Economic Justice in Islam", Sh. Muhammad Ashraf, Lahore, 1971.

CHAPTER 18

Planning and Development in Islam

18.1 Economic Planning in Islam:

(a) Its Meaning

(b) Objectives

(c) Execution of planning

(d) Method of Financing

(e) Necessity of Planning in an Islamic State

18.2 Economic Development in Islam:

(a) Its Meaning

(b) The prerequisites for Growth and Islam as a Factor of Development

18.3 Some Aspects of Economic Development in Muslim Countries.

(a) Development Experiences and the Scale of Poverty

(b) Minimum Provisioning For Living

(c) The importance of social appropriateness in the transfer of technology

(d) The 'Ulamā' and Development

18.4 Summary and Conclusions.

Planning

Economic Development

18.5 Selected Further Reading.

"He sends down water
From the skies, and the channels
Flow, each according to its measure:
But the torrent bears away
The foam that mounts up
To the surface. Even so,
From that (ore) which they heat
In the fire, to make ornaments
Or utensils therewith,
there is a scum likewise
Thus doth God (by parables)
Show forth Truth and vanity.
For the scum disappears
Like froth cast out;
While that which is for the good
Of mankind remains
On the earth. Thus doth God
Set forth parables."

(*Al-Qur'ān, Sūrah* XIII. 17)

"It is the predicament of our age that we realise that planning is necessary, but also know that wrong planning may be disastrous. It has always been open to question how far institutions can foster religious experience . . . but now mankind is engaged in a life and death struggle for civilization, even the engineer realises that society is rooted in deeper layers of the human soul than he ever thought."

Karl Mannheim, *Diagnosis of Our Time*

18.1 Economic Planning in Islam

(a) Its Meaning.

Economic planning in Islam seems to provide a realizable synthesis of planning by inducement and planning by direction. Various injunctions of the Holy *Qur'ān* and the *Sunnah* have confirmed this, although no evidence has been found to indicate any systematic treatment of the subject. However, we all know that Islam stands for a happy blending of the spiritual and material values of life. Therefore, worldly occupations are recommended again and again both in the *Qur'ān* and the *Hadith*. The *Qur'ān* says:

"And when the Prayer
Is finished, then may ye
Disperse through the land,
And seek the Bounty of Allah".

(*Sūrah* LXII. 10)

Modern planning is nothing but the utilization of this "bounty of Allah" in a systematic manner to achieve certain objectives keeping in view the changing needs of the community and values of life. In a wider sense planning refers to the preparation of schemes for any and every economic activity. As Professor Robbins has observed, all economic life involves planning. The consumer spending his income and the producer deciding what to produce are both planning. But we cannot accept this view of planning mainly because of the fact that there is usually more than one individual involved. The different plans may come into conflict with each other resulting in disorder and economic chaos, and this chaos may lead to wastage of resources. But the *Qur'ān* has condemned all wastage of resources, human and material. Therefore, the modern concept of planning, which should be understood in a restricted sense, is recognized in Islam, because such planning implies the best possible exploitation of the resources which God has provided for man's subsistence and comfort.

Needless to mention that all the original resources of wealth—the sun, the moon, the stars, the earth, the clouds that bring rain, the winds that drive the clouds and carry the pollen, all phenomena of Nature—are the gift of Allah to the whole of mankind. There are two ways of using "this gift of Allah". One way is planning by direction and the other planning by encouragement. In communist countries we find planning by direction. In this approach, the problem of finding resources is approached from the standpoint of estimating the resources needed for achieving predetermined targets of national income, employment and production. Here all the resources of the community are regarded as available for being pressed into development work. This necessarily means the imposition of extensive controls in order to direct all resources into the desired channel for achieving the prescribed targets. This approach to planning is based on the materialistic interpretation of history and the economic theory of exploitation. This type of planning is foreign to Islam because of Islam's faith in private ownership, individual freedom and democracy.

Moreover, Islam does not believe in Marx's materialistic interpretation of history. The *Qur'ān* recognizes the diversity of capacities and talents, which in itself is beneficent, and, consequently, the diversity of earnings and material rewards (*Sūrah* V. 32). It does not approve of dead-level equality in the distribution of wealth, as that would defeat the very purpose of the diversity and would amount to denying the favour of Allah (*Sūrah* XVI. 71). Therefore, in the Islamic state the problem of finding resources should be approached from the standpoint of estimating the maximum amount of resources which the community will be willing to devote to development either through public or private saving. This does not necessarily mean that Islam believes in planning by inducement only. If need be, the Islamic state may direct all resources—material and human—toward the benefit of the community as a whole, as is apparent from the early history of financial administration in Islam when, beginning with persuasion and recommendation, duties were enforced with all the power that society could command. This was true of *Zakāt*. The history of Islam records many incidents where the State enforced payment of *Zakāt* and the Caliph Abū Bakr waged war against those who defaulted in the payment of it. Again, private ownership is recognized in Islam. But the *Sharī'ah* of Islam lays down that the owner of the property must discharge his social responsibilities in a manner consistent with the injunctions of the Holy *Qur'ān* and the *Sunnah*, otherwise the state can intervene and deprive him of ownership.

All these instances bear ample testimony to the fact that planning in Islam relied largely on individual initiative while the State took upon itself the dual role of a brake and an accelerator. Thus, Islam seems to provide the best realizable synthesis of the two opposites; incentive to work is retained by recognizing the restricted private ownership of property and perfect socialist effects are produced by enforcing compulsory distribution of excess of income and property. The structure of the Islamic economy is capitalist in outline though largely restricted by socialist institutions.

In fact, co-operation between public and private sectors is the basis of economic planning in Islam. In the case of failure of co-operation the state can intervene in order to achieve the social objectives of planning.

(b) Objectives.

We have already mentioned that modern economic planning is done to achieve certain objectives. The theoretical reason for a statement of objectives is that it defines ends from which a choice of criteria can be derived. In this way value judgments can be made by responsible leaders at the beginning of the planning operations and the remainder of the planning work can be turned into a merely technical process of deciding and applying criteria that select the set of actions which will best serve the selected objectives.

Thus what is a beneficial objective to the community depends both on the conditions of that community at a particular time and on the values of life. Therefore, the objectives of modern planning vary from state to state. Islam maintains a balance between exaggerated "opposites". No doubt, objectives of economic planning in Islam are relative to the needs of the community and this changes with the changing circumstances subject to the injunctions of the Holy *Qur'ān* and the *Sunnah*. The soundness of the objectives of Islamic planning will be judged by the principle of beneficence and care for the poor. Planning in Islam must move towards a viable synthesis between the claims of economic growth and social justice through the pursuit of pragmatic policies, consistent with the spirit of Islam. Many subsidiary objectives may be formulated from these basic objectives. Of course, there might be a conflict between various objectives under the Islamic framework of planning. But in all cases, a balance will have to be sought between various interests, and the predominant intention will be to promote benefits and prevent harm. The noted jurist Ibn al-Qayyam says:

"If one contemplates the laws which the Almighty ordained for His creatures one finds that they are all designed to ensure a balance of benefits and that where there is a conflict preference is given to the more important as against the less important. The laws also seek to prevent the infliction of harm, but where harm is inevitable, the lesser of evils is preferred. These are the principles implicit in the laws of Allah, which eloquently speak of His wisdom and compassion."

Therefore, the planners in an Islamic state must keep in view this basic principle in formulating the various objectives of planning. Let us now take up the principle of execution of planning.

(c) Execution of Planning.

For achieving the objectives of economic planning in Islam we are to depend on the universally recognized principles of *Shirākat* (i.e. co-operation). That is, the execution of planning will be made through the participation of both public and private sectors on a partnership basis. This will, we are sure, work through the application of the eternal principle of *Muḍārabah*, where labour and capital can be combined together as partners. It is not merely a partnership in the modern sense of the term. It is something more than this because Islam has provided a code of economic ethics. This code will have to be adhered to when the principle of *Muḍārabah* is put into practice. Industrial, commercial and agricultural projects within the framework of planning can be worked on this principle, combining the various units of production. The income resulting from such enterprises can be shared proportionately after deducting all legitimate expenses. There is little chance of loss in the Islamic system of planning because, as a result of co-operation between the public and the private sectors, there will be more chances of healthy investment, pushing the march of economic progress ahead. There will also be less possibility of depression under such a system of planning. If depression takes place owing to some reason, the Islamic system will be better suited to face the situation than the capitalist system of planning, because the fixed rate of interest which retards recovery from depression will not be allowed to exercise its tyrannical influence on levels of employment and production.

(d) Method of Financing.

The question of execution of a plan is vitally connected with the question of finding financial resources. So far as the method of financing is concerned there is an element of similarity between the Islamic and modern planning systems, but their difference lies, not only in its emphasis, but also in its method of utilizing the resources. There are usually a number of ways of raising resources and achieving targets, the two fundamental sources of finance being internal or domestic resources and foreign assistance.

(i) Internal Finance.

Internal finance may take two forms: private saving and public saving.

Private Saving.

In underdeveloped Muslim countries it is difficult to increase the volume of current domestic savings partly because of low incomes and partly because of an increased desire for consumption of luxury imports or sumptuous goods, etc. Much can be done by encouraging investment in the fields of greatest urgency and production. Unlike modern planning, in Islamic planning strategy saving can be married with economic development not through the differential rates of interest but through co-operation. Niggardliness is condemned in the *Qur'ān* (*Sūrah* IV. 37). The other extreme, extravagance, is equally condemned. Even when giving to, or sharing with others, a person should not go so far as to render himself in turn an object of charity (*Sūrah* XVII. 29). Therefore, when unnecessary consumption retards the process of economic development, the Islamic state can intervene to control such consumption and direct control of investment policy.

Public Saving.

Again, where private saving is insufficient much can be done by adopting the policy of progressive taxation which is always regarded as an important method of financing a development plan. Raising revenue by taxation is justified in Islam. The *Hadith* says: "There is always due besides *Zakāt*." But in Islamic planning undue emphasis on indirect taxes can hardy be justified. The fundamental point which is to be borne in mind, in order to better appreciate the nature of taxation in Islam, is to understand the double sanction, spiritual and temporal, behind government taxes in the Islamic state. Both these aspects are welded together to create an equilibrium in man with his complex nature. Thus, as I have already pointed out, the objectives of planning in Islam must be guided by the principle of benevolence and care for the poor. Judged by this standard the modern system of indirect taxation comes under heavy fire because the burden of indirect taxes generally falls on the shoulders of the poor. From the point of view of having a progressive tax structure direct taxes are certainly much more desirable. If a policy of full employment requires a high marginal propensity to consume, progressive taxation is apparently necessary for transferring wealth from the rich to the poor. In many Muslim countries we find excessive dependence of the fiscal system on indirect taxes. But efforts should be made to intreduce an element of progressivity in the structure of indirect taxes by exempting certain necessities of life.

The Islamic system of taxation must ensure that only the rich and prosperous, who have enough to spare, bear the main brunt of taxation. Probably, it is for this reason that incomes are not taxed at source, but only savings or hoardings.

(ii) *Zakāt*

Another unique source of revenue which an Islamic state can utilize for financing a development plan is *Zakāt*, which cannot be spent in any way an Islamic state may want. It must be spent in the way prescribed in the *Qur'ān* which says:

"Alms are for the poor
and the needy, and those
Employed to administer the (funds)
For those whose hearts
Have been (recently) reconciled
(To Truth); for those in bondage
and in debt; in the cause of God;
and for the wayfarer:
(Thus is it) ordained by God,
And God is full of knowledge
And Wisdom."

(Sūrah IX. 60).

Keeping in view these items of expenditure on which *Zakāt* revenue can be spent, the modern social security schemes and social welfare projects of Islamic planning programmes may be financed out of the surplus of *Zakāt* revenue. *Zakāt*, if collected in a systematic manner, may check the tendency to hoard idle cash resources and provides a powerful stimulus for investing idle stocks. This stimulus gets momentum from the fact that Islam allows profits and sleeping partnerships in which profit and loss are shared. Some have taken *Zakāt* to be a voluntary private charity, whereas it is a compulsory tax on saving and property at a rate varying from $2\frac{1}{2}$ to 20 per cent.

(iii) Deficit Financing.

Another resource in the public sector is deficit financing which means government's borrowing from the banking system of the country when available resources are not enough for financing development expenditure. What makes deficit financing a key variable in underdeveloped countries and a major guide to the financial position of the government is the fact that most of the public debt in these countries is held by the banks and the possibilities of borrowing from the non-banking sector are often very limited. Under the Islamic system of planning there is no harm in resorting to deficit financing. The only fundamental difference from modern planning lies in the fact that interest will not, under Islamic planning, be allowed to exercise its harmful effects on production, employment and social justice. In the Islamic socio-economic set-up, banks must act as partners in trade, commerce, industry and development plans. A happy fusion of the financial experience of the bank and the investor's knowledge of investment and business must be made in order to achieve the objects of planning, realization of which would ultimately lead to a stage of society based on true social justice and the universal brotherhood of man.

Let us now turn to the problem of financing development plans through foreign assistance.

(iv) Foreign Assistance.

Foreign aid is important for planning, not only to bridge the gap between resources required and those available within the country, but also to supply a specific type of resources for which no domestic substitute is available, i.e. foreign exchange. The foreign exchange component of expenditure has to be found abroad in foreign loans and grants to the extent that the balance of payments position of the developing country does not permit the release of foreign exchange for its own purposes out of its own earnings. It is because of this unfavourable balance of payments position and the acute shortage of technical know-how, that the use of foreign funds becomes particularly important in developing states.

The following systematic attempts may be made towards solving the problem of foreign exchange of Muslim countries. A systematic policy of promoting exports is recommended. This is not un-Islamic, because Islam has encouraged international trade. (If one studies the history of commercial law, one can see that the enlightened Muslim Moors used to have extensive trade links with the Levant from Barcelona and other places. Their goods reached Indian and Chinese ports and they traded along the African coast as far as Madagascar.)

Obviously, for the exploitation of the vast natural resources of Muslim states what is required is huge public expenditure. Since interest is prohibited on loans it is an appropriate time for the Islamic Development Bank to contribute by pooling the resources of the Muslim world, to be supplemented by grants, and aid from the World bank, the I.D.A., the Asian Development Bank, and other friendly Governments, which may undertake joint projects, particularly when individual Muslim states are not in a position to finance the projects themselves. Muslim states may try to persuade foreign investors to invest on a partnership basis without any political strings. The funds may be private or governmental or may be supplied by intergovernmental agencies.

Lastly, a state may take loans from abroad on payment of interest. One may differ with me but the fact remains that Muslim states cannot impose their religious injunctions on non-Muslims, this being obviously against the spirit of Islam. So if foreign exchange becomes absolutely essential for the establishment of a just society where a viable synthesis between the claims of economic growth and social justice is achieved, loans may be taken from abroad on payment of interest just as wine is permitted in special circumstances. Where harm is inevitable, the lesser of the evils is to be preferred. Therefore, in the larger interests of society it is a lesser evil to have interest transactions with a non-Muslim state on the analogy of the action of the Caliph 'Umar who permitted the levying of customs duties and tolls on the articles of trade of a non-Muslim neighbouring state in *reprisal* to the same extent as were levied by the latter. This is, in a nutshell, the way by which the foreign exchange requirements of development planning of Muslim states can be met.

(e) Necessity of Planning in an Islamic State.

Our present discussion will remain incomplete if we do not answer a preliminary question: "Why plan at all in Muslim countries?" The following reasons may be put forward.

(1) The Muslim states, despite their numerical strength and geographical distribution all over the world, are today, by and large, under-developed. But from Morocco to Indonesia and from Mauritania to Malaysia without exception all countries possess vast natural resources and rank amongst the world's most important growers of primary commodities and producers of mineral wealth. Obviously, for the systematic exploitation of these vast natural resources, what is required is comprehensive economic planning.

(2) The world's Muslim population is increasing so rapidly that it is impeding the economic growth of respective Muslim countries. The figures issued by the World Muslim Congress at its fifth world meeting in Baghdad in 1962, as amended to date, give the estimate at certainly over 700 million. The logic of the circumstances suggests that an attempt should be made not only to adjust population growth to resources but also to adjust resources to population. The first attempt calls for adoption

of a comprehensive population control policy, and the second one a comprehensive programme of economic planning in all Muslim countries.

(3) The *Qur'ān* says: "After finishing the prayer, seek the bounty of God" (*Sūrah* LXII. 10). Again, the Prophet (peace be upon him) is reported to have said: "When you finish your morning prayer, do not sleep until you strive for your livelihood." Now, the question of earning one's livelihood in a decent manner depends on the opportunities of getting employment. Planning not only solves the problem of unemployment by bringing about a happy marriage between saving and investment, but it also faces the ugly problem of unemployment by creating new avenues of employment. As Professor Benham says, "It is true that planning organisations as a whole including all those engaged in obtaining information would absorb a considerable proportion of the personnel and other resources of the community."

(4) Islam has condemned wastage of all kinds. The *Qur'ān* says: "But waste not, by excess, for God loveth not the wasters". (*Sūrah* VI. 141). In the economic sphere, the chance of waste is the greatest where there is no economic stability. Economic planning brings about the required economic stability in society, whereas a planless society is not stable because here the individual entrepreneur is guided by his own study of the market conditions. This leads either to overproduction or underproduction.

(5) Islam views with extreme disfavour the monopoly of resources by a few self-seeking millionaires. The *Qur'ān* says: "In order that the (wealth) may not (merely) make a circuit between the wealthy among you" (*Sūrah* LIX. 7). Again the Prophet (peace be upon him) is reported to have said: "Riches (*i.e. Zakāt*) should be taken from the rich and returned to the poor" (Bukhārī). Again, he says; "If any Muslim has his brother holding a position inferior to him, he should let him partake of what he eats and what he wears" (Bukhārī).

All these instructions go to prove that Islam views with disfavour the idea of inequitable distribution of wealth. But it is economic planning which helps to secure a more equitable distribution of income and wealth. Experience shows that private enterprise has failed to bring about an equitable distribution of the benefits of economic growth among the different sections of the community.

(6) It follows that planning is of supreme importance for avoiding the monopolistic exploitation, speculative businesses and anti-social wastes of the competitive system. Islam has condemned not only monopoly business but also speculative business. Thus it is related that the Holy Prophet (peace be upon him) said: "He who accumulates stocks of grain during the period of scarcity (with a view to profiteering later) is a great sinner" (Muslim and *Mishkāt*). But, unfortunately, the actual course of economic development almost everywhere has been to increase the power of the monopolies, and a monopoly-dominated economic order is the fabric of capitalist societies. Thus, resources are misdirected because the monopolist restricts output and employment. Under a planned economy,

the monopolist will lose his power of artificially raising the price and of restricting the use of the resources.

Lastly, Islam regards war as an abnormal and destructive activity to which recourse should be had only as a last resort. The *Qur'an* says: 'If aggression were not repelled by force, the earth would be filled with disorder and all beneficence would disappear" (*Sūrah* II. 252). Therefore, from the viewpoint of total welfare some sort of peace-time preparation for war is necessary to face any eventuality. So some kind of planning is necessary even in times of peace in order to facilitate the easy transition of a country's economy to a war basis. Various strategic factors are, for instance, taken into consideration in the location of industries even in times of peace. So, planning in some form or other is necessary not only for a peace-time economy but also for a war economy.

It is thus abundantly clear that there is an imperative need for comprehensive economic planning in all the Muslim countries of the world. True it is that, in spite of many intrinsic merits, modern planning cannot be carried out without huge bureaucracy with all its evils of red-tapism and the potential threat to personal freedom. Yet we feel that planning in an Islamic state will be free from the vicious influence of bureaucracy for two reasons:

(*a*) The very basis of Islamic planning is co-operation—a principle which will be applied in all aspects of economic activity. The influence of bureaucratic red-tape would be the minimum.

(*b*) The whole conception of planning in an Islamic state is not dependent on material welfare to the utter neglect of spiritual and moral development. In the Islamic state all economic problems will have a moral slant.

Since, under the Islamic scheme of society, there is not much room for the capitalist trinity—the sovereignty of consumers, the tyranny of the price system, and the quest for huge profits—planning in Islam is definitely free from many of the shortcomings of modern planning.

18.2 Economic Development in Islam.

(a) Its Meaning.

In modern secular economics, "Economic development refers to the process whereby the people of a country or region come to utilize the resources available to bring about a sustained increase in per capita production of goods and services." Professor Snider tells us: "Economic growth refers to the long-run or secular increase in per capita productivity." According to Professor W. A. Lewis, "Growth is taking place if output is increasing per hour of work done." In his book *Process of Economic Growth*, Rostow tries to explain economic development in terms of a number of propensities: the propensity to develop fundamental science; the propensity to apply science to economic ends; the propensity to accept innovations; the propensity to seek material advance; the propensity to consume or to save and the propensity to have children. These propensities summarize the effective response of a society to its environment at any period of time through its existing institutions and leading social groups.

Thus economic development is defined as an increase in the *per capita* income of the people at a given period of time. It views the economic organization of a society as a production unit. Economic growth measures the capacity of the economy to increase the supply of goods and services. So, in other words, it means the increase of national income, but both the money cost and real cost remain unaltered, for, if they increase in proportion to the increase in national income, it cannot be called economic development in the real sense of the term.

To determine whether an economy is a 'developed' one or not, the following three general tests are used: (1) its per capita income must be a fairly high one; (2) the per capita income must be a rising one; (3) the rising trend in per capita income must be a continuous and self-sustained one. Judged by these tests, Kuwait may not be called a developed country, in spite of the fact that her *per capita* income is well above the level of any country of the world because it is the result of oil royalties. Similarly, Japan's *per capita* income in 1953 (*a*) was less than half that of Israel, Puerto Rico and Uruguay; (*b*) was considerably less than that of Lebanon, Chile, Colombia, Portugal, Spain, Turkey, and Brazil, and (*c*) was about equal to that of Mexico, Yugoslavia and, perhaps, Costa Rica. And yet, Japan is commonly regarded as a developed country, while all these others are not. This is because Japan has consistently maintained a rapid rate of growth of *per capita* income for every year since 1868.

The Islamic concept of economic development is much wider than the concept of development in secular economics. Despite the fact that the Islamic basis of development is multidimensional, having moral, social, political and economic dimensions, moral and spiritual development are integrated into the very concept of economic development right from the beginning. This is what is called "*Tazkiyah al nafs*" following the verse: "By the human soul, By Him who perfected it, Who endowed it with a capacity for righteousness as well as for unrighteousness. Felicitous is he who ennobles it. Wretched is he who degrades it" *Qur'ān* (*Sūrah* XCI 7–10) and other similar verses.

Thus, economic development in Islam is *not* simply materialistic development. The spiritual and moral phases are assigned great importance, and they are made explicit in "*takaful*" or "*tadamūn*" or the mutual social security of Islam. The ideal pattern of Islamic belief contains enough motivational properties which encourage people to work and which can influence actual patterns of Muslim behaviour. It is possible to motivate economic achievement, thereby accelerating economic development through psychological training. For instance, in Islam "work" for the purpose of efficient utilization of Allah's resources is also a worship. The *Qur'ān* has said that "when the prayer has been ended, disperse through the land and seek the bounty of Allah" (*Sūrah* LXII. 10). The Prophet (peace be upon him) is reported to have said that no one eats better food than that which he eats out of the work of his hand" (Bukhari).

Besides payment of *Zakāt*, benevolent loans, voluntary and obligatory intrafamily and intracommunity obligations carry the double notion of benefits; they do not merely bring material benefits to takers, but also confer benefit on the givers, both morally and socially.

Furthermore, even in the material area, emphasis on the increase in the *per capita* income and on sustaining rapid growth over a period of time may not ensure Islamic conditions for economic growth simply because it does not control the extent of inequality in the distribution of income – a central question in Islamic economics.

(b) The Prerequisities for growth and Islam as a Factor of Development.

There are many prerequisites for economic growth of which the most important are two: one is natural resources and the other human behaviour. As Professor Lewis has observed: "The growth of output per head depends on the one hand on the natural resources available, and on the other hand on human behaviour." But our empirical observation suggests that rich resources cannot alone promote economic growth since countries with similar resources show dissimilar vigour at different times in their history without any obvious change in their resources. Natural resources determine the course of development and constitute the challenge which may or may not be accepted by the human mind. "At every stage of development," observes Kindleberger, "we can find countries of the same level of income, one having ten times the arable land per capita of the other—1 hectare per capita to 0.1 hectare: Australia and Switzerland; Argentina and the Netherlands; Syria and Japan; Liberia and Haiti. As for industrial resources, there are many examples of countries having developed despite the lack of some of the basic industrial raw materials and minerals; for instance, Britain with little oil or non-ferrous metals; Switzerland with none except hydro-electricity; Japan with little coal and no oil; and New Zealand with hardly any important mineral of her own to speak of. The Middle East has fabulous resources of oil, but still continues to be an underdeveloped area. Britain did not possess indigenous sources either for cotton or jute, which were among the first industries established on her soil. Denmark, Iceland and Netherlands have developed with little domestic sources of industrial metals. Japan has built up an impressive iron and oil industry based on imported raw materials. The existence of rich natural resources is not a sufficient condition for economic development, or even a necessary one."

From the above analysis it is proved beyond doubt that human behaviour which is indicative of the desire for growth plays a very crucial role in economic development. As a matter of fact, development is a complex process; economic, political, religious, social and cultural conditions must be favourable. But, unfortunately, in all undeveloped Muslim countries like Pakistan and Bangladesh we find enough economic resources but adverse human behaviour. So what is needed is a painful readjustment—the creation of a favourable atmosphere on the ruins of adverse social, economic, legal and political institutions.

The moulding of human behaviour is a painful process in the underdeveloped countries. These countries should either abandon their development programmes in the face of unfavourable social, economic and political institutions or adopt coercive measures to achieve the targets of economic development. Islam does not rule out the need for coercive measures, if need be, for achieving the greatest good of the greatest number of people. Yet the possibility of getting favourable human behaviour suited to the requirements of economic development is greater in an Islamic state than in secular states in at least three ways.

In the first place, unlike other religions, Islam gives equal recognition to both metaphysical and material needs for life. In Christianity, it is thought that a man of God has no business to bother with politics or economics; his duty is only to be morally good and preach only love and goodwill towards mankind. Similarly, in Buddhism metaphysics is far more emphasized than the actual life of man. Buddha attempted to prove that all manifested and created existence is unreal. It is obvious that such a teacher could have nothing to do with the economic remoulding of society or with the politics of an actual or ideal state. In Hinduism, in like manner, the doctrine of the transmigration of souls and the weary round of incarnate life is preached and a believer is urged to get rid of this weary round by annihilating his desire and resorting to monastic life. Religion, in this way, becomes complete worldliness, asceticism and renunciation of the natural and physical world. All this is against the spirit of Islam. Here, the world is not considered to be an illusion or Maya; it is regarded as a reality and a fact which cannot be suppressed by any monasticism or spirituality. For it the concept of the salvation of the individual as an isolated entity is absolutely wrong. Islam deals with man not as an individual man but as a member of society. Moreover, it regards it as an obligation on every Muslim not to be contented with his personal piety and righteousness but to spread and propagate it and at the same time to fight against evils prevalent in society, whether in the field of ethics or economics or politics.

Thus the Holy *Qur'an* points out that "after the (morning) prayer is finished, one should seek the bounty of Allah" (*Surah* LXII. 10). The tradition of the Prophet also runs like this: "Earning of livelihood (honestly) is next to prayer in order of importance". Besides this, there are many other directives both in the *Qur'an* and the *Sunnah* which go to prove that the proper utilization of economic resources means fulfilment of Allah's desire. Therefore, the idea of economic development is inherent in the faith of the Muslims. This very fact reflects a new approach to the whole problem of economic development. Herein lies the superiority of the Islamic concept of development over the modern concept.

Secondly, the teachings of early Islam can profitably be utilized to contain the undesirable side effects of material development, which has both economic and social dimensions, evidenced by rises in personal income and productivity as well as the presence of hopes of high achievement, strong self-motivation and rising expectations. While traditional societies are characterized by a static balance, the stresses and strains involved in developmental endeavours bring about a dynamic disequilibrium and personal frustration on a massive scale, because people realize the possibility of improvement in their conditions and look to increasingly higher goals. The more they achieve, the higher become their expectations. Paraphrasing William James and benefiting from some of the recent research findings in behavioural sciences, it may be stated that: (*a*) expectation achievement (i.e. expectation divided by achievement) equals the prevailing degree of frustration; and (*b*) expectations rise in a geometric progression whereas achievements are added in arithmetic progression. The gap between expectations and achievements indicates the level of frustration.

It is, therefore, necessary to deal rationally with these undesirable side effects of the otherwise desirable development process. Here we have some very important lessons to learn from Islam. If the teachings of Islam are injected into the minds of young people through a sound educational system, we are sure to get a new generation; the individual would be conditioned to thinking in terms of social achievement rather than personal achievement. Service above self may appear a trite maxim but in it alone lies the salvation and peace of mind for the individual and the survival of a nation. Personal frustration on a massive scale, inevitable in a rapidly developing nation, would otherwise lead inexorably to class warfare, group strife and regional conflicts. Rightly or wrongly, Mao's thought has produced a miracle in so far as the development of China is concerned. I find no reason why Islamic thought, if properly propagated, could not have lasting and decisive effects on the development of the world of Islam.

Lastly, secularism has become the keynote of the technology-oriented development process of today. The continuous erosion of the established value system results in a moral vacuum. The individual is left without a reference point for his conduct and is deprived of a spiritual bedrock to support him in the stresses and crises inherent in change. Here also Islam can fill the gap of a moral vacuum, introducing a stabilizing element in the process of growth.

The scientific method, some of the outstanding earlier discoveries in natural and applied sciences, the contribution of basic importance to the social sciences, and technological developments in chemistry, mathematics, medicine and architecture, were all the products of minds influenced by and infused with the spirit of Islam. The appeal to reason, rational analysis and the study of empirical facts and the use of science for the conquest of Nature and for the development of human society are some of the basic distinguishing attributes of early Islam. A proper appreciation of Islamic injunctions and a careful study of our cultural heritage would, therefore, remove the incompatibility between the present-day secular trends and religious doctrines. (Indeed, the so-called secular movement was, originally and in some of its useful aspects, a borrowing from medieval Islam, not completely consistent with the notions then prevalent among the Europeans.)

The fact is that Islamic principles concerning appeals to reason and the harnessing of all the resources given by Allah for the benefit of man need to be brought out so that the motivation for action in the society is provided by the belief that 'the best of you is not the richest and the most powerful but the virtuous'. Unless this fundamental principle of Islam is practised in every-day life even material progress will be frustrated by the decay of moral and spiritual values which are the only safeguards against waste and inefficiency resulting from corruption, exploitation and personal greed. We must not allow the opportunities of rapid economic development to obscure our moral values and destroy the best of our social institutions. The fact of the matter is that a renaissance of true Islamic thought can serve as a positive factor of development.

In this connection it is interesting to quote a French scholar, Professor Jaques Austruy, who, in his recently published article entitled "Islam's Key Problem—Economic Development," observed: "The economist must here play the part of midwife, helping to bring into the world the materialized result of latent ideas and possibilities. He must contribute to the birth of development, and the economy, which is limited to human possibilities, must seek out the most suitable types of structural arrangements for any particular civilization, as thoroughly as it would strive for the best possible results from the mechanisms of any given structure. This widening of the economic horizon shows the great utility which respect for its own values represents for each community. It also shows the importance of the powerful motives which an economic orientation, emerging from the essential vocation of this community, can bring to development. Here the moral is combined with the practical, and the long-term prospects are initiated by the most immediate and effective form of action." It is, therefore, essential to relate the economic development of Islam to religious and cultural factors.

Unfortunately, many of the Muslim countries of the world like Bangladesh, Pakistan, Afghanistan, Indonesia, Kuwait, Iraq, Iran, Syria, Turkey, Egypt, Libya, Sudan, Algeria, Morocco, Tunisia, Jordan, are underdeveloped compared to other advanced countries of the world like the U.S.A., the U.K. and Japan. There is immense scope for development in all these Muslim countries, both from the point of view of natural resources and from the point of view of human resources, because a happy combination of these two factors determines the actual course of development. In other words, Muslim countries are in a better position to make development efforts compared with other underdeveloped countries for two reasons: (*a*) many resources unknown in the nineteenth century are today accessible to Muslim countries; (*b*) unlike other religions Islam can be used as a factor of economic development in so far as the moulding of human behaviour is concerned.

Now I may draw a brief pen-picture of the natural resources of the Muslim countries. From 1945 to 1958 the contribution of the Middle East to the world production of oil rose from 7.5 per cent to 25.4 per cent. But the size and importance of the deposits discovered grew even more rapidly. In 1920, these reserves were estimated to be 5 per cent of the world reserves. Today the figure is approximately 85 per cent. According to experts on oil, if the deposits in the Middle East continue to be worked at the same rate there will still be enough oil to last for 150 years, particularly in Saudi Arabia.

Additional major discoveries have been made in Libya and the prospects of finding more oil in Tunisia, Algeria and remote parts of the Sahara are generally believed to be good. In the event that new discoveries are made on a large scale, Europe's energy problem for the future may well be considerably eased. At the same time these resources may provide an economic basis for improving the political relationship between France and the emerging states of North Africa. Moreover, Indonesia and Malaysia meet the world's major requirements for tin and rubber. Bangladesh has a virtual monopoly of jute. Egypt is amongst the largest of the world's cotton growers.

At this stage it might be profitable to examine the strategic importance of the Muslim world as we find it on the map of the world today. Turkey, the master of the Bosphorus and the Dardanelles, stands guard on the northern gateway of the Mediterranean. In fact, the Mediterranean Sea has been considered to be more than 60 per cent a Muslim lake. Egypt controls the eastern gateway to the Mediterranean through Port Said and the Suez Canal. The Red Sea is also very largely a Muslim lake controlled on either side by Islamic states. Likewise, the Arabian Gulf enjoys complete Muslim control. In South-East Asia, Indonesia is the furthest outpost of the Muslim world in the Pacific Ocean. From the south-western borders of China to the south-western borders of Russia a large block of Muslim countries is spread out in multi-pronged penetrations to guard many vital frontiers and to stand as valiant sentries to protect, socially and politically, the lands of Islam.

But these vast natural resources and the strategic importance of the Muslim world are not sufficient conditions for growth. Muslim countries must realize that natural resources cease when the extent and scope of knowledge ceases. Here, by knowledge, we mean knowledge of both modern science and technology as well as true knowledge of the Islamic values of life. On both fronts we shall have to work very hard. Muslim countries will have to accept the challenge of time. They should not only borrow modern ideas of sciences and technology but also imbue the Muslim populations of Muslim countries with Islamic values and ideas so that an urge for development comes from within.

18.3 Some Aspects of Economic Development in Muslim Countries.

(a) Development Experiences and the Scale of Poverty.

The need for an alternative strategy of development in Muslim countries arises from the fact that the past three decades of development experiences of Muslim countries (excepting some oil-rich Muslim countries), in general and of the least developed countries in particular, is disappointing. Relatively speaking, the least developed member countries of the Islamic conference (L.D.M.C.) are poorer than ever before.

Out of the thirty-one countries listed as least developed countries by the United Nations Committee for Development Planning (1971 and 1975), sixteen Muslim countries are classified as least developed in terms of the following three basic criteria:

(a) *Per capita* domestic product;

(b) The share of manufacturing in total domestic production being ten per cent or less; and

(c) Literacy rate – production of the literate in the age group of fifteen years or above of twenty per cent or less.

Even if the five World Bank criteria (1981) ((a) G.N.P. per capita, (b) average annual growth (per centage), (c) *per capita* food production, and (d) per capita consumption of energy) are applied, fourteen out of the sixteen least developed Muslim countries come under the heading of low income countries.

It is to be noted that the above criteria are neither wholly reliable nor sufficient in themselves in the sense that they do not provide a complete picture of the economic situation of the countries concerned.

There is a consensus of opinion that the measurement of economic welfare in terms of *per capita* income is not a very satisfactory basis for policy action. It does not tell us anything about the extent of inequality in the distribution of income in these countries; a matter with which Islamic economics is vitally concerned. It gives us an approximation of the general level of the economic conditions of the countries as they are, not as they ought to be. Again, the criterion of the literacy rate as adopted by these surveys does not indicate the availability of critically needed skilled manpower for economic development. While there is a need for further refinement, the fact is that over 160 million people of the L.D.M.C., who constitute about thirty per cent of the Muslim population of the *Organization of Islamic Conference* (O.I.C.), are still living in absolute poverty with inadequate food, shelter, education, health care and even safe drinking water. This figure does not include the poor of the remaining twenty-six developing Muslim countries of the O.I.C. For many of them there has been little or no improvement in the standard of living, and for some there was actually a decline in the standard of living in the 1970s. The current World Bank (1981) estimate suggests that during the 1980s the outlook for reducing poverty is likely to worsen. The G.N.P. is projected to grow at only 1.8 per cent a year in low income countries while the gap between the poorest group and the middle and industrialized countries will widen further. In 1980, income per person in the industrialized countries was about five times that of the developing countries as a whole, and twelve times that of the low-income oil importers. But on an exchange-rate conversion basis, the differences would be much larger. The gap is expected to widen during the 1980's. (World Bank Report, 1981, pp. 16–17). So the basic problem facing these countries is how to accelerate the process of economic development and to reduce the number of people living in absolute poverty, thereby ensuring an equitable distribution of income-one of the most important objectives of an Islamic economy.

In general, experience suggests that the distribution of income is likely to worsen in the course of economic growth. But even if disparities increase, the income of the poor can rise. Where people in the L.D.M.C. are living at a subsistence or starvation level, the Islamic economy must be more concerned with how to *raise* the income levels rather than with closing their relative positions in the distribution of income.

The Muslim world's forming a part of the Third World developing countries forces us to raise some basic questions: why are the Muslim countries (with some exceptions) so pitiably poor as a whole? Why do half of the least developed or underdeveloped countries belong to the Muslim world? Furthermore, historically speaking, why, for instance, did Byzantium, which was economically much more advanced in contrast with Crusader Europe, fall into decline? In the past, it was common to attribute their backwardness to either geographic or climatic causes. The development experiences of Japan, Korea and Argentina, however, do not support this view. Backwardness is also attributed to the fact that these countries are culturally-bound, traditional societies which have developed neither the mechanism of command nor the markets to sustain the process of growth. Thus while Max Weber (1963, p. 265) and others put forward the hypothesis that Islam, with its thoroughly traditionalist ethics, is an obstacle to development, this hypothesis is again not supported by facts. It is also common to attribute Muslim countries' backwardness to European colonial exploitation.

The fact is that there are no simple answers to these complex issues, which need in-depth separate treatment. Here we look upon the Western experience of development *not* as the paradigm and model to follow but as a special case in which various peculiarly favourable activating factors encouraged the historic economic development of the West. Here, development is seen only in a materialistic sense. But the basic question facing Muslim countries is how to realize the goals of the Islamic concept of economic development, which are to be defined not merely in terms of Gross National Product and increases in *per capita* income but also in terms of raising the absolute income levels of the poor to eradicate poverty, simultaneously meeting material and non-material human needs, and conserving natural resources, wildlife and the ecological environment. All these goals will be accompanied by the preservation of moral and spiritual values as reflected in the concept of "*tazkiyah*" (moral purification plus growth).

(b) Minimum Provisioning for Living.

While the *Sharī'ah* encourages the individual to earn a livelihood, yet it is also recognized by the *Qur'ān* and the *Sunnah* that a state of poverty and deprivation entitles one to the community's support, since the guarantee of a minimum level of living is to be provided by an Islamic state. The following *Hadīths* and the Qur'anic verses confirm this:
The Prophet (peace be upon him) said:

"To earn an honest livelihood a duty (ranking) next to the chief duty (of offering prayers)" (Mishkat).

"And when the prayer is finished, then disperse in the land and seek of Allah's bounty"

(*Al Qur'ān, Sūrah* LXII. 10)

"And the earth have we spread out and placed therein firm hills, and caused each seemly thing to grow therein. And we have given unto you livelihood therein and unto those for whom you provide not."

(*Sūrah* XV. 19, 20)

The *Qur'ān* also declared:

"And in those wealth there is a right acknowledged for the beggar and the destitute".

(*Sūrah* LXXX: 24, 25)

Again it is said:

"The alms are only for the poor and the needy, and those who collect them, and those whose hearts are to be reconciled, and to free the captives and the debtors, and for the cause of Allah, and (for) the wayfarers, a duty imposed by Allah. Allah is Knower, wise."

(*Sūrah* IX. 60)

In any scientific study of human poverty in Islamic economics we have to find out the Islamic solution to the question of why some individuals cannot earn according to their capacities. What are the factors involved and what type of Islamically justified economic, social, institutional and legal measures are needed to ensure the minimum guaranteed income to meet the basic needs of the individual?

The fact is that the concept of poverty changes throughout time resulting from the changes in the estimates of minimum guaranteed income. Objectively, poverty can be measured in terms of the proportion of currently agreed-upon basic necessities such as food, shelter, clothing, education and health care that income can buy. Poverty is a condition under which people are unable to obtain this "subsistence". In line with the spirit of the *Sharī'ah*, it should be possible to develop a "three level band concept" to synthesize the definitions of poverty. They are "minimum subsistence", "minimum adequacy" and "minium comfort" which can actually be ascertained by surveying what families actually buy, thereby arriving at the money equivalent of the "subsistence", "adequacy" and "comfort" minimums subject to periodic price adjustments.

This attempt to integrate "subsistence", "adequacy" and "comfort" is rooted in the *Sharī'ah*. This position has been affirmed by many Muslim jurists from time to time such as Al-Ghazāli (1058–1111 A.D.), Shatibi and many others. Al-Ghazāli stressed the need for preservation of one's own life and for maintaining it in a state of efficiency along with protection of religion, reason, progeny and property. Shatibi also expressed similar views when he argued in favour of provisioning for the basic needs of individuals, not as an end in itself but as a means to an end (i.e. the protection of religion). The satisfaction of wants, including comforts, adornment and ornamentation of life is permissible and quite lawful in Islam. The Holy Prophet advised his companions to enjoy the good things of this world which God had created for their use. There are many savings of the Holy Prophet which testify to the fact that enjoyment of the beautiful things of life is not repugnant to the teachings of Islam.

But when people are living at a subsistence or starvation level, the *Sharī'ah* demands that we attack absolute poverty rather than relative poverty as a matter of priority. One who is relatively poor may still be in comfortable circumstances, as an automobile company executive with a six figure income is poor in comparison with, say, the heirs of Henry Ford. The feeling of deprivation of goods arising from such relative poverty is not considered to be justified in the *Sharī'ah* as this type of subjective poverty may increase one's unhappiness and greed, with the associated urge for exploitation of less fortunate people. The Prophet (peace be upon him) is reported to have said that "when one of you looks at someone who is superior to him in property and appearance, he should look at someone who is inferior to him" (Bukhari and Muslim). A version by Muslim has "look at those who are inferior to you and do not look at those who are superior to you, for that is more liable to keep you from despising God's favour to you" (Mishkat al-Masabih).

The fact is that "the derived notion of poverty or deprivation – in the apparent objectivity of a package of specific needs – reflects society's judgements of differences in social function and status. In practice, the minimum which a family needs to maintain physical efficiency is ascertained by surveying what families actually buy. The separating minimum needs of those on relief from those who use the community agencies for non-monetary services is done by asking what the latter have and what they spend it on". At all times there have persisted differences in what a society considers "subsistence", "adequacy" and "comfort" in a given period of time.

There is no hard and fast rule regarding the "subsistence", "adequacy" and "comfort" levels of goods and services. They are relative to the stage and level of socio-economic conditions of the community. Although provisioning for the minimum subsistence in respect of food, clothing, shelter, education and health care is the primary concern of an Islamic state, yet it is highly desirable to achieve levels of sufficiency, which are necessary to further the cause of religion and the well-being future generation. This is what the *Sharī'ah* actually demands.

But in the context of today's reality, it is very difficult to give a categorical answer to whether all Muslim countries (excepting a few oil-rich countries in the Middle East) are capable of giving guarantees of a minimum provisioning for food, shelter, clothing, education and health care to their people. In the case of many least developed Muslim countries the minimum provisioning for shelter alone can, perhaps, utilize the whole of the available budgetary resources leaving practically nothing for other items of vital expenditure. When a state cannot provide a guarantee of a minimum provisioning to its poor people as required by the *Sharī'ah* due to its resource constraints, it should perhaps identify an order of priority in terms of minimum provisioning, thereby providing a guarantee for at least high priority needs, although it may be a guarantee for sub-minimum provisioning. This is not to suggest that this second best solution should be a permanent feature of any Muslim society. Attempts should, however, be made to exploit resources in such a way that it becomes possible to break the vicious circle of poverty. This is perhaps an Islamically justified approach to the problem.

(c) The Importance of Social Appropriateness in the Transfer of Technology.

It would be a mistake to assume that the transfer of technology, its development and use are value-free. On the contrary, it should be possible to demonstrate that Islamic social, moral and economic values can come into conflict with the transfer, development and use of technology. For example, the importation of certain advanced technology for an urban area in a Muslim country may require huge inflexibility capital that may be committed to the needs of large organizations, a large market and large manpower – both skilled and unskilled. On the one hand, it may lead to internal migration of agricultural labour from rural to urban areas which may disturb the social and moral equilibrium. On the other hand, it may lead to the concentration or accumulation of wealth in the hands of a few and consequently more unequal distribution of income. The social, moral and economic consequences of both possibilities may not be acceptable to Islam.

The very complexities introduced by development and the moderniz-ation processes of advanced countries make the developing Muslim states and their people dependent and prevent these countries from initiating Islamic reforms in existing institutions. Thus the introduction of modern technology into the context of Muslim countries must take into account the socio-economic values of Islam, because technology is not merely a tool but it is a tool using human behaviour too.

It is true that technological transformation and adaptation would undoubtedly remain the *sine qua non* of economic progress. But an appropriate solution to the development problem in developing Muslim countries cannot overlook the need to encompass and draw the socio-economic and socio-cultural systems of these countries into the development, use, transfer and application of technology. Therefore, what is important is to encourage development of appropriate technology so that the machine suits the man, that is, technology is scaled to the needs of a society with a view to enhance the quality of life and the ecological environment. This should include finding technologies which can maximize the use of local factors and input so that grass-root innovation has a chance to develop and the desire for self-help is promoted.

(d) The '*Ulamā*' and Development.

Since the rural population forms a great part of all the Muslim countries of the world, the '*Ulamā*' or *Imāms*, who still have a great hold on the people, may be associated with the development suited to the requirements of the respective economies of Muslim countries. This association may be of great significance in the field of agricultural development because food deficits are steadily mounting in all Muslim countries in spite of efforts by the respective governments to increase agricultural production. This is indicative of the fact that the total involvement of the people is needed to meet this intractable situation.

A vast majority of Muslim farmers are unaware of the tremendous improvements in agriculture brought about by modern science and technology. They are chained to traditionalism and dangerously misleading travesties of what their religion really stands for. As religion occupies a very important place in the lives of the Muslim people and has more to do with determining their attitudes than any other factor, the '*Ulamā*' can render invaluable service to the nations by helping to create psychological and ideological conditions favourable to the progress of the agricultural population. The propriety and desirability of the '*Ulamā*'s participation in a campaign for agricultural progress becomes obvious when we consider the past and present activities of religious leaders of other faiths in the field of agricultural development. In the United States of America, for instance, the churchmen in the rural areas do their utmost to equip themselves with scientific and technological qualifications in order to better serve the rural communities. Along with religious education, they acquire proficiency in agriculture and related specialities. Thus, the movements of conservation of land, co-operation, youth organizations, social reform and education started by religious groups in the U.S.A., especially promoted by the Catholic Church, have acquired a near religious sanctity and people believe in and act in accordance with them as if they were essential articles of their faith.

As a first step towards participation by the '*Ulamā*' in agricultural development, Muslim countries may try a scheme like a mosque community and farm guide centre which should envisage the training of village *Imāms* in certain special trades and skills, including breeding of poultry and fish, poultry vaccination, better farming through improved seed, agricultural implements, fertilizers, etc., and making them the torch-bearers of progress in the countryside. The scheme may provide for the sale of improved seed, for fertilizers, etc., through the *Imāms* who would get commission on the sales, and thus improve their own financial position as well. Thus the basic requirements of agriculture would readily become available at the farmer's doorstep.

There should be a follow-up programme, also, to ensure that the interest of the '*Ulamā*' do not sag in the project. The Pakistan Academy for Rural Development, Peshawar, launched such a programme covering five Union Councils only. The results, however, are very encouraging. In addition to the proposed use of mosques as centres of adult and agricultural education, purposefully conceived and planned series of sermons and *Khuṭbahs* can be a powerful means of creating the spirit of the dignity of labour and co-operation which is essential in an economy like Pakistan's where the size of the land-holdings of individual farmers is extremely small and uneconomic. The need for such association gathers further momentum from the fact that it will create a desire for growth among the so-called fatalist farmers of rural areas. This desire is vital from the point of view of growth.

Farm Chambers. Another important step which the governments of Muslim countries may take is to encourage the formation of farm chambers. If the agriculturists organize themselves into regional chambers on the pattern of the chambers of commerce and industry, this would enable the agriculturists to project their problems. The approach should be one of persuasion and motivation, not of force. An environment is to be created where such a sense of co-operation comes from within, not from "outside".

On successful implementation of the mosque community and farm guide scheme, the governments of Muslim countries will have to touch the Islamic law of inheritance which is apparently responsible for the subdivision and fragmentation of holdings. This can be done by prescribing the limit of economic holdings.

If governments fix the limit of minimum economic holdings without violating the Islamic laws of inheritance, this may act as a powerful inducement for co-operative farming, vital for Muslim countries. Egypt has already introduced such legislation. I find no harm in framing such laws in other Muslim countries in the larger interests of society. The possibility of giving insurance cover to the farmers of Muslim countries on the model of insurance cover to industrial labourers may also be explored.

We must not, however, forget that mere financial assistance does not ensure the fulfilment of the socio-economic goals of the Islamic state in the sphere of agricultural economy. The forces of change in a traditional society are generally weak and hence they require a powerful impetus if they are to assert themselves. The role of the Islamic state or the state-sponsored bodies in the management and functioning of agricultural credit institutions as well as in creating congenial conditions for the development of agriculture through a large number of smallholders, thus assumes crucial importance.

18.4 Summary and Conclusion

Planning.

The modern concept of planning which refers to the utilization of the resources of the country to attain certain objectives is recognized in Islam. Economic planning in Islam is nothing but a synthesis of planning by inducement and planning by direction. Various injunctions of Holy *Qur'ān* and sayings of the Prophet (peace be upon him) have confirmed this. Co-operation between public and private sectors is the basis of economic planning in Islam. The objectives of economic planning in Islam are relative to the needs of the community and can be changed with the changing circumstances subject to the injuctions of Holy *Qur'ān* and the *Sunnah*. The soundness of its objectives can be judged by the principle of beneficence and care for the poor. The execution of planning will be made through the participation of the public and private sectors on a partnership basis which will work through the application of the principle of *Muḍārabah*. It is because of this that there will be little chance of loss and fewer possibilities of depression under the Islamic system of planning.

There are two fundamental sources for financing a development plan. One is internal or domestic resources and the other foreign assistance. Internal finance may take two forms: private saving and public saving. In the Islamic state much can be done by encouraging the investment of small savings in the fields of greatest urgency and production. But when unnecessary consumption retards the process of economic development the Islamic state can intervene to control such consumption and direct control of investment policy. In respect of public saving the government of an Islamic state may adopt the policy of progressive taxation with less emphasis on indirect taxes which are often regressive in character, particularly if the taxed commodity happens to be a necessity of life. Again, keeping in view the items of expenditure on which *Zakāt* revenue can be spent, modern social security schemes and social welfare projects of planning may be financed out of the surplus of *Zakāt* revenue. Moreover, under the Islamic system of planning there is no harm in a government resorting to deficit financing. The only fundamental difference from modern planning lies in the fact that interest will not be allowed to exercise its harmful effects on production, employment and social justice. Here banks must act as partners of trade, commerce, industry and development plans.

For solving the problem of foreign exchange which is vital for development planning, we propose the following courses of action: (1) a systematic policy of promoting exports, (2) assistance from the Islamic Development Bank (I.D.B.), (3) encouraging foreign investment on a partnership basis, (4) taking loans from abroad on the payment of interest in extreme cases. However, the necessity of economic planning in Muslim countries arises for the following reasons:

(1) to exploit the vast natural resources of the Muslim countries which are poor and backward;

(2) to adjust the resources to the rapidly increasing population all over the Muslim countries;

(3) to bring economic stability and to reduce wastage, which is condemned in Islam;

(4) to help secure a more equitable distribution of income and wealth, which is recognized in Islam;

(5) to avoid the monopolistic exploitation, speculative business and anti-social wastes of the competitive system;

(6) to bring about an overall structural change in the economy of Muslim countries rapidly;

(7) to facilitate an easy transition of a country's economy to a war basis so that aggression, which is condemned in Islam, may be repelled.

In fact, planning in Islam is free from many of the shortcomings of the modern planning.

Economic Development.

The superiority of the Islamic concept of development, which refers to increasing output per hour of work done, over the modern concept of the term lies in the fact that the urge of economic development in Islam comes not only from the eternal economic problem of man but also from the divine inducement of the Holy *Qur'ān* and the *Sunnah*. We have seen that growth of output per head depends, on the one hand, on natural resources and, on the other hand, on human behaviour. But natural resources are not a sufficient condition for economic development, not even a necessary one. Human behaviour plays a very crucial role in economic development. But the moulding of human behaviour is a painful process in underdeveloped countries because it involves readjustment of social, economic, legal and political institutions. Unlike other religions, Islam recognizes both the metaphysical and the material needs of life. Therefore, the problem of moulding human behaviour in an Islamic state is not that acute compared to secular states.

Islam can be treated as a factor of economic development. The economists must here play the part of midwife, helping to bring into the world the materialized result of latest ideas and possibilities which may be related to the religious and cultural factors of Islam. Muslim countries are now in a better position to make greater development efforts for two reasons: (1) Many resources unknown in the nineteenth century are today accessible to Muslim countries. In 1920 the oil resources of the Middle East were estimated to be five per cent of the world's resources. Today the figure is approximately eighty-five per cent. (2) The Islamic values of life may be utilized for adjustment of adverse socio-economic and socio-political institutions and for moulding human behaviour. The development experience of Muslim countries since the 1950s (excepting some oil-rich Muslim countries) in general and of the least developed countries in particular is disappointing. Relatively speaking, the least developed Muslim countries are poorer than ever before. It has been stressed that the provisioning for the minimum subsistence level in respect of food, clothing and shelter is the primary concern for an Islamic state.

Again, it is pointed out that, while efforts should be made to exploit resources, emphasis should be given to social appropriateness in the use, development and transfer of technology.

However, all-round efforts should be made to develop the Muslim countries. Since a vast majority of farmers of Muslim countries are unaware of the tremendous improvements in agriculture brought about by modern science and technology, attempts may be made to associate the '*Ulamā*' or *Imāms* of mosques with development activities. As a first step towards participation by '*Ulamā*' in agricultural development, Muslim countries may try a scheme which would envisage the training of village *Imāms* in certain special trades and skills and making them the torch-bearers of progress in the countryside. Besides this, encouragement should be given to the formulation of farm chambers on the model of chambers of commerce and industry. Apparently, it appears that the Islamic law of inheritance is responsible for the subdivision and fragmentation of land-holdings. Muslim countries should come forward to fix the limit of minimum economic holdings. This may act as a powerful inducement for co-operative farming, vital for Muslim countries.

18.5 Selected Further Reading

Abu Saud, Mahmud, "Economic Policy in Islam" in *Islamic Review*, London, 1957.

Ahmad, K. "Some Thoughts on a Strategy for Development under an Islamic Aegis" in *Islam and a New International Economic order: The Social Dimension* Geneva I.I.L.S., 1980.

Ali, Ahmad Mohammad, "The Role of the Islamic Development Bank in the Future Economic Order", in *The Muslim World and The Future Economic Order*, The Islamic Council of Europe, 1979.

Cook, M. A. "Economic Developments" in *The Legacy of Islam* 2nd edn. ed. by Joseph Schacht and C. E. Bosworth, Oxford, 1974.

Daley, T. W. and Puligandia, R. "Islam and the Concept of Progress', *Islamic Review*, vol. 58, No. 2, London, 1970.

Hasan Z. "Distributional Equity in Islam", a paper presented at the Second International Conference on Islamic Economics: Development, Finance and Distribution in an Islamic Perspective Islamic University, Islamabad, 19–23 March, 1983.

Hug, A. "Poverty, Inequity and the Role of some Islamic Economic Institutions", a paper presented at the Second International Conference on Islamic Economics: Development, Finance and Distribution in an Islamic Perspective Islamic University, Islamabad, 19–23 March, 1983.

Hussain, Muzaffar, "Motivation for Economic Achievement in Islam", All Pakistan Education Congress, Lahore, 1974.

Ibrahim, Yousif, "The Contributions of Islamic Ideology to the Field of Development", International Institute of Islamic Banking and Economics, paper 4/3 for "First Advanced Course on Islamic Banks", Cairo, 1981.

Jomo, K. S. "Islam and Weber Rodinson on the Implications of Religion for Capitalist Development" in *Development Economics*, Tokyo, 1977.

Mannan, M. A. "The Economics of Poverty with special reference to Muslim Countries", a paper presented at the Second International Conference on Islamic Economics: Development, Finance and Distribution in an Islamic Perspective, Islamic University, Islamabad, 19–23 March, 1983.

Mannan, M. A. "Development experience and Choice for the Muslim World: A Search for Policy Alternatives in Development Planning in an Islamic Framework", in *The Making of Islamic Economic Society: Islamic Dimensions in Economic Analysis*, Chapter 16, International Association of Islamic Banks, Cairo, 1984.

Mannan, M. A. "The Strategy of Economic Development in an Islamic Economy", a paper presented at the Second International Conference on Islamic Economics: Development, Finance and Distribution in an Islamic Perspective, Islamic University, Islamabad, 19–23 March, 1983.

Al Naggar, Ahmad, "The Healthy Path Towards Economic Development: The Islamic Alternative", *Proceedings of International Seminar on Islamic Social Justice*. A. B. U. Zaria, 1983.

Naqvi, S. N. H. "An Islamic Approach to Economic Development" in Islam and a New International Economic Order: *The Social Dimension*, I.I.L.S, Geneva, 1980

Quraishi, Marghoob A. "Investment and Economic Development in Muslim Countries".*Proceedings of Third Seminar* Association of Muslim Social Scientists, Indiana, U.S.A. 1974.

Rauf, Muhammad Abdul, "The Islamic Doctrine of Economics and Contemporary Economic Thought", American Enterprise Institute, Washington, D. C., 1979.

Rushdi, A. A. "Effects of Elimination of Riba on the Distribution of Income", a paper presented at the Second International Conference on

Islamic Economics: Development, Finance and Distribution in an Islamic Perspective, Islamic University, Islamabad, 19–23 March, 1983.

Sajidin, M. "The Concept of Agricultural Development in Islam", in *Economic System of Islam*, National Bank of Pakistan, Karachi, 1980.

Sharif, R. "The Concept of Economic Development in Islam", a paper presented at the Second International Conference on Islamic Economics: Development, Finance and Distribution in an Islamic Perspective, Islamic University, Islamabad, 19–23 March, 1983.

Sutcliffe, Claud R. "Is Islam on Obstacle to Development?" *The Journal of Developing Areas*, Illinois University, 1975

Ulgener, Sabri F. "Monetary Conditions of Economic Growth and the Islamic Concept of Interest – The Definition of Riba" in *The Islamic Review*, vol. 52, London, 1964.

Appendices

(a) **Basic socio-economic indicators for member countries of the Islamic Development Bank (I.D.B.).**

(b) **Selected publications on Islamic Economics by the author in different languages.**

(c) **Readers' views and peers' opinions on the works of the author; selected excerpts.**

Appendix (A) Basic socio-economic indicators for member countries of the Islamic Development Bank (I.D.B.)

Table 1 *Basic Indicators for member Countries-1*

Country	Area '000 km²	Total Population (million) Mid-1981	Density (persons per km²) 1981	Average Annual Growth of Population % 1970–80	Arable Land and Land under Permanent Crops 1000 ha 1979	Irrigated Area (1000 ha)	Labour Force in Agriculture % 1980	Labour Force in Industry % 1980	Life Expectancy at Birth Years 1980
1	2	3	4	5	6	7	8	9	10
Afghanistan	648	16.36	25	2.5	8,050	2,600	78	8	37
Algeria	2,382	19.21	8	3.2	7,497	300	50	25	56
Bahrain	(620 km²)	0.36	580	2.8	2	1	..	..	67
Bangladesh	144	89.94	625	2.6	9,230	1,520	84	11	46
Burkina Faso	274	7.09	26	1.8	2,563	5	81	13	39
Cameroon	475	8.72	18	2.2	6,912	8	81	7	47
Chad	1,284	4.55	4	2.0	3,150	3	84	7	41
Comoros	2	0.40	200	4.0	90	..	64	..	47
Djibouti	22	0.38	17	2.3	1	..	..	..	45
Egypt	1,001	42.87	43	2.1	2,848	2,850	50	30	57
Gabon	268	0.55	2	1.1	450	..	76	..	45
Gambia	11	0.62	56	2.8	265	30	78	..	42
Guinea	246	5.60	28	2.9	1,570	10	80	11	45
Guinea Bissau	36	0.58	16	1.5	285	..	82	..	42
Indonesia	1,905	147.40	77	2.3	19,418	5,360	55	13	62
Iraq	435	13.53	31	3.3	5,450	1,730	40	26	56
Jordan	98	3.28	33	3.4	1,370	85	26	20	61
Kuwait	18	1.44	80	6.0	1	1	2	34	70
Lebanon	10	3.22	322	0.7	348	85	10	27	66

Country									
Libya	1,760	3.10	2	4.1	2,564	140	16	28	56
Malaysia	330	14.42	44	2.4	4,300	360	48	16	64
Maldives	(300 km²)	0.16	533	2.5	3	..	11	26	47
Mali	1,240	7.16	6	2.7	2,050	100	87	12	43
Mauritania	1,031	1.68	2	2.5	195	8	83	5	43
Morocco	447	20.65	46	3.0	7,719	500	51	21	56
Niger	1,267	5.48	4	2.8	3,290	36	88	3	43
Oman	212	0.92	4	3.1	41	..	62	..	48
Pakistan	804	82.44	103	3.1	20,175	14,450	54	20	50
Palestine	..	..	..	..	..	..	..	..	..
Qatar	11	0.23	21	5.4	2	..	..	..	58
Saudi Arabia	2,150	8.74	4	4.4	1,105	395	60	14	54
Senegal	196	5.82	30	2.8	5,200	180	74	10	43
Sierra Leone	72	3.57	50	2.6	1,760	6	65	19	47
Somalia	638	3.73	6	2.3	1,066	165	80	8	44
Sudan	2,506	18.90	8	3.0	12,400	1,700	77	10	46
Syria	185	9.30	50	3.6	5,686	539	48	31	65
Tunisia	164	6.51	40	2.1	4,970	140	41	33	60
Turkey	781	46.45	59	2.4	27,940	2,050	54	13	62
Uganda	236	13.62	58	2.6	5,610	5	81	6	54
U.A.E.	84	0.80	10	13.2	12	5	..	..	63
Yemen A.R.	195	6.06	31	2.9	2,790	243	75	11	42
Yemen P.D.R.	333	2.02	6	2.4	205	67	59	15	45

(.. not available)
Sources: 1. UN Monthly Bulletin of Statistics, July 1982, UN
2. World Development Report 1982, World Bank
3. 1980 Production Yearbook, Vol. 34, FAO.
Reproduced from the seventh Annual Report of the Islamic Development Bank, (1982)

Table 2 *Basic Indicators for Member Countries-3*

Country	GNP at Market Prices (US$ Mn) 1980	GNP per capita (US$) 1980	Average Annual Growth of GNP per capita Real (%) 1970-79	Growth Rate of Real GDP % 1979-80	Gross Domestic Investment as % of GDP 1980	Gross Domestic Savings as % GDP 1980	Consumer Price Index (1975=100) 1980	External Public Debt (Disbursed only) (US$ Mn) End 1980	Debt Service as % of GNP 1970	Debt Service as % of GNP 1980	Exports of Goods and Services 1970	Exports of Goods and Services 1980
1	2	3	4	5	6	7	8	9	10	11	12	13
Afghanistan	3,644[a]	241[a]	3.9	−3.4	14[e]	11[e]	148.8	1,094.5	2.5	1.4[a]	..	..
Algeria	36,410	1,920	2.8	7.2	41	42	159.6[e]	15,989.7	23.9	9.0	9.7	37
Bahrain	2,350	5,560	0.7[b]	..	..	..	177.4	—	—	—	—	—
Bangladesh	11,470	127	0.8	4.8	17	.2	144.0	3,495.3	7.1	0.7	3.4	0.3
Burkino Faso	1,110	190	−1.2	2.0	18	−9	166.4	323.0	6.8	1.4	2.8	0.6
Cameroon	5,660	670	3.1	3.2	25	23	166.1	1,773.9	0.8	3.6	3.2	1.8
Chad	530	120	−2.4	7.4	13[e]	−14[e]	..	159.3	1.0	3.1	3.9	0.8
Comoros	100	300	−4.3	4.3	36	..	..	50.4	..	0.5	..	4.8
Djibouti	170	480	−4.9	3.5	21[a]	4[a]	156.6[a]	32.0[e]	..	..	..	..
Egypt	23,140	580	5.3	8.8	31[e]	16[e]	183.1	13,053.6	18.9	6.9	5.3	1.9
Gabon	2,420	3,680	5.2	5.2	47	..	183.8	1,259.3	15.1	12.1	4.4	3.5
Gambia	150	250	0.4	−3.5	..	..	162.4	85.1	..	0.1	..	0.1
Guinea	1,590	290	0.6	5.6	11	14	..	1,068.4	24.6	6.6	5.9	1.6
Guinea Bissau	130	160	3.1[e]	−4.3	16	..	..	55.5	30.0	4.1	..	18.1
Indonesia	66,554	451	4.6	9.6	22	30	207.9	14,940.3	8.0	2.7	3.7	1.2
Iraq	39,550	3,020	9.3	6.2	33	59	..	—	—	—	—	—
Jordan	3,270	1,420	6.0[d]	7.1	48	−27	173.3	1,266.2	5.4	3.7	2.3	1.6
Kuwait	30,900	22,840	1.4	..	11	63	141.0	—	—	—	—	—
Lebanon	..	..	..	..	..	..	..	194.0	0.2	..	—	—
Libya	25,730	8,640	−1.6	5.0	25	59	..	—	—	..	—	—
Malaysia	22,410	1,670	5.4	7.6	29	32	124.7	3,103.4	2.3	1.4	1.4	0.9
Maldives	40	260	−0.7	..	..	..	..	23.8	..	1.0	—	—
Mali	1,340	190	2.5	−2.0	15	−3	..	621.1	0.2	0.8	..	3.6
Mauritania	530	320	−0.7	3.9	51	14	163.4	713.8	11.5	5.9	4.9	2.5
Morocco	17,444	860	3.5	2.3	21	11	158.9	7,097.5	28.0	6.7	14.5	3.5

Country												
Niger	1,760	330	−1.2	5.1	29	21	198.4	398.7	5.7	2.2	2.3	0.9
Oman	3,900	4,380	3.8	..	..	..	..	345.5	4.2	3.5	0.6	0.5
Pakistan	24,870	300	1.5	5.8	18	6	153.9	8,775.3	10.9	2.4	4.4	1.0
Palestine	..	..	..	..	..	..	..	−	..	..	..	..
Qatar	6,020	26,080	−1.2	..	..	..	151.5	..	−	−	−	..
Saudi Arabia	100,930	11,260	9.6	..	26	59	138.8	905.6	0.8	6.9	2.7	..
Senegal	2,560	450	0.1	−5.6	15	−2	189.6	343.9	2.9	4.2	10.1	18.4
Sierra Leone	950	270	−1.2	1.4	15	6	273.8	693.0	3.5	0.5	0.9	0.1
Somalia	516	136	4.1	−0.6	16	3	233.3	3,097.5	17.4	1.8	1.9	0.2
Sudan	8,640	470	1.5	3.2	12	10	163	2,492.7	15.2	3.2	3.7	0.8
Syria	12,030	1,340	4.6	9.7	25	25	140.4	2,955.0	11.8	4.9	5.5	2.3
Tunisia	8,340	1,310	5.7	7.0	28	18	722.6	13,998.5	1.3	1.2	16.3	11.6
Turkey	66,080	1,460	3.5	−0.4	27	2	..	669.0	0.6	0.4	3.4	11.9
Uganda	3,750	280	−3.5	−2.0	3	73	..	..	−	−	−	..
U.A.E.	26,850	30,070	2.4b	..	30	−20	..	..	..	..	..	..
Yemen A.R.	2,680	460	4.3	1.5	44	..	..	619.9	1.7	0.7	0.3	0.1
Yemen P.D.R.	810	420	6.2	−4.9	..	..	123.7e	536.5	3.3	1.8	0.7	0.4

.. not available
— nil

a refers to 1978
b refers to 1975–79
c refers to 1960–79
d refers to 1972–79
e refers to 1979

Source: 1. Development Co-operation 1981, OECD, Paris.
2. Handbook of International Trade & Development Statistics, 1981 Supplement, UNCTAD.
3. International Financial Statistics (Supplement on Price Statistics).
4. World Bank Atlas 1981, World Bank.
5. World Debt Tables 1981, World Bank.
6. World Development Report 1982, World Bank.
Reproduced from Seventh Annual Report of the Islamic Development Bank (1982)

Table 3 Basic Indicators for Member Countries-5

Country	Exports (F.O.B.) (US$ Mn) 1981	Exports as % of GDP 1980	Average Annual Growth of Exports % 1970–1980	Imports (C.I.F.) (US$ Mn) 1981	Imports as % of GDP 1980	Average Annual Growth of Imports % 1970–1980	Trade Balance (US$ Mn) 1981	Terms of Trade (1975 = 100) 1960	Trade 1980	International Reserves (US$ Mn) End 1981	Exchange Rate National Currency Per US $ September 30, 1982
1	2	3	4	5	6	7	8	9	10	11	12
Afghanistan	263	:	3.7	484	:	8.1	−221	82	106	519.3	50.00
Algeria	14,056	31	2.2	11,505	24	12.7	2,551	39	177	3,922	4,705
Bahrain	3,541	:	30.3	4,385	22	30.5	−845	201	84	1,551	0.376
Bangladesh	791	7	−1.9	2,542	34	3.5	−1,751	88	89	155.3	23,012
Burkina Faso	133	5	2.0	323	27	7.9	−190	106	123	71.3	356.90
Cameroon	1,862	25	2.5	1,760	32	7.2	102	98	96	97.2	356.90
Chad	141	13	−4.0	137	28	−2.2	4			11.76	356.90
Comoros	9	17	13.0	42	37b	11.8	−27				356.90
Djibouti	50	14b	9.1	177	21	9.4	−166	92	79		177.72
Egypt	3,233	13	−0.7	8,782	28b	8.8	−5,549	47		1,491	0.70
Gabon	2,196	51b	33.3	956	29	30.5	1,240	104		204.0	356.90
Gambia	25	8	15.4	164	16	27.4	−139			3.95	2.363
Guinea	428	23	28.5	351	38	18.7	77		255		22.9956*
Guinea Bissau	15	14	20.2	52	16	2.9	−37	63	135		40.9882
Indonesia	22,101	31	8.7	13,520	29	11.9	8,581	25	170	6,076	670.50
Iraq	9,372	74	2.2	18,903	109	20.5	−9,531	78	59		0.2953
Jordan	682	20	18.4	3,908	24	13.5	−3,226	23	171	1,087	0.3600
Kuwait	16,561	73	−8.5	8,042	81	16.3	8,519	87	84	4,180	0.2909
Lebanon	1,107	19	0.7	3,946	31	2.4	−2,839	31	183	1,906	4.42*
Libya	16,391	72	−6.5	14,642	45	16.8	1,749	150	109	9,147	0.2960
Malaysia	11,198	58	7.4	11,578		7.0	−380			4,193	2.3780

Maldives	9	22[a]	11.3	36	17[a]	7.7	−27	107	91	..	7.55*
Mali	154	14	9.4	370	21	3.4	−216	149	77	17.4	713.80
Mauritania	325	40	−1.1	265	52	5.6	60	75	57	168.3	53.55
Morocco	2,160	13	2.1	4,487	23	8.5	−2,327	98	80	253	6.248
Niger	297	15	12.8	449	26	15.8	−152	..	..	105.8	356.90
Oman	4,416	58	34.6	2,221	31	44.9	2,195	..	..	1,209	0.3435
Pakistan	2,880	12	1.2	5,410	25	4.3	−2,530	102	74	1,507	12.428
Palestine	..	..	..	..	..	..	..	..	..	..	..
Qatar	3,978	95	34.5	1,571	..	39.6	2,407	27	165	..	3.6399
Saudi Arabia	113,328	20	5.4	35,268	26	35.2	78,060	71	63	32,422	3.435
Senegal	416	26	1.2	1,035	45	4.1	−619	121	84	9.9	356.90
Sierra Leone	277	12	−4.8	238	45	−3.0	39	145	88	16.0	1.275
Somalia	133	8	5.5	199	21	7.2	−66	83	86	37.5	15.207
Sudan	820	16	−5.7	1,942	22	3.5	−1,122	69	120	17.0	0.90
Syria	2,205	30	6.8	4,603	32	13.0	−2,398	64	99	291	3.925
Tunisia	2,209	5	4.8	3,994	48	10.6	−1,785	..	71	542.7	0.6356
Turkey	4,703	4	1.7	8,961	14	3.3	−4,258	..	130	1,444	176.75
Uganda	317	69	−8.5	395	3	−9.8	−78	..	..	..	99.55*
U.A.E.	20,939	..	6.1	9,549	29	27.7	11,390	123	162	3,387	3.671
Yemen A.R.	39	1	16.0	1,699	57	53.8	−1,660	..	..	961.9	4.5625
Yemen P.D.R.	421	56	10.0	1,096	121	12.1	−675	..	..	256.3	0.3454

.. Not available

a Refers to 1978

b Refers to 1979

* Figure for September 29, 1982

Sources: 1. Direction of Trade Statistics Yearbook 1982, IMF
 2. Financial Times, October, 1982
 3. Handbook of International Trade & Development Statistics 1981 Supplement, UNCTAD
 4. International Financial Statistics, November 1982, IMF

Reproduced from Seventh Annual Report of the Islamic Development Board (1982).

Table 4 *Three Top Export Commodities and their Total Weight in Exports, 1975 (3 digit-SITC Group)—IV*

	Total Weight (%)	Commodity Group
Algeria	93	Crude petroleum; Petroleum products; Alcoholic beverages
Bahrain	87	Petroleum products; Aluminium; Mineral tar and crude chemicals from petroleum
Bangladesh	83	Textile fabrics; Made-up articles, wholly or chiefly of textile materials, Jute
Burkina Faso	80	Live animals; Oil seeds, oil nuts and oil kernels; Cotton
Cameroon	65	Cocoa; Fresh meat; Petroleum products
Chad	87	Cotton; Fresh meat; Petroleum products
Gabon	98	Crude petroleum; Ores and concentrates of non-ferrous base metals; Rough wood
Gambia	97	Oil seeds; Fixed vegetable oils, soft; Feedstuff for animals
Indonesia	82	Crude petroleum; Rough wood; Petroleum products
Iran	96	Crude petroleum; Petroleum products
Iraq	99	Crude petroleum
Jordan	61	Crude fertilizers; Fresh fruit and nuts; Aircraft
Kuwait	91	Crude petroleum; Petroleum products, Mineral tar and crude chemicals from petroleum
Libya	100	Crude petroleum; Natural gas; Petroleum products
Malaysia	51	Crude rubber; Fixed vegetable oils other than soft; Tin
Maldives	100	Fish, fresh and simply preserved
Mali	70	Cotton; Live animals; Oil seeds
Morocco	69	Crude fertilizers; Fresh vegetables; Fresh fruit and nuts
Niger	85	Ores and concentrates of non-ferrous base metals; Live animals; Fixed vegetable oils, soft
Oman	100	Crude petroleum
Pakistan	46	Rice; Cotton; Cotton fabrics
Qatar	99	Crude petroleum; Manufactured fertilizers
Saudi Arabia	99	Crude petroleum; Petroleum products
Senegal	57	Petroleum products; Fixed vegetable oils, soft; Crude fertilizers
Somalia	81	Live animals; Fresh fruits and nuts
Sudan	83	Cotton; Oil seeds, oil nuts and oil kernels; Crude vegetable materials
Syria	82	Crude petroleum; Cotton
Tunisia	65	Crude petroleum; Crude fertilizers; Fixed vegetable oils, soft
Turkey	43	Cotton; Fresh fruit and nuts; manufactured tobacco
Uganda	93	Coffee; Cotton; Tea and mate
U.A.E.	98	Crude petroleum
Yemen A.R.	80	Cotton; Coffee; Hides and skins
Yemen P.D.R.	76	Petroleum products

Source: Summary of Statistics (1980). Page 35. Statistical, Economic and Social Research and Training Centre for Islamic Countries, Ankara, Turkey, Organization of Islamic Conference.

Table 5 *Share of Some Muslim Countries In the World Export Market Of Selected Commodities Average 1975–77 (Percentage)-V*

Country	Commodity								
	Jute	Rubber	Ground Nuts	Tin	Phosphate Rock	Baux- ite	Petro- leum	Ground nut Oil	Palm Oil
Bangladesh	63.9	–	–	–	–	–	–	–	–
Gambia	–	–	5.3	–	–	–	–	3.8	–
Guinea	–	–	0.3	–	–	25.3	–	–	–
Indonesia	–	22.1	0.3	10.9	–	1.2	4.3	0.1	16.6
Iran	–	–	–	–	–	–	15.3	–	–
Iraq	–	–	–	–	–	–	6.6 (98.4)	–	–
Jordan	–	–	–	–	3.2	–	–	–	
Kuwait	–	–	–	–	–	–	5.6	–	–
Libya	–	–	–	–	–	–	6.2	–	–
Malaysia	–	52.2	0.3	39.8	–	0.7	–	0.5	59.2
Morocco	–	–	–	–	34.4	–	–	–	–
Nigeria	–	1.0	–	1.6	–	–	6.4	–	0.3
Saudi Arabia	–	–	–	–	–	–	24.1	–	–
Senegal	–	–	4.9	–	4.0	–	–	42.4	–
Sudan	–	–	20.0	–	–	–	–	1.1	–
Tunisia	–	–	–	–	3.8	–	0.3	–	–
Total:	63.9	75.3	30.8	52.3	45.4	27.2	68.8	47.7	76.1

Source: Islamic Development Bank,
SEG/WP/111–5/IDB, Jeddah,
Saudi Arabia, 1979.

Table 6. A. *World Export Shares (percentage of total value)*

	1960	1970	1973	1974	1975	1976	1977
World	100.0	100.0	100.0	100.0	100.0	100.0	100.0
USA	15.9	13.6	12.2	11.6	12.2	11.4	10.6
EEC	32.7	35.7	36.4	32.6	33.8	32.8	33.7
O/C[1]	5.3	6.2	7.6	14.2	12.6	13.5	12.1
Oil Exporting[2]	3.5	4.3	5.8	12.4	11.0	11.8	11.2
Others	1.7	1.9	1.8	1.9	1.7	1.7	1.0

B. *World Import Shares (percentage of total value)*

	1960	1970	1973	1974	1975	1976	1977
World	100.0	100.0	100.0	100.0	100.0	100.0	100.0
USA	11.0	12.1	11.6	12.5	11.4	12.7	13.6
EEC	33.3	35.2	36.2	34.2	33.0	33.6	33.3
OIC[1]	5.0	4.3	4.9	5.4	7.0	7.1	8.0
Oil Exporting[2]	2.5	2.0	2.6	3.0	4.4	4.7	5.4
Others	2.5	2.3	2.2	2.4	2.6	2.4	2.7

Source: UN Trade Statistics
(1) Members of the Organization of Islamic Conference (OIC) reproduced from: *Areas of economic co-operation among Islamic countries* by SESRTCIC, Ankara, (OIC), P. 34, 1980.
(2) Figures include Algeria, Indonesia, Iran, Iraq, Kuwait, Libya, Oman, Qatar, Saudi Arabia, U.A.E.

APPENDIX (B)

SELECTED PUBLICATIONS ON ISLAMIC ECONOMICS

by the author in different languages

1. *PUBLICATIONS IN ENGLISH LANGUAGE.*

1.A. *Books/Monograph on Islamic Economics*

—*Islamic Economics; Theory and Practice*, book of 386 pages, published by Sh. Mohammad Ashraf, Lahore, Pakistan, 1970, (Awarded best-book Academic Award by Pakistan Writters' Guild, 1970) reprinted 1975 and 1980 in Pakistan. Reprinted in India, 1980.

—*The Making of Islamic Economics Society*: Islamic Dimensions in Economic Analysis: published by International Association of Islamic Banks, Cairo, and International Institute of Islamic Banking and Economics, Kibris (Turkish Cyprus) 1984, p. 534.

—*The Frontiers of Islamic Economics*, published by Idaraht-Ada'biyah, Delhi, India, 1984, p. 207.

—*Economic Development in an Islamic Framework* (Edited/forthcoming).

—*Key Issues and Questions in Islamic Economics, Finance and Development* (forthcoming).

—*Abstracts of Researches in Islamic Economics* (edited), KAAU, 1984.

1.B. *Research Papers/Articles on Islamic Economics since 1962.*

—*"Islam and Trends in Modern Banking* – Theory and Practice of Interest-free Banking" – First Presented at a seminar, Serajgong College, University of Rajshahi, Bangladesh in 1962; its modified version published in *Islamic Review and Arab Affairs*, Vol. 56, Nov./Dec., London, 1968, pp. 5–10, and Vol. 57, January, London, 1969, pp. 28–33, U.K.

—"Fiscal Policy and Budgeting in Islam" in *Voice of Islam*, University of Karachi, Vol. 16, Karachi, 1967/68, pp. 658–675.

—"Trade and Commerce in Islam" in *Voice of Islam*, University of Karachi, Karachi, Vol. 16, Karachi, 1967/68, also appeared in *the Criterion* Vol. 6, No. 6, Karachi 1970, pp. 19–29.

—"Modern Labour-Capital Relationship in Islam" in *Islamic Literature*, September issue 1967, Lahore, Pakistan.

—"Concept of Private Ownership in Islam" in *Islamic Literature*, November, 1968, Lahore, Pakistan.

—"Some Aspects of Public Finance in Islam", in *Contemporary Affairs*, Bureau of National Research (B.N.R.), Rawalpindi, Pakistan, 1968.

—Distribution of National Income and Wealth in Islam, in *Contemporary Affairs*, B.N.R., 1969, Rawalpindi, Pakistan.

—"Islam as a factor of Development" in the *Criterion* Vol. -6. No. 3, Karachi, 1971, pp. 10–19, also appeared in *Islamic Literature*, 1969, Lahore, Pakistan, August.

—"Consumption Loan in Islam" in *Islamic Review and Arab Affairs*. Vol-58, March, 1970, London, U.K.

—"Islamic Theory of Capital and Interest" in *Islamic Literature*, Vol-16, No. 4, Lahore, 1970, p. 23–34, also appeared in *The Criterion*, Vol-5, No. 3, Karachi, 1970, pp. 60–69.

—"Islamic Social Framework – Its Meaning and Scope" in the *Criterion*, Vol-5, No. 1, Karachi, 1970, pp. 5–12.

—"Concept of Welfare State in Islam" in *The Criterion*, Vol-5, No. 6, Karachi, 1970, pp. 63–73.

—"Superiority of Islamic Concept of, Brotherhood and Co-existence" in *Islamic Literature*, January, 1970, Lahore, Pakistan.

—"Analysis of Modern Prices" in *The Criterion*, Vol-5, No. 5, Karachi, 1970, pp. 19–28.

—"Islam and other Isms – Ideologies of Capitalism, Socialism, Fascism and their effects on Man's behaviour", in *Islamic Review and Arab Affairs*. Vol-59, January, London., U.K. 1971, pp. 5–11.

—"Rent and Wages in Islam" in *The Criterion*, Vol-6, No. 4, Karachi, Pakistan, 1971, pp. 34–40.

—"Principles of Consumption in Islam" in *The Criterion*, Vol-6, No. 5, Karachi, 1971, Pakistan, pp. 23–29.

—"A Muslim World Bank – Urgent Need" in *The Criterion*, Vol-6, No. 1, Karachi, 1971, Pakistan, pp. 15–20.

—"Islamic Social Framework: An Outline of its Structure and Criteria": published by the *Muslim Institute, London*, 1980.

—Scarcity, Choice and Opportunity Cost: Their Dimensions in Islamic Economics", published by *Journal of Social Sciences*, University of Kuwait, Hijra Issue, 1981, reprinted by Muslim Institute London", and *International Centre for Research in Islamic Economics* (I.C.R.I.E.), King Abdulaziz University, Jeddah, 1982.

—"Institutional Settings of Islamic Economic Order" published by the International Centre for Research in Islamic Economics (*I.C.R.I.E.*), King Abdulaziz University, Jeddah, 1981.

—"Indexation in an Islamic Economy: Problems and Prospects" in *Journal of Development Studies*, vol. -IV, 1981 N.W.F.P., Agricultural University, Peshawar, Pakistan.

—"Islamic Perspectives on Market Prices and Allocation" published by the International Centre for Research in Islamic Economics (*I.C.R.I.E.*), King Abdulaziz University, Jeddah, 1982.

—"Why is Islamic Economics Important" published by *ICRIE*, King Abdulaziz University, (KAAU), Jeddah, 1982.

—Islamic Economics as a Social Science, ICRIE, KAAU, Jeddah, 1983.

—Non-formal Education: Where Does Islamic Economics Values Enter?

1.C. *Seminar Papers and Research Reports/Books On Islamic Economics and Muslim Countries:*

—"Allocative Efficiency, Decision and Welfare Criteria in an Interest-free Economy: A Comparative Approach" paper presented at the International Seminar on Monetary and Fiscal Economic of Islam held under the King Abdulaziz University at Makkah, 7–12 October, 1978: Also published by *Muslim Institute, London*, August, 1980.

—"Special Policy Imperatives for Economic Development and Social Change in least Developed Muslim Countries of Islamic Development Bank" 170 page report, Jeddah, April, 1979.

—Islamic Perspectives on Islamic Banks" An analysis of nine unconventional role and operational strategies: Published in *Thoughts on Islamic Banking* by Islamic Economics Research Bureau, Dhaka, Bangladesh, 1980, presented at an International Seminar on Islamic Banking, held in Dhaka, Bangladesh.

—Review article on "Risk-bearing and Profit-sharing in Islamic Framework" presented at Monetary Economics seminar at Islamabad, Pakistan, 1981.

—"The Economics of Poverty in Islam": presented at the Second International Conference on "*Development, Distribution and Finance*", held at Islamic University, Islamabad, Pakistan, March, 1983.

—"The Strategy of Economic Development in an Islamic State", Working paper presented at the Second International

Conference on "*Development Distribution and Finance*", held at Islamic University, Islamabad, Pakistan, March 19–23, 1983.

—Review article on a book: Issues in Islamic Banking, ICRIE, KAAU, (1983).

"Guidelines for Key Issues in Islamic Economics"

a paper presented at Joint International Conference on Research in crime prevention held in Riyadh 23–25 January, 1984, sponsored by Arab Security Studies Centre and United Nations Social Defence Research Institute, Rome, Italy.

"The Frontiers of Islamic Economics;
Some philosophical underpinnings"

Presented at the third International seminar 1984 in Kuala Lumpur, Malaysia sponsored by International Institute of Islamic thought Washington, DC. U.S.A.

"When does Economic Development and Social Change begin in Muslim Society?

Presented at a Seminar of Islamic Approach to Development of Bangladesh, Dhaka, sponsored by Islamic Economics Research Bureau, Dhaka, Bangladesh (1985).

—Review article on "A Model of Educational Planning and Development in Islamic Perspective" (forthcoming).

—Review article on a book: *Outlines of Islamic Economics, Journal of Research in Islamic Economics*, KAAU, 1984, Vol. 2, No. 1.

"International Islamic Bank in Financing Development in the Muslim World"

Presented (1984) at International Seminar of Financing for Development, sponsored by the Faculty of Economics, University of Kebangsaan Bangi, Sclangor, Malaysia and the Public Bank of Malaysia.

1.D. *Text Books: (Published in Bangladesh and Pakistan):*

—*An Introduction to Applied Economics*, published by the Pakistan Book Corporation, Dhaka, Bangladesh, 1963, pp. 210.

—*Economic Problems and Planning in Pakistan.* 1st edition 1968, 4th edition 1970. Published by Ferozesons Ltd., Lahore, pp. 423.

1.E. *Unpublished Research just Completed or in Progress:*

—"Securities Market in an Islamic Framework: A Comparative Analysis", (Monograph/just completed to be published by Islamic Development Bank, Jeddah, Saudi Arabia.)

Abstracts of Completed Studies by Functional Category: (1977–1984) under ICRIE Research Programme (Abstracted and edited/forthcoming).

—Understanding Macro-economics from Islamic Perspectives (Text book in progress).

—The Structure of Structural Change: Towards Islamic Theory of Development, A case study of Bangladesh (in progress).

2. PUBLICATIONS ON ISLAMIC ECONOMICS IN ARABIC LANGUAGES

2.A —*Islamic Economics; Theory and Practice*, originally published in English by Sh. Mohammed Ashraf, Lahore, Pakistan (1970), translated into Arabic by Dr. Mansour Al-Turki, published in (1973) reprinted in 1975, 1976.

2.B —"Zakat: its disbursement and intra-poor distributional equity, Al-Muslim", Al-Musir, Quarterly, Kuwait Scientific Research House, No: 37, Al-Muharram, 1404.

2.C —"Scarcity, Choice and Opportunity Cost; their dimensions in Islamic economics" originally published in English by *Journal of Social Science*, University of Kuwait, Century Hijra Issue, 1981, reprinted and translated into Arabic by the International Centre for Research in Islamic Economics, King Abdulaziz University, Jeddah, Saudi Arabia.

2.D —*The Making of Islamic Economic Society; Islamic dimension in economic analysis*; original published in English, International Association of Islamic Banks, Cairo and International Institute of Islamic Banking and Economics, Cyprus, (Arabic version forthcoming).

2.E "Guidelines for Key Issues in Islamic Economics"

a paper presented at Joint International Conference on Research in crime prevention held in Riyadh 23–25 January, 1984, sponsored by Arab Security Studies Centre and United Nations Social Defence Research Institute, Rome, Italy.

3. PUBLICATIONS ON ISLAMIC ECONOMICS IN TURKISH LANGUAGE

3.A —*Islamic Economics; Theory and Practice*; originally published in English by Sh. Mohammad Ashraf, Lahore, Pakistan (1970). Translated into Turkish language by Dr. Bahri Zengin, Turkey, first published in 1973, reprinted in 1975, 1976, 1980.

3.B —"Islam and Trends in Modern Banking – Theory and Practice of Interest-free Banking" originally published in *Islamic Review and Arab Affairs*, vol. 56, Nov./Dec., London, 1968, pp. 5–10, and vol. 57, January, London, 1969, pp. 28–33, U.K. Translated into Turkish by M. T. Guran Ayyildiz Matahassi, Ankara (1969).

3.C —*The Making of Islamic Economic Society; Islamic dimensions in economic analysis*: original publisher in English: International Association of Islamic Banks, Cairo and International Institute of Islamic Banking and Economics, Cyprus (Turkish version forthcoming).

4. PUBLICATIONS ON ISLAMIC ECONOMICS IN BENGALI LANGUAGE

4.A —*Islamic Economics; Theory and Practice*: originally published in English by Sh. Mohammad Ashraf, Lahore, Pakistan (1970). Translated into Bengali by A. A. Rushdi, Department of Economics, University of Dhaka, Bangladesh.

4.B —"Trade and Commerce in Islam", originally published in Voice of Islam, University of Karachi, vol. 16, Karachi, 1967/68, translated by the author in Bengali and published in Bengali Journal *Sandan* of Islamic Research Institute, Islamabad, 1967.

4.C —"Islam and other Issues" published in English in *Islamic Review and Arab Affairs*, vol. 59, January, London, 1971. Its original Bengali version by the author appeared in Bengali Journal *Sandhan* of Islamic Research Institute, Islamabad, 1968.

4.D —"Interest-free Banking" published in English in *Islamic Review and Arab Affairs*, vol. 56, Nov./Dec., London, 1968, its Bengali version by the author appeared in Bengali Journal *Sandhan*, Islamic Research Institute, Islamabad, 1969.

4.E —"Land Tenure System under Hazrat Umar" translated into Bengali by Sharif Hossain and published by Islamic Economics Research Bureau, Dhaka, 1982.

4.F —Scarcity, Choice and Opportunity Cost; their dimensions in Islamic economics.

5. PUBLICATIONS ON ISLAMIC ECONOMICS REPORTED TO BE IN PROGRESS IN OTHER LANGUAGES SUCH AS GERMAN, FRENCH, KOREAN, MALAYAN AND THAI LANGUAGES.

—*Islamic Economics: Theory and Practice*: book of 386 pages, originally published in English (1970) by Sh. Mohammad Ashraf, Lahore, Pakistan.

—"Scarcity, Choice and Opportunity Cost; their dimensions in Islamic Economics" in Malayan languages by Syukri Salleh, University of Sains, Malaysia, (1981).

—*The Making of Islamic Economic Society*: Islamic dimensions in economic analysis (Malayan version forthcoming)

6. *PUBLICATIONS REPORTED TO BE IN PROGRESS IN SPANISH LANGUAGE.*

"Guidelines for Key Issues in Islamic Economics"

a paper presented at Joint International Conference on Research in crime prevention held in Riyadh 23–25 January, 1984, sponsored by Arab Security Studies Centre and United Nations Social Defence Research Institute, Rome, Italy.

(Note: Most of the English publications listed here are reproduced from a recently published bibliography on *Islamic Economics literature in English and German* by Dr Volker Nienhaus, Koln, West Germany, 1982. Author's other publications on economics of education and development Economics by Michigan State University, (U.S.A.) Fergoman Press (Australia), Institute of Developing Economies (Japan) are not cited here for obvious reasons.)

APPENDIX (C)

Reader's views and peer's opinion on the works of the author, Prof. M. A. Mannan, in Islamic Economics.

—In: "Modern Labour Capital Relationship and Islam" the author (M. A. Mannan) elucidates that Islam is a self-contained organism and has, therefore, its own system of economics . . . . . "

> Editor, Islamic Literature
> Lahore, Pakistan
> September Issue, 1967.

—In: "Trade and Commerce in Islam", the author (M. A. Mannan) has succintly summed up the basic principles on which trade and commerce should be carried out according to Islam . . . . "

> Editor, Islamic Literature
> Lahore, Pakistan
> March Issue, 1968.

—Islam as a factor of Development—" this is a thought provoking article . . . . ".

> Editor, Islamic Literature
> Lahore, Pakistan
> August issue, 1969.

—"Consumption Loan in Islam": It provides a discussion of the unique mechanism an Islamic state should adopt to handle consumption loan"

> Editor, Islamic Review
> and Arab Affairs,
> London, U.K.
> Vol-58
> March issue, 1970.

—"The most important point which the author: (M. A. Mannan) has raised in his book: *Islamic Economics: theory and practice* is the founding of a Muslim World Bank of Development to better utilize the vast resources of the Muslim countries. This is not a Utopian notion but a practical and useful suggestion . . . . "

Dr Charles S. Benson,
University of California
Berkeley, U.S.A.
June 2, 1970.

(Note: Islamic Development Bank (I.D.B.) formally came into existence on 20th October 1975 (15th Shawal 1395H). Its present membership consists of 44 Muslim countries. The Headquarters of the I.D.B. is
in Jeddah, Saudi Arabia).
—". . . . . I like your articles on Islamic Economics very much . . . . "

Abdullah Jan
Editor, The Criterion: Journal
of the Islamic Research
Academy, Karachi, Pakistan.
November 9, 1970.

—"Your book: *Islamic Economics – theory and practice* (1970) has hit the
mark and won you a National Bank Prize for literature – 1970. Please
accept my congratulations on this achievement. The award is well
deserved . . . . ".

S. H. Mohammad Ashraf
Ashraf Publication,
Lahore, Pakistan
February 23, 1971.

—"Mannan is extremely competent with regard to comprehension of
complex theoretical and conceptual formulation, and he also has the
ability to keep such theory in a broad perspective . . . . His book:
Islamic Economics shows his broad range of interest, especially on the
religious cultural and institutional context in which economic change
and growth take place . . . .".

Dr Mitchell Stengel
Dept. of Economics,
Michigan State University, U.S.A.
February 14, 1972.

—"Dr M. A. Mannan, who comes from Bangladesh is a man who will
make a contribution to the field of economic development . . . . . His
interest in developmental change reflects high motivation, reinforced
by his strong interest and continued study of religion, ethics and
justice . . . . "

W. Paul Strassmann
Professor of Economics
Michigan State University
East Lansing, U.S.A.
Feb 20, 1973.

—"*Islamic Economics – theory and practice*" is a very interesting and informative book . . . . "it is very useful to the Islamic Development Bank . . . . "

> Dr Ahmad Mohamed Ali
> President,
> Islamic Development Bank
> Jeddah, Saudi Arabia
> June 23, 1977.

". . . . Your joining of the International Centre for Research in Islamic Economics, King Abdulaziz University, Jeddah has "strengthened the Centre and given confidence to all of us that Inshallah the Centre would achieve its objectives and carve out an honourable place for itself . . . . "

> Prof. Khurshid Ahmed
> Islamic Foundation, U.K.
> July 20, 1978.

". . . I am indeed pleased to find that some one of Dr. Mannan's calibre, who has been at work in the area of Islamic economics for more than a decade, has been agreed to offer this course (a *six-lecture course on key Issues in Islamic economics*), Possibly the first of its kind in London, U.K. . . . ."

> Dr Kalim Siddiqui
> Director, The Muslim Institute,
> London, U.K.
> May 8, 1980.

". . . . We are very keen to have someone like yourself to lecture in Islamic Economics as it is new field to be introduced in our school . . . . . . The Course content you sent looks very good and I am sure the student would like to attend the course . . . . . "

> Dr A. H. Baharuddin
> Chairman,
> Division of Economics
> University of Sains
> Penong, Malaysia
> January 30, 1981.

—"This book: (*The Making of Islamic Economic Society*) to our knowledge offers the most comprehensive account of Islamic economics in the English language. It is likely to be adopted as an undergraduate text book by many Islamic Universities . . . and to attract a variety of general readers in Europe and North America . . . . . "

> Macmillan Press
> London, U.K.
> (in its pre-publication Review)
> June 7, 1981.

"Islamic perspectives on Islamic Banks" – a very well written paper containing many relevant and innovative ideas . . . . . "

> M. Azizul Haq
> Sonali Bank
> Dhaka, Bangladesh
> July 22, 1981.

"We hope that Dr Abdul Mannan will give a short series of lectures on Islamic economics, a subject *not* included in own present curriculum. The course outlines that Dr Abdul Mannan sent to us sounds most interesting and we would be delighted if he could join us in September."

> Prof. Michael C. Hudson,
> Director, Centre for
> Comtemporary Arab Affairs,
> Georgetown University, U.S.A.
> March 26, 1982.

"On behalf of the faculty and students at the Center for Contemporary Arab Studies, I would like to thank you for your lecture series on Islamic economics. Dr Oweiss and the others in attendance were very impressed with your presentations."

> Prof. Michael C. Hudson
> Director, Center for
> Contemporary Arab Studies
> Georgetown University, U.S.A.
> October 15, 1982.

"Islamic Perspectives on Market Prices and Allocation"—a high-calibre academic research work . . . .

> Anonymous referee
> December, 1982.

"I am glad to remind you that I attended your lectures on *Key Issues in Islamic Economics* at the Muslim Institute in London in the summer of 1981. My interest in the subject has increased with additional readings . . . . The faculty here is developing a programme in Islamic Economics . . . . . I shall be glad to receive your assistance . . . . . "

Dr Uzir Abdul Malik
National University of Malaysia,
Malaysia
March 22, 1983.

—"Your presence (Dr M. A. Mannan) in our workshop entitled: Workshop on Curriculum Development in Islamic Economics will be most invaluable not only as a participant but also as a resource person . . . "

Dr Uzir Abdul Malik
National University of Malaysia
April 29, 1983.

—*The Frontiers of Islamic Economics* will help further the cause of Islamic Economics . . . . it is a valuable addition to our literature . . . . . . "

Dr M. O. Zubair,
Professor of Economics and
ex-President,
King Abdulaziz University,
Jeddah, Saudi Arabia
June 28, 1983.

Securities Market in an Islamic framework: It is an "excellent research" on the subject and a "Pioneering study" . . . . . .

Anonymous referee
November 20, 1983.

Securities Market in an Islamic framework: " . . . . an excellent monograph. I am not aware of any literature ever written so extensively on the subject in English language. The author has shown considerable expertise in blending knowledge of modern economics with the knowledge of the *Shari'ah* . . . . "

Anonymous referee
November 20, 1983.

The Making of Islamic Economic Society – is "an influential work" . . . .

Dr M. O. Zubair
Professor of Economics,
King Abdulaziz University,
Jeddah, Saudi Arabia
1983.

"I am indeed pleased to write the foreword of the revised edition of Dr M. A. Mannan's academic award winning book: *Islamic Economics: theory and practice*, the first edition of which was published in 1970 when few scholars in Muslim World showed serious interest in the study of Islamic Economics as a distinct branch of knowledge . . . . . "

> Dr Abdullah O. Nassiel
> Secretary-General, The World
> Muslim League,
> ex-President and Professor,
> King Abdulaziz University,
> Jeddah, Saudi Arabia
> December 10, 1983.

"A critical and comparative analysis of Islamic Economics vis-à-vis Capitalist and Socialist Economics is a very urgent need of the day for removing the ignorance and misunderstanding of Islamic Economics and Dr Mannan's book (*Islamic Economics: theory and practice*) admirably serves this purpose . . . . . "

> Dr M. N. Huda
> formerly Professor of Economics
> Dhaka University
> from the Foreword of the Bengali edition
> of the book
> December 30, 1983.

The Making of Islamic Economic Society "is a valuable work of research . . . . . providing the basis for further research work in Islamic economics and banking . . . . . "

> Prince Mohammad Al Faisal Al-Saoud
> Chairman, Dar-ul-Maal
> Islami Geneva
> from the "Foreword" of the book (1983)

. . . . . Interested in translating the revised edition of your valuable book: *Islamic Economics: theory and practice* into Arabic language . . . . . "

> Dr Abdullah Abid
> Faculty of Commerce,
> Al-Azhar University,
> Cairo, Egypt,
> (1983).

"*The Making of Islamic Economic Society* is one of the pioneering works in Islamic Economics . . . . ".

Prof. (Dr) Ahmad Al-Najjar,
ex-Professor of Economics and
Secretary General of
International Association
of Islamic Bank,
Cairo, Egypt
(1983)

"It was my pleasure to translate your esteemed work of 'Zakat: its disbursement and Infra-poor distributional equity', published in '*Thoughts on Economics*' Vol. 4 No. 8 Jan-March 1983, pp 1–24 into Arabic language . . . "

Muhyiddin Aliyyah,
Scientific Research House,
Kuwait
January 29, 1984.

"The Centre is fortunate to have you as its first full time research Professor since its establishment six years ago. Your sincere and devoted contribution towards the development of academic, organisational and administrative structure of the Centre can hardly be overestimated. I shall continue to remember your contribution with respect."

Dr Omar Z. Hafiz
Director
International Centre for
Research in Islamic Economics,
King Abdulaziz University,
Jeddah, Saudi Arabia
February 12, 1984.

"I am extremely pleased with your work on 'Guidelines on Key Issues in Islamic Economics' . . . . "

General O. W. Mueller,
Distinguished Professor of
Criminal Justice,
Rutgers: The State University
of New Jersey, U.S.A.
March 26, 1984.

"It was the first time in which I was presented with a comprehensive perspective on fundamental issues of Islamic economics. Your paper: 'Guidelines for Key Issues in Islamic Economics' is a decisive elucidation of the subject . . . "

Index

Wadīʿa sale 203
wages: differentials 117–18, 315; Islamic attitude 115–17; Marginal Product Theory 116
wants, Islamic priorities 47–8 *see also* comforts, luxuries
Waqf property 100, 253
war, condemned by Islam 373
water rights 69
wayfarers, assistance 228
Wazifah 248
wealth, concentration condemned 351
Wealth of Nations (Adam Smith) 13
Weber, Max 381
weights and measures 286
welfare 171; early Islamic state 228–9; and fiscal policy 240, 241; guiding principle 152; Islamic approach 20–1, 68; and the market 148; scientific basis 20; and socialism 317; state systems 263; state's responsibility 155, 353–4; Western and Islamic view distinguished 10, 55–6
well-digging 58
Wells, H. G. 254, 310, 337, 348, 353
Whither Islam (H. A. R. Gibb) 347
Wicksell, K. 60
widows and widowers, inheritance rules 133–6
wills 138, 139
wine, prohibition 55–6
women: economic position 361; inheritance and participation in economic activity 140–1; self-realization and birth control 85
work, as worship 374
workers: and capitalist system 89; categories 117; rights and duties in Islamic state 116–17; share in production 88–9 *see also* labour

World Bank 210, 371 *see also* Muslim World Bank
world peace, and interest payments 130–1

Yahyab Ibn Adam 23
Yemen 185
Yemen A.R.: export commodities 400; socio-economic indicators 394–9
Yemen P.D.R.: export commodities 400; socio-economic indicators 394–9

Zahrah, Shaikh Muhammad Abu 257
Zakāt (revenue) 13, 14, 31, 87, 132, 178, 204, 221, 228, 234–5, 237, 245, 267, 291, 334, 352, 353, 360, 375, 387; anti-hoarding effects 163; 164; assessment 257–8, 270; collection 256; compulsory payment 366; distribution 240; early Islamic state 245–6; and economic planning 369–70; expenditure restrictions 263, 264; on idle money 159; inadequacy 68; on industrial machinery 258–9; and inflation 260–1; liability to 255–6; modern significance 253–4; non-Muslims and 228; Pakistan 273–81; payment to poor 159; private property 67, 73; proposed certificates 266; and public finance 261; rates 229–31, 237, 276–81; redistribution mechanism 171; on rent 259–60; revenue deposition in *Bait-ul-Māl* 176; on safe deposits 165; six governing principles 255–6; social advantages 263–6, 337–8; *Sūrah* 21; tax advantages 261–3
Zamīndārī system (landlordism or feudalism) 77; condemned by Islam 78–9
Al-Zarqa, Shaikh Mustafa 302
al-Zawawi, Al-Syyid Yusof bin Ali 106–9
Zimmis see Dhimmīs
Zubair bin Rafiʿah 79